State and Society in
Independent North Africa

This volume is the first
of a series published by
The Middle East Institute

in honor of the late
JAMES TERRY DUCE
from the proceeds of
THE JAMES TERRY DUCE MEMORIAL FUND,
established in the honor
of the Institute's President
1961–1963

The Members of the Board of Governors of
The Middle East Institute

are the Trustees of the Fund

State and Society in Independent North Africa

Edited with an Introduction by
LEON CARL BROWN

THE JAMES TERRY DUCE MEMORIAL SERIES
VOLUME I

THE MIDDLE EAST INSTITUTE
Washington, D.C.
1966

Copyright © 1966 by The Middle East Institute
Library of Congress Catalogue Card Number 66-20316

PRINTED IN THE UNITED STATES OF AMERICA
BY GARAMOND/PRIDEMARK PRESS, BALTIMORE, MD.

Publisher's Preface

The 18th Annual Conference on Middle Eastern Affairs of the Middle East Institute was held in May, 1964. The title of the Conference was: "North Africa: State and Society, 1964." The usual practice of the Institute is to prepare a Proceedings of these Conferences. In this case, it was felt that the need for works in English on independent North Africa exceeded the capacities of a Proceedings, and it was decided to rework the Conference papers into the present volume.

Some of the material presented at the Conference does not appear here and material from other contributors has been added. The original papers presented in May, 1964, have been revised and brought up-to-date to the time of going to press. Topicality, however, is not the sole—or primary—aim. That is, rather, faithfully to represent the title—*State and Society in Independent North Africa.*

The Institute is most grateful to the Editor, Leon Carl Brown, of Harvard, to the Harvard Center for Middle Eastern Studies, where the major part of the work of preparation went on, and to the thirteen contributing authors. The officers of the Institute repeat their thanks to members and to financial contributors, who make these offerings possible, and to the host of the original Conference, Georgetown University.

It is also a matter of solemn gratification that this work appears as the first in a memorial series in honor of the late President Emeritus of the Institute, James Terry Duce.

Table of Contents

I. INTRODUCTION 1
   Leon Carl Brown

II. POLITICAL PARTIES IN INDEPENDENT NORTH AFRICA 22
   Clement H. Moore

III. NORTH AFRICAN FOREIGN POLICY 41
   I. William Zartman

IV. LANGUAGE AND IDENTITY 73
   Charles F. Gallagher

V. THE ROLE OF ISLAM IN MODERN NORTH AFRICA 97
   Leon Carl Brown

VI. IMPLICATIONS OF RAPID URBANIZATION 123
   Roger Le Tourneau

VII. TRADE UNIONISM 146
   Eqbal Ahmad

VIII. THE RURAL SYSTEM OF THE MAGHRIB 192
   Jacques Berque

IX. POLITICAL ASPECTS OF RURAL DEVELOPMENT 212
   Douglas E. Ashford

X. ECONOMIC PLANNING IN NORTH AFRICA 234
   A. J. Meyer

XI. PLANNING: WHY, HOW AND WHAT RESULTS? 258
   Charles Issawi

XII. OIL IN THE NORTH AFRICAN ECONOMY 269
   John Lichtblau

XIII. PROSPECTS FOR NORTH AFRICAN UNITY 286
   Benjamin Rivlin

XIV. THE COLONIAL IMPRINT 303
   Elizabeth Monroe

XV. MODERNIZATION OF THE MAGHRIB 313
  Jacques Berque
Select Bibliography on Modern North Africa 317
The Contributors 321
Glossary 325
Index 327

List of Illustrations

FOLLOWING PAGE 70

King Mohammed V of Morocco

President Habib Bourguiba of Tunisia

Boulevard Youcef Zirout, Algiers

New apartments in Tripoli, Libya

The old sector of Algiers

An Algerian classroom

FOLLOWING PAGE 166

Moroccan women voting in municipal election

A Berber woman

A Berber nomad in the Middle Atlas mountains

Moorish women beating wheat at harvest-time

Weighing the harvest from an experimental plot for the development of new seeds in Libya

Young men at Agadir attending class in the mechanics of modern farm machines

Koutoubia Mosque, Marrakesh

FOLLOWING PAGE 262

Fruit and vegetable stalls in Tangier

Small shop in Tangier

Trailer living quarters for the French Oil Company in Algeria

Hassi Messaoud oilfields

Port of Casablanca

Algiers firemen destroying the *bidonville* in the old section of Mahieddine

1
Introduction

Leon Carl Brown

On July 3, 1962, with the independence of Algeria the formal process of decolonization in North Africa was completed. Only eleven years earlier all of that vast stretch of land extending from Egypt's western border to the Atlantic had been under outside control. Now four sovereign states—Libya, Tunisia, Algeria, and Morocco—actively participate in international organizations from the United Nations to the Arab League, and are busily engaged in ambitious domestic plans and policies. A large proportion of the present leadership is drawn from those who only a few years earlier were in prison, exile, or the *maquis,* and on the other hand many names which in the very recent past symbolized traditional power and influence are disgraced or even forgotten.

The first (and what many perhaps mistook as the final) step of the revolution is over for North Africa. Independence has been achieved. Gone are the hardships of the nationalist struggle, replaced by the routine burdens of day-to-day government and administration. Gone also is something of that extra unity and cohesion most easily fostered in any struggle against an identifiable outside enemy. Different forces have already begun to fill the void left as the *élan* generated in a struggle for independence was consumed both by its very success and by the disappointments of the post-independence period. There are already new calls to unity—to "fight underdevelopment" or to achieve a "Greater Maghrib." There are also many old forces of disunity; Berber *v.* Arab, nomad *v.* sedentary, city *v.* rural, and the confrontation, itself now venerable with age, of traditional and modern.

The former political mold which was the colonial system has been broken. Of this there can be no doubt, as diplomatic recognition, new treaty relations, and indigenous ministries and civil servants bear witness. How many other molds—in the religious, social, economic, or political life of these four countries—have been broken or modified beyond repair? Here the answer is not nearly so simple. No single factor—be it levels and sources of foreign aid, language of instruction in the schools, status of traditional religious leadership, rate of urbanization, number of tractors, or the amount of oil revenues—can answer such questions with the same sharp clarity. Everyone agrees that these four countries, only a few years ago legally dependent, are now legally independent, but from this point onward, agreement becomes more difficult.

As in any time of rapid change, a thorough re-examination of all aspects of state and society is in order for those who would know what is taking place in North Africa today and what is most likely to happen in years to come. Such a re-examination should subject to especially close scrutiny the old assumptions which formed the received wisdom of an earlier generation of Western scholars—the pervasive influence of Islam, the depth of Berber-Arab antagonism, or the alleged inability of native leadership to transcend provincialism and tribalism and create unified states. The re-examination should be equally circumspect in accepting newer ideas or slogans which would claim to explain the most important points—neo-colonialism, the revolution of expectations or the "take-off stage."

These considerations suggest two reasons for this book: now is the proper time for attempting to understand the new circumstances prevailing or still emerging in North Africa. Second, considering the uncertain nature of our knowledge and understanding in this time of transition, a collective effort is indicated. In such a situation, asking the right questions is almost as important as finding the answers, and there is a pressing need to have a whole spectrum of "right questions" posed.

The major purpose of this book is to pose the right questions and thus locate the essential elements which must be considered in any study of what is taking place in North Africa. Such an approach forces the emphasis on the background, underlying impersonal aspects of reality. Those who seek detailed information on even a few of the many colorful personalities in present-day North Africa will be disappointed as will those who want the four countries neatly labeled according to their position in the present international political spectrum. Amazingly, the many contributors have been able to write their chapters with hardly a reference to communism, neutralism, or pro-West leanings.

This is in no sense a misreading of the importance of the Ben Bellas, Boumediennes or Bourguibas* as flesh-and-blood persons. Nor is there any reluctance to recognize the eventual impact of foreign policy orientations now being hammered out, but first things first.

In a sense, this book is a collective effort to seek out and describe the political, social, and economic setting of a North Africa still in its first generation of post-independence groping. The approach taken here necessarily gives second place to daily domestic and diplomatic events and to the interplay of personalities, but it is the hope and belief of those contributing to this volume that such an attempt to set the stage will also serve to give a heightened understanding and appreciation of the actors involved. For surely no appraisal of this or that political leader is reliable unless based on an accurate estimate of the choices available to him—that is, he must be carefully fitted into the framework of his own immediate environment.

The four countries of North Africa have many of the same problems as the rest of the formerly colonized world: shaky state administrations with a woeful shortage of trained personnel, high rates of illiteracy, a population explosion, a "dual economy" or the the uneasy juxtaposition of modernized economic sectors participating in world trade and a traditional sector barely rising above subsistence levels—to name only a few of the most commonly recognized. For this reason the lessons to be learned from North Africa's experience should be of interest and application in other parts of the world facing identical problems, just as North Africa has much to learn from their trials and efforts.

Still, beyond these many points of similarity with the former colonized world of Africa and Asia stand basic differences growing out of North Africa's heritage. Whether today the most important issues for North Africa are those shared with other former colonial possessions or those stemming from a peculiarly North African background is a question about which observers continue to argue. Several of the contributors in this book will be seen placing considerably more emphasis on one or the other

---

*The contributions forming this book were written before the June 19, 1965, Army coup in which Boumedienne ousted Ben Bella. The book has been carefully reviewed in the light of this event, but no changes (except where appropriate from present to past tense) have been made. Since the book sets as its task "the background, underlying impersonal aspects of reality," the reader is entitled to use the ouster of Ben Bella (and other such changes when they occur) as an appropriate means of judging our efforts. *(The Editor)*

side of the balance. In either case, knowledge of these unique aspects of North Africa's own history and background has generally been assumed in the following chapters. Therefore, it might be useful to mention very briefly some of the things that have shaped North African history and distinguished the region from its neighbors.

North Africa—*jazirat al maghrib* (the westernmost island) to the medieval Arab geographers—is indeed an "island" bound by the Mediterranean Sea, the Atlantic Ocean, and the world's largest desert land mass, the Sahara. These natural physical boundaries have served to give the region a distinctiveness *vis-à-vis* her neighbors throughout the centuries, and one can speak meaningfully of a North African history and heritage. Only the eastern end of the Maghrib (now the state of Libya), lacks sharpness in its physical boundaries. This helps to explain the quandary of present-day Arabists (and editors of books such as this)[1] in deciding whether Libya belongs more nearly to the Arab East or the Arab West. In fact, throughout history Libya has tended to serve as link—and buffer—between the two with the eastern portion, Cyrenaica, usually tied more closely to Egypt and the Middle East and the western part, Tripolitania, looking more westward toward the Maghrib.

Geography has not only given the Maghrib a certain natural identity. It has also created other obstacles to unwanted intrusion from outside:

1. Few good natural harbors, and most of these are circumscribed by mountains blocking easy access to the interior.

2. No navigable rivers.

3. The internal barriers of the Atlas mountain chain, which might well be viewed as the backbone of the region, extending from the southwest corner of Morocco northeastward through that country and then more nearly in an easterly direction until it dies out at the Mediterranean in Tunisia.

This combination of natural characteristics was especially important until at least partially offset by the technology of the modern age with its roads, railroads, airplanes, and improved harbors. Geography did not enforce isolation upon North Africa —the legacy of Carthage, Christianity's Saint Augustine, the Arab

1. As well as many of the contributors to this book. Several have not included Libya in their chapters, some pleading a lack of knowledge based on first-hand experience, others finding that Libya did not fit neatly into the typology or general approach they were able to use with good results in considering the other three countries. Unfortunately, as a result Libya has been somewhat slighted.

role in Spain and the Islamization of West Africa from the north bear witness to this—but it certainly facilitated the task of any ruler from within who chose isolation, as Morocco tended to do in the 19th century. This helps explain how a rich, attractive country literally visible from Europe on a clear day (at the six-mile-wide Straits of Gibraltar) escaped European domination until 1912, long after remote, virtually unknown reaches of Africa and Asia had been gobbled up.

There is, however, another aspect to these geographical barriers. They have also made infinitely more difficult the imposition of central government from within and have helped preserve different cultures and even languages. The fundamental Berber/Arab dichotomy is the best known, and as will be seen later[2] even today after over a millennium of Arabo-Islamic presence, Berber (which makes no pretense to being the vehicle of a literary tradition) remains the native tongue of some 30 percent of the Moroccan and 22 percent of the Algerian population. It is not accidental that in Libya and Tunisia, the least mountainous and most accessible of the four, Berber has—for all practical purposes —died out in favor of Arabic. Nor is it surprising that opposition to the present regime in Algeria has tended to center in the mountainous Kabylia region which lies roughly between Algiers and Bougie. It is perhaps helpful in understanding one aspect of this opposition to reflect that the same region has given trouble in the last 2,000 years to the French, Turks, Arabs and Romans.

In Morocco the difference between that area where the sultan's rule was accepted (*blad al makhzan*) and the rest of Morocco beyond central government authority (*blad al siba*) is the key to understanding the entire medieval period, but this fundamental division also helps to explain why the French and Spanish had such trouble in conquering the Rif leader Abd al Krim in the 1920's or why the final French "pacification" of Morocco was delayed until 1934. Nor are flickerings of the same impulse to resist central authority lacking in the post-independence period for Morocco.

The contrast and frictions between nomad and sedentary, between "desert and sown," are well known, and the nomadic way of life has been another major determinant in North African history. One need only recall the great nomadic Berber dynasty of the Almoravides or the Bedouin Arab invasions of the Beni Hillal and Beni Sulaym (whose destructiveness Ibn Khaldun

2. See Chapter 4.

compared with a "plague of locusts")—both bursting upon the political scene in the 11th century. Even today in Libya many of the stresses in the existing structure can be traced to the antipathies between the population of Cyrenaica, the center of Sanusi strength and still closely attuned to the Bedouin way of life, and the more settled culture of Tripolitania.

North Africa has inherited not one but two of the major problems which physical geography has devised for human societies: the desert *v.* the sown and the mountaineer *v.* the plainsman. The great challenge of reconciling desert, plain and mountain has always formed the background of the North African scene.

A second major influence upon present-day North African society is its long, intimate link with Arabo-Muslim culture. The first Arab reached North Africa by the 640's, just over a decade after the death of Mohammad, and by 711 the Arab conquerors were using Berber auxiliaries in their conquest of Spain. This would appear to suggest that North Africa offered little resistance to Arabic and Islam. Actually, the process of Arabization and Islamization was the slow work of centuries. The last Christian dioceses disappeared as late as the 1150's (in the wake of Almohade persecution), and the tenacious survival of Berber has already been noted. Even so, if the process was slow it was thorough, and Islam eventually penetrated to the remotest parts of North Africa in a way no other great influence coming from outside (be it Carthage, Rome, Christianity, or France) was able to equal.

From the time the Arabs first established themselves in North Africa most of the major political upheavals have been intimately linked with Islam. In 740 the Berbers added a new element to their almost ceaseless resistance to the Arab invaders by revolting in the name of Islam. Embracing the puritanical, fanatical Muslim credo of Kharijism (provoking the great Dutch orientalist Dozy to comment that in North Africa the Muslim Calvinism had found its Scotland) the Berbers set a pattern of politico-religious revolt which has prevailed down to modern times. The Fatimids, Almoravides, Almohades, and the rise of Sufi brotherhoods resisting the incursions of the Portuguese and Spanish from the 15th century—all attest to the peculiar combination of political protest and Islamic reformist movements in North African history. Several observers would be inclined to argue that the emphasis on Islam and religious reformism in the modern nationalist movements was, after all, no more than a modern variation on this theme. Certainly the modern experience of the Sanusiya of Libya, the Algerian Association of Ulama, and the Moroccan Muslim reformists from Al-Dukkali to Allal al-Fassi all seem to fit in quite neatly as links in this long chain.

North Africa thus became and has remained part of the Arabo-Muslim world. Nevertheless, centuries before the advent of modern colonialism, geography and history had conspired to limit contacts with the Arab East and give North Africa its own special variety of Islamic culture. Political ties between Arab East and Arab West began to slacken within a century after they had begun. The Umayyads of Spain (from 756) and the Idrisids of Morocco (from 789) ruled over the first major Muslim areas to break away from the central caliphate just as the Aghlabids (800-909) of *Ifriqiya* (modern Tunisia and eastern Algeria) created the first autonomous dynasty remaining formally within the framework of the caliphate. Neither the Fatimids who got their political springboard to power in North Africa (beginning in the late 9th century) nor the Ottomans who took over all of North Africa except Morocco in the 16th century really breached the gap between East and West. The Fatimids soon turned their backs on North Africa after moving to Egypt and founding Cairo in 969. Ottoman rule in the three states of Algiers, Tunis, and Tripoli was more in the nature of a protectorate or loose alliance by comparison with the Ottoman control in the Balkans or the Arab East.

Culturally, also, North Africa had its own lodestar in Muslim Spain, and significant differences of architecture, poetry, and music bear witness to the special Western Islamic subculture which emerged.

This relative gap between Arab East and West was, of course, widened during the period of modern colonialism. As a result, today the two areas, although sharing the really important matters in a cultural tradition—religion, language, and a sense of identity—still find great gaps in the present state of their mutual knowledge which can lead to misunderstandings and friction. Culturally, they are perhaps as close as the Americans and the English, which is to say there still remain some not inconsiderable differences.

It should already be clear that North Africa is not distinguished by its uniformity. There are vast differences between Berber and Arab, urban and rural, plainsman, mountaineer, and nomad, and throughout the centuries Islam had been enmeshed in the political struggles which reflected these several differences. Eventually, however, a religious uniformity emerged. The native Christian church disappeared, only a small native Jewish minority remained, and virtually all of Muslim North Africa opted for orthodox Sunnism. Nothing could be more striking than this great religious uniformity of North Africa in contrast to the Arab East with its Sunnis, Shi'ites, Druze, and a large minority of native Christians of all rites. Because of this uniformity, Islam in North Africa is the common denominator, *par excellence,* transcending and mitigating (but not eliminating) the difference of tribe, language, and way of life. As a result, Islam in North Africa has served and could still serve as a rallying point for unity just as Arab nationalism (the sense of common Arabness) can help transcend religious differences in the East.

The third major influence shaping present-day North Africa and distinguishing it from the underdeveloped and/or formerly colonized world is its special colonial experience. In the rest of Africa and the Middle East the vagaries of the scramble for colonies left a crazy quilt of British, French, German, Italian, Belgian, Spanish, and Portuguese colonial administrations existing in uneasy juxtaposition often not even graced with feasible boundaries. In North Africa it was a different situation. Over 90 percent of North Africa's population shared the common experience of French colonialism. Only the two ends of the North African "island" escaped: Northern Morocco which was administered as a Spanish protectorate[3] and Libya which fell to Italy. Also, the two areas outside of French rule were less populated, less urbanized, and (until the discovery of oil in Libya) less well endowed economically. For all practical purposes, colonialism in North Africa meant France.

This common French experience has had an especially important effect in fostering the sense of unity and identity among the three states of North Africa (and conversely it poses an obstacle to the integration of former Spanish Morocco into the rest of Morocco just as it adds yet another major factor distinguishing modern Libya from the rest of the Maghrib). The educated elite of all three countries speaks the same Western language. The

---

3. In addition, a small, thinly populated segment of Southern Morocco, Tarfaya, was administered as part of the Spanish Protectorate. Tarfaya was returned to Morocco in 1958.

same French systems of education, administration, law, public finance, agriculture, and industry have invaded all three countries, challenging traditional ways. North African political parties and trade unions have all found inspiration and models from the ideologies and structures of the French left. The very idea of North African unity was first bruited in this century by Algerian, Tunisian, and Moroccan students who discovered in Paris how much they had in common.

Also distinguishing more than 90 percent of North Africa which shared French colonialism from most of Africa and the Middle East was the intensity of French colonization. The French conquest of Algeria began in 1830, fully half a century before the great scramble for colonies in Africa. Colonial rule began much later in Tunisia (1881) and Morocco (1912), but all three countries were characterized by the rapid buildup of settler populations. In most of Africa and all of the Middle East (except Israel) the colonial presence meant an army of occupation, a small cadre of upper-level colonial administrators and a handful of merchants, teachers, and missionaries from the metropolitan power. North Africa had all of this plus French farmers, industrialists, small retail merchants, middle grade civil servants, teachers, and even workers who organized trade unions. At one time in Algeria (1906) the European population formed 13 percent of the total, and during most of the 20th century until independence one person out of every ten in Algeria was European. In Morocco and Tunisia the European population formed between six percent and eight percent of the total during the last few decades before independence. (Even Spanish Morocco and Libya shared with the rest of the Maghrib the fate of literal colonization. Almost 10 percent of the population of these two areas were respectively Spanish and Italian at the peak periods of colonization.)

By contrast the Europeans in the "settler colony" of Kenya never exceeded one percent. To find comparable areas in percentages of white settlers plus a massive influx of modern industrial society, one must look to South Africa and Southern Rhodesia at the other end of the continent.

Now that independence has been achieved in all of North Africa and the great majority of Europeans have departed, it can be seen somewhat more clearly in retrospect that this mass influx of settlers left as legacy a curious mixture of curses and blessings. Largely because of the work (and pressure on home governments) of these settlers the economic infrastructure of North Africa—

roads, railroads, light industry, pockets of modernized farming—is impressive. Yet some would argue that this "unnatural" development of certain parts to the exclusion of others has thrown into even bolder relief the differences between the "traditional" and "modern" sectors[4]—thus the exacerbated problems of a dual economy.

The existence of a large *colon* population did not automatically provide more schooling for the native population than in non-settler colonies. North African nationalists, just as nationalists in most other colonies, had cause to complain of inadequate educational facilities.[5] Still, the first-rate French education which the *colons* insisted upon for their children was there to benefit a handful of lucky North Africans and also to serve as a yardstick for the "Franco-Arabe" systems designed for the native populations. However, the situation created by the *colons* tended also to emphasize rather than reconcile the problems of bilingualism and biculturalism.

The large number of settlers served as living examples of Western techniques which a modernizing society wants to learn, but the advantage this might have brought was probably more than offset by the manner in which these same large numbers of settlers monopolized not only top but even middle and occasionally lower positions in government, business, and the professions. As a result, all too few North Africans received even lower level training in these many requisites for operating a modern state and society. The post-independence plight is seen most clearly in Algeria. There, a quite modern administration and economy (potentially a great boon for the new Algeria) was monopolized by the settler class. With their mass exodus there were almost no trained Algerians to move in and keep things going. The physical shell of modern urban agglomerations taunts most of a native population who are strangers in their own land.[6]

4. See Chapter 8.
5. It is only fair to point out that in all three countries France began an imposing educational program following the Second World War. Nor is it historically sound to judge the general problem of native education during the colonial period according to present-day standards. Even in Britain and France the idea of universal, compulsory, free primary education gained legal acceptance only late in the 19th century. Still, the educational gap faced by these newly independent states was staggering. In 1954, which might be taken as the last "normal" year of the colonial era (i.e., the outbreak of the Algerian revolt and roughly one year before independence for Tunisia and Morocco), only one out of every five Muslims of French North Africa of primary school age was actually in school.
6. See Chapter 6.

There are certain broad generalizations which can be made about the impact of modern colonialism upon the colonized societies everywhere. If anyone made an itemized list of these many changes, distortions and improvements which have stemmed from modern colonialism, he would probably not be too wide of the mark if he simply added alongside each entry, "in French North Africa it was more so." French rule in North Africa was both more constructive and more destructive than colonialism in the Middle East and most of Africa. Whether these excesses on both sides of the ledger balance out, show a net loss or a gain is still being pondered and disputed by North Africans and outsiders. Probably the answer varies according to the special combination of factors in each country.

The above suggestion leads quite naturally to a final major consideration: although it is both justified and often quite useful to speak of North Africa as a single region, it nevertheless contains four separate, sovereign states which necessarily means four different approaches. In several of the succeeding chapters these distinctions will loom large, but usually somewhat circumscribed according to the immediate subject being discussed. For example, the economist might find valid reasons for optimism in a country which the political scientist sees only in the most somber tones. Yet there are a few basic distinctions giving individuality to each of the four countries under consideration which need to be noted before turning to the many specialized ways of comparing and contrasting the four which will be found in the following chapters.

Tunisia. It is always easiest to begin with Tunisia, the smallest in area and by far the most cohesive and uniform. Tunisia, about the size of Louisiana with a population of some 4,300,000, is blessed with relative geographical unity. The mountainous areas which do exist in the western part of the country are in no way comparable as pockets of particularism to Algeria's Kabylia or Morocco's Rif. There are, indeed, sectors in the west and the south shading off into the Sahara which are economically much more backward but they are not so distant from the more developed centers as to be out of touch.

There is no Berber/Arab problem in Tunisia, and all Tunisians are Arabic speaking.

The essential unity of Tunisia can be seen in the existence of a single major city, Tunis, which serves as the hub for all of this small country's activities. There is no great tension of rival regional "capitals" such as Marrakech, Casablanca, Fez, Tangier, and Rabat in Morocco or Oran, Algiers, and Constantine in Algeria (or the system of the rotating dual capitals—Tripoli and Benghazi—in Libya which reflects the regional differences in that country).

Tunisia has historically been the most accessible means of entry into North Africa and the most open to outside influences. Out of this heritage has come a certain ability to adapt and absorb outside influences in a more orderly fashion. The French colonial period is but the last great example of this trait. Without losing its national identity Tunisia was able to assimilate large doses of new, Western ways of doing things. Of course, the institution of a protectorate instead of outright control (as in Algeria) helped. Nor should it be overlooked that the colonial experience in Tunisia was relatively lacking in violence. There was nothing of the brutality characterizing the conquest of Algeria and Libya, nor the long period of "pacification" which Morocco experienced. Tunisia was quickly conquered and during the 75-year colonial period the energies of the native leadership could be concentrated upon taking the measure of the new culture rather than in barren physical struggle.

Tunisia is small as modern states go, and it has mercifully been denied the means to follow the temptations of imperialist expansion at the expense of its neighbors. Somewhat like Lebanon in relation to the Middle East or Switzerland in Europe, Tunisia has the psychology of a small state which must learn to live with more powerful neighbors.

Tunisia is also blessed with a continuity of leadership. The ruling Neo-Destour Party[7] was founded in 1934 and has had the advantage of over thirty years' experience. More like the pattern in settled political systems which have enjoyed independence for decades, there are several generations of political leadership in Tunisia from the party founders such as Bourguiba himself down to present cabinet ministers still in their thirties as Ahmad Ben Salah.

Accordingly, it is understandable that Tunisia's post-independence adjustment appears a bit more thorough and less exposed to the dangers of complete breakdown than that of her neighbors. It is therefore perhaps not always just to the other three countries to make comparisons and "progress reports" without giving proper emphasis to the built-in advantages Tunisia possesses.

7. Renamed the Destourian Socialist Party in the October 1964 Party Congress.

On the other hand, however, it is equally important to remember that it takes leaders and groups in every age to put natural advantages to use. Even in relatively fortunate countries there is nothing automatic about ordered progress, and thus both the virtues and faults of the present Tunisian leadership must also be given their due.

Finally, it is worth noting that Tunisia is not (in contrast with Morocco and Libya) blessed with great riches or economic resources. The permissible economic margin of error in Tunisia is slight. Unlike Morocco or Libya, Tunisia cannot afford the luxury of many serious mistakes or delays in her plans for economic development. Given her more modest resources, even a spirited program of development will not necessarily yield great results in absolute terms.

Morocco. Slightly larger than California, Morocco boasts a population of about thirteen million. Here, indeed, is a land of contrasts. In an age which appears to view monarchies as anachronisms, Morocco is a Muslim-type kingdom. Nor is this Moroccan monarchical state a latter-day creation as tended to be the case in the Arab East. The roots to the present system can be traced all the way back to the 8th century, and the ruling Alawi dynasty assumed power over three hundred years ago. The sultan or king is also a religious leader or *imam* of the Moroccan Muslim community. It is not without significance that the 1962 Moroccan Constitution gives the king the title always assumed by Muslim caliphs—*amir al mu'minin* (Commander of the Faithful).

Morocco is also one of the very few formerly colonized countries in which the traditional leader, Sultan Mohammed V (reigned 1927-1961), served as symbol and leader of the struggle for independence. In most cases, the traditional leadership, be it a single leader or a class, was itself a casualty of the concomitant process of modernization and nationalism. In Morocco the sultanate was, in fact, revitalized during the colonial period—first, by the unification French rule achieved, obliterating (at least in terms of positive law) the age-old difference between *blad al makhzan* and *blad al siba* and second by the early nationalists themselves who chose to win over Mohammed V as the symbol of Morocco rather than resist him as a "French puppet."

Yet, if Morocco is a revitalized monarchy and if the present French-educated ruler, Hassan II, is a would-be modernizer, it remains true that grass-roots support for the monarch comes from the most backward and traditional areas of the country. The parliamentary elections of 1963 in which the king actively intervened revealed this with inescapable clarity.

In addition to these traditional areas there is another Morocco more in touch with the modern world—Casablanca, thriving port and industrial center with a population of just under a million (it was a sleepy port numbering only about 10,000 at the turn of the century), the Moroccan trade union movement with a membership of some 300,000, the some one million hectares of modernized agricultural lands, the Morocco of a brand new major industry—tourism, etc.

In economic potential Morocco is the richest country in North Africa, an asset all the more important in that its wealth is a balance of many factors, not just a single predominant asset as is oil for Libya and—to a lesser extent—Algeria. Yet proper utilization of this potential wealth along modern lines requires stability, consensus and trained cadres. Morocco has always been a difficult country to govern. It remains so. Especially dangerous for the long run would be a polarization of political forces in Morocco solely along the lines of traditional *v.* modern. Then the so-called leftist forces (most likely to grow in numbers as modern education, industry, agriculture, etc., spread) would become more alienated and the monarchy, feeling the threat, would become more traditional. Under such baleful circumstances nothing much would be achieved except accumulated frustrations most likely to lead to some sort of social explosion.

With just a few changes of emphasis one can achieve a more optimistic prognosis. Morocco is indeed a country of contrasts and varied interests. In the existing scene, these many interests do have some outlet for expression. Morocco comes closer than any of the other North African countries in providing a relatively free and genuinely diversified press. The somewhat chaotic pluralistic political system perhaps reflects accurately the pluralistic Morocco society. Seen in this light, the present situation provides a proving ground for the diversified dynamism of Morocco to probe and experiment.[8]

Certainly, Morocco's record thus far in terms of plans achieved or consistency of purpose is hardly enviable. On the other hand, it could be argued that no doors have been definitively closed. Morocco still has a full spectrum of options to choose from, and perhaps the present inchoate period is providing a needed long period of gestation for modernization *à la marocaine*.

8. See Chapter 2.

Algeria. Algeria is a huge country of some 850,000 square miles, if the vast Algerian Sahara is included, but over 90 percent of Algeria's some eleven million population is found in a non-desert area about the size of New Mexico lying along the Mediterranean and seldom extending more than a hundred miles inland. Until the discovery of oil, the Algerian Sahara with an average of just over one person per square mile could have been considered a different world (which it was and still is) and virtually ignored by the rest of Algeria (which it was but is no longer). The Sahara now represents a great economic and financial asset. Eventually, the more effective integration of the Sahara's sparse population into the rest of the Algerian state and economy will be posed (just as in other oil-rich desert areas), but the critical period of that problem is well in the future. It is still possible at this time to concentrate on Algeria north of the desert which in any case has problems enough.

Algeria could well serve as a classic example of the evils of colonialism. The balance sheet one could attempt to draw up on the effects of French colonialism[9] might well find a net gain in Morocco where French rule laid the administrative and economic groundwork for a unified, modern state. In Tunisia, French rule certainly appears to have greatly facilitated the modernizing process while avoiding abrupt destruction leading to social breakdown. In Algeria, however, there can be little doubt. Colonialism was a net loss, both for Algeria and France.

The mode and longevity of the French conquest in Algeria established a tradition of violence and mutual distrust between colonizer and colonized which culminated in the long (1954-1962), brutal armed struggle for independence.

The large number of settlers was not only enough to monopolize middle and top positions in all sectors of modern state and society; the cumulative impact of their presence and the society they brought with them destroyed much of the traditional Algerian society.[10] It is, of course, a commonplace to observe that under the circumstances of colonialism and its accompanying modernization, tribal chiefs, the traditional urban bourgeoisie,

---

9. See this chapter, pages 8-9.
10. This is not to imply that Algeria was a viable, cohesive state (or nation) before 1830, or to deny that considerable destruction of traditional Algeria would have been necessary in any case for the creation of a modern state and society. It is, however, deemed important to emphasize the *imbalance* between destruction of old and creation of (native) new which seemed to characterize Algeria's colonial experience.

the religious elite, the artisan class—all suffer a radical decline. However, it is important to realize just how pervasive the process was in Algeria. Further, there was not even the usual balancing advantage—the creation of a numerically significant new class, products of Western education.

Writing in 1930 at the time of the Centennial, the French historian of modern Algeria, Augustin Bernard, could affirm with apparent equanimity that French colonialism "has torn up Algeria like a sharp-toothed harrow. It is a flock of sheep without shepherds. . . ."[11]

The shepherds, when they came, proved to be a tough breed. Algeria's struggle for independence was based on a politics of despair. Leadership in the Algerian struggle for independence did not come from a native middle class (too small and weak for such a role) nor from a group whose nationalism was mitigated by ideals of liberal democracy learned in Western universities. Ferhat Abbas has symbolized and led the small number in Algeria who represented this tendency, and the inability to gain concessions in time through protest and negotiation had undermined their position. The FLN was the creation of desperate men convinced that only violent, desperate measures would achieve results. The ultimate tragedy of Algeria is that they were probably right.

The many dislocations endemic in the Algerian colonial system were quickly exacerbated during the Algerian war. Algerian casualties might be estimated quite conservatively as some 200,000. Nearly two million Algerians had been moved from their villages and "relocated" by the French army in its massive attempt to isolate and crush the rebellion. Some 160,000 refugees found their way beyond the borders to Tunisia or Morocco. Then, after the last-ditch stand of the European terrorists (OAS) had failed, there was in 1962 a panic flight of Europeans from Algeria, leaving perhaps one-tenth of the original community in Algeria one year later. This was the final twist of irony. Those very *colons* who by their monopoly had stunted the growth of a native Algerian cadre for modern society could have been of considerable value in the immediate post-independence period by giving the

11. Augustin Bernard, *L'Algérie*, Vol. II in *Histoire des Colonies Françaises et de l'Expansion de la France dans le Monde*, eds. Gabriel Hanotaux and Alfred Martineau (6 vols.; Paris: Société de l'Histoire Nationale, 1929-33), p. 534. With the optimism characteristic of that period in French Algeria, Bernard went on to say "but this society which has lost its own framework is preparing to enter into ours."

new government needed time to select and train Algerians. With their flight following the final crescendo of violence, Algeria was left with yet one more liability—the physical plant of modern state and society but virtually no one to operate it.

Some observers have been attracted by the very cataclysmic nature of change in Algeria. The idea of such violence as a social catharsis, rapidly clearing away outmoded traditions and other obstacles has been espoused by the late Frantz Fanon, based on his own extensive experience in Algeria during the years of the war.[12] A handful of Trotskyites have tended to view Algeria as the best human laboratory for their ideas since the downfall of the Spanish Republic. And, of course, the violent nature of decolonization in Algeria fits into the ideological line adopted by Communist China.

Others are not nearly so optimistic, perhaps especially orthodox economists who see in Algeria a pauper nation relying for its very existence on outside aid.[13]

Certainly the list of liabilities inherited by the new Algerian government is long. Added to the many cumulative dislocations already alluded to is another major question—can the tradition of violence now be halted? Can the desperate men who fought and won a seemingly impossible war now be content with internal development, or are links with Cuba and Communist China plus the manifest desire to play an active role in Africa basically the conditioned reflexes of politico-military activists who find it difficult to settle down?

Also, Algeria—just as Morocco—has always been a difficult country to govern. The near civil war on the morrow of independence and the later troubles in Kabylia suggest that Fanon was at least partially wrong. Many of the age-old differences are still present.

In Algeria today there are probably more obstacles to success (even if success is defined conservatively as simply the attainment of a viable state and society) than in any other North African country, but perhaps sufficient in itself to overcome such a heavy burden is a fortitude and tenacity in the Algerians themselves so clearly demonstrated during the war years.[14]

Libya. Libya is a huge country (over two and one-half times

---

12. Cf. his *L'An V de la Révolution Algérienne* (Paris; Maspero, 1959) and *The Damned,* trans. from the French (Paris: Présence Africaine, 1963).
13. See Chapter 10.
14. See Chapters 8 and 9.

the size of Texas) with a small population—about 1,300,000. These two figures alone are sufficient to suggest that in Libya one is dealing with an arid, largely desert country. It is equally not surprising to find that Libya is characterized by a large percentage of nomads or semi-nomads.

Desert, the heritage of nomadism as a way of life, and (since 1959) the existence of oil in commercial quantities—all this sounds very much like Saudi Arabia. And if to this is added the fact that the ruling families of both countries are identified with modern puritanical Muslim reformist movements—the Wahhabi for Saudi Arabia and the Sanusiya for the ruling Sanusi family of Libya—then the parallel is striking indeed.

It has already been mentioned how Libya does not fit easily either into Arab West or Arab East, but serves as buffer and link between the two. This much can be seen by any political map of the region, but there is much more than mere accident of juxtaposition. Here the comparison with Saudi Arabia is helpful, for Libya is not just in between the Arab East and North Africa but in its basic geographical and ecological circumstances is different from *both* and much more like Saudi Arabia, just as Saudi Arabia is quite different from the sedentary culture of the Fertile Crescent and Egypt. Further, similar to Saudi Arabia, Libya faces the whole range of problems which oil revenues, international commerce and the challenge of modernization can present a traditional society attuned to a rough balance of subsistence agriculture and pastoralism.

Libya is also different from all her neighbors in being the only Arab country colonized by Italy—a colonization which began in 1911, and was marked by intermittent agreements and bitter struggles between Italy—firmly installed only in the sedentary and coastal areas—and the Sanusi forces who controlled the hinterland down to the 1930's.

The mass colonization which might have made Libya's experience somewhat more like that of her three neighbors to the west actually began in earnest only in the mid-1930's, and was of course halted by the outbreak of World War II. The long Libyan campaign completely wiped out Italian colonization in Cyrenaica (which had changed hands three times) and left only 40,000 Italians in Tripolitania, almost half of whom were in the city of Tripoli.

A war among outsiders achieved for Libya what the long Algerian war brought to Algeria—the virtual elimination of the settlers and the preconditions for independence. After the war a diplomatic struggle which involved great power interests and had no immediate connection with Libya[15] resulted in the creation of the independent Kingdom of Libya in December 1951.

Ironically, the North African country least prepared with trained cadres and most wracked with internal division (especially the old tension between more sedentary and urban Tripolitania where the Sanusi movement is weakest and the more pastoral Cyrenaica, bastion of the Sanusiya) was the first to attain independence.

Libya's oil revenues are also a mixed blessing. They force the pace of change, perhaps to the breaking point. Even more important in the short run, oil makes Libya an object of outside interest—the United Arab Republic, the oil companies concerned, the Western powers only now beginning to liquidate their base holdings, and the rest of North Africa which can be expected to increase its interest in the rich neighbor to the east.

As a result of these internal weaknesses and the combination of foreign interests, Libya's short-run future is more likely to be determined by outside pressures than by internal initiatives. To a sensitive Libyan this is hardly a happy state of affairs, but if the countervailing outside influences neutralize each other in something approaching a stable equilibrium, then this huge country with a small population could be granted just what it needs most—time.

In any collective effort perhaps the major problem is to achieve unity without sacrificing the special qualities, talents and viewpoints of each contributor. This book has attempted to strike that balance in the following way. 1) Each contributor was urged to stress the broad, general framework even if at the risk of glossing over interesting and timely detail. 2) Where subject matter and personal experience made it possible, each contributor was asked to treat all four North African countries. Some found it impractical to include Libya, but with this occasional exception each chapter is a general study of the entire area. 3) In the orig-

15. The USSR at one time (before the Italian elections of 1948) supported Italian trusteeship, but later switched to the idea of a collective trusteeship which the West feared as a Soviet foothold in the Mediterranean. The chief Western idea—the Bevin-Sforza plan—giving Italy trusteeship over Tripolitania, Britain over Cyrenaica, and France over Fezzan, with the creation of an independent state within ten years, was defeated in the General Assembly. Finally, independence emerged as the only acceptable alternative.

inal selection of subjects and contributors an attempt was made to achieve an interdisciplinary approach. Among the contributors are historians, political scientists, economists, sociologists, and at least one who conforms more closely to the 18th century ideal of the learned man.

Subject to these general guidelines, however, each contributor has been left completely free to deal with his chosen subject as he sees fit. Each chapter can stand alone and for that reason they can be read in any order. However, the ordering of the chapters does attempt to satisfy the demands of those who prefer a rather less random approach, and for that matter, it follows quite closely the original schema arrived at well before any of the chapters had been written. Briefly, the classification is as follows:

The first two chapters following this introduction deal with two important aspects of the political process. Clement H. Moore discusses the role of political parties in North Africa and I. William Zartman concerns himself with the varying approaches to foreign policy which the four states have chosen.

The next two chapters discuss two important influences in any culture. Charles F. Gallagher considers the problem of language and identity and L. Carl Brown treats the role of Islam in the modern context.

Four chapters then follow which might best be placed under the general rubric of sociology: those of Roger Le Tourneau and Eqbal Ahmad dealing with the urban environment, and those of Jacques Berque and Douglas E. Ashford concerned with the rural scene.

Then come three chapters discussing more directly economics and the development plans. A. J. Meyer presents the general guidelines of the existing plans in the four countries with some observations on progress to date. Charles Issawi gives a critique of the planning process—what to expect and what not to expect—based on the North African experience. John H. Lichtblau gives a succinct treatment of oil production, costs, revenue, and prospects in North Africa.

Remote as it now seems, the achievement of a "Greater Maghrib" could have such far-reaching implications that it is important to trace the development of this idea and present some prognosis of its future. This is done in the chapter by Benjamin Rivlin.

The last two chapters fit together as an appropriate conclusion for a collective work on such a subject. The era of modern European colonialism has come to an end in North Africa, and Elizabeth Monroe offers some reflections on what will be the enduring legacy of the colonial period. The North African states today are addressing themselves to social and economic development. A brief chapter by Jacques Berque contains at one and the same time methodological suggestions for studying the developmental process in North Africa and a needed exhortation for a more humanizing approach.

2

Political Parties in Independent North Africa

Clement H. Moore

Political parties, the architects and prime instruments of national independence, have been called to unprecedented tasks in many new nations. Unlike the parties of stable constitutional democracies in the West, their function has not been limited to selecting leaders and competing for electoral support. Rather, graced with the mantle of victory, they have considered it their mission to forge new political orders. In Tunisia, the Neo-Destour was successful in the absence of any countervailing force. In Morocco, less politically developed before independence, the Istiqlal lacked the necessary internal cohesion and became one of a number of parties competing for the favor of the king. In Algeria the National Liberation Front (FLN) disintegrated at independence but paradoxically became the armature of a new order.

Under these circumstances it is instructive to compare the roles of the parties in the three political systems. For, despite real differences in social structure and national policy, the three systems display remarkable similarities with respect to the power structure. Despite variations in constitutional wording and personal style, Habib Bourguiba of Tunisia, Ahmad Ben Bella of Algeria,* and King Hassan II of Morocco all exercise broadly comparable, comprehensive powers in the absence of effective opposition. Each leader has successfully consolidated power by playing off rival groups and factions and eliminating them as threats to his personal

---

*On June 19 an Army coup led by Col. Houari Boumedienne overthrew Ben Bella. It is still too soon to up-date this chapter on the basis of Boumedienne's leadership record. More important, the analysis based on the pre-June 19 situation is still pertinent. (See also the footnote on page 3. *The Editor*)

power. Wide consultation prevails in all three countries, but no procedures have been accepted that might bind the ruler to implement proffered advice.

Though party competition lies at the heart of what is generally meant by democracy in the West, the requisite of legitimate channels for resolving partisan differences does not yet exist in North Africa. Even in Tunisia, the most homogeneous of the three countries, the rivalry in 1955 between Bourguiba and Salah Ben Youssef led to bloodshed and a virtual civil war. During the power struggle of 1962 in Algeria, the ultimate arbiter was the organized military strength of the People's National Army (ANP), while in Morocco since independence party officials have been assassinated and tribes have occasionally revolted. Relatively little blood has been shed in independent North Africa, but the threat of violence underlies all political controversy.

In such a context Ait Ahmad, subsequently the leader of an armed insurrection against Ben Bella, was probably correct in saying that "democracy is not possible unless one renounces the spirit of partisanship."[1] Partisanship is too intense to permit conflicts to be resolved democratically. North African politicians intensely distrust one another, and political disputes become personal vendettas. Power is conceived as a coercive instrument rather than a cooperative process; indeed, to cooperate with someone is a sign of weakness, for the project must belong to one or the other. Before the French colonized the area, such attitudes toward power were appropriate because the sphere of politics was limited, authority was distant, and distrust was mitigated by the ideal of piety and the personal consultations of the good Islamic ruler. But the imposition of modern, impersonal administration, especially in Algeria where traditional rulership was eliminated, reinforced the native distrust of authority while radically expanding the scope of power and politics. The repression of nationalist movements hardly encouraged a more cooperative conception of power but rather served to cloak the political process in the shadowy garments of conspiracy and clandestine action; especially in Algeria, but to a lesser extent in Morocco and Tunisia, politics become synonymous with organized violence. To the traditional habit of tribal insurrection were added new ones of revolutionary warfare and terrorism.

This political culture precluded classic Western-type party activity although the North African parties, modeled on those of

1. *Jeune Afrique* (Tunis), October 1, 1962.

the French left, succeeded in discrediting most structures of the traditional societies. Their respective styles of anti-colonial agitation, coupled with the differing colonial impacts upon social structure, largely shaped their new activities, which would vary considerably after independence in the respective countries.

In Tunisia the Neo-Destour was able with relative ease to found a new order, because in a sense even before independence it constituted a functioning political system. Founded in 1934, the party was the oldest and best organized in Africa. With a disciplined and well-trained 100,000 members twenty years later, it had acquired the political experience to staff a new state while retaining its organization. Its greatest asset was the remarkable national cohesion it had engendered, a product not only of organization but also of the new social forces it represented. A new middle class had come into being, shaped by French education which was more accessible to Tunisians than to either Algerians or Moroccans. Not only the sons of traditional notables but those of the peasants of the Sahel acquired university degrees, and, even before World War II, they succeeded in displacing the traditionally-minded urban bourgeoisie as an effective political force. Thus by independence the dispute common to many Islamic countries between modernizers and traditionalists had been resolved, and the Neo-Destour under the remarkable leadership of its founder Bourguiba was able to tackle the problems of development in an atmosphere of relative consensus. The party's political style was decisively shaped by the manner in which independence had been won—a judicious mixture of negotiation by stages accelerated by occasional well-planned acts of mass agitation. The legacy of this pragmatic style encouraged the formation after independence of a political order dominated, to be sure, by the single party, but characterized by the flexibility of its tactics in pursuing the revolutionary goals of a modernizing society.

The Istiqlal in Morocco, on the other hand, was neither well organized nor socially cohesive. Founded only in 1944, it did not succeed before independence in transforming itself into a tightly disciplined mass party like the Neo-Destour. As a result, when the French deposed Mohammed V in 1953, the Istiqlal was unable to channel expressions of popular discontent. Urban terrorism, a tactic used sparingly for political effect in Tunisia, escaped the Moroccan party's control. Moreover, the deposed sultan, the martyr of Moroccan nationalism, displaced the Istiqlal as its prime symbol, whereas in Tunisia after the death in 1948 of the beloved

Moncef Bey, no royalty could outshine Bourguiba and his party. At the root of the Istiqlal's inadequacy was the nature of Moroccan society, rent by natural divisions exacerbated by the unequal impact of the colonial situation. The French legacy did not include a triumphant new middle class as in Tunisia, but rather a small, mixed elite dominated by the traditional Fassi bourgeoisie. Therefore the Istiqlal would be unable to express any modernizing consensus; instead, after independence younger elements in the party would break away from the yoke of the Fassi notables to form a new party, the National Union of Popular Forces (UNFP). Moroccan society was far more heterogeneous than that of Tunisia, centered on the Sahel's cluster of Mediterranean towns and villages. In Morocco tribesmen, Arab and Berber, resisted the central authority until 1934, just as they would subsequently resist Fassi domination by creating a rival party, the Popular Movement. The traditional bourgeoisie would also be unable to contain the workers of a modern industrial sector that was larger than Tunisia's. In Morocco neither a party nor a class nor a program, but only a king could be an instrument of national unity, eliciting whatever agreement might be possible in the fractured social setting.

Algeria, too, until the founding of the FLN in 1954, displayed a diversity of parties and outlooks reflecting different social forces—the liberalism of a weak new middle class, the reformist Islam of traditional urban and village elites, and the revolutionary nationalism of a proletariat that included hundreds of thousands of emigrants to France. The FLN tried to represent these disparate forces together with a sub-proletariat that the exactions of a million European settlers had created not only in the new cities but in the countryside. Certainly by the end of the eight-year guerrilla war everyone in Algeria had become tragically involved, whatever the extent of his actual military participation. But violence, which Frantz Fanon worshipped as the praxis of disalienation and national unity,[2] by definition is mute, and it was not clear which outlook or social force the FLN would represent after independence. Moreover, the nature of guerrilla warfare precluded the development of a coherent, centralized political structure; with respect to organization as well as to doctrine, the FLN was indeed a front rather than a political party. But the war, the culmination of 132 years of destruction of the Algerian social fabric, swept away all alternatives to the FLN. It would be the uncontested leader of

2. Frantz Fanon, *Les Damnés de la Terre* (Paris: Maspero, 1961), pp. 29-70.

the social revolution its violence had consecrated; hence like the Neo-Destour it would be the armature of a single-party regime. But Algeria, the dikes of tradition cut, enjoyed even less social cohesion than Morocco. At independence Algeria was brought to the verge of anarchy when the leaders of the FLN could not agree whose revolution they were to pursue. Clearly the FLN's path could not follow that of the dominant party in cohesive Tunisia; the pragmatic balancing of social forces would not ensure government, much less development, in Algeria.

TUNISIA

The plight of the Neo-Destour in independent Tunisia illustrates some of the dilemmas that parties face in emergent one-party systems. They must play conflicting roles: in the name of national unity to serve the new government, yet in the name of the people to supervise the government and ensure that its policies reflect the general will. The thorny problem of party-state relations is especially interesting in Tunisia, where no Leninist blueprints are permitted to serve as a guide. It was not by accident, but with the embarrassment befitting a liberal democrat, that Bourguiba established his single-party regime; significantly, the Constitution of 1959 nowhere mentions the party though it is the center of Tunisian political life.

In the name of the people, the party easily eliminated the bey, Tunisia's traditional absolute monarch, shortly after independence. The party lists swept the elections of March 25, 1956, for a constituent assembly which, on July 25, 1957, deposed the bey and proclaimed Bourguiba President of the Republic. But Bourguiba was careful, pending the elaboration of the constitution, to inherit all of the bey's powers and hence sidestep any effective parliamentary control. The cabinet of Neo-Destour leaders was responsible only to the President of the Republic, who temporarily enjoyed full legislative as well as executive powers.

With the full support of the party, Bourguiba ensured national unity by reducing all dissident centers of power. When Ahmad Ben Salah advocated integral economic planning and the rapid nationalization of foreign properties, Bourguiba was able to eliminate him from the leadership of the powerful General Union of Tunisian Workers (UGTT) by playing upon schisms within the trade union. The fact that its two subsequent leaders were members of the party's political bureau helped to assure harmony between trade union and party on the latter's terms. By the force of example the other national organizations, representing businessmen and artisans, farmers, youth, and students, were encouraged to obey the political bureau.

But after Bourguiba had consolidated his power over the national organizations with the aid of the party, he used his new position as Head of State to assure his hegemony over the party. The government apparatus which the party had staffed at all levels now had to take precedence over the party. On October 2, 1958, Bourguiba launched a sweeping reform of party structure. At the regional level, the party's democratically elected federations were supplanted by commissioners appointed by the political bureau. Thus many party veterans could be eliminated who were obstructing the activities of the provincial Governors by their demands for special privileges. A number of high party officials were also disciplined for improper interventions into governmental affairs. During this period the upper levels of the party hierarchy were unofficially transformed into docile sounding boards for the government. The representative organs of the party, such as the national congress and the national council, were rarely convened. By 1959 the party's representative role at the provincial and national levels seemed virtually nonexistent; the transmission belt between the government and the people seemed to turn only one way. Even at the very top, the fifteen-man political bureau, under the impact of presidential government, became an increasingly ceremonial body. Bourguiba had in fact replaced the bey as Tunisia's new monarch—a popular one, to be sure, but concentrating in his hands more effective power than any bey or French Resident General had ever enjoyed.

Under these conditions the once powerful mass party was in danger of withering away. Indeed, there were some signs of apathy and disaffection. Four years after independence, paid party membership had declined by half in its historic Sahel stronghold despite offsetting gains elsewhere. Activist students unsuccessfully tried to break the party's control of their organization. Autonomist tendencies similarly asserted themselves on occasion within the weakened trade union. The party's youth organization grew weaker as careerist ambitions submerged the revolutionary *élan* of an earlier period.

Yet the party continues to fulfill one crucial function in Tunisia's new political system. It is the source of its legitimacy, indeed the only source, surprising as this may seem. It is possible for Bourguiba to play the role of monarch, but the monarchy as a traditional institution was forever destroyed. Moreover Bourguiba's personal prestige as the *moudjahid al akbar* (Supreme Warrior) of the independence struggle is too fragile to provide legitimacy. For especially since his campaign in 1960 against the fast of Ramadan, he is vulnerable to religious objection in what remains an Islamic culture. Technically the people are the source of legitimacy, but the constitutional procedures by which the people exercise their sovereignty are of little significance in the one-party state.

The Neo-Destour gives legitimacy to the government and to the most important of its decisions by constant expressions of confidence. The confidence is not the outcome of democratic deliberation but is nonetheless important for its symbolic value, even as the well-orchestrated mass manifestations suggest popular participation. The party provides legitimacy not so much by what it does as by what it is, an intangible symbol of national unity, the repository of national history.[3] Thus the actual procedures by which decisions are reached do not affect their legitimacy, as long as the party supports them. Quite possibly the party may more effectively play its legitimizing role if it is less involved than other bodies in actual decision-making. Without responsibility, it can conserve its prestige.

Yet the symbol, to be convincing, must express some political reality. The party must indeed be able to retain popular support, to justify its claim to embody the nation. Were the party to be seen by Tunisians as a mere appendage to the government, its usefulness as a legitimizing agency would soon be at an end. It must constantly display signs of its representative quality. But this does not require the practice of internal democracy; rather, it means that the party must on occasion represent the aspirations of the nation by recapturing the revolutionary *élan* of the independence struggle. Thus Bourguiba revivified the party during the Bizerte crisis of 1961-62; more recently, in May 1964, he seized the remaining million acres of settler land, despite the nefarious consequence of losing French economic and financial assistance.

By subordinating the party to the state, Bourguiba has been

---

3. For an interesting parallel which more explicitly applies Max Weber's conception of charisma to a political party, see W. G. Runciman, "Charismatic Legitimacy and One-Party Rule in Ghana," *Archives Européennes de Sociologie,* IV (1963), 148-165.

able to transform the former into a powerful instrument for mobilizing popular support for development projects and economic planning. Through the party, too, he is able effectively to balance the interests represented by the national organizations. But the danger of mass depoliticization and disaffection is always present. Moreover, the national organizations are not always quiescent, as the UGTT's hesitation in endorsing the government's devaluation of the dinar suggested in October 1964. But the alternative of allowing greater internal democracy within the party and greater party responsibility in government decision-making would also have posed problems. Party veterans are often jealous of the young technicians whom Bourguiba brought into the government, yet without them, Tunisian development policies would certainly have been less rational. Furthermore, the party veterans, if allowed a freer rein, might have transformed the party into a ruling caste. Under the guidance of an arbiter who like Bourguiba is open to new ideas, Tunisia's political system has been able more easily to recruit new blood. Without Bourguiba's personal support, Ben Salah could not have succeeded in launching economic planning; the new Neo-Destour "socialism" (since the congress of October 1964, the party has been renamed the Destourian Socialist Party) had many enemies among the veterans.

Probably the carefully engineered reorganization of the party in 1964 would also have been impossible. By expanding the political bureau to fifty members, Bourguiba was able to include young leaders like Mohammed Sayah, a dissident student leader until 1961, in addition to all the members of his government and of the old bureau. The president's unchallenged control over both party and government has probably also helped to mitigate the tensions between political militants and administrative technicians —both elements remaining essential to a balanced politics of development. Under Bourguiba's tutelage the consolidation of a closed ruling caste has been avoided, and the system seems sufficiently flexible to respond to the new demands and interests of an expanding elite. In the long run, economic planning may pave the way for more effective popular participation.

ALGERIA

More visibly than in Tunisia, the single party in Algeria appears to dominate every facet of political life. As the central instrument of the constitution it drafted, the FLN is the "single vanguard party" (Art. 23) that "defines the policy of the nation and inspires the action of the state" (Art. 24). No rival party is permitted. It nominates the candidates to the National Assembly and may revoke the mandate of a deputy with the support of two-thirds of his colleagues. Though the President of the Algerian Republic, unlike Bourguiba, is responsible to the Assembly, he enjoys the latter's broad emergency powers and in fact is general secretary of the FLN. Within the party, despite the traditional Algerian distrust of the personality cults, Ahmad Ben Bella like his Tunisian counterpart was supreme. He was elected by the FLN Congress of April 1964, while his colleagues on the 15-man political bureau were named by the 74-man central committee elected by the Congress. The underlying political fact was that Ben Bella since the summer of 1962 had consolidated his power by eliminating his rivals among the founders of the FLN as well as others in the Provisional Government. But unlike Bourguiba, who had the support of a well-structured party, Ben Bella succeeded with the assistance of an exile army, the only organized force in the hectic months following independence. Then, with control of the government, he proceeded to rebuild the FLN and attempted to incorporate all but his most irreconcilable adversaries. By the end of 1964 the task apparently remained unfinished.[4] Indeed, in one important respect Ben Bella's position was probably not as strong as Bourguiba's: the apparatus of the FLN, on which the Algerian leader must depend, seems unable to exercise full control over the army. The ANP is nominally subordinate to the political bureau but it remains under the command of the powerful Vice-President and Defense Minister, Houari Boumedienne—the man who more than any other assisted Ben Bella to power.[5] No one in Tunisia has such strong claims on Bourguiba.

Paradoxically the weaker Algerian party is summoned to a greater revolutionary role than its Tunisian equivalent. It is not only a symbol of legitimacy, nor merely the subservient instrument of the government that controls the national organizations

---

4. In the quasi-official party weekly *Révolution Africaine* the editorials of 1964 often highlighted the need to strengthen the party. See, for instance, the editorial of November 7, 1964, calling for greater activism.

5. Inside the political bureau, Boumedienne is in charge of military affairs. The FLN congress decided that, while there would be overall political control of the army, the party in the interests of military discipline would not organize cells in the army. See *Révolution Africaine*, April 25, 1964.

and mobilizes the masses whenever popular support is necessary. It is also supposed to make policy and, according to the program adopted by the FLN Congress, to supervise the government bureaucracy. Thus, if the danger in Tunisia is that the party might wither away in the shadow of the government, the risk in Algeria is that it could become the government.

In his speech to the congress in April 1964, Ben Bella recognized this possibility and pointed out that the confusion of party and state would lead to the destruction of the authority of each. Therefore the party was not systematically to intervene at all levels of administration but rather to serve the more modest function of providing "political impulsion." To avoid losing its identity, it was to keep a majority of its leading cadres out of government while ensuring that its members in the state bureaucracy obey party directives. It was at all costs to shun the routine management functions of government. The precedent of the confusion of political and administrative functions in the Provisional Government before independence had served as a warning to the architects of Algeria's new order.

But in practice, though a majority of political bureau members do not have government positions, the most important party leaders do. Ben Bella's five ministers on the bureau were in charge of party activity in their respective ministerial fields. It is difficult in any event to imagine how Ben Bella's government might be held accountable by Ben Bella's party on crucial matters of state. Mohammed Harbi, one of the President's advisers, recognized the difficulty of the party supervising the state bureaucracy when the best party cadres, catapulted into government, are exposed to new pressures.[6] The exercise of governmental responsibilities, after all, had brought a decrease of party influence in Tunisia.

Generalizing from Tunisian experience, however, may be risky. Given the dislocations of the war and the mass exodus of the French, the Algerian revolution has proceeded since independence at a dizzy pace, guided by a more articulate and revolutionary variant of socialism than that of the Neo-Destour. Ideology, being the monopoly of the party, may enhance its influence and cohesion. For the socialism that both Ben Bella and Harbi proclaim points to a class enemy inside the state bureaucracy as well as the society. The party has the task of purging this enemy and also of ensuring

6. See his very interesting lecture, "Party and State," recorded in *Révolution Africaine*, November 7, 1964.

that a new caste of functionaries, subject to the temptation of bourgeois comforts, does not "confiscate the revolution."

Though a vanguard rather than a mass party, the FLN is to be constantly renewed, lest it become the preserve of professional politicians who might themselves become a ruling caste. The cure proposed by the ideologues of the FLN is a socialism in some respects more akin to Proudhon than to Marx: a dynamic process of democracy inside the party safeguarded by decentralization and effective self-government at the local level. The original quality of Algerian socialism as its creators perceive it lies in the self-management committees spontaneously created on deserted settler farms. The eventual goal of the FLN is to generalize them to all enterprises; in 1964 self-management was practiced on one-third of the cultivated land and in one-tenth of Algerian industry.

The future role of the FLN may depend largely on how successfully it can channel local energies, once its structure is in place. Despite the emphasis its programs place on self-management and communal reform, there are signs that the party is becoming increasingly hierarchical, like the Neo-Destour. For the first time, during the summer of 1964, free elections were to be held in each FLN cell (the lowest party unit), but the suppression of the intermediary sections reinforced central control over cells. The party has also tried to limit the role of the General Union of Algerian Workers (UGTA), especially in the self-managed sectors of the economy. The FLN's practice of organizing cells parallel to the local UGTA *syndicats* may inhibit the latter's freedom of action, as the UGTT discovered in Tunisia.

Like the Neo-Destour, the FLN quickly consolidated its authority over the national organizations after independence. At the stormy UGTA Congress in January 1963, the party organized truckloads of sometime workers to take control of the meeting and change the trade union leadership. The National Union of Algerian Students (UNEA) was also captured, though dissident Algerians studying in Paris were permitted to speak at its congress in 1964 before being excluded. It seemed that the national organizations were becoming satellites of the ruling party.

Repeatedly, however, Ben Bella and official party documents stressed the importance of trade unionism in Algeria and indicated that the UGTA was not to be a simple transmission belt for party or governmental commands. The dispute in the winter of 1964 over what to do with the profits of self-managed farms suggested that the UGTA still played a somewhat independent political role, even though Ben Bella's decision to distribute fixed bonuses diverged from the trade union's position that the profits should be used to create new jobs. The UGTA continued to play a variable role in the self-management sector, while fomenting occasional strikes, probably in agreement with the party, in the private industrial sector. But it seemed that the party would determine whether and how the 300,000 man trade union federation would wield its influence in policy-making affecting the workers.

Weaker than the Neo-Destour, the FLN would probably not exist at all if limited to the former's functions in the political process. To provide legitimacy, the FLN has more need of proving that it has a mission than does the Tunisian party. The latter, after all, has palpable structures and a continuous thirty-year history, whereas the FLN existed only in name during the power struggle of 1962. The effective separation of party and state, however, is extremely difficult if not impossible in a newly independent nation. If the FLN is not to become an appendage of the administration, strong ideological conviction will be needed to maintain its sense of purpose as an entity separate from the state. In a climate that, as Charles Gallagher has suggested, "shouts excess"[7] the prolonging of the revolution and the articulation of an ideology justifying it may prove possible. Islamic socialism in Algeria is not an empty phrase, but means rather the wholehearted acceptance of Marxist-Leninist insights as the economic means of achieving the good society safeguarding an Arab-Islamic identity. Though the contradictions here are obvious, the effort to resolve them might be significant. Armed with an ideology and practicing a measure of internal democracy, the FLN conceivably might avoid becoming a subservient instrument of government.

MOROCCO

Although the Constitution of 1962 expressly forbids the construction of a one-party system in Morocco, the role of parties under the constitutional monarchy resembles that of the Neo-Destour more than that of classic multi-party systems in the West. The outcome of party competition neither at the polls nor in parliament can decisively affect the composition or policies of the king's government. Like the Tunisian party under Bourguiba,

7. Charles F. Gallagher, "The Algerian Year, Part II: Choices and Interpretations," American Universities Field Staff Report, North Africa Series, IX, No. 7 (July 22, 1963).

the Moroccan parties have been largely subordinated to the king, who rules as well as reigns. Indeed, Mohammed V and Hassan II were able to pit one party against another, just as Bourguiba played off one faction against another within the Neo-Destour and the UGTT, in order to avoid the crystalization of a political force strong enough to threaten the position of the monarchy.

In a sense the parties of Morocco are collectively more impotent than the Neo-Destour, for the latter, even though it only ratifies government policy, does serve as a symbol of legitimacy and national identity, whereas in Morocco this function is performed by the monarchy. But in the give-and-take of Moroccan politics, where only the Communist Party is outlawed, there is no danger that the parties will wither away. Even when included in the government, neither the Istiqlal nor the UNFP became so identified with it as to give up the chance to criticize it and place the burden of unpopular policies on others. Precisely because no one party can attain a monopoly of power in Morocco's fractured political setting, the organizational vitality of each is assured.[8]

Thus far, however, the diffusion of political responsibility has resulted in immobilism. To the solid Tunisian achievements in economic planning could be contrasted the utter failure of Morocco's Five Year Plan (1960-64). Beside the careful Tunisian and the precipitous but not unsuccessful Algerian agrarian reforms could be noted the absence of any coherent Moroccan policy. It would appear that Moroccan parties and pressure groups are sufficiently strong to veto any policy that threatens the interests of any organized social sector. Or when, as at a colloquium on educational policy held in 1964, the parties are able to agree, the decision (immediate Arabization in this case) is a futile and demagogic protest against the existing policy.[9] In contrast, the one-party regimes of North Africa have been able (usually through compromise) to marshal support for coherent programs.

Possibly Moroccan immobilism is less the result of a multi-party system than the reflection of a society that is more complex and more divided than that of either proletarian Algeria or middle-class Tunisia. The parties faithfully mirror the social forces and

8. However, Douglas E. Ashford has pointed out that Istiqlal had lost membership since independence and, more generally, that "cumulative, widespread group activity cannot be depended upon to create a more effective, more responsive political system." See his "Patterns of Group Development in a New Nation," *American Political Science Review*, LV (June 1961), 328, 332.

9. See "Le Colloque sur l'Enseignement," *Maghreb* (Paris), No. 4 (July-August 1964), 17-20.

psychological tensions of a society which underwent more rapid change. The Istiqlal tried to be national, but though Allal al Fassi is too complex to be called a traditionalist, it could not bridge the gap between the older generation and younger leaders who were less equivocal modernizers. Class cleavages were superimposed upon generational ones, as the leaders of the National Union of Popular Forces rejected Al Fassi's vague Islamic socialism for more rigorous Marxist formulae. In their eyes the old Fassi bourgeoisie was less dangerous than the new class of businessmen and modern landowners it was spawning. With the creation of the UNFP, the workers were divided into two trade unions, although by 1962 the Moroccan Federation of Labor (UMT), wary of intellectuals without troops, was steering a political course increasingly independent of the UNFP. Against the threat of "Fassi dictatorship," the Popular Movement was formed in 1957 as a loosely-structured party representing primarily Berber rural elements. Loyal to the king, it constituted the numerically most important backing of the Democratic Front for Constitutional Institutions (FDIC) formed in time to contest the first elections under the 1962 Constitution for the House of Representatives. Though after by-elections the FDIC could claim a majority of the seats, the alliance broke up in 1964. Ahmad Reda Guedira and other politicians close to the king formed the Democratic Socialist Party (PSD), representing modern commercial and palace interests. Together with the Popular Movement and officers of the Royal Armed Forces, it governed the country in 1964. The Istiqlal, loyal to king and constitution, was the dominant opposition party since its elimination from the government in January 1963. The UNFP, with 27 of the 144 seats in the lower House, but with some of its top leaders in prison or exile for alleged conspiracy against the king, seemed divided as to the legitimacy of the regime it had unsuccessfully combatted in the 1962 constitutional referendum. In 1964 the king was unable to bring the two opposition parties into a new government of national unity, much less to achieve agreement among them on such controversial issues as agrarian reform.

Under the new constitution, however, Hassan II would seem to have the necessary powers to launch needed development policies. The constitution reflects the political ascendency of the monarchy that Mohammed V had clearly demonstrated in May 1960 by taking personal charge of the government. Despite a formal separation of powers, there are few checks or balances to executive authority. Though the cabinet, responsible to the king, is also responsible to the House of Representatives, the latter's weapon of censure, requiring an absolute majority, is permitted only once a year, as is the royal weapon of dissolution. Votes of no confidence, taken on the Prime Minister's initiative, also require an absolute majority. Selected by the king, the cabinet is essentially a royal agent serving him like those of de Gaulle under the Fifth Republic, as a shield from partisan pressures. The domain of law, narrowly defined, effectively excludes such controversial matters as education from the field of legislative competence. The House's role in budgetary matters is, in effect, purely consultative. The government may make decree laws during the eight months that parliament is not in session. Moreover the House of Councillors, elected in a way that ensures a large royalist majority, can virtually veto, if the king desires, any unpalatable legislation the lower House might pass (Art. 62). If the government, enjoying useful procedural weapons, fails to get needed legislation passed, or if the king wishes to veto laws passed by both houses, his power to initiate a referendum, like that of de Gaulle, could be used to great effect.

Hassan II probably has much more definite programs in mind than his father had. By exercising presidential control over key policy sectors, he may be able to circumvent the ministerial rivalries that plagued earlier efforts at reform. Formally speaking, the parties in the House, where the king commands a majority personally loyal to him, do not have sufficient power to upset his plans. But successful development requires more than good legislation. It requires competent administration, which Hassan, surrounded by a growing number of capable non-partisan technocrats and assisted, too, by a much larger number of French experts than Tunisia, may be developing. It may also require one asset that the king does not yet have, namely, an organizational weapon at the local level for stimulating popular motivation. National Promotion, launched in 1961 as a panacea for growing Moroccan unemployment and economic stagnation, failed in part for lack of a coordinated administration but in part, too, for lack of local cadres that Tunisia's Neo-Destour provided for a similar and more successful program. It is conceivable but unlikely that Guedira's party, the PSD, might develop adequate mass structures. A functional alternative might be to encourage the communes, launched in 1960, to take a more active role in development. But the powers of the communes remain highly circumscribed by a central government bent on maintaining its prerogatives. The potential of the army as an agent of development would also seem limited, though a number of officers serve as provincial governors and in other key capacities. Called upon to manage National Promotion, the army could not generate sufficient grass-roots cooperation.

In pluralistic Morocco a broadly based consensus on development policies is probably impossible. But the king, whether or not he brings the opposition into a new government,[10] seems sufficiently strong, his power consolidated, to override the vetoes of special interests represented by the parties. The presidential technocracy intimated by the new constitution may be sufficient, even in the absence of the popular mobilization single parties provide, to encourage economic development. Morocco has more varied resources than the other North African countries, and may therefore be able to develop without the massive governmental intervention required in Tunisia. In addition to political parties, Morocco offers a number of other channels of social mobility for ambitious young technocrats—not only in the bureaucracy but also in the agricultural and industrial sectors that are being gradually Moroccanized by private means. Underlying a politics of apparent stalemate is a society that is highly dynamic. Though technocracy alone is incapable of radical social engineering, this perhaps is not necessary. Indeed, that the scope of politics, paralyzed by dissensus, remains limited may be a positive advantage. When, as in Algeria, all facets of social activity are politicized, the load may be too great for the political system to bear. The cost can be increasing cynicism, depoliticization, and stagnation.

If Tunisia has in this respect achieved a relative balance, it can be explained by a relatively high degree of social cohesion that does not exist in Morocco. Each political system has in different ways achieved legitimacy in the eyes of large majorities of their respective populations. But in Tunisia, where legitimacy rests on the party, the demands of policy-making have led to a relative depoliticization, reflected in the decline in vitality of the Neo-Destour. In Morocco, on the other hand, where the monarch is the symbol of legitimacy, parties have retained their vitality but are unable to agree upon constructive policies.

In one respect the more fluid Moroccan pattern of multi-party politics seems more promising for political development than the Tunisian one-party pattern. Moroccan parties remain free to

---

10. He apparently had tried and failed, but his new government formed on August 20, 1964, was expected to be a stopgap pending further negotiations with the opposition parties. See *Le Monde,* August 21, 1964.

articulate the varied demands of the society and to bring new sectors into the political system. In Tunisia, on the other hand, the openness of the system is guaranteed more by the president than the party. Were Morocco to have become a one-party system under the Istiqlal, its Fassi leadership would probably have blocked the entrance of other groups into the political arena.

Another function that multi-party systems may be better able to perform than one-party systems is to transmit an effective political culture to the society. To be sure, the single parties can mobilize popular support, but without the practice of democracy inside the party, they are unable to communicate an agreed style for resolving conflicts. In Tunisia, political differences are aired in private; apart from rumors, the public is only made aware of issues on which agreement has been reached. Possibly differences are aired more publicly in Algeria, but it is doubtful that the FLN, once consolidated, will remain as open to debate and controversy. In Morocco, on the other hand, a framework for the public resolution of conflict exists. Even without achieving agreement, the party system can foster more widespread political education, and perhaps eventually more effective popular participation. Elections, mere spectacles of national unity in Tunisia and Algeria, are in themselves meaningful and instructive in a climate of real competition, even when the issues are abstract and divorced from policy-making.

Within a single-party regime, a prime task of the party may be to achieve an orderly succession. In Tunisia a muted struggle over Bourguiba's successor has probably already commenced. But in such a system the president cannot afford to allow any other individual or faction sufficient power to ensure victory. Unless the president continues to balance one group against another, he is in danger of prematurely losing his own title to rule. Acutely aware of the problem, Bourguiba in 1964 told the Neo-Destour Congress that, when the time came, the enlarged political bureau was to select his successor within twenty-four hours.[11]

Whether the party could agree upon a successor would depend upon whether it meanwhile could develop internal procedures of deliberation which everyone might consider legitimate. Perhaps discussion within the party is more possible today precisely because of its subordination to the government. There is less risk that it might upset the latter's policies. In Algeria, on the other hand, if the FLN retains a greater role in policy-making than the

11. *L'Action* (Tunis), October 21, 1964.

Neo-Destour and avoids being subordinated to the government, it will have been by virtue of an ideology that would discourage dissent. Under these circumstances the revolutionary single party may have difficulty in assuring orderly successions—more so, indeed, than the more pragmatic type of ruling party.

Paradoxically, the Moroccan multi-party system, which has no role in selecting kings and a rather tenuous one in the choice of prime ministers, may have the greatest chances of developing procedures accepted among the parties for ventilating their disputes. Indeed, the Moroccan political arena, displaying diversity as well as unity, may provide the stage for a new Maghribi political culture to develop. Given the realities of power and participation in all three executive-dominated systems, politics remains a spectacle for most North Africans. But if parties become one-way transmission belts for those in power, they will lose touch with the people and thus lose their political relevance. New attitudes toward power and new styles of participation are needed that a multi-party system may be better able to provide, if parties are to remain a significant factor in North African politics.

SELECTED BIBLIOGRAPHY

Books

Ait Ahmed, Hocine. *La Guerre et l'Après-Guerre.* Paris: Editions de Minuit, 1964.
Ashford, Douglas E. *Perspectives of a Moroccan Nationalist.* Totowa, N.J.: Bedminster Press, 1964.
———. *Political Change in Morocco.* Princeton: Princeton University Press, 1961.
Bedjaoui, Mohammed. *Law and the Algerian Revolution.* Brussels: International Association of Democratic Lawyers, 1961.
Boudiaf, Mohamed. *Notre Révolution,* Vol. I: *Ou Va l'Algérie?* Paris: Librairie de l'Etoile, 1964.
Debbasch, Charles. *La République Tunisienne.* Paris: Librairie Générale de Droit et de Jurisprudence, 1962.
Fanon, Frantz. *Les Damnés de la Terre.* Paris: Maspero, 1961.
Gallagher, Charles F. *The United States and North Africa: Morocco, Algeria and Tunis.* Cambridge, Mass.: Harvard University Press, 1963.
Lacouture, Jean and Simonne. *Le Maroc à l'Epreuve.* Paris: Editions du Seuil, 1958.
Le Tourneau, Roger. *Evolution Politique de l'Afrique du Nord Musulmane, 1920-1961.* Paris: Colin, 1962.

Mandouze, André (ed.). *La Révolution Algérienne par les Textes.* 2nd ed. Paris: Maspero, 1961.
Micaud, Charles A., with Leon Carl Brown and Clement Henry Moore. *Tunisia: The Politics of Modernization.* New York: Praeger, 1964.
Miner, Horace and George De Vos. *Oasis and Casbah: Algerian Culture and Personality in Change.* Anthropological Papers No. 15, Museum of Anthropology. Ann Arbor: University of Michigan Press, 1960.
Moore, Clement H. *The Dynamics of One-Party Government: Tunisia since Independence.* Berkeley: University of California Press, 1965.
Nouschi, André. *La Naissance du Nationalisme Algérien.* Paris: Editions de Minuit, 1962.
Ouzegane, Amar. *Le Meilleur Combat.* Paris: Julliard, 1962.
Rézette, Robert. *Les Partis Politiques Marocains.* Paris: Colin, 1955.
Robert, Jacques. *La Monarchie Marocaine.* Paris: Librairie Générale de Droit et de Jurisprudence, 1963.
Zartman, I. William. *Destiny of a Dynasty: The Search for Institutions in Morocco's Developing Society.* Columbia, S. C.: University of South Carolina Press, 1964.
———. *Morocco: Problems of New Power.* Atherton Press, 1964.

Articles

Abdallah, Ridha, "Structures et Evolution du Néo-Destour," *Revue Juridique et Politique d'Outre-Mer,* XVII (1963), 385-428, 573-657.
Ashford, Douglas E., "Contradictions of Nationalism and Nation-Building in the Muslim World," *Middle East Journal,* XVIII, No. 4 (Autumn 1964), 421-430.
———, "Patterns of Group Development in a New Nation: Morocco," *American Political Science Review,* LV (January 1961), 321-332.
Beling, Willard A., "Some Implications of the New Constitutional Monarchy in Morocco," *Middle East Journal,* XVIII, No. 2 (Spring 1964), 163-179.
Gallagher, Charles F., American Universities Field Staff Reports, North African Series, Vols. IX and X (1963 and 1964).
Maghreb (Paris), No. 1 (Jan.-Feb. 1964) and subsequent issues.
Marais, Octave, "La Classe Dirigeante au Maroc," *Revue Française de Science Politique,* XIV (August 1964), 709-737.
Marie, René, "Problèmes Algériens," *Revue de la Défense Nationale* (March-April 1964), 382-403, 578-592.
Robert, Jacques, "La Constitution de la République Algérienne, Démocratique et Populaire," *Revue du Droit Public et de la Science Politique en France et à l'Etranger,* LXXX (March-April 1964), 293-388.
Schaar, Stuart, "King Hassan's Alternatives," *Africa Report* (August 1963), 7-12.
Silvera, Victor, "Le Régime Constitutionnel de la Tunisie: La Constitution du 1 Juin 1959," *Revue Française de Science Politique,* X (April 1960), 336-394.

3
North African Foreign Policy

I. William Zartman

I

As the states of North Africa attained independence, a number of conflicting schools arose concerning different levels of relations with the external world. These can be stated schematically, without relation to any particular state, to serve as a reference point for later analysis. Since independence was the starting point for formal foreign relations, the first level concerned the consequences of independence. One school thought that independence was merely the first step in a struggle that would not end until all North Africa (and beyond) was liberated from colonial rule. To this point of view, the state was a temporary creation of colonial rule, and the nation—Arab, African, or Maghribi where the two overlapped—cut up by artificial boundaries into many states, was the only relevant reality. The other view also held that independence was only a prelude, but its emphasis was on domestic development; foreign policy was to assure the defense of state and society and the maintenance of good relations with other countries as state interest may direct, while major efforts were to be channeled into development, distribution, and enjoyment of the benefits of independence. Coincidentally, this debate had its roots in the independence struggle, where the advocates of violence contended with those who felt that independence could be gained by political pressure, reforms, and gradualism. The "state diplomacy" school prevailed over the "national revolution" school for numerous reasons, but most importantly because of the subtle but powerful influence of the environment in which the new states were operating, where the primary unit of international relations was recognized to be the sovereign state and not a disembodied movement.

Another debate concerned the meaning of independence. One

school saw the rupture of ties of political dependency on the metropole as only the beginning of a series of similar moves designed to remove all special privileges and break up all relationships where a predominantly bilateral pattern between former colony and metropole existed. This school not only looked to immediate evacuation of colonial troops and the removal of land from the hands of foreign owners—matters inherited from colonial times—but also sought to diversify the sources of input into the society after independence—such as military supplies, foreign aid, and trade. The other school was not in so much of a hurry to carry its slogans of independence to logical extremes. It enjoyed the protection, stability, and privileges that continuing association with the metropole afforded. It felt that political independence allowed this option to be made freely instead of being imposed, and it felt that there was sufficient fulfillment of nationalist ambitions in being able to gather the golden eggs of independence themselves, rather than going on to kill the goose. However, frequently this school's domestic policy involved no change in the social structure of the country, whereas its opponents felt that the political revolution of independence was meaningless without a domestic corollary of social revolution that would radically change the make-up of those who ate both the golden eggs and the goose. The confrontation of the two schools has produced mixed results: in the short run, the "complete independence" school has been able to impose the liquidation of many tangibles of colonial heritage, but the limited possibilities for diversification of input sources, more than the political power of the "bilateral association" school itself, has kept old patterns of trade and aid in force.

Meanwhile, another argument concerned the shape of the new world into which the states had entered. One school interpreted independence as the acquisition of membership in the family of sovereign states, where relations were conducted according to established rules and customs, variously listed as diplomatic practices and international laws, and where power was the means to ends defined in terms of state interests. Membership in the family was accepted unconditionally by the other members thanks to current myths of state equality, although the reality of world politics meant that, in general, the new states were classed among the small or weak, with less power to attain their goals than stronger states such as the metropole. Membership then meant legal equality, political inequality, and a need to develop internally in order to increase state power for the defense of state interests. The other school accepted independence, membership, and equality as a chance to join together with other states in a similar position, now a majority in the family, and overthrow the established rules and relations. It rejected the international law that sanctioned colonialism, the power politics that allowed the domination of the weak by the strong, and the Cold War system of international relations which threatened innocent bystanders with destruction in a mismanaged conflict over selfish ambitions cloaked in irrelevant ideological terms. It sought to impose a new international system based on equality, rights, and justice, goals it found more justifiable and more attainable than power and might. Armed with its rights—and a vigorous propaganda campaign that was its only instrument of power—this school sought to tighten relations with other states of similar views—thus adopting another classical tactic of power—and impose on the developed states the obligation to restore, in the form of stringless aid, the wealth of the underdeveloped world by which they had developed.[1] This argument between the "acceptance" and "revisionist" schools came to a draw by circumstance and by default. The "revisionists" found that power was necessary, even if not sufficient, to right wrongs, and that rights no more made might than might made right; they therefore found themselves forced to use the methods of the "acceptance" school, without, however, changing their aims.

The sides on each of the three levels of the debate have thus tended to group into two opposing arguments, each with its own internal cohesion and logical structure; when added together, the six schools fit into two distinct clusters of reasoning. The "national revolutionaries," the "complete independence" school, and the "revisionists" form a general approach to foreign policy that can be termed "revolutionary-idealist." The "state diplomacy," "bilateral association," and "acceptance" schools may in turn be called the "conventional-realists." Despite possible connotations of these terms (and despite certain admitted sympathies of this analyst), there is no attempt to attach a value judgment to the two arguments. The "revolutionary-idealists" wanted to change the world, radically and rapidly, and neither their success nor their failure was complete. Nor was that of the "conventional-realists."

---

1. Thus this school was, in fact, only advocating a struggle for power redefined.

However, it has been seen that, if one camp did from time to time gain the upper hand in the argument, it was at least as much because of the pressure of the situation or environment as of the schools themselves. While the "revolutionary-idealists" pressured the "conventional-realist" school into adopting certain of their goals, the world situation pressured the "revolutionary-idealists" toward "conventional-realism," particularly in their means, and a balance was established in the influence of the two schools. This fact in turn only further convinced the "revisionists" that they had to change the world in order to make it safe for their ideals. Thus foreign policy in North Africa has been characterized by a low degree of control over environmental factors, a low incidence of power in world politics, and a limited choice of real alternatives.

The arguments continue. Although in some cases one side has prevailed, the deciding force has frequently been the force of events or the pressure of the situation, imposed by the need of the state to interact with other states in conducting foreign relations. In other cases, neither camp has been the complete winner, and even where one argument appears to gain the upper hand over the other, the "meanwhile" has been filled with policies in which both camps have had their rôle and their influence. Perhaps most significant is the fact that each argument has given rise to new ones as time moves, situations change, and options become more complex. As all this occurs, North Africa develops a foreign policy. Its content may bear similarities to that of other states in the underdeveloped world rather than to the goals and aspirations of the metropole and its developed allies; its policy-makers may follow patterns of action established in other small states—developed or underdeveloped—instead of those used by the great powers and superpowers.[2] But the most important characteristic of the foreign policies and relations of North Africa is their developing complexity. Whatever the policy content and the behavioral patterns, policy is no longer made on the basis of a single goal—independence—and relations are no longer carried out within an exclusively bilateral framework. In short, the

---

2. Theoretical insights into the actions of small states are found in Annette Baker Fox, *The Power of Small States* (Chicago: University of Chicago Press, 1959). A similar treatment of developing states' foreign policies is found in Zartman, *Developing International Relations* (Englewood Cliffs: Prentice-Hall, 1965). For an earlier study of decolonization, see Maurice Flory, "Le Maroc, la Tunisie et la France," in *Les Nouveaux Etats dans les Relations Internationales*, eds. J-B. Duroselle and Jean Meyriat (Paris: Colin, 1963), pp. 285-319.

subject under analysis here is the decolonialization of foreign relations.

II

A transition from the above background to the foreign policies of the individual countries can be made easier through a few typical quotations from national leaders, to help establish the flavor of each state's policies and their relation to the various schools of thought. The clearest statements have been made by Tunisian President Habib Bourguiba, whose frequent speeches have outlined the process of progressive acquisition known as Bourguibism.

> Our objectives are well-known: Liberating the country from the last vestiges of colonialism, Raising the standard of living of the people, . . . [and] Leading the country to progress in order to gain strength and become less vulnerable. . . . Dignity comes first. Once we have assured dignity, we will concentrate on the economic and cultural aspects; we will consider common interests and cooperation and we will work with the object of achieving progress and prosperity. . . . At the start, our independence, like the independence given to Algeria, was only on paper. In order to make it real, we had, as Algeria will have, to engage in many struggles. . . . [The economic and the evacuation] struggles are in fact one and have the same objective, which is to assure the dignity of the Tunisian people. In order to secure this, two factors are necessary: full national sovereignty over the whole territory and guaranteed conditions of a decent life for all. . . . The aim [is] the reconquest of our national sovereignty so as to free the nation's potentialities in all fields: cultural, social, and economic.[3]

A more radical view is predominant in Algeria. A typical example is found in the words of the collective authors of the Tripoli Program, close to attitudes later to be expressed by President Ahmad Ben Bella.

> For the Algerian people, the Evian Accords represent an irreversible political victory which puts an end to the colonial regime and to foreign secular domination. . . . However, as

3. Quotations taken from Bourguiba's speeches, August 11, 1961, October 12, 1961, July 2, 1962, October 27, 1961, and November 7, 1960, issued by the Tunisian Secretariat of State for Information.

> a counterpart to independence, these Accords foresee a policy of cooperation between France and Algeria. This cooperation, . . . implies the maintenance of ties of dependence in the economic and cultural fields [and] gives precise guarantees to the French in Algeria . . . The Evian Accords constitute a neocolonialist platform that France is preparing to use to install and maintain its new form of domination. . . . The French government will not only utilize its armed forces and the French minority to influence the evolution of Algeria. Above all, it will exploit political and social contradictions within the FLN and will try to find within this movement objective allies likely to detach themselves from the Revolution to turn against it. . . . Sovereignty has been reconquered but everything remains to be done to give content to the national liberation. . . . Thus the foreign policy of Algeria should be oriented, within the neutralist current, toward an alliance with those countries who have succeeded in consolidating their independence and are liberated from the grip of imperialism. . . . This foreign policy is the indispensable corollary of our internal objectives. It will permit our country to attain the goals of the people's democratic Revolution and to participate in the construction of a new world.[4]

In contrast, Moroccan monarchs have shown a deep sense of history and its continuum, and have viewed independence as the restoration of sovereignty to an old state. During the early years of independence, Mohammed V said:

> Our aim is the recognition of Moroccan independence and the creation of new, freely negotiated relations between our country and France. . . . Interdependence should emanate from independence. Thus, before defining the relations of interdependence, our unconditional and unlimited independence must be recognized. It is for the French and Moroccan governments to define the particular areas where Franco-Moroccan cooperation is necessary for the reinforcement of their independence and the safeguard of their common interests. . . . Peace in Algeria . . . concerns our security, the stability of the North African ensemble, and the future of the friendly relations that the three [North African] countries sincerely wish to maintain with France. For these reasons, we admonish those responsible to hasten the solution of this problem and thus to bring an end to so much

---

4. Selections taken from Front de Libération Nationale, *Projet de Programme* (Algiers [?]: *Al Chaab*, n.d.), pp. 5, 9, 14, 49, 51.

human suffering.... Then these three countries—free, stable, and at peace—can undertake constructive works and great enterprises, in collaboration with France. Maghrib and France can then develop their common riches, in friendship, cooperation, and liberty.[5]

Hassan II, half a decade later, continued to reflect similar attitudes.

> Today, in the era of independence and decolonization, Morocco opens wide its arms to capital and technicians that wish to participate—under conditions established by its government—in the development of its natural resources. But we do not want an economic, financial, [or] cultural neo-colonialism to take root or grow in the country of ours that has so hardily reconquered its political independence. So, while maintaining mutually advantageous cooperation with the highly industrialized countries, we work to develop our exchanges with the African states.... This unity of our continent should be built on a program of courageous action, capable of ridding the African states forever of dependence, underdevelopment, ignorance, and hunger.[6]

A representative spokesman for Libya is harder to find, particularly since King Idris has made few important declarations on foreign affairs. A former prime minister and Libyan ambassador, Muhieddin al-Fikini, set a typical tone, however.

> The efforts displayed by the responsible Libyans in order to settle the relations of their country with the main Western powers ... may also pave the way for the heralding of a new era of friendly and fruitful cooperation between this geographical and human ensemble [the Arab world] and the Western world provided that there is readiness for comprehension on the basis of a mutual and genuine disposition in view of attaining the sacred values of dignity of the individual and the free determination of peoples.... [Italo-Libyan] relations, based on mutual respect and fructuous cooperation in the framework of dignity, equality and the respective independence of the two countries, illustrate the best example of the manner in which the relations between some of the Western powers and the African peoples should be settled, instead of the present errings, which confront the

---

5. Selections taken from Mohammed V, *Le Maroc à l'Heure de l'Indépendance* (Rabat: Ministry of Information, n.d. [1958]), pp. 237, 315, 134, 120.

6. Quotations from interviews with Hassan II by Georges Vaucher, *Sous les Cèdres d'Ifrane: Libres Entretiens avec Hassan II Roi du Maroc* (Paris: Julliard 1962), pp. 231-232.

principles of the United Nations and the Free World with the most painful trial, expose the relations with the African states to serious difficulties, and accentuate the danger of threats to tranquility and peace in the world.[7]

With these statements as a background, we can turn to the Moroccan, Algerian, Tunisian, and Libyan experiences in decolonization of foreign relations, examining first their relations with developed countries (especially the metropole). A priority item of decolonization has been military evacuation. Morocco, Algeria, Tunisia, and Libya (Fezzan) were still occupied by French troops after independence; there were also American and Spanish bases in Morocco, and British and American bases in Libya. The situation in Libya was slightly different from the other three countries, however, in that the French, British, and American bases were granted by agreements signed after Libyan independence.[8] Strengthened by its signature in 1953 and 1954 of the British and American agreements, which included provisions for substantial sums of aid, Libya then reversed its position and began to press France for evacuation of its bases in the Fezzan. The diplomatic pressure was successful, and the evacuation agreement of August 10, 1955, established a precedent for North Africa.

It was not long before Tunisia and Morocco took up demands for evacuation of colonial troops.[9] Official pressure began in Tunisia in mid-June 1956 and in Morocco in October, after the French kidnapping of Ben Bella. Diplomatic insistence was supplemented by mounting propaganda by the two states' political parties and their press, and eventually by direct political action, including strikes, roadblocks, demonstrations, and other incidents. The campaigns were pushed to a fever pitch in 1958, first by the French retaliatory attack on Sakiet Sidi Youssef, and then by the

---

7. Quotations from a speech by Al Fikini to the Commonwealth Club of San Francisco, August 14, 1959 (mimeographed, Libyan Embassy).

8. The agreements are dated December 24, 1951, July 29, 1953, and September 9, 1954, respectively. For background information, see Majid Khadduri, *Modern Libya: A Study in Political Development* (Baltimore: Johns Hopkins Press, 1963), pp. 258-261, 226-231, 252-258, respectively.

9. For background information on military evacuation in Morocco and Tunisia, see Zartman, *Morocco: Problems of New Power* (New York: Atherton Press, 1964), pp. 22-61; Douglas E. Ashford, *Political Change in Morocco* (Princeton: Princeton University Press, 1961), *passim;* Charles Debbasch, *La République Tunisienne* (Paris: Librairie Générale de Droit et de Jurisprudence, 1962), pp. 87-94; and Habib Bourguiba, Jr., "Tunisia," in Joseph E. Black and Kenneth W. Thompson, *Foreign Policies in a World of Change* (New York: Harper and Row, 1963), pp. 351-375.

French army's rôle in the May 13th revolt in Algeria; there was fear on both sides of Algeria that France might move in to reoccupy its former protectorates, as it had after the conquest of Algeria, and that French bases in Tunisia and Morocco would be used to facilitate the attack. Moroccan and Tunisian pressure, coinciding with the Gaullist strategy of bettering relations with the wings while concentrating power on the center of the line in Algeria, led to an agreement on evacuation of all Tunisian bases except Bizerte on June 17, 1958, and a major withdrawal from scattered Moroccan installations at the same time.

Despite this progress, the idea that independence was incompatible with continued occupation remained as powerful as ever, encouraged rather than satisfied by its first victories. The attitude was only further roused by the reasons against evacuation which had been given by France in 1956 and which still governed French policy in 1959: "cover Algeria, insure the security of the Frenchmen until North Africa is entirely pacified and the two governments are able to insure security themselves, [and] insure permanent participation in the defense of the Mediterranean."[10] Internal pressure was increased, in Tunisia, by the fact that Bourguiba felt he had been given a promise by de Gaulle that evacuation of Bizerte would be negotiated, and, in Morocco, by Mohammed V's success in negotiating an evacuation agreement for American bases that was signed by President Eisenhower on December 22, 1959. It was not difficult for France to accede to rising Moroccan pressure and sign an evacuation agreement on September 1, 1960, since the bases were primarily training schools and were useless in the Algerian war, and internal security was effectively assured by the Moroccan army. Evacuation was completed in a year and a half, and was accompanied by the withdrawal of Spanish troops from Moroccan bases. In regard to Tunisia, however, France was reluctant to break up the Bizerte-Toulon-Oran (Mers al-Kebir) naval defense triangle and de Gaulle had made public commitments not to negotiate under pressure. But Bourguiba was equally committed to his method of progressive decolonization, including the use of violence when negotiations proved unsuccessful. The result was the bloody clash of July 1961, ending in over a thousand Tunisian deaths, the temporary reoccupation of Bizerte town by the French, and a

10. Speech of French Foreign Minister Christian Pineau, cited in Debbasch, *La République Tunisienne,* p. 88. On the Bizerte affair, see *Bizerta: 15th October 1963* (Tunis: Secretariat of State for Information, 1963).

hardening of Tunisian policies. Negotiations resumed in 1961, leading finally to an evacuation of the base on October 15, 1963, when the Algerian war was over and de Gaulle was ready to withdraw.

Meanwhile, the Evian Accords of March 19, 1962, had created a somewhat different situation in Algeria by providing fixed dates for the evacuation of French troops from designated and non-designated sites.[11] Ben Bella was not a direct party to the Evian Accords and his attitude toward them was at best equivocal. When he called the military clauses of the Accords into question in March 1963, following French use of designated Saharan sites for atomic testing, France accelerated its military withdrawal; when it became apparent that there were few remaining Frenchmen in Algeria to defend and that the French army was relatively impotent to insure their security, evacuation of non-designated sites was further accelerated and was completed by mid-June 1964, a year ahead of schedule. When Bizerte was evacuated, the Mediterranean defense triangle lost one leg to stand on and Mers al-Kebir was downgraded from a strategic to an ordinary base; the need for its garrison to live out the fifteen-year guarantee of occupancy became less apparent, and evacuation of the base as well as other designated sites may well be hastened in order to avoid pressure from Algeria.

Withdrawal in all three states was delayed—above all because of the Algerian war—to the point where military advantages were outweighed by political repercussions. French bases in the area were interrelated. It was in the border regions that French troops in Tunisia and Morocco might have helped the efforts of their comrades in arms in the Algerian war, but once independence had been granted to Algeria's neighbors their freedom of action was limited. French troops in the Moroccan and Tunisian countryside were unnecessary to defend the security of Frenchmen, who no longer lived there, but once the troops were withdrawn, the remaining bases in the cities were also of lessened importance. Once the Algerian war was over, even Bizerte was politically less tenable, but once Bizerte was evacuated and the French exodus from Algeria had taken place the bases in Algeria were unimportant. The whole point of debate was then only one of timing, but it was crucial. "Our rights," Habib Bourguiba, Jr., has writ-

11. For background information on the military evacuation in Algeria, see Zartman, "Les Relations entre la France et l'Algérie," *Revue Française de Science Politique,* VI (December 1964), 1087-1113.

ten, "were recognized only after the Sakiet Sidi Youssef incident, added to many others, had destroyed confidence and made cooperation doubtful."[12]

In this process, there are two notable aspects to the foreign policies of the North African states. One was the fact that their concrete acts of pressure and even violence had little effect on the chain of events; this was partly due to the effective stubbornness of France's policy, but stubbornness was possible simply because the North African states could not bring meaningful pressure to bear on France. Second was the fact that Tunisia's, Morocco's, and Algeria's contribution to the evacuation struggle was thereby thrown onto the vaguer, perhaps unconscious, but no less effective level of propaganda. Continual reiteration by party and government of their sincere conviction—not simply tactical stand—that bilateral military association was incompatible with independence achieved the major goal of propaganda: to decree the unthinkable. This effort was aided by the Algerian war, which gave an additional reason for demanding evacuation, but even after the war was over, no "new era of cooperation" was suggested. By this time, evacuation was a policy accepted even by France.[13]

The situation in Libya confirms this observation. There was little pressure for abridgment of the British and American base agreements until February 1964, when Nasser turned his attention to the remaining Western bases in the Arab world. His efforts to decree the unthinkable—or spread it to Libya—bore rapid fruit within the context of Libyan domestic politics, and Libya asked for an early evacuation date. Both the British and the American structure of Mediterranean bases had been weakened by earlier evacuations elsewhere—Morocco, Malta, Cyprus, and Suez; although this made the bases more important militarily, the precedent rendered them less tenable politically. Early evacuation was agreed to in principle during 1964, and Britain began evacuation in 1965. The "complete independence" school had reversed attempts at bilateral association in the military field.

Civilian evacuation is another aspect of decolonization, not because of intrinsic dislike of the "colonialists" (who lost their political rights and power with the granting of independence),

---

12. Bourguiba, Jr., "Tunisia," p. 365.
13. What is more remarkable is that this agreement on the unthinkable did not cross the Sahara, where continued French military presence was frequently accepted as desirable and was finally reduced during 1964 as an economy measure by France, with few political ingredients from either side in the decision.

but because they occupied national land and drew disproportionate profit from the national economy. However, much more than military evacuation, civilian evacuation has a disruptive effect on the development of the country, for it generally removes the highest producing and consuming group in society as well as the largest source of private savings and investment. Whereas military evacuation does not involve any conflict between demands of independence and security, civilian evacuation poses a basic dilemma between criteria of independence and development, and so proceeds more slowly. In North Africa, the heat was taken off what might have been an even more burning question than it was, by the voluntary evacuation of much of the civilian population before any direct pressure was necessary. In no North African state was terrorism or violence a significant method of forcing evacuation—although there is no doubt that it would have been in Algeria if *colons*, with the advice of their embassy, had not quietly given in to the wave of summary seizures in 1963.

Algeria was not the first North African state to benefit from a mass exodus. Although the absolute figures differ widely, Libya, like Algeria, had a colonial minority equal to 10 percent of its population on its soil before World War II. In Libya, however, all Italian civilians were evacuated from Cyrenaica before 1942, and few came back, although property remained to be settled. Negotiations were carried on sporadically after independence, ending finally in an agreement of October 2, 1956, guaranteeing private property rights and even transfer of funds from sale of vacated property. In Tunisia and Morocco, the French population was larger, although the proportion was smaller. In both areas, independence meant a drop in this figure and then a leveling off. In Tunisia, early nationalization of major public utilities, progress toward military evacuation in 1958, agrarian reform on *habous* and tribal lands, and the hardening line towards France all made the situation ripe for Bourguiba to raise the question of colonial landholdings in November 1958. Two years of diplomatic pressure and negotiations brought an agreement for the recovery of 240,000 acres in 1960; indemnity was to be paid out of funds lent by France to Tunisia for the purpose. Other agreements followed annually on the same pattern, until 1964. In Morocco, pressure for recovery of colonial lands came from the Istiqlal Party, but was so inextricably bound up in questions of general agrarian reform and internal politics that no results were accomplished. Token distributions of public land by the king were timed in 1956, 1957 and 1959 so as to take the edge off the pressure, and a royal survey commission combined with further distributions in 1960 served the same purpose.[14]

It was Algeria that finally served as a catalyst for its neighbors. Although ideas of complete independence were clearly expressed in the FLN's Tripoli Program, and agrarian reform was sanctioned and provision made for its financing in the Evian Accords, the decolonization of the domestic Algerian economy did not come from any careful plan provided by the nationalist leadership, but from a peasant ground swell with innocuous beginnings. The first lands taken over were actually vacated and their temporary occupation by hired hands and sharecroppers was accepted by the Franco-Algerian provisional executive. Once begun, the movement was impossible to stop; the best Ben Bella could do (although it was by no means against his own inclinations) was to legalize the seizures as they moved from physically vacated lands to farms that were vacant only by *ex post facto* decree. The March 1963 crisis, set off by the French atomic test, provided a covering incident for further legalizations, although the decree was actually prepared before the atomic incident occurred. The final step was triggered by a similarly extraneous—but this time domestic—event as the Kabyle revolt gave Ben Bella the need for a dramatic gesture to rally support; on October 1, 1963, all French lands were expropriated. Throughout the period and afterward, expropriation of French urban commercial and industrial property continued.

The sequence of events in Algeria could not fail to have an effect on politics and policies in the neighboring countries. In Morocco, where political forces were pluralized, the elections of 1963 (despite a partial boycott by the opposition) and the installation of a multi-party parliament gave the forces of complete decolonialization an increased means of pressure. Inherent in the government parties' reaction was a fear of Algerian influence spreading throughout the hitherto inert rural masses, who might then take matters in their hands in an Algerian fashion. Plans for agrarian reform were drawn up in the ministries, leaked to

14. For background information on civilian evacuation and the land question in North Africa, see Khadduri, *Libya*, pp. 275-277; Debbasch, *La République Tunisienne*, pp. 94-104; Zartman, *Morocco*, pp. 118-153; Charles Micaud, Leon Carl Brown, and Clement H. Moore, *Tunisia: The Politics of Modernization* (New York: Praeger, 1964), pp. 159-167; *Le Fellah Maghrebin* (Paris: *Confluent*, Nos. 45-46, 1964); and Zartman, "Les Relations."

the press, promulgated by decree in September 1963, before parliament met, and countered by more vigorous opposition proposals in a special legislative session. As under Mohammed V, the government attempted to enact a minimum program to take the wind out of the opposition's sails, but the result was nevertheless a full-scale attack on colonial holdings, with the debate limited again to timing and indemnification. In Tunisia, where political forces were more nearly monolithic and decision-making more direct, the Algerian example was followed more closely. Bourguiba broke off negotiations with France on the question of indemnification in May 1964 and nationalized 250,000 acres of French land.

In both cases, as in Algeria, the exodus facilitated expropriation and expropriation accelerated the exodus. By 1965, there were about 130,000 Frenchmen in Morocco, 120,000 in Algeria, and 25,000 in Tunisia, nearly all of them in the cities. As in the case of military evacuation, the major policy instrument of the three states was propaganda, both in making continued French landholding unthinkable, thus reducing foreign reactions to government measures, and in strengthening internal pressure on one government and then the others for complete independence. However, contrary to the process of military evacuation, the states involved could take direct action, and the absence of French military forces and the political inhibitions on their use even if they were present—again, the unthinkable—removed chances for retaliation on North African soil. Decolonization has its own logic, wherein each step not only created pressures for the next, but also reduces the possibility of counteraction by retreating colonial forces.

It should not be thought that the ex-colonial states are powerless in their retreat, however. As decolonization moves forward, it moves onto less and less sure ground: less sure because the line between the thinkable and unthinkable becomes obscure and less readily propagated, less sure as decolonization thus moves into areas where the metropole has strong foreign policy advantages, and less sure since the decolonizing elites find themselves pressing forward into the jaws of a dilemma made up of their own primary values: independence and development, dignity (in the Bourguibist sense) and interest. The pressures of interest against ideology, or reality against idealism, have served to slow down the further process of decolonization as it moves to change postcolonial input sources.

All four states of North Africa leaned heavily on the metropole's financial injections into their public budgets before independence.[15] After independence, the need for these injections continued, and even increased as domestic economic activity temporarily fell following the colonial exodus. Not only was it generally assumed that aid would continue to flow from the metropole, but it was also often thought that this aid was owed by the metropole as a debt to the former colonies for exactions made during the colonial period. In Algeria, the Evian Accords provided for continued French aid over three years at the preindependence level. It soon became evident, however, that the metropole, far from accepting the colonial reparations argument unquestioningly, would use aid as a political weapon, its most important arm of pressure against other aspects of decolonization. Even in the matter of financial assistance, therefore, and despite moral feelings about restitutions, North African states began to look for complete independence instead of bilateralism.

In Morocco and Tunisia, the question was quickly decided. In Morocco, after the French kidnapping of Ben Bella in October 1956, negotiations with France were broken off; French aid during 1957 dropped to half the figure of the previous year and in 1958 dried up completely.[16] Morocco turned to the United States, but American aid, although steadily increasing since 1957, has been able only partially to replace the former French support, and Morocco has drawn heavily on its hard currency holdings. The 1957 franc devaluation was followed with grumbling, but the second devaluation two years later finally led (after a period of indecision and high political tension) to a national currency, devalued but unpegged from the franc and occupying a special position within the franc zone. In Tunisia, it was again the Algerian war, and Tunisia's "cobelligerency," which caused France to cease all economic aid in 1957. Bourguiba first covered his flank by creating a Tunisian national currency, in 1958, and then, on the occasion of the 1959 devaluation, unpegged the dinar from the franc, refused to follow the devaluation, denounced the

---

15. Good reviews of economic and financial relations are found in René Gallissot, *L'Economie de l'Afrique du Nord* (Paris: Presses Universitaires de France, 1961, [Que Sais-je, No. 965]); Nevill Barbour (ed.), *A Survey of North West Africa: The Maghrib* (2nd ed.; London: Oxford University Press, 1962); and *Revue France Outre-Mer*, special issue on French-speaking Africa, No. 409 (March 1964).

16. Much of the aid was replaced by sizeable loans to private companies in Morocco; *Tableaux Economiques du Maroc* (Rabat: Service Central des Statistiques, n.d. [1960]), p. 267.

bilateral customs union, and adopted exchange controls putting Tunisia "halfway out" of the franc zone.[17] Again, the alternative was American, and since 1957 the US aid program has partially replaced former French assistance.

In Algeria, in a more delicate situation, both sides played their hands more carefully. Independent Algeria has never called French aid into question, has not unpegged its new currency from the franc or restricted its membership in the franc zone, but, of course, has also not suffered from a major foreign policy disagreement such as the Algerian war was to Tunisia and Morocco. France, on the other hand, has not posed alignment as a political condition for aid, but has annually pared off sums to pay *colons* for confiscated land and has intimated a drastic reduction of aid after the three-year Evian guarantee expires. The Algerian alternative to French aid, an aid which riles the Algerian sense of decolonization while it keeps the Algerian economy afloat, has been the Eastern bloc. Russia has granted important loans, and China and the satellites have followed suit, without as yet replacing the predominantly French source of assistance.

Thus all three countries found, in one or the other of the leading Cold War antagonists, an alternative to reliance on French aid: Tunisia and Morocco turned to the United States, and Algeria to the Soviet bloc (while Libya until 1962 relied heavily on the United States and Britain). This alternate relationship lacked the possibilities of political pressure created by the presence of other ties with France and of French populations and investments on North African soil, and there has been remarkably little fear lest aid by the two Cold War protagonists be used to enforce alignment. However, in 1962, Morocco negotiated a restoration of French aid, and in July 1963 Hassan II visited de Gaulle for the purpose of increasing the sum and to consummate a rapprochement that was both personally and politically based. When the Bizerte issue (and the Algerian war) was settled, Tunisia too returned to France for aid and, in August 1963 and February 1964, contracted for a renewed financial assistance program.[18] The answer of Algeria and Libya to the problem of decolonizing sources of assistance has been to accelerate state intake of increasing oil revenues. While there is continued aware-

---

17. Tunisia then devalued in September 1964.
18. This program was in turn interrupted when Bourguiba nationalized remaining colonial land in May 1964.

ness of the problems of bilateral association, the notion of colonial reparations appears to have fallen by the wayside.

Equally important for Tunisia, Algeria, and Morocco has been their continued reliance on French cultural and technical assistance.[19] It has riled the "complete independence" school that Tunisian, Moroccan, and Algerian education is still kept alive by French teachers, and Bourguiba has frequently said that "we are determined to work out a plan so that our education will no longer be at the mercy of foreign assistance."[20] Algeria and Libya have gone the farthest in using Egyptians and other Arabic speakers to teach in their schools, but even in Algeria the vast majority of technical assistance still comes from France. Cultural and technical assistance has continued in all countries despite recurring political crises, and even the Bizerte incident and the seizures in Algeria had little effect on the number of schoolteachers willing to remain, contrary to initial fears. Although the trend throughout North Africa has been to shift from direct participation to the use of technical assistants as advisors and trainers, the exigencies of development in this field have won over the demands for independence, to the point where some Moroccans wonder if aid is not becoming a habit.[21] The continuance of bilateral association in this field has also reflected both France's unwillingness to use technical assistance directly as a political weapon, and, at the same time, the high place accorded to cultural foreign policy in France's post-colonial relations. Telecommunications assistants in Tunisia were charged with constituting a spy ring in February 1959, and teachers in Morocco were among the 481 signatories of a petition to end the Algerian war in 1960. But, for the most part, teachers and advisors have been beyond the reach of politics. Perhaps the reason lies in the fact that both sides consider technical assistance a value to be preserved, and hence hesitate to endanger it by bringing it into the bargaining process. Whatever the reason, the record of technical assistance shows that complete independence is neither an absolute nor an

19. For background information, see David C. Gordon, *North Africa's French Legacy: 1954-1962* (Cambridge, Mass.: Center for Middle Eastern Studies, 1962); and Charles Gallagher, *The United States and North Africa: Morocco, Algeria and Tunisia* (Cambridge, Mass.: Harvard University Press, 1963).
20. Speech of October 12, 1961.
21. For an official review of French aid programs, see *France: Aid and Cooperation* (New York: French Embassy, Press and Information Service, No. 6, 1962). The problem of cooperation from the North African side is well treated in *La Coopération Technique et Culturelle* (Paris: *Confluent*, Nos. 29-31, 1963).

imperative, and that, whatever its limits, bilateralism still has a future, especially when development is at stake and alternatives are scarce.

One aspect of foreign aid, however, is political by nature, is unrelated to development, and is full of alternatives. This is military assistance. Here the rules are different and the results— despite a certain advantage to standardization—more diversified even than in economic aid.[22] Because of its "cobelligerency" with the FLN, Tunisia was early refused French military aid; it threatened to turn to the East as it expanded its army during the tense days of 1958, and the threat brought a quick American response. Arms have continued to come from the United States, with additional aid from Britain; the air force is Swedish supplied, and the navy has former French ships. Morocco benefited from considerable French and Spanish aid at the time of its army's creation, with French assistance continuing thereafter. In 1960, miffed at French evacuation delays, Crown Prince Moulay Hassan turned to the Soviet Union for airplane purchases, although in previous years Morocco had been shipped Eastern bloc arms, presumably destined for Algeria. Algeria received military aid mainly from Russia, Eastern Europe, Egypt, and China, during the revolutionary war; other supplies were inherited from withdrawing French troops after independence. The Algero-Moroccan border war of October 1963 showed Algerian arms to be in need of modernization, and new supplies and trainers streamed in from Russia, China, Egypt, and Cuba. Libya has also had diversified sources of military aid, drawing on supplies and training from Britain, United States, Italy, Turkey, and Germany. The trend throughout all North Africa has been toward multiple sources of military assistance, and notions of complete independence have become accepted by military suppliers and receivers alike—although only in Morocco have Russia and the United States aided the same army. As a closing evaluation of the various types of aid, it can be said that military assistance quickly fell under the arguments of "complete independence," technical assistance has remained largely a matter of "bilateral association," and economic aid has been a battleground for the two concepts and a matter of political bargaining.

22. The best review of North African armies is found in Helen Kitchen (ed.), *A Handbook of African Affairs* (New York: Praeger, 1964). American military aid figures to Morocco and Tunisia are classified, and estimates of other countries' aid vary widely.

Trade is as important to North African foreign relations as the other aspects of decolonization, but is also the slowest to change, except by drastic measures. Commercial bilateralism is a fundamental condition of colonial relations, and to the Marxist is practically synonymous with colonialism;[23] when combined with hidden political intent, it becomes neocolonialism in current jargon. Even those nationalist leaders who see benefit in continued close economic relations with the metropole seek some change in the colonial pattern, usually expressed as a demand for higher, guaranteed prices for their raw materials and agricultural exports, and a policy of higher, protectionist tariffs to shelter their infant industrial development. Thus, Tunisia and Morocco were no exceptions when they raised duties on French products after independence, but sought to retain preferential treatment for their own products, and looked for new markets elsewhere. The effect on the general pattern of relations has been slim.[24]

Libya and Morocco have gone furthest in diversifying trade, and Algeria is moving fast to catch up. Both Morocco and Tunisia have signed commercial agreements with more than thirty countries in an effort to increase markets and diversify trade. Yet, as in the case of economic aid, the tendency has been to retain bilateral patterns of trade, at least for the moment; again, the absence of significant alternatives plays an important role. The three former French territories benefit from important tariff preferences with France, usually within established quotas. Commercial relations have then been a subject of debate, but rarely a subject of politics or an ingredient in diplomatic bargaining on other matters. An analysis of the Tunisian experience, examining the situation after the *demi-sortie* from the franc zone, is relevant to all the countries of North Africa: "The ties are no longer imposed. Henceforth they are discussed by the two parties. The desire for independence has won out. But in the minds of the nationalist leaders this desire does not exclude cooperation.

23. *Fundamentals of Marxism-Leninism* (2nd ed.; Moscow, 1963), lists all four North African countries among those "which have won their political independence and pursue an independent foreign policy, which have freed themselves from imperialist enslavement but remain in the capitalist system of economy." Cited in Thomas Perry Thornton (ed.), *The Third World in Soviet Perspective: Studies by Soviet Writers on Developing Areas* (Princeton: Princeton University Press, 1964), p. 49; see also p. 22 for a more detailed breakdown of Soviet categories.

24. Because of the presence of other chapters on economics and the distinction between foreign policy and economic policy, this aspect of decolonization will be treated only briefly here.

The basis of relations between the two states has not been drastically modified. The interdependence of several decades of colonization has not been changed—in the interest of both sides."[25]

Despite important differences from state to state, several general features stand out in the decolonization of relations between North Africa and the metropole. The "complete independence" school *has* won out, in political and military matters, in thought and in ideology. Thanks to the surge of the independence, concepts such as interdependence and bilateral association have been buried among the unthinkable, and their disappearance has been accepted on both shores of the Mediterranean. From the new position of independence, real ties, influences, and sources of input can be accepted or changed. From Algeria to Morocco (on the ideological spectrum), economic aid, technical assistance, and commercial exchanges have been accepted on a continuing bilateral pattern, and the latter two fields have to a large extent been exempted from the political bargaining process. Complete independence, as a state of mind, has been asserted, and at the same time development, as an economic necessity, has been fostered. The tense employed should not suggest that the argument has been settled forever, but rather that a temporary balance has been achieved. For in fact the two values are interdependent, and it is this relation that assures the balance. Independence as a frame of mind is necessary if the state leaders are to evaluate opportunities according to criteria of state interest, and development is necessary if the state is to continue to assert successfully its independence.

A second relation lies between pressures and obligations. The Evian Accords set up a delicate system of counterbalancing obligations between Algeria and France, designed to tie the two states to a close policy of cooperation. In a sense, either the Accords left Algeria with a conditional independence, or the obligations were not absolutes at all but were merely subjects of continuing negotiations. The exodus destroyed the balance between inter-community and inter-state obligations, lifted the conditional nature of independence, and placed the obligations on the negotiating tables—where they have been the subject of bargaining ever since. The independence of Morocco, Tunisia, and, even more so, Libya, was somewhat different in nature, although both Tunisia and Morocco soon broke away from economic obligations

---

25. Debbasch, *La République Tunisienne*, p. 97.

within the franc zone and, even more important, from the implicit supposition that they would follow their former metropole in political attitudes toward the Algerian war. In the process, economic and diplomatic relations were sometimes broken, and then both sides could set about freely to restructure these relations. At this point the balance sheet may appear to be dangerously out of balance, for what chance do the weak states of North Africa have to put pressure on a stronger state such as France as they bargain for continued aid and trade preferences? The answer is ironic, but it puts the bargaining table back on level ground. France entered the bargaining process with material goods to give, but also with interests to preserve and its own feelings of obligation to assuage. The Fifth Republic has felt it important to keep lines of communication open to the former territories of the Maghrib, despite or even because of their differing policies, and has even contributed to keeping power diffused among the three states; it has seen this as its interest. But it reinforces this interest with feelings of obligation—a sense of *noblesse oblige* and *mission civilisatrice* rolled together—that are an important basis to its technical assistance and foreign aid program. The countries of former French North Africa have been willing participants in this process, since it advances their development without placing obligations on their independence.

III

Independence and development have been seen to be one dilemma that the new states of North Africa have had to reconcile. The other foreign policy dilemma is between independence and unity. Whereas independence means the development of identity, interests, and decision-making within a state framework, unity means modifying and limiting these three elements by consideration of other nationalisms, interests, and governments, until— if the process is completed—political sentiments, rationales and processes are transferred to larger entities and higher values. The first stage involves independent state action, the second alliances and cooperation, and the third the ultimate formation of a new, larger state. Despite the many pan-movements in history, the third stage is a rarity. North Africa has been no exception. But in the ex-colonial areas, myths of unity and solidarity have been strong inheritances from the anti-colonial struggle, and new states have frequently sought unity as a means of achieving strength against more powerful and more developed countries. Since the North African states shared these myths and methods, and strongly felt ties of similarity and solidarity with many other areas of the world, they joined the rest of the new nations in seeking a satisfying definition of unity that would nevertheless preserve the separate independence for which they had all struggled so long.

North Africa is part of many worlds. It makes up its own region, the Maghrib.[26] This very name also implies that the region is the West of the Arab world where notions of nation and unity are strong. The European name for the region, North Africa, also implies membership in the African world, whose attempts to find an agreeable definition of unity parallel those of the Arabs, at a distance. In the largest sense, Arab Africa is part of the Afro-Asian group of states who share an antipathy to colonialism, a search for an acceptable meaning to neutralism, and a need to overcome a common underdevelopment. Each of these circles have provided a context for Moroccan, Algerian, Tunisian, and Libyan foreign policy and relations.

Until the independence of Algeria, North African relations with the rest of the Arab world were touchy at best. The three states which achieved independence during the 1950's waited a year or two before joining the Arab League, and Tunisia attended its first meeting only long enough to read a list of charges against Egypt and then leave. When the League met in Casablanca for the first time in 1959, Mohammed V's closing remarks proclaimed, "If the League has known an Oriental period, it now has its Maghrebi period."[27] The North African states avoided involvement in the Middle East balance of power system that swung around alliances, rivalries, ideologies, and personalities. Yet there was some interaction between the Middle East and North Africa. The states of the Maghrib and the FLN rallied to support Egypt during the Suez crisis in 1956 and opposed American intervention in Lebanon in 1958. The assassination of Feisal II in Iraq the same year came as a severe personal and political shock to Mohammed V, and the formation of the United Arab Republic was greeted with reserve in North Africa. Egypt, which had served as the haven for Allal al Fassi, Ben Bella, Bourguiba, and Idris I before 1956, also continued after North African independence

26. See Chapter XV.
27. *Petit Marocain* (Casablanca), October 9, 1959. Iraq's role in bringing Tunisia back into the League was an attempt to rally anti-Nasser votes and thus to involve North Africa in the Middle East balance of power.

to harbor Abdulkrim al Khattabi, who castigated the Moroccan regime, and Salah Ben Youssef, who plotted to overthrow the Tunisian regime; an Egyptian attaché in Libya tried to subvert the king's authority in 1956, and an Egyptian plot against the Libyan regime was discovered in 1958. After independence, Bourguiba exerted serious and finally successful efforts to move the FLN External Delegation from Cairo to Tunis, where it would be away from Nasser's influence and more accessible to Tunisian councils of moderation.

Given the Arab unity myth and the great similarities between the two Arab regions, how can the five years of tense relations between Arab East and West be explained? The answer is complex and must be found on many levels, but in summary it is that the similarities were taken for granted and the differences magnified by feelings and events. The North African countries felt justifiable pride in their own independence, and resented not only Egyptian attempts at interference but also a frequently expressed Egyptian feeling of superiority, rightness, and "having been there before." Egyptian support for Ben Youssef gave these feelings a concrete focus in the Tunisian case; Egyptian republicanism and Nasser's support for the 1958 Iraqi coup and regicide worried Morocco. Neither Morocco, Tunisia, nor Libya felt any particular debt to Egypt for their independence; their gradualism was opposed to Egyptian advocacy of violence, revolution, and socialism. Finally, Moroccan and Tunisian cultural orientation and political experience was closely tied with their French experience, whereas Egypt's Arabism was unsullied by any predominant Western source of influence.

Slow changes have taken place in this picture. As early as 1959, a new activist government in Morocco developed closer ties with the Middle East; Premier Abdullah Ibrahim toured the Arab states in June, the Arab League held its only North African meeting in September, and Mohammed V visited Arab heads of state in February 1960. In January 1961, Iraqi persuasion and a desire to mend fences brought Tunisia back to the League meeting at Baghdad, but it took the Bizerte crisis in July and the elimination of Ben Youssef by assassination to create a new basis for understanding and a restoration of diplomatic relations with Cairo in October 1961. "Bourguibism is dead, but Bourguiba lives," it was said; "Ben Youssef is dead, but Youssefism lives."[27a] However, such ruptures and rapprochements lack the deeper

27a. Gordon, *North Africa's French Legacy*, p. 101, n. 21.

grounding that would give them permanence. In the March 1965 meeting of Arab foreign ministers, Morocco, Tunisia, and Libya dissented from the other states' attitudes toward Israel and West Germany; yet at the same time Hassan II was warmly welcomed on a state visit to Cairo, while Bourguiba in Beirut and Amman was roundly castigated by the Middle East press for his conciliatory statements on the Palestine problem.

The independence of Algeria the following year and the accession of Ben Bella to power completed the change. After 1952, Ben Bella's nationalist experience before his kidnapping and imprisonment was mainly in Egypt; Algeria's experience was revolutionary, republican, socialist, and indebted to Egyptian support; the new Algerian leadership was favorably predisposed to Arab solidarity and strongly felt the need for a cultural reaction against France. Algeria's attitude, in turn, had diverse effects on the other North African countries, according to their geographic position and their other attitudes. When the Addis Ababa meeting took place in May 1963, it was the occasion for a public reconciliation of Bourguiba with Ben Bella and Nasser. When Michel Aflaq of the international Baath Party cited Algeria as the only North African state among the "liberated Arab countries," Bourguiba, offended, tried to prove him wrong but Hassan II, unconcerned, merely went to Paris to tighten relations with de Gaulle. When the Algero-Moroccan border war broke out in October 1963, Egypt gave concrete support to Algeria and Rabat broke diplomatic relations with Cairo. At the January Arab League summit and at the second Organization for African Unity (OAU) summit in August, both held in Cairo in 1964, all North African heads of state attended, but Hassan II has continued to be absent from smaller meetings, in Tunis and Algiers, where Nasser was present.

Although the general pattern of relations between North Africa and the rest of the Arab world has changed since the independence of Algeria, it is impossible to see a consolidation of solidarity within the Arab world to the exclusion of ideological differences. Nor is such a development likely in the future. The Maghrib is not a rival center of attraction within the Arab nation,[28] nor has it ever been; it is merely a separate region of the Arab world, with separate interests and separate attitudes. On the Israeli question,

---

28. As claimed by Jacques Baulin, *The Arab Role in Africa* (Baltimore: Penguin, 1962), p. 141.

its sympathy with Arab policies is unquestioned but it is further from the scene of conflict. It still remains untouched by many of the elements—negative and positive—that make the Middle East a separate system of action and interaction, elements such as the attraction of political unity, the presence of the international Baath Party, direct involvement in the historic Baghdad-Cairo rivalry, felt threats to security by the existence of Israel, and the political attraction of Gamal Abdul Nasser. On Arab issues, there is Arab unity—when there is not Arab interference on issues of national importance.

The attraction of the Arab world is also weakened by the competing—and rising—attraction of the African world. The three independent states had no diplomatic contacts with Black Africa when they were invited to send representatives to the first Conference of Independent African States in Accra in 1958. Their participation, along with that of Egypt, had an important symbolic effect on Black African relations, for it broadened the African unity movement to include the entire continent. In doing so, it led Black Africa to consider the Algerian war as part of the continental independence movement, rather than as simply an extension of Arab national self-assertion. African support for the Algerian war was strongly felt by the FLN, whose organ *El Moudjahid* gave more space to African solidarity than to Arab states' support.

But the Algerian war also served to split Africa into two groups, and was reinforced in this effect by the ideological split introduced after 1960 by Congolese events. Thus the special African foreign ministers' conference held in Monrovia in August 1959 was attended by North African representatives and, for the first time, by an officially-recognized GPRA delegation. But the moderate states, especially the host, Liberia, worked to delay final action on Algeria until the second Conference of Independent African States in Addis Ababa in 1960. There, the moderate majority limited its stand to support, not recognition, of the GPRA. Earlier the same year, Tunis was host to the second meeting of the All-African Peoples Conference, which had the important effects of impressing Algeria with African support, convincing Tunisia of its African role, and pressing Bourguiba to renew the Bizerte affair. However, when Morocco made an attempt in early 1961 to call a pan-African summit to consolidate support for the GPRA and Lumumba, as well as to find allies for its Mauritanian policy, Tunisia found itself in agreement on only one of these three issues—the Algerian question—and the Casablanca Group was formed of only six African governments: Morocco, Egypt, Guinea, Ghana, Mali, and the GPRA. Libya attended, but it too found the company incompatible with its policies, and withdrew quietly. Tunisia and Libya then joined in the Monrovia meeting of the moderate African states, with whose policies there was more agreement. When the group held its second meeting in Lagos in January 1962, Tunisia and Libya were unable to maintain their membership because of the one issue on which they agreed with the Casablanca Group—Algeria.[29] Africa, in its search for a minimum definition of unity, could only wait until the divisive issues of Congo and Algeria had been settled by time and the course of events.

As the two divisive issues disappeared and pressure rose for a continental reconciliation, some states took an active part in preparing a pan-African summit meeting. One of these states was Tunisia, which had had trouble in finding its place in the African groups. The third Conference of Independent African States was scheduled for Tunis in 1962. The conference was thrice postponed and finally abandoned, as its functions were absorbed by the new foreign ministers' and summit meetings at Addis Ababa. But in the process, the Tunisian preparations for the conference entered into the general moves of reconciliation and paved the way for final success at Addis Ababa. Algeria also made its contribution, in a negative way; having gained its independence, it lost its interest in the Casablanca Group, and finally, with Egypt, declined to attend a final group meeting, an announcement that was tantamount to dissolution of the group. Only Morocco clung to the hope of maintaining an alliance that would support its Mauritanian policy. When its allies deserted, Morocco refused to attend the founding meeting of the Organization for African Unity.

Although Morocco's absence from Addis Ababa had no effect on the success of the meeting, the subsequent role of the OAU in Moroccan affairs was a significant victory for the new African

29. Tunisia was also active in the formation of the African Trade Union Confederation (ATUC), which did not insist on disaffiliation from other labor internationals, while Morocco was instrumental in forming the All-African Trade Union Federation (AATUF), which advocated disaffiliation. The International Confederation of Arab Trade Unions (ICATU) does not have active affiliates in North Africa. See Jean Meynaud and Anisse Salah-Bey, *Le Syndicalisme Africain: Evolution et Perspectives* (Paris: Payot, 1963); and Werner Plum, *Gewerkschaften im Maghreb: UGTT, UMT, UGTA* (Hannover: Verlag für Literatur und Zeitgeschehen, 1962).

organization. When the Algero-Moroccan border war broke out, it was to the OAU that both sides finally turned for mediation; the good offices of the Arab League were rejected, particularly by Morocco who considered the League biased in Algeria's favor. An important step in the integration of North Africa in the African system—a step begun in 1958 in Accra—had been consummated. At the second OAU summit, held in Cairo in August 1964, all North African states were present. But African unity, and with it the solidarity of North Africa, soon sundered on the revived problems of Congo.[30] Algeria gave direct aid to the Congo rebels. Morocco, Tunisia, and Libya, while opposed to the government of Moise Tshombe and sensitive to his castigation of "Arab imperialism," had enough experience with subversion by their neighbors to deplore foreign-based attempts at overthrowing a legally constituted government, and, at the OAU council of ministers meeting in December 1964, to side with the moderate minority in deploring all intervention. The remarkable fact of both the Algero-Moroccan border war and the Congo rebellion was that, unlike the earlier Algerian and Congolese problems, they caused no formalized split of Africa into opposing groups, and no suspension of cooperation among African states.

The Maghrib's consciousness of its membership in the African community is an important event of the 1960's. While the Sahara remains an important communications barrier,[31] feelings of solidarity born of the nationalist movement and policies of interaction resulting from independence have tied "Black" and "White" Africa together in many real ways. Tunisia's *Jeune Afrique* is widely read throughout the continent, and Algeria's *Révolution Africaine* has been a potential competitor; like these two weeklies, the Istiqlal's new daily, *La Nation Africaine,* proclaims the Maghrib's African membership in its title. Morocco has offered economic aid in the form of credits to Mali and Guinea, and cultural aid to Senegal; Tunisia has offered cultural aid to Mauritania and Niger. Moroccan and Algerian assistance to insurgent movements in Portuguese Guinea, Angola, and—in Algeria's case—Congo has tied their policies to new sub-Saharan

---

30. Tunisia is a member of the OAU *ad hoc* committee on Congo, and Algeria is a member of the OAU Liberation Coordination Committee.
31. A conference of Saharan states met in Algiers in May 1964 under the auspices of the UN Economic Commission for Africa to plan a trans-Saharan road, most of which would lie within Algeria. For the position of the Sahara in area politics, see Zartman, *The Sahara—Bridge or Barrier?* (New York: Carnegie Endowment for International Peace, 1963 [International Conciliation, No. 541]).

states and territories. Tunisia and Morocco sent troops to the UN operations in Congo, although Tunisia's troops were temporarily withdrawn for the Bizerte affair in 1961 and Morocco's troops were permanently removed at the time of the Casablanca Conference (after serving a major role in support of the Congolese army and the Kasavubu-Mobutu government). As more developed and slightly older members of the African community, the North African states have much to offer to the newer nations as models for development, sources of assistance, and allies in cooperative endeavors toward common goals. North Africa has been able to find its place in the African unity movement because unity has been defined in minimal terms of policy and cooperation and has not threatened independence.

Arab Africa is also part of the neutralist, underdeveloped Afro-Asian world. Tunisia, Morocco, and Algeria (GPRA) proclaimed their formal membership in the non-aligned world by attending the Belgrade Conference of September 1961, and were joined by Libya in the successor meeting in Cairo in October 1964. All four countries agreed to attend the second Bandung meeting of Afro-Asian states, scheduled for Algiers the following spring. However, North African policies have frequently shown the limits of the non-alignment that Afro-Asian states were seeking to define. Algeria has strained the bounds of neutralism to its Eastern limit by its close association with Soviet policies, particularly evident during Ben Bella's visit to Moscow in May 1964. Tunisia's admiration for the United States, until the moment of disappointment in the Bizerte incident, has often been criticized as pushing non-alignment to its Western limits, and the Anglo-Libyan mutual defense treaty—the only alliance with a European power in North Africa—has kept Libya outside the strict definition of non-alignment. In between, Morocco has wavered, from the early days when Mohammed V advocated a Mediterranean defense triangle with Spain and France, through the moments of greater radicalism under domestic pressure during 1960 and 1961, to somewhat closer relations with France and the United States thereafter.

These differences among the states are the natural consequence of the varying independence struggles, which still leave their mark on foreign policy. Libyan independence was achieved without violence through the efforts of the Western powers within the United Nations. Libya has never had occasion to invoke Communist support against Western powers in order to strengthen its stand on an important issue. Tunisia and Morocco combined diplomacy with insurgency to win independence; they benefited from American sympathy during their diplomatic efforts at the United Nations and owed little to the Communist bloc. Only when the West has failed them on policies they deemed essential—Mauritania for Morocco, Bizerte for Tunisia—have the two states turned to the East. Algeria, on the other hand, fought long for independence from a France armed with NATO weapons and backed by benevolent American and British neutrality. During the war, the FLN received important quantities of Communist arms and varying degrees of Communist diplomatic support; after independence, the FLN adopted a policy of revolutionary socialism that built further ties of sympathy and solidarity with Cuba, Yugoslavia, Russia and China. There was neither gratitude, nor sympathy, nor a common value structure with the West—such as Tunisian and Moroccan leaders have proclaimed—to counterbalance these leanings.

The Maghrib states have been active members of the Afro-Asian group in the United Nations, although, like new members, they have frequently abstained on votes. Morocco and Tunisia have sat on the Security Council, and Mongi Slim of Tunisia has been president of the General Assembly. Solidarity among the three states admitted to membership in 1955-1956 has been high, as has been their independence from East and West.[32] North Africa gave support to the West during the Hungarian crisis in 1956, but it abstained in 1961 on both Hungary and Tibet; it has supported the admission of Communist China to the United Nations but accepted the credentials of the Kasavubu government in 1960. The states split on the Cuban complaints of 1961 and 1962. The arrival of Algeria among the United Nations members in 1962 added a new voice more favorable to Soviet positions, creating strains on the solidarity of North Africa.

As members of the Afro-Asian world, the North African states are caught up in the rivalry between Russia and China, although only in the case of Algeria is there any relevance to the statement that neutralism has shifted from an East-West context to a Russia-China context. Morocco, Algeria, and most recently Tunisia have recognized Communist China, and all carry on some trade with it.

32. Solidarity here means identical votes or abstention. African members of the Arab group in the U.N. (including Sudan and Egypt) were opposed to the United States on about 40% of the votes, and opposed to the USSR on about 8%, through 1962; figures on identical voting are 28 and 72%, respectively. Thomas Hovet, *Africa in the United Nations* (Evanston, Ill.: Northwestern University Press, 1963), pp. 169, 177.

Only in Algeria was Chinese Premier Chou En-Lai's visit in January 1964 an occasion for warm greetings and increased cooperation, and even Ben Bella has wished to avoid choosing sides between the two Communist colossi. None of the North African states have given vocal support to Indonesia's withdrawal from the United Nations, a move that has received hearty Chinese approval. In all cases, however, it would be difficult to conclude that a final policy has been made; North African states, fascinated by the activity of China and fearful of its size, watch its rise with a careful eye on their own interests.

A closing analysis can be made of prospective world views within the context of foreign policy, although even this approach must be taken on several different levels. Do the North African policy-makers look to the creation of a new order of world affairs, or do the governments seek merely to take their place among others in an established state system? In the terms of current Indonesian acronyms, are the North African countries among the new emerging forces (NEFO) or the old established forces (OLDEFO)? In one sense, there are noticeable differences. Some North African states have recognized and aspired to change the establishment; others have recognized and accepted it. Tunisia's policy, with the clear guidelines given in Bourguiba's frequent speeches, has been directed almost exclusively to the removal of limitations on state sovereignty and the enhancement of state efforts to develop itself as a full-grown member of the established community of nations. Foreign policy development in Tunisia has, in fact, progressed to the point where the government has a well-defined view of national interests and of instruments of national policy, as well as a comprehension of classical tactics of diplomacy and rules of mutuality in dealing with other states. Libyan views are similar, but lack the development so prominent in Tunisian policy. Morocco, too, aspires to full acceptance in an established community of nations, a view based on the long history of the state as a sovereign entity. Official Moroccan attitudes also reflect this background by recalling old Islamic notions of the state and applying them as justification for a policy of irredentism against other states of the western Sahara, an atavism absent from Tunisian or even Libyan policy. Even during its more radical days in the Casablanca Group, Morocco failed to share the revisionism of its allies in its policy statements.

Algeria, in contradistinction, has given a clear expression of revisionism, limited only by the vagueness characteristic of ideal-

King Mohammed V
of Morocco

President Habib Bourguiba of Tunisia (Wide World Photo)

Boulevard Youcef Zirout, Algiers

Above: *New apartments in Tripoli, Libya.* Opposite: *The old sector of Algiers*

Education for all is the goal

istic politics with which it sees the new order.[33] Ben Bella's speeches inveigh against the established world order, which is the source of all injustice, in the name of the people, in whom there is only justice and right. Rather than to the state, with its national interests, it looks to the oppressed peoples (in an African, Arab, or Afro-Asian framework) as the agent of international relations, with the vague implication that the state is to remain only as an administrative organization for masses of people who outmode independence with the basic characteristic of unity. Such views are not mere demagoguery, idealism, or utopianism; they show a basic difference in goal conception from those of the rest of North Africa.

In another sense, all the ex-colonial states appear to be participating in the creation of a new order. By helping to destroy the old colonial system which tied much of the world to a Europe-centered pattern of international relations, they have posed the problem of a new system. The characteristics of this system are not yet clear, and the continuance of power differentials and bilateral relations indicates that the change is not—and may never be—complete. The effect of the breakdown of colonialism and the loosening of bipolar ties has been to accentuate the characteristic of highly diffused power among many separate units—often termed the balance of power system. The continued weakening of the United Nations has removed, at least temporarily, the possibilities of a concert system or a universal international system.[34] The regulator mechanism—the means for solving conflicts and maintaining equilibrium in the system—appears to continue to lie in the classical gamut of instruments from diplomacy to war, and in the operation of regional organizations to solve intra-regional disputes. The limited effectiveness of the latter, however, prevents any present consideration—contrary to what was once thought to be a visible trend—of a world of blocs, where regional concerts or organizations would replace states as the effective unit of a world system. Thus, the loosening of colonial ties has disrupted the established pattern of relations less than might be supposed. It has

---

33. No reference to revisionism would be complete without citing Frantz Fanon, *Les Damnés de la Terre* (Paris: Maspero, 1961), one of the most coherent statements of revisionist idealism. See also discussions in Morton A. Kaplan (ed.), *The Revolution in World Politics* (New York: Wiley, 1962).

34. Discussions of systems and regulators are found in Morton A. Kaplan, *System and Process in International Relations* (New York: Wiley, 1957) and Richard N. Rosecrance, *Action and Reaction in World Politics: International Systems in Perspective* (Boston: Little, Brown, 1963).

merely brought a large, and possibly unmanageable, number of new members into an old state system, now worldwide, without bringing any new "rules of the game" to govern this sudden multiplication of possible relations. Again, the result has been to bring out a previously-noted characteristic of North African foreign policies—the relative inability of the new states to control their environment. Even their contribution of propaganda has been unable to bring any new "rules of the game" into the realm of the thinkable or relegate any old rules—except for colonialism itself— beyond the pale of the unthinkable. Caught between internal pressures to act like independent states and external pressures of a system of like units, Morocco, Algeria, Tunisia, and Libya have been moving—remarkably fast although sometimes willy-nilly— into full status in the family of nations.

4
Language and Identity

*Charles F. Gallagher**

"Qui ten la lengo ten la claou"
—Mistral

Decisions regarding linguistic identification and the teaching of a common, working tongue are of vital importance in the struggle to shape the future of the countries of North Africa, and also serve as an indication of their present character. In the modern world people are often known for their words as much as for their deeds. So it is with the Arabs, who base their identity in large measure upon the use of a common tongue. Equally true of the French is the belief that language will play a predominant role in the cultural orientation of a man or of a nation.

Today in the Maghrib, language serves both as this kind of symbol—of affinities and aspirations, as direction and identification—and as a tool for reordering, re-creating, and seeking propitious ground in which to put down renewed roots. Both opportunities and dangers abound amid the prospects aroused by an educational and cultural drive which combines elements of birth and rebirth. There is the chance to unbar the gates to modernism and progress on the one hand, and to rediscover an intellectual attic filled with ancestral treasures on the other. Either act may in its turn impose new norms of self-assessment and understanding leading to even greater adventures of the unknown for the collective soul. These chances and perils are expressed in the traditional Arab antithesis of the *qadim* and the *jadid,* the Old and the New; in the tension between the Secular and the Godly, between the Self and the Other; and most markedly in the need to resolve the boundary

---

*©American Universities Field Staff. The Editor and the publishers are grateful to AUFS for permission to use Mr. Gallagher's paper in this volume.

lines between the Symbolic and the Utilitarian, which now tend to mark off the areas in which, respectively, revelation and reason dominate. This search for the proper tongue is perhaps the true North African dilemma, the problem which distills the essence of all other problems facing the area, beyond that of mere peasant existence.

The outstanding expression of the linguistic dilemma is the split between official dogma and observable reality. The three countries of the Maghrib: Tunisia, Morocco, and Algeria,[1] are by self-proclamation Islamic in spirit and Arabic in language. The Tunisian Constitution in its preamble declares the "Will of this people . . . to remain faithful to the teachings of Islam, to the unity of the Greater Maghrib, to belong to the Arab family . . . ," and Article 1 establishes Arabic as the language of the state. Likewise, the preamble of the Moroccan Constitution defines the Kingdom as a "sovereign Muslim state, whose official language is Arabic," but significantly separates language from other areas by making no mention of Arabism as a concurrent social or political phenomenon. The Algerian Constitution, adopted in September 1963, after describing Algeria as an "Integral part of the Arab Maghrib, of the Arab World, and of Africa" in Article 2, continues in Article 5 to state that "Arabic is the national and official language of the state." By provisions of Article 73, however, "French can be used provisionally along with Arabic." In all three cases Islam is described as the state religion, a statement with as many repercussions in the language field as elsewhere.[2]

1. Because its linguistic and cultural development has been so different, no mention is made here of Libya. No real problem of bilingualism or Arabization exists there; the underlying reasons for this fact and the policy of the Libyan government, however, are interesting in themselves.

2. A different categorization of the North African states, and one useful in exhibiting French views on the question of cultural penetration and influence, appears in one of the few official French statements which discuss the cultural orientation of various countries to France. This is a report on *La Politique de Coopération avec les Pays en Voie de Développement* (the so-called Jeanneney Report) published in 1964. In Annex 12, p. 201, countries are divided into four categories according to "the importance of the French language in the countries considered." These are:

(A) A first group of countries having its own national language and a sufficiently structured and adequate teaching system. Example, Latin America.

(B) Some other countries where formerly there was strong implantation of French teaching and where our language was widely spread, but where a national educational system in the language of the country predominates. . . . Examples, Lebanon, Cambodia, Laos, Vietnam.

(C) A third group of countries characterized by the existence of a double system, national and French (with a well-stocked Cultural Mission), a heavy inte-

To the bustling graduate student arriving in the area from the United States to work in political science or economics, these official statements would be a clear indication of the language training needed to carry out successful research, just as they would serve to reassure a businessman from the Levant that he would have no difficulty from the communications point of view in opening a branch office in Casablanca, or as they would console religious authorities visiting from Saudi Arabia to know that they would be understood by the urban masses of Algeria. How wrong they all would be emerges from a glance at the actualities underlying these pronouncements.

Today one can observe the leading figures and high officials of the Algerian Republic using French overwhelmingly as their means of communication with the Algerian people. President Ben Bella in the spring of 1964 called for the revision of the military clauses of the Evian agreements in French before a National Assembly (significantly not using the earphones available for simultaneous translation) which in August 1963 had called for "the use of Arabic in all administrations at the same level as French" and recommended "the translation of the Official Journal into Arabic." The late Foreign Minister, Mohammed Khemisti, was unable to speak directly to President Nasser in Cairo because they had no common language. A distinguished American scholar of Arabic vainly suggested to President Bourguiba during an interview in French that they might switch to Arabic. Journalists at press conferences held by the King of Morocco must be able to follow the monarch's impeccable French, but they need not know a word of Arabic. Considering only the question of external communication (internal exchange between North Africans will be discussed later), the scholar, visitor, or tourist will find French spoken everywhere throughout the administrations in Maghrib countries, and used as a *de facto* working language, not only at state functions and receptions, but to the point where the Post Office (in Morocco, for example) has refused to accept telegrams written in Arabic and most government offices insist that bilingual forms be filled out in French by preference. The foreigner will note that French is the overwhelmingly used language of enter-

---

gration of our agents in the national system, an extremely vast diffusion of our language in the administrative structure, and the existence of an important French minority.

(D) A last group where our language has the character of a national language. . . . Example, Black Africa.

tainment in cinemas, theaters, and cabarets, and is widely, but far from exclusively, employed as the vehicle for information communication. The most widely read newspapers in North Africa are French-language journals,[3] and radio newscast bulletins in French which use directly incoming European-language cables are more up-to-date and reliable than their Arabic translations. To illustrate the dangers to the unwary by paraphrasing Simeon Potter[4] on the nonunderstanding of American English in London before World War II, a foreigner in Algiers today who knew only Arabic might well die of a heart attack in the street before he could find a pharmacy, explain what specific medicine he required, and make himself understood.

The fact that independent North African states came into being burdened—if that word may be used, for in the long run the benefit may prevail—by these linguistic vagaries is not accidental, in the strict sense, nor can more than a small part of the problem be attributed to Machiavellian maneuvers by colonialism. It is rather the direct result of history at its extremes in time, space, and men: North Africa received too few Arab speakers, spread out too far from their original homelands, and strung over too many centuries, while it was blanketed in the colonial period by too many Europeans in too intense a concentration.

Upon a permeable but finally ineradicable Berber substratum which has left about 20 percent of the entire area Berber-speaking today, the Arab invasions poured out over some six centuries a series of diverse groupings: perhaps 150,000 soldiers in the first waves of the 7th and 8th centuries, plus the merchants, functionaries, women and hangers-on around them, and a doubtful 200,000 in the Hilalian invasions of the 11th and 12th centuries. A further infusion came in the later Middle Ages in the mass migration of Andalusian Moriscos from the towns and *huertas* of Spain. In between, trickling arrivals of individuals and smaller groups, usually from the Arab centers in the East or Spain, came to the cities of the Maghrib, leaving large parts of the countryside untouched. And, finally, came centuries of much reduced intercourse tantamount to isolation. North Africa, accordingly, has never been "Arab" in race or blood—although we should shy away from any attempt to use the word "Arab" on other than a culturo-

3. E.g., *Jeune Afrique* and *La Presse* in Tunis. *La Dépêche* in Algiers had an estimated circulation of 95,000 before it was closed down in the autumn of 1963. Estimates on Moroccan papers vary widely, but it is generally agreed that *Le Petit Marocain* distances the field.

4. Cf. Simeon Potter, *Our Language* (London: Penguin Books, 1954).

linguistic basis. Eventually the heterogeneity of the immigration and its insufficient quantity produced what might be expected: in the long-established traditional cities, like Tunis and Fez, an often distinguished urban *bourgeoisie* speaking a dialectal but rich Arabic and possessing some literacy; in those parts of the countryside settled early and open to urban influence, like the Jbala in Northern Morocco, an older, city-type speech; in the mountains, dialects influenced by Berber, particularly in consonantal degradation and dentalization, others reflecting more or less clearly their Bedouin ancestry in the Orient, (some of these, as is true everywhere in language refuge-areas, of exceptional purity-in-archaism). There are Berberophone pockets of some size in the more rugged regions, and a heavy infiltration of Berber in most rural speech, having to do particularly with the names of flora and fauna, tools and utensils, toponymy, and a special vocabulary fitted to the settled agriculture of the area.

The potential of the French language as a force toward homogeneity was never fully invoked either. For over 130 years, from 1830-1962, North Africa was inundated, consciously and unconsciously, with a more massive dose of metropolitan culture than that bestowed on any comparable subject area. The French conquest had several powerful means at its disposal. First, there were the sheer numbers of the colonization. It is interesting to reflect that in 1931 the 1,400,000 Europeans[5] in a total population of 14 million represented probably as large a minority as the Arabs had some seven centuries earlier. Their political and economic power positions were much the same, but the communications facilities of the latter-day conquerors were infinitely superior. Moreover, France appeared with a will to impose itself, centered in terms of assumed cultural, and therefore linguistic, superiority as much as or more than in other domains. A methodical policy of deracination and deculturization was followed in Algeria in the 19th century, was repeated to a lesser extent in Morocco over a shorter period, and carried out most slightly in Tunisia. Finally, this policy was carried forward with the certitude of the morally right (and the victorious), and was in devious ways abetted by the semicomplicity of the vanquished to whom one of the most expressive symbols of power became the magic new language.

Despite the French conception of themselves as fulfilling a

5. Not all the Europeans were French, of course, and a small minority did not speak the language; but French was the language of the European community in French-held territories in North Africa. (This does not include Spanish Morocco.)

mission civilisatrice, there was little energy expended in forcing French thought and language down the throats of recalcitrant Arab millions in the Maghrib. The minuscule number of North Africans receiving a modern, French education in 1939 (about 100,000), and the obstacles often put in their way, testified to the rigidity of a traditional policy of educating and assimilating a small elite. For the masses, indifference and disdain were the keynotes, and the main effort, if any can be said to have been deliberately made, was to destroy the colonized by a complete denigration of their fundamental values. Algerian peasants were often physically forced off their lands in the 19th century and turned into little more than scavengers for scraps; the natural cultural counterpart of this was the conviction that they needed no more of a native vocabulary than that suitable for gathering nuts and berries (or esparto grass), and just enough French to obey commands. Only much later, with the coming of modern industrial fringe activity, was it thought necessary to teach them the rudiments of a technical lexicon so as to let them occupy the essential bottom rungs of the new hierarchy.

While a generalized, low-level knowledge of French inevitably came to be widely spread among these masses, the colonial ruling group had from the start a healthy fear of contact between the culturally dispossessed *indigène* and classical Arabic.[6] Distant and dead as that might seem to the non-literate North African at the turn of this century, both because of desuetude and systematic discouragement by the colonial authorities, it represented a threat to *colon* supremacy vaguely but deeply felt by the settler community. The vicissitudes undergone by a young Maghribi rising through the French educational system were on the whole nothing compared to those suffered by him if he chose to vest himself with a fully Muslim-Arab education, especially if he compounded this by trying to wed the prestige of this tradition to the forbidden realms of political action.[7]

In the end—which began to take shape with the awakening of

6. A gross but useful simplification for non-specialists would be to suggest that the relationship between classical Arabic and the North African dialect(s) resembles that between Latin and Spanish (or, in the Moroccan extreme, Portuguese). The general directions of changes in morphology and syntax over more than a millennium have been similar in both cases as well (reduction of verb endings, elimination of cases, etc.).

7. There were important differences in what was allowed, where, and when. What was impossible in Algeria, and usually difficult in Morocco, might be permitted in Tunisia, as the example of the Khalduniya, among others, shows.

the 1930's—North Africans of the previous generation started to understand that both these "exotic" languages were weapons to be used in separate ways. French was increasingly learned by young modernists as a means of combatting the Other, the enemy of his own terrain, and for ferreting out his secrets. The study of classical Arabic, meanwhile, became a way of preserving one's identity and of restoring to the Self a dignity which had fallen away through oppression and neglect over decades and centuries. Religious schools everywhere, and groups like the *ulama* in Algeria, encouraged young men along this path wherever they were politically free to do so, but their efforts were limited by official restraints which increased as World War II approached.

After the war, French policy turned in the direction of opening up education (always in French) on a much wider scale, and by the mid-1950's, when independence for at least part of the Maghrib had become certain, a still small but much more respectable number of North Africans than that of ten years before was receiving a full or modified form of French-inspired teaching. Moreover, by this time French had clearly been established as the *lingua franca* of the three countries, both on an administrative and literary basis, and as an external, vulgate tongue for communication in all cases between natives and non-natives. Its dominant position was unstable, however, because it represented domination and humiliation as well as access to the outside world of modern thought. It was written and spoken well by only a tiny minority of the indigenous population and there clung to it an odor of foreign impurity. It was an infidel in the Muslim household faced with a potential rival of great prestige and emotional attraction. To an observer in 1955-56, speculating on the linguistic future of North Africa was fascinating but difficult—just as it is today.

The linguistic realities of today, after nearly ten years of independent orientation in Morocco and Tunisia and a short two years in Algeria, are very different from those of a decade ago and in some ways surprising. They can be summed up *grosso modo* as regards quantity in Table I.[8]

As can be seen, dialectal Arabic is the common tongue of North Africa, spoken by everyone except a portion of the Berberophones,

---

8. The estimates in this table are highly approximative. They have been arrived at, except in the case of Algeria, by taking as a base the number of graduates at the primary level, presumably literate, from national schools before and after bilingual instruction was introduced, plus graduates from private schools, free

Table I. Approximate Number of Persons Normally Using or Having a Knowledge of

Country	Estimated 1964 Population	Dialectal Arabic (speaking)	Berber (speaking)	Classical Arabic (reading)	French (speaking)	French (reading)
Morocco	13,000,000	11,000,000	4,000,000	1,000,000	4,000,000	800,000
Algeria	11,500,000	10,000,000	2,500,000	300,000	6,000,000	1,000,000
Tunisia	4,500,000	4,500,000	—	700,000	2,000,000	700,000
Total	29,000,000	25,500,000	6,500,000	2,000,000	12,000,000	2,500,000

(Totals do not tally horizontally, of course, because many individuals fall into several categories.)

mostly women, who are little in contact with the outside world. The dialects in North Africa are, by and large, mutually intelligible with little effort (the writer has observed Moroccans with a very limited classical background functioning without problems in Tunisia a few weeks after their arrival there) and they could be considered one. Technically they should be subdivided into at least two subdialects of a group which extends roughly from Tripolitania westward. The dialect is not written under normal circumstances, although French colonial policy sometimes attempted this in order to avoid using classical Arabic. (A few outdated railway carriages in Morocco still have bilingual notices which use vulgar Arabic written in the 1920's.) One immediately apparent difficulty is that the verbal bond between North Africans is made up by a richly expressive and lively spoken tongue which is, particularly from the standpoint of vocabulary, quite inadequate to the needs of modern, technical civilization.

The estimates given for classical Arabic presuppose the ability to read and understand tolerably well a local newspaper. The number of those speaking a degree of the classical, or what the speakers themselves consider some facsimile of it, would be very different; so, too, would the number of those able to understand and repeat with reasonable accuracy the content of a radio news

schools, religious institutions, and the cultural missions. Another breakdown might be:

TOTAL NUMBER OF LITERATES (Estimated)

	Tunisia	Morocco	Algeria
Arabic only	300,000	400,000	100,000
Bilingual	500,000	700,000	300,000
French only	100,000	100,000	900,000
Total	900,000	1,200,000	1,300,000
	20 percent	10 percent	12 percent

broadcast. Widespread inculcation of classical Arabic, on a very limited and rote-learned basis, has been achieved by religious teaching and memorization of Koranic passages. Thus, nearly every male in the area knows a fair number of set phrases and passages which permit him, depending on individual ability, to extend this understanding to other spheres. The knowledge in such cases almost always remains passively conceived, however. Two socially important notations should be made with regard to classical Arabic: first, that it is used by two kinds of elites, one a traditional and religious group, the other a modern, educated group which includes much of the administrative hierarchy; second, that the age-curve is significantly low—that is, there is a steadily rising percentage of young North Africans becoming fluent in it. Ten years ago there were far fewer than 500,000— and this is probably a very generous estimate—who could read an Arabic-language newspaper in North Africa. Today there are four times as many, and from 200,000 to 250,000 join them each year.

Like vulgar Arabic, Berber is only a spoken language; occasionally but rarely, as in Kabylia, one may see it written in Roman letters. Several facts stand out about the Berber dialects: (1) They are confined to specific geographical areas in Morocco and Algeria, all in the mountains; (2) They seem to be gradually losing ground but at an extremely slow pace; (3) There is some mutual intelligibility (Kabyles and Riffians claim to be able to understand each other, and (4) most adult male Berber-speakers are forced to learn another language—Arabic or French—for their dealings with out-groups, so that about half of all Berberophones are at least bilingual. Official policy in both Morocco and Algeria toward Berber as a language has been complicated by the political overtones in Berber areas. Flurries of self-interest approaching a form of separatism have occurred and caused problems. Still, aside from occasional misunderstandings, administrative tendencies have been to leave the language as is without encouraging it— but pointedly rejecting the previous French-colonial policy of distinguishing Berber speakers from those of Arabic. Government radios broadcast several hours a day in Berber dialects and the central administrations have become more careful in appointing regional officials who can be understood by the population.

Taken as a whole, some general conclusions which can be drawn from the above figures are:

(1) North Africa is still very much an illiterate area. Literacy

seems to vary from about 10 percent to 20 percent, with important variations between city and country as well as between men and women.

(2) With 29 million individuals producing 44 million speakers of one or another language, there is a high degree of bilingualism and some trilingualism.

(3) There is an important diglossia between the primary spoken language (dialectal Arabic) and the standard written form of that language (classical Arabic). In fact, the sharpness of the difference—much greater than for comparable dialects in the Middle East *vis-à-vis* the classical—may help explain why a mélange akin to the "third language" of the Arab East has not really developed in North Africa. However, the brief time span in which classical has been taught, and the much wider use of French, may be equally inhibiting factors.

(4) Only one of the three spoken tongues is written as such.

(5) The secondary spoken language (French) is a vehicle of literacy for more individuals than the written form of the primary spoken language.

This linguistic structure appears to have become solidified in the Maghrib in recent years through the instrument of generally similar educational policies. Morocco and Tunisia adopted their present educational systems soon after independence (in 1958 in both instances), and Algeria, although still operating somewhat *ad hoc,* seemingly intends to follow much the same path. The basic principles guiding the governments of the Maghrib in educational matters are these: (1) Full, public education for all nationals, as opposed to the formation of an intellectual elite, is felt necessary—every child has a right to education; (2) It is considered that Arabic culture and the Arabic language have been neglected in favor of an approach uniquely stressing European civilization and its values; And (3) it is recognized how difficult it would be to attack the problem of mass education rapidly while simultaneously shifting the whole emphasis of instruction as well as substituting one language for another. The importance of the third principle was reinforced by the disaster suffered by Morocco in 1956-57 through an overhasty Arabization of curriculum and methods. In consequence, the 1958 reforms in that country, and in Tunisia, were impregnated with a spirit of moderation and gradualism. The basic aim laid down was to nationalize instruction by unifying the complex system of school types which previously existed, by progressively Arabizing the course content, and by using Arabic as the vehicle of instruction.[9] In practice, the compromise adopted was to institute a functional bilingualism in the educational system. Thus, the beginning student was given preparatory instruction in classical Arabic, following which he was to use both Arabic and French as languages of instruction on an equal or nearly equal basis (15 hours for each in Morocco, a slight excess of Arabic in Tunisia) during the remaining years of elementary schooling. In the secondary schools in both countries, French predominates (20 out of 33 hours in Morocco), often more in reality than on paper. In Algeria during the first year of independence seven out of 30 hours were given in Arabic; this was increased to ten hours during the 1963-64 school year.

As to how well the North African governments have been able to carry out the twofold task of extending education and Arabizing, the first part at least is statistically demonstrable (Table II).

TABLE II. PRIMARY SCHOOL ATTENDANCE IN NORTH AFRICA

	1955-1956 (excluding Europeans)		1962-1963	
	Number	Percentage of School Age Children	Number	Percentage of School Age Children
Morocco	307,000*	18	1,020,000	43
Algeria	272,000	18	940,000**	43
Tunisia	224,000	26	527,000	55

*As of November 1956.
**As of the end of the school year. Not all were enrolled at the beginning owing to internal upheaval.

In examining the more subtle but crucial second part of the problem—Arabization—two questions come to mind. Can Arabization become effective according to schedule under present circumstances? As a corollary, do the governments concerned mean what they say about making it work?

The first question has two distinct aspects, one dealing with the material and personnel problems involved, the other with the problems inherent in the language itself. Before all else, and

9. For a thorough discussion of this subject, cf. David C. Gordon, *North Africa's French Legacy, 1954-1962* (Cambridge, Mass.: Center for Middle Eastern Studies, 1962), especially Chapter VIII "Arabization and Modernization." Some interesting general comments on the subject by a leading Algerian nationalist, Mostefa Lacheraf, are presented in "Réflexions Sociologiques sur le Nationalisme et la Culture en Algérie," *Les Temps Modernes* (March 1964).

assuming that purely budgetary questions have been taken care of (in itself a great assumption), strenuous requirements in textbooks and teachers must be met. So far, Tunisia has made the best showing on all scores, by establishing its own educational office for printing textbooks and setting up the most coherent system of teacher training. Morocco is following suit and now prints texts which are translations from other Arab sources or from Western languages, but complaints are heard about the quality of the translations. The dimensions of the problem of finding and training an adequate number of teachers in Arabic, and of borrowing them from abroad in French, can be seen in Table III.

TABLE III

Number of Teachers Available in North Africa (1963)			Contribution of French Nationals Under Co-operation Programs	
	French or Bilingual	Arabic	Total	Teaching in Cultural and University Missions
Morocco	14,000	13,000	8,196	1,867
Algeria	21,000	3,800	14,872	3,700
Tunisia	4,500	6,000	2,293	1,112

In none of the countries is the number of Arabic-language instructors sufficient for thoroughgoing Arabization, and all three are still very dependent on French nationals, especially in secondary and specialized education. Algeria is in the worst position by far, particularly in the matter of teacher-training facilities. The figures strongly suggest that the near-million Algerian children in school cannot possibly be receiving ten hours instruction in Arabic each week, although in 1964 history and civics in primary school were scheduled to be taught entirely in Arabic. Nor do numbers alone tell the whole story. Algeria faces the same problems of poor teacher quality encountered by its neighbors nearly a decade ago. In most country schools there is recourse to monitors whose intellectual horizons are at times only slightly less limited than their pupils. The situation in the two exprotectorates is infinitely better now than it was some years back,[10] but it is still agreed that a one-to-one correlation cannot be made in terms of "instruction

10. See *Morocco Goes Back to School* (CFG-10-'58) by Charles F. Gallagher, American Universities Field Staff, September 1958.

value" between the average local product and a teacher imported from France. Of course, not all Arabic-language instructors are North Africans. Tunisia uses no Middle Eastern teachers except those on special assignments or visiting lecturers at the University, but Algeria has been bolstered by over 1,000 incoming Arabic teachers and Morocco had more than 500 in 1963-64, mostly Egyptians whom it expelled in the fall when the United Arab Republic supported Algeria during the border clashes. Another weakness in the program is clear from this: the degree to which North Africa is dependent on outside sources and the political considerations which may intrude. The Bizerte crisis led to a massive departure of French teachers from Tunisia in 1961, and such events as the Moroccan-Egyptian rupture play havoc with the orderly attainment of objectives. Now the main danger comes in Algeria where many French teachers, dissatisfied because of new fiscal burdens added to many other material and psychological problems, planned not to renew their contracts in 1964-65. A look at Table III shows what a blow to Algerian educational progress the loss of a sizable number of these teachers would be.

As to the ability of Arabic itself to cope with the demands of industrial and scientific civilization, few subjects raise stronger emotions among Arabs, including North Africans. Since so much of the Arab Renaissance of today has been intimately bound up with the repolishing of a language which itself was, and still is, closely interlocked with a sacred area of religious culture and history, this is understandable. If the subject is raised, there is usually a heated defense of the genius of the tongue and those special qualities which it has shown in history and which none will deny: the creation of a great literature in poetry and prose, the ability to stir men's hearts at the most profound levels of response, a mastery of evocatively nuanced imagery and phrasing, a rigorously formal framework of construction, and many others. Its more objective defenders are less certain of its qualities of preciseness—the very richness of vocabulary presents problems and has been contrasted by opponents of Arabic with the clarity of French—and inventiveness, and of its ability to translate with exactitude the batteries of modern terminology being spewed out by the West. The retort of the defense is that on the historical record Arabic showed itself capable of translating and transmitting Greek thought, and showed great inventiveness in such fields as mathematics and medicine.

Despite a tendency to public apologetics, not all North Africans are convinced that Arabic is suitable, however. The Algerian weekly organ of the FLN (National Liberation Front Party), *El Moudjahid,* explaining that the literacy campaign in Algeria would be conducted bilingually (in fact much more work was done in French), remarked on the "more functional character" of French.[11] The former director of the Bureau of Arabization in Rabat noted that "conversation between bilingualists is automatically in French as soon as the subject of conversation reaches a certain level and becomes technical."[12] Several prominent Moroccan officials have confided to this writer that they consider Arabic technically useless in their work, and the director of one important autonomous office in Rabat thinks all teaching in Arabic should be abolished. The present head of the Bureau of Arabization described the language as "underdeveloped" and "not ready to play a role in technical matters." To cite such opinions is not to imply that they form a majority; but they do represent a considerable—and, in this writer's judgment, growing—minority which questions whether Arabic can indeed do the job alone, and thus whether Arabization is the answer.

Objectively viewed, Arabic faces some grave problems if it is to adapt itself to the efficient transmission of technical information. It is burdened with an inadequate and ossified script which needs overhauling and simplification. The present-day hesitancy of the language (which has not been true at all times in the past) to borrow directly is a sign of weakness. The inability to prefix and suffix easily and to build combining forms is a serious handicap in a world whose vocabulary is being enlarged every day with compound constructs. But, above all, as Vincent Monteil has pointed out in his admirable summary of modern Arabic, "the fundamental question is that of setting up a unified scientific and technical terminology."[13] Here, the political anarchy of the Arab countries seems reflected in what Pellat called the "semantic anarchy of this language which hesitates to fix itself." Today, as the result of disparate efforts by academies in Cairo and Damascus and by intellectuals working on their own, terminology is not unified to the point where serious scientific work can be exchanged in Arabic with the certainty of exact comprehension. Another part of the problem, that of scientific translations, is steadily getting more acute as new vocabulary is formed in the West at ever-

11. *El Moudjahid* (Algiers) June 22, 1963.
12. As quoted in Gordon, *op. cit.,* note 9, p. 115.
13. Cf. Vincent Monteil, *L'Arabe Moderne* (Paris: Klincksieck, 1960).

increasing rates. It is enough to point out that, even in fairly static sciences like zoology and botany, Arabic has no standard binominal scientific classification, and the terminology of social sciences like anthropology and sociology is so imprecise as to make translation of little value.[14] On the other hand, the performances of Syria and Egypt in recent decades, while technically difficult to judge in terms of the long-range effects of Arabization—one does not know what would have happened in other circumstances— prove that an Arab country can function using Arabic almost exclusively in all fields of endeavor without running up against insurmountable problems.

The reform of modern Arabic is a problem which concerns all Arabs, not primarily those of the Middle East who are closer to the spiritual nexus of their culture and who took the lead in resuscitating and revivifying their language in the last century. A quite subjective impression derived from many North African intellectuals is that they are somewhat detached from this issue in the sense that they feel themselves to be "secondhand" in any case, condemned to have ideas and the symbols which express them passed on to them from either the Middle East or from France, from one or the other "mainline" culture. This is a fairly common attitude, difficult to pin down, and not limited to the question of language. One senses almost that here, as in many domains, some North Africans see the future in terms of observing and comparing the performances of the Arab East and the Occident (which means, in effect, France) with the notion of accepting specific items that look promising, from whichever source. This tendency to look upon culture as a kind of *joteya*, a secondhand bazaar where bargains (and short cuts) can be found, is disturbing, and it is allied, at least in this writer's mind, with that elusive quality described elsewhere, which pervades what is a basically non-idea-producing society.

If one wishes to follow the progress of Arabization, a visit to the Bureau of Arabization in Rabat is instructive. The Bureau is busy translating, co-ordinating, preparing lexicons, and drawing up lists. It is working on a lexicon of tourism (Arabic-French-English) of 700 words, and on a sports lexicon of 1,000 words. It keeps in touch with special congresses held in Arab countries (like the one on medicine in Alexandria) and records and collates the vocabularies used at them. A year ago it began to study

---

14. On the question of Latin terminology in the sciences, cf. Monteil, *op. cit.*, note 13, pp. 177-181; on the social sciences, pp. 204-205.

primary-school texts used in various Arab and European countries. From this effort it has now extracted a 7,500 word vocabulary as used in French schoolbooks. This list will be circulated to committees set up in the Ministry of Education in each Arab country, which will then start preparing new Arab texts with terms which are to be both exact translations of the French terms and standard in all Arab countries. At the same time, the Bureau is undertaking a census of French administrative terms for which a similar procedure will be followed.

The results so far are disappointing to the director, who is a learned and sympathetic man. There have been great delays in countries responding. Inter-Arab political problems intervene and on several occasions have caused communications to be broken off. Moreover, he volunteered that the Arabs "were not serious" and refused to work hard at this task. In Morocco, he put much of the blame on the Ministry of Education which had not shown enough initiative. It had issued a circular "urging" the use of Bureau terminology in schoolrooms, but in fact practically none of the sciences were taught in Arabic and secondary instruction was still almost exclusively in French. In an interview, conducted entirely in French, he explained that he was bilingual: he thought in French but spoke Arabic. This is the contrary of the claim made recently by President Ben Bella to the effect that although he spoke in French he thought in Arabic.

The question as to how serious some governments are about Arabization is partially answered here. There is very little frank discussion of the pros and cons of the subject in North Africa,[15]

---

15. Just as this chapter was being finished, a National Conference on Education began in Rabat (April 1964). The general tone at the beginning confirmed that the subject of Arabization in all its implications would not and could not be discussed with frankness, but some interesting overtones came out. In his detailed opening remarks, King Hassan II made an impressive and reasoned appeal for the application of common sense to all educational questions. Sounding like a distressed parent in any country, he commented on what he considered the insufficiency of a 30-hour school week (and noted that he had studied 50 hours a week for eight years in higher education), on the problems of technical instruction, on the place of teachers in the national life, etc. Without making any direct reference to Arabization, and passing over Arabism in total silence, he stated:

> We must organize our culture and our instruction as seems necessary, and reform what must be reformed, in order to turn it into an instrument capable of shaping our children, who hope, thanks to it, to become citizens of their country, and of their continent which does not speak Arabic. We live in a continent which speaks English and French. [In fact, the total population of those countries which considered themselves Arabic-speaking in Africa is about 70 million out of a total African population of about 230 million.]

and responsibility for some of the embarrassing operational results connected with it is usually covertly passed to another office. Conversations with Ministry of Education officials produce the same type of generalities as those uttered in all high places, but the blame is put elsewhere. Few seem to be true believers themselves, and it is worth noting that most ministry personnel in these countries, like the people working in the Bureau, are bilingual. This may create personality problems for them as individuals, but it also creates a personality type, one which tends to oppose or look askance at monolinguals, meaning in practice Arabophones. Sometimes this attitude stems from the fact that the bilingual individual is not completely sure of himself in either of his languages; sometimes it is the linguistic professional who, in the end, is more interested in making lexicons than in seeing society progress; and sometimes the bilingual expert likes to be in the position of dividing and ruling. Thus many bilinguals in key positions—and most people in these positions in the Maghrib are bilingual—profit from the present state of affairs, they do not want to upset their apple cart, they have no real interest in seeing (any) one language predominate, and consciously or not they tend to brake progress. All in all, it is hard to avoid concluding that if a *de facto* bilingualism seems to be becoming institutionalized it is due in large measure to bureaucratic inertia combined with personal status advantages.[16]

> Our country, which has transmitted the beams of culture, has no intention of living shut in on itself or of preventing our culture from spreading. We have the will to restitute to our present the prestige of our past. If we make our children citizens living in a Muslim country but also children equipped to live in a great ensemble speaking French and English, we will be armed to face our difficulties and our choices. We will have made our teaching an homogeneous teaching, preparing us to be citizens of our country, of the African continent, and of the world.

The Minister of Education followed this address with an exposé of the problems facing Moroccan education and raised the possibility that the government may be considering abandoning the present primary system for one which divides the student body into two groups and reintroduces an elitist concept based on bilingualism. Developments along this line would be extremely important.

16. Commenting in a revealing way on the opening of the Conference on Education in Rabat, and on the state of education in Morocco, was Rabat's *Al Alam* (April 13, 1964), organ of the Istiqlal Party and spokesman for a large, conservative, usually traditionally oriented group of the urban middle classes and rural notables:

> It is truly stifling to speak seven years [sic] after independence of the Moroccanization or the Arabization of anything whatever; still less of the school, which should have been transformed into a school with Moroccanized teachers

Because an effective bilingualism appears to be taking root among ever larger segments of the North African population, it might be useful to look briefly at the way it functions, how it affects the individual in his environment, and to assay its advantages and disadvantages.

The subject can perhaps best be illustrated by tracing the steps in an average educational career. The child, who has already learned his dialect as a maternal language and possesses the vocabulary of his family, the home, and the immediate community of daily life around him, enters school at six or seven and studies classical Arabic for two years. The languages have the same background and a good deal of similar vocabulary, but the complex grammatical apparatus of the classical language and the problems of its script are beyond this age group at this time. A voluntary effort is usually made because of the prestige of the written language, but there is an undeniable strain.[17] At eight or nine the child is introduced to French—just at the time when classical Arabic is catching hold—and plunged into using this as the vehicle for learning mathematics and natural sciences, while he applies his classical Arabic to the study of geography, history, civics, and such. The most common complaint of teachers and observers at this juncture is that neither language has been satisfactorily learned at the end of the elementary period. The total number of hours given in French, for example, varies from 1,600-1,800, compared to the more than 4,000 hours considered necessary by

---

and with a language and spirit Arabized from the first hours of our independence. . . .

. . . We have inherited as the backwash of colonialism a language of instruction and programs of foreign study. We have kept them like something sacred which cannot be touched. In fact, under the banner of independence, we follow out a course which colonialism could not dream of applying as strictly. . . .

If we persevere in this path, before ten years French will have become the first language of the country, spoken in the plains and in the mountains, and used in the schools, the administration, the factories, and—why not?—the mosques, too. Arabic will be relegated to second place, known only by those interested in ancient civilization, and in questions of the Orient, that is, by those who are called "orientalists."

17. The November 1962 issue of *Esprit,* entitled "Le Français, Langue Vivante," was entirely given over to the question of French linguistic and cultural penetration overseas. Part III, "Le Débat avec l'Autre," pp. 753-794, contains much valuable testimony by French experts and teachers working in North Africa. The section has a piece by Selim Abou on "Bilinguisme au Liban" (Bilingualism in Lebanon), which the author also treats exhaustively from every point of view (much of it pertinent to and with references to North Africa) in his *Bilinguisme Arabe-Français au Liban* (Paris: Presses Universitaires de France, 1962).

French pedagogues for full mastery of the language. Nevertheless, some authorities argue that the child graduating with this modicum of double culture is better fitted for living and working at a modest level in his country, all uncertainties of the near future blindly weighed, than he would be under any other system feasible at this point.

Some teachers insist that intellectual and personal difficulties deepen early in the secondary cycle. The low level of most actual Maghrib primary instruction, and the high level of traditional French secondary instruction (fairly well kept up by the transfusion of so many French teachers at higher levels) creates a gap often hard to bridge for the North African student whose basic language foundation is shaky. He often feels insecure linguistically, at times extends this to the whole intellectual field, and occasionally compounds his difficulties by splitting his personality into two parts, justifying his failure to keep up with the "Cartesian" world (for that is what usually escapes him) by taking refuge in a literary mysticism which rejects the "practical" and scientific attitude. Equally poignant in human terms, of course, is the case of the student who fully takes to a Western education and comes to disdain his own cultural background and reject his family. In all cases the pitfalls facing the secondary student are manifold. He must be proficient in French if he wishes to continue his studies abroad at the university level. The equivalence of *baccalauréats* between North Africa and France is a salvation rope for solid higher learning and material successes, but it means a stiff examination in which the student must show a very considerable mastery of the other side of his double culture.[18] Although most students strongly prefer to study abroad if possible, many must remain in their own countries; and even in the Maghrib itself there is a preponderance of French-language instruction at university level. In 1962-63 at the Law Faculty in Rabat, 1,790 students followed courses in French and 1,193 in Arabic, while all courses in the Faculties of Medicine and Science were given in French. In Tunisia, 64 French nationals and 59 Tunisians, many of them bilingual, were teaching at the university in Tunis in that same year.

---

18. A recent reform in the Algerian *baccalauréat* system instituted a separate "Algerian" examination, with a higher coefficient for Arabic, alongside the "French" examination. Unless agreement is reached between governments for an *équivalence* for the new examination, this will pose new problems for many students in Algeria who will feel it necessary to take both examinations.

The bachelor's degree or the university *licence* leads to careers in which government service predominates. It may be stated flatly that in Morocco and Tunisia today the non-French-speaking candidate has no chance of getting a good government job and advancing himself in any ministry except Justice, Religious Affairs, or in specialized functions in the Interior (police work) or Education. High-level posts in key ministries like Foreign Affairs, Commerce and Industry, Planning, Public Health, Defense (except in Algeria), and Agriculture, as well as in the many specialized offices dealing with production and technical matters, are virtually closed to the monolingual Arabophone, not to mention jobs in important commercial or industrial enterprises in private business. In sum, from the third year of primary school on, there is an unrelenting pressure forcing the individual to adapt himself to a double set of goals, both of which ideally should be equally striven for. If the student cannot compete on both levels, he may withdraw from one sector of the battle at the cost of mortgaging his future in one way or another, or he may be led to drop out altogether as soon as possible, a problem now beginning to preoccupy some education specialists in the region.

Since one of the most valid objectives of a bilingual, bicultural formation is to avoid splitting youth into two groups, one deracinated in terms of its own civilization and the other withdrawn into its cultural cocoon, it is necessary to insist on the phenomenon, easily observable among many students, that the split may occur within the individual as well as within society as a whole.[19] The personality division may take many forms, too, from benign to malignant. Many bilingual individuals in North Africa—the most successfully adjusted ones—do use their second language much as a Scandinavian uses English, or as a Zurich banker visiting Geneva speaks French; it is merely a division of communication for the convenience of the situation and the person spoken to. Others vary their language according to the social situation, using it like a code either to communicate with special ingroups or deliberately not to communicate with certain outgroups. One example of this is the tendency of bilingual North African officials to address each other in Arabic in front of technical advisers for whom they reserve French; the latter thus have access to only part of the communication. There are infinite variations, however, and the

---

19. Not always, however. A more optimistic view of adaptability is taken by Blondel and Decorsiere in "Une possibilité d'Enrichissement," *Esprit, op. cit.,* note 17, especially pp. 790-791.

weapon can be directed as effectively against Arabic-speaking monolinguals, and often is. In such interaction the fluent bilingual experiences a sense of power and mobility. When he amuses himself with friends in French, his bantering attitude, indeed his whole character, is quite distinct from that expressed by his more robust joking in Arabic. His normally authoritarian attitude toward his wife and children at home in Arabic, changes publicly under the influence of Western convention and the use of French in a *salon de thé*. Most of all, traditional male attitudes toward women are wrenched about in the new circumstances. It is fascinating to see how a completely new etiquette has had to be improvised in a country like Tunisia to deal with the social (and professional) situations involving men and women shifting back and forth between two language worlds. (Mohammed Khemisti's secretary, an *évoluée* Algerian lady married to a French consultant, observed when she accompanied the late Algerian Foreign Minister to Rabat early in 1963 that Moroccan men usually ignored her and refused to rise or shake hands, until the quality of her French impressed them sufficiently to make them revise their opinions. It was not rudeness in her opinion, rather a compartmentalization of behavior triggered by language.) The bilingual also often reflects his sense of subtle class and other differences in the language vehicle he selects; his choice may reveal some of his deeper inner value judgments about what, or who, is modern, aristocratic, pious, properly oriented politically, or the opposite.

In most cases, though, the bilingual individual operates at a cost to himself. Within the wide spectrum of all those that fall inside the definition, there are few who can move freely and without trauma between two quite disparate views of life. These fortunate ones, who constitute a socio-intellectual asset of the highest worth to their countries, reap the true and substantial advantages of a double culture: an easier mastery of technical problems, a sense of universalistic belonging, and an understanding heightened by a comparative scale. But the great majority of the others too often represent an unstable compound which at times breaks down into insoluble constituents. In large measure these are individuals who are uncertain about some of the most basic values of their lives—and for this who can blame them?— just as their own society as a whole is unsure. It has been said that the man who cannot make up his mind is greedy; the biculture of North Africa, and a common type it is now producing, is—with reason—just that. This culture wants to be supremely rational and delightfully unpredictable at one blow. It values the mantle of tradition but delights in experimenting with the exciting and the untried. And, at the heart of the matter, one part of it, frightened of the future it seems to be heading toward, fervently wants to keep the Sacred it has long known and venerated, while another part, discouraged by this very past, seeks to put Caesar and God on the same level and separate them decisively.

Here we enter the most sensitive domain of the language question, in which foreigners should tread warily. For language is ultimately more than mere communication, and the pull it exerts is more than that explicit in its manipulability, usefulness, and aesthetic style. Language is the verbalization of the shared beliefs, fraternal bonds, communal historical ties, and the joint expectations of a people. It is only a mirror of existential reality, however, and, accordingly, as the beliefs and expectations are strong and fully shared, or slight and in the process of weakening, these truths will be reflected in the thinking, writing, and general creativity of the times.

For North Africa, the major historical frame in which these shared beliefs and experiences have been assembled has been the Community of Islam. This has been elaborated most satisfactorily for a great peasant majority by an ensemble of folk cultures, assimilated to and forming part of Islam, and by a folk language adequately expressing it. This culture is still buoyant and vibrant in many regions, untouched seriously by outside influences, and to the extent that it is, the folk language and the self-view of it as a means of expression, is undisturbed. For an elite and smaller group, the elaboration was that of a firmly set traditional urban civilization, which, while employing a language much akin to the language of the peasantry, leaned heavily on its access to a great historical heritage through the keeping alive of the classical written language as an implement in the service of God, his knowledge and science. Unlike the rural masses, the traditional elite has been shaken from its complacency by recent history, and its apologetics cover the language problem as only one of the aspects of a civilization in which many of its more active and restless members no longer wholeheartedly believe, a civilization which some of them have in fact completely abandoned. Evidence for this abounds in the political literature, belles-lettres, and experimental theater, and in the flowering of the hitherto restricted representational fine arts of sculpture and painting. It is too much to say that the Maghrib is in a Golden Age of intellectual effervescence—although the change from half a century ago is remarkable—but new ideas and new forms are spreading everywhere outside the traditional paths, and often in opposition to them.

As far as language is directly concerned, the one point that should be noted is the existence of, at least, a one-way crosslinkage of religious and linguistic disuse: Less Arabic does not always mean a weakening of religious practice or faith, but religious disobservance or disbelief will always mean less Arabic, usually in ascending order as the passive disobservance turns into more active disbelief. Naturally, there are found in North Africa as in all Muslim areas, many variations on "modernism," within or without Islam in a formal sense. This is not the subject under discussion here, but something can be noted. Many individuals are seeking in diverse ways a large accommodation with a revitalized faith which will enable them to solder together the best of their own tradition and the most useful from other sources of inspiration. Some, however, are frankly not seeking this. The extreme left and a considerable group around it in all three countries are at best indifferent to the place of religion in their vision of the new state. They are correspondingly interested in language (unlike *Al Alam*) only for its social efficiency, or in temporarily using it for ulterior political purposes. Where the left is potent and numerous, as in Algeria where the best test seems likely to come, it looks inevitable that the conflicting pull toward secularism and the counterreaction stimulated among those who resist it will someday lead to a showdown. When President Ben Bella said, that "there are some men who still hesitate to associate their efforts for the realization of our socialist objectives, proclaiming that this policy is contrary to Islam,"[20] he was forced to protest too much precisely because he was trapped between these two forces.

In the end, the most searching questions raised in this field are unanswerable, but they merit reflection. Can a foreign language representing an impersonal, secular, unbelieving way of life coexist with one fundamentally opposed to it in ethic, provided that the crosslinkage of the latter with its religious foundation remains as reasonably strong as it is today? Or, since the

---

20. *Le Monde* (Paris) March 25, 1964.

movement of individuals between traditionalist and modernistic groups (of one or another kind) is, at this point in history, moving in only one direction and accelerating, are we to expect a modulation or weakening of religion which will have repercussions on the linguistic future of the area? Summing everything up, the final question—which should perhaps have been the first —is one which many North Africans in positions of the greatest responsibility hesitate to put to themselves: Who are we? And, by hesitating, they prolong the crisis. Everything revolves around this query: the alternatives for political development, the chances of building true nation-states, and the issues of co-operation within the Maghrib, or outside it in the Arab World; the problems relative to joining the European Economic Community in some form of association, plus the crucial issue of the steady emigration which is forming a European subproletariat; the issue of regional associations of all kinds, and notably the recent, burning flirtation with Africanism which has been an attempt to suggest an answer. To come full circle, the whisper of an answer may come as suggested in the first paragraph of this piece. They will know what they are and who they are only as they think it, formulate it, and express it, and by expressing it become the product of whatever their will permits and their imagination refuses to limit. The rebate on the price being paid by North Africa in its present dilemma is that it is potentially as openended a society as exists on this planet. The hidden dividend for suffering through a crisis of identity is that there is a valid choice. Not until North Africans make it will we have our answer.

5

The Role of Islam in Modern North Africa

Leon Carl Brown

Any observer fascinated by the phenomenon of radical change of major social institutions within a very few years will be attracted to the modern Maghrib. It is a commonplace to point out that many of the most important social patterns and institutions of fifty years ago, or in many cases even a single generation, would hardly be recognized today in their revolutionarily different casts.

Yet, even within this area where radical change has become the rule it is quite likely that no modification has been so pervasive and deep rooted as that which has taken place in North African Islam—in religious law, ritual, popular customs and beliefs of religious content, religiously-based social organizations, the educational system, and the social standing of the religious élites.

North Africa at the turn of the century and for at least two or three decades thereafter appeared to be essentially a theocentric society whose most important guides and spokesmen were those endowed with a religious authority, both the orthodox *ulama* and, even more important, the saints and leaders of the pervasive Muslim brotherhoods—the *marabouts*.

The Western scholars of this age, such as Doutté, Rinn, Coppolani, and Westermarck, stressed the intensity of religious feeling in North Africa and the system of taboos and popular beliefs which created an elaborate popular, or as some saw it, "primitive," religion. The Berber substratum with its alleged tendencies toward anthropolatry was a common theme.

Today, on the contrary, the scholar, both native North African and foreign, seems less concerned with Islam, and when his attention turns to Islam he is ineluctably drawn to the factors indicating decline: an *ulama* class reduced from prestigious lions under the throne to poor unfortunates, the wasting away of the previously widespread system of Sufi brotherhoods, the secularization of ideas, laws, education, etc. Most observers today doubt the importance of Islam as a factor shaping present-day aspirations and behavior in North Africa. Some even question the idea that many present-day values and institutions can profitably be seen as springing from an Islamic matrix.

The apparently revolutionary contrast between the North African Islam into which were born Habib Bourguiba (1903), Ahmad Ben Bella (1919), and Hassan II (1927) and that of today presents an intriguing problem. Has there really been that much change? It would certainly seem so. There is no reason to question the earlier scholars of North African Islam who were meticulous observers even if one might be inclined to dispute some of their underlying assumptions.

Perhaps, then, they were simply bad "prophets," completely missing the indicators pointing the way in which North African Islam was moving. Reflection on this suggestion should provoke equally doubts about present-day prophecies concerning Islam in North Africa: a process of irrevocable change, a pattern of decline in Islam and Islamic values, or rather the low point of a cyclical movement to be followed by some form of resurgence?

An attempt to answer these questions needs a framework for interpreting the recent history of Islam in North Africa in order to measure the extent of change and indicate the immediate steps leading to the present. The following three factors are suggested as providing such a framework:

I. The decline—one could almost say collapse—of the Sufi religious brotherhoods.
II. The role of the Muslim reformist movement which was, *inter alia,* the major reason for the decline of the brotherhoods.
III. The intimate link between Islam—usually reformist Islam—and the origins and growth of the nationalist movements.

THE SUFI BROTHERHOODS

The brotherhoods represent the organizational form eventually adopted by Islamic mysticism or Sufism. In North Africa Sufism began to flourish only from the 11th century, much later than in the Arab East,[1] and Sufism organized into mass brotherhoods was later still. It was not until the 15th and 16th centuries in North Africa with the breakdown of internal order and the foreign threat posed by the Spanish and Portuguese that the brotherhoods became mass movements and potent political forces extending out into the countryside. From that period until modern times these brotherhoods formed a major social and political (as well as religious) fact of life in North Africa.

Earlier scholars have clarified many of the doctrinal and organizational peculiarities of the brotherhoods:

1. The fundamental role of the founder of the order (*tariqa* or "way") and of the chain of his successors, all believed to possess *baraka* (charisma or powers of intervention with the divine).

2. The importance of obedience to the founder, his successor or immediate representative—a principle of unquestioning submission well preserved in the sayings: "He who has no shaykh has the devil as his shaykh."[2] "The initiate must be in the hands of his shaykh like the corpse in the hands of the washer of the dead."

3. A vague, but important, hierarchy according to ability to comprehend the esoteric.

4. A doctrine which claims only to supplement orthodox Islam but in practice tends to replace it.

5. Thus, the possibility of tension with the representatives of orthodox tradition (*ulama*), a tension which was generally solved in the late medieval period by a mutual tolerance or even an informal alliance between Sufi shaykhs and members of the *ulama* class (e.g., many of the *ulama*, themselves, belonged to a brotherhood).

There is no need to name the major brotherhoods, list their dates of origin extending from the 12th century right to the present century (there was a constant tendency for a dynamic person raised in the precepts of a certain *tariqa* to split off and with his own disciples form a new order), or cite the several differences in doctrine or popular practice. These matters today probably seem about as unnecessary to most modern observers as the fine points of medieval Christian scholasticism.

More significant and immediately pertinent to the cause for their decline in recent times was the social and political role of

---

1. Cf. Georges Marçais, *La Berbérie Musulmane et l'Orient au Moyen Age* (Paris: Editions Montaigne, 1946), p. 293.
2. A statement which can be traced back to Al Ghazzali.

the brotherhoods. In an age when the central government seldom had effective control of outlying areas and, in any case, the "state" tended to be a small élite interested in its own perpetuation and willing to settle for limited relations with the society it governed, these brotherhoods assumed real social functions.

In other words, as the political scientists would tend to look at the problem, the Sufi brotherhoods were a quite natural manifestation of the *de facto* extreme political decentralization characteristic of the Maghrib in the late medieval period. This has been noted by early scholars. Doutté referred to the "almost territorial jurisdiction" of the Muslim *marabouts*,[3] and de Foucauld recounted being met in the Tadla region of Morocco with the independent claim, "Here there is neither sultan nor *makhzan* —only God and Sidi Ben Daoud."[4]

Seen in this light, the brotherhoods lived in a workable symbiosis with, on the one hand, the central government and the orthodox *ulama* and, on the other hand, the tribal structure. Obviously, there were countless variants from region to region and especially as between rural and urban elements, but the brotherhoods were important everywhere. It was not simply a "quaint custom" that the right of asylum tended to be recognized in most *zawiyas* or that the shaykh of the *tariqa* often mediated between the central government and the tribal leaders.

Thus, at the beginning of modern times the pervasive system of brotherhoods, led and personified by the shaykh or *marabout*, filled real social and political functions and could claim the veneration which comes from longevity in traditional societies. Most important, the brotherhoods were strengthened by a religious sanction, justly won as the major instrumentality for the spread of Islam among the urban masses and the rural population in the late medieval period. From this situation the brotherhoods commanded political power, often as nebulous as their membership,[5] but nevertheless very real—a power perhaps best described

3. Edmond Doutté, *Notes sur l'Islam Maghribin: Les Marabouts* (Paris: Leroux, 1900), p. 19.

4. Charles de Foucauld, *Reconnaissance au Maroc* (Paris: Challamel, 1888), p. 52.

5. One can find estimates for membership in the brotherhoods starting as early as the late 19th century in the works of Depont and Coppolani, Doutté, the various editions of the *Annuaire du Monde Musulman*, etc., but they vary so widely as to be of limited use. Cf. also G. H. Bousquet, *L'Islam Maghrebin: Introduction à l'Etude Générale de l'Islam* (4th ed.; Algiers: La Maison des Livres, 1954), pp. 156ff. Further, what criterion would be used to determine membership —active participation or rather more passive identification? If the latter, one

as in inverse ratio to the effectiveness and strength of the central government.

This latter point suggests a major reason for the decline of the brotherhoods. With French rule came centralization and pacification.

> ... the organization of modern means of transportation has considerably reduced their [the brotherhoods] function as lodgings on the road; the pacification of the country has almost entirely eliminated their mission as mediators; the limitation of governmental arbitrariness has restricted their right of asylum.[6]

While French rule was having the unplanned result of making the socio-political role of the brotherhoods anachronistic, a more conscious policy of French administrators to work through the leadership of the brotherhoods served to make them vulnerable to any future nationalist movement.

This change in the material situation that came with French rule was in itself enough to confront the brotherhood system with the prospect of radical adjustment or decline. However, it was the attack from within the indigenous society, from within Islam, which insured the collapse of the brotherhoods. This attack from within was Islamic reformism or the *salafiya* movement.

THE ISLAMIC REFORMIST MOVEMENT

The origins of Islamic reformism in North Africa, just as the origins of Sufism centuries earlier, can be traced to the Arab East. Jamal al-Din al-Afghani, Mohammed Abduh, and the latter's disciples who formed the *manar* group provided the stimulus and doctrinal basis for North African reformism just as they did at the other end of the Mediterranean. The stimulus from the East was, in fact, transmitted by an amazingly small number of persons, for intercommunication of men and ideas between the

---

might go so far as Ganiage in discussing pre-Protectorate Tunisia in maintaining, "All Muslims sedentary or nomadic belonged to one brotherhood or another, often several at the same time." (Jean Ganiage, *Les Origines du Protectorat Français en Tunisie: 1861-1881* [Paris: Presses Universitaires de France, 1959], pp. 164-65.)

6. Roger Le Tourneau, "North Africa: Rigorism and Bewilderment," in *Unity and Variety in Muslim Civilization,* ed. G. von Grunebaum (Chicago: University of Chicago Press, 1955), p. 250.

Maghrib and Mashriq was (and remains) limited. A few of the founders such as Morocco's Abu Shuaib al-Dukkali, Algeria's Bashir al-Ibrahimi and Tayyib al-Uqbi, and Tunisia's Abd al-Aziz al-Thaalbi either studied or lived many years in the Arab East. Others, including the dynamic leader of Algeria's reformists, Abd al-Hamid Ben Badis who studied at Zitouna in Tunis, received the inspiration more indirectly.

Scarcely more than a spark from the East was needed to start Islamic reformism in the Maghrib. One is tempted to go further and assert that French rule, more than Shaikh Mohammed Abduh, created the *salafiya* movement in North Africa. As already noted, French rule made the brotherhoods both anachronistic and suspect. French rule also presented a general cultural challenge, posing most acutely for Algeria but to a lesser extent elsewhere as well the basic problem of cultural identity. In short, there was a time of troubles and Muslim North Africa tended to respond as so often in its past with a puritanical, reformist Muslim movement.[7]

Just as was the case with Sufism and brotherhoods, it is quite possible to analyze the rise of the reformist movements in social and political terms. A small body of those who had received an orthodox religious training reacted to the foreign threat to their religion and society by preaching salvation through a return to the religious fervor and daily practices of the early Muslim community—an appeal to the myth of the golden age, a classic theme in Muslim culture.

In Morocco this school was championed by Dukkali, already mentioned, and by his disciple Moulay al-Arabi al-Alawi. By the 1920's the former in Rabat and the latter in Fez[8] had collected circles of followers from among the students and graduates of religious training, including the young Allal al Fassi.

Reformism in Algeria began in the mid-1920's under the inspiration of Ben Badis, and the group was formalized from 1931 in the Algerian Association of Ulama.

Interestingly, in Tunisia Muslim reformism never had a strong separate identity. The leader of the Old Destour, Abd al-Aziz al-Thaalbi had been identified with the *salafiya* movement at the

7. Cf. Leon Carl Brown, "The Islamic Reformist Movement in North Africa," *Journal of Modern African Studies* II, No. 1 (March 1964).
8. Cf. Jamil Abun-Nasr, "The Salafiyya Movement in Morocco: The Religious Base of the Moroccan Nationalist Movement," *St. Antony's Papers, No. 16, Middle East Affairs, No. 3* (London: Chatto and Windus, 1963).

turn of the century, and some echoes of the major reformist program—the fight against the brotherhoods—could be found in the Old Destour writings of the 1920's, but for the most part the absence of dynamic leaders such as Ben Badis and working compromises with the established *ulama* class in Tunis tended to take the cutting edge off Muslim reformism in Tunisia. This probably explains at least in part the success of a thoroughly Westernizing Neo-Destour in the 1930's.

In all three countries—varying only according to the strength of the movement, itself linked to the intensity of the challenge—the reformist program was similar:

1. A stern message for a return to the strength and primitive simplicity of early Islam. This created a preference for the stricter Hanbali school and for the teachings of Ibn Taimiya (1263-1328).

2. A complete rejection of institutionalized mysticism which was anathematized as *shirk* (association of anything or anyone with God). In this way, the worship of saints (and the reverential awe with which the brotherhood leaders had been approached worship) and the many popular "superstitions" involving visiting tombs, use of amulets, etc., were all condemned as *shirk*.

3. An equally strong stand was taken against Christian missionary activity.[9]

4. The positive aspect of the reformist program revolved around a more effective dissemination of Arabic and Islamic teachings. For this reason the amazingly successful campaign for Islamic primary schools, with education in Arabic, built by private subscription was a priority consideration.

5. A strict moral code barring both major sins such as drunkenness, but also minor lapses such as ostentation, overly lavish weddings, dowries, etc.

Results of the reformist activities were soon manifest. By the early 1930's in Algeria the leaders of the brotherhoods had reacted by forming their own newspapers and a central organization somewhat misnamed the "Council of Sunni Ulama"[10] and in May 1933 a paper representing the brotherhoods openly asked for a cease-fire in this struggle with the reformers, by arguing

---

9. It is interesting to note the correlation between stepped-up—or at least less subtle—missionary activity and the rise of Muslim reformism. This was especially marked in Morocco.

10. Cf. Joseph Desparmet, "Un Réformateur Contemporain en Algérie," *Afrique Française* (March 1933).

for toleration and liberty of conscience, "that essential principle of modern civilization."[11]

Before the end of the 1930's the brotherhoods had declined so much as to be hardly an issue in Tunisia, at the death of Algeria's Ben Badis in 1940 they were a spent force in Algeria, and even in Morocco reformism had made great inroads on that more conservative society. The political influence of Abd al-Hay Kettani and his Kettaniya brotherhood right until Moroccan independence, an apparent exception, can in large measure be explained by French backing.[12]

Muslim reformism had brought about the collapse of the system of brotherhoods. No observers dispute this negative contribution, but what about any lasting positive contribution of reformism in North Africa? This leads to the religious bases of North African nationalism.

ISLAM AND NATIONALISM IN NORTH AFRICA

It is surely significant how major turning points in the nationalist development of all three countries were linked with religious issues.

In Morocco it was the ill-advised "Berber *dahir*" forced by French administration upon the young Sultan Mohammed Ben Youssef in 1930 which gave a coterie of young Moroccan nationalists the opportunity to find mass support. What was the Berber *dahir*? Essentially, it was one part an attempt to regularize a *de facto* situation and two parts a crudely obvious plan to divide the presumably more "assimilable" pure Berbers from the rest of Morocco by assuring them their own customs and laws.[13]

However, the recognition of Berber law meant the exclusion of Koranic law. The Berber *dahir* was resisted as an attack on Islam and on Moroccan unity, and in a very real sense the two were seen as one and the same thing. Out of the ensuing campaign fought on these Islamic terms Moroccan nationalism was born.

In Tunisia it was the naturalization campaign started almost

11. Quoted in Desparmet, "Deux Manifestes Indigènes," *Afrique Française* (December 1933).
12. As was the case with Thami al-Glaoui, pasha of Marrakech.
13. A thorough historical treatment of this French illusion about the "assimilable" Berber as opposed to the "unassimilable" Arab as it developed in Algeria is found in Ch-R. Ageron, "La France a-t-elle eu une Politique Kabyle?" *Revue Historique* (April-June 1960).

by accident in December 1932 when an obscure *mufti* of Bizerte ruled that a Tunisian Muslim who had accepted French citizenship did not have the right to be buried in a Muslim cemetery. An angry crowd gathered to stop the burial. This led to a series of identical incidents at funerals of other *naturalisés* until the Protectorate government capitulated several months later and created special cemeteries for those unfortunate French citizens whom their coreligionists classed as apostates. Leading this campaign were Bourguiba and his colleagues who in the following year (1934) would create the Neo-Destour. They managed to accomplish several purposes:

1. Place their nationalist activities within a Muslim framework.

2. Score their conservative rivals in the Destour who were rather more cautious.

3. Castigate the "pusillanimous" official *ulama* who tried to find[14] a face-saving formula for all concerned, and to show that by contrast it was the Western-trained younger generation of Tunisians (those whom the conservatives accused of being godless) who in time of crisis proved to be the staunchest supporters of Islam.[15]

Again, a religious issue provided a major turning point in North African nationalism, an issue described years later by President Bourguiba as of "enormous influence" in the origin and early influence of the Neo-Destour.[16]

In Algeria, even the dramatist with full liberty of fictional creativity could hardly produce a more poignant and symbolic example of the Islamic role in nationalism than the dramatic 1936 public statement by Ferhat Abbas and the reply of President Ben Badis of the Algerian Association of Ulama. It was on this occasion that Abbas, at the end of his many years of attempting to secure political change within the framework of France through adopting the policy of "assimilation," issued his statement so often quoted afterwards both in and out of context:

> If I had discovered the "Algerian nation" I would be a nationalist . . . but this nation does not exist.

The reply of Ben Badis appeared in the April 1936 issue of the

---

14. Cf. *Action Tunisienne*, April 20, 1933.
15. Cf. the letter to the editor entitled "Our Revenge" in *Action Tunisienne*, April 27, 1933.
16. Interview by the author with Bourguiba, October 1961.

Arabic-language organ of the Algerian Association of Ulama, *Al-Shihab:*

> We too have searched in history and in the present, and we have discovered that the Algerian Muslim nation does exist. . . . This Algerian Muslim nation is not France, cannot be France, does not want to be France.

ISLAM IN NORTH AFRICA TODAY

It is tempting to elaborate on this idea of the Islamic coloration of North African nationalism and especially the fundamental importance of the Algerian Association of Ulama as a formative influence in the 1930's. However, the subject here is Islam in North Africa today, and it is perhaps time to meet the argument of those who would suggest: This past history is all very well, but it is a closed chapter. Islamic reformism played a decisive role in clearing away the brotherhood system and other remnants of a previous theocentric age, but it has played its role and has gone down with its enemies leaving the arena open for a modern secular mentality.

It might help to anticipate somewhat the viewpoint to be developed in considering the above argument, which is no doubt a cogent one. Certainly, even though any measurement of the intensity of religious expression in a society is admittedly nebulous and difficult, it can be agreed that North Africa is today less intently Muslim than it was at the turn of the century or even a generation ago. At the same time it can be readily accepted that nothing thus far developed in the previous pages (suggesting the extent of change in North African Islam in modern time by tracing: 1) the collapse of the brotherhoods; 2) the role of Islamic reformism; and 3) the link between Islam and the development of nationalism) in any way contradicts the argument that the recent Islamic past is now a "closed chapter." However, the opposite is not self-evident either. It is not demonstrable that the Islamic impulses generated in previous decades have cancelled themselves out.

This is the ultimate justification for the historical approach used thus far—the need to avoid prejudging the question: Has North Africa passed a watershed and is now in a "post-Islamic" or at least "de-Islamized" age?

Finally, even though many of the subjects treated up to this point may seem quite remote from 1964 it must be emphasized that the "historical approach" adopted here has in fact covered somewhat less than the life span of those presently in power in North Africa.

THE ARGUMENT: ISLAM A DIMINISHING FORCE

Those who would argue that the role of Islam—in the form of reformism—was transitional and merely smoothed the way for the present more secularizing world view need not in any way understate the earlier role of reformism.

For example, no one seriously disputes the importance of the reformers in destroying an earlier mentality of passivity and fatalism by stressing the religious importance of deeds accomplished in this world. It is not accidental that more activist and this-worldly passages from the Koran and *hadiths* have increased in popularity in modern times.

God does not change a people until they change themselves.[17]

Work for this world as if you would live forever, work for the next world as if you would die tomorrow.[18]

In fact, this latter *hadith* brings to mind the statement made by Shaikh Bashir al-Ibrahimi at the 1935 Congress of the Algerian Association of Ulama which summed up in a striking manner the new dynamism arising in Algeria, in large measure under reformist guidance:

> The Algerian *umma* has gained vitality and strength. There is an awareness of the present shortcomings, and awareness of corruption is the first stage to reform. This awareness is manifested in various aspects of [Algeria's] public life: in the economic life by entry into business enterprises formerly not open to Muslim Algerians, in cultural life by the creation of various clubs and societies, in education by a responsiveness to instruction in both Arabic and French, by a diligent pursuit of knowledge and even emigration in quest of it, in religion by the creation of mosques in villages

---

17. Significantly, this quotation appears in Malek Bennabi's *Vocation de l'Islam* (Paris: Editions du Seuil, 1954) at the head of the chapter entitled "Le Mouvement Réformateur."
18. As early as 1921 Othman Kaak, now director of the Bibliothèque Nationale in Tunis was writing in the short-lived Tunisian Communist newspaper *Habib al Umma*, "Let us abandon resignation. A *hadith* has said 'Work for this world as if you would live forever.' Let us look at our condition as it is, not as we saw it once in the past."

with funds from the nation itself, and in the ideological field with serious, right-guided thought, self-reliance in the above-mentioned subjects, and faith in the existence of something called the nation [*umma*]—all of this after the nation had relied for this world on the government and for the next world on the *marabouts* and shaykhs of the *tariqas*.[19]

In the same way, the fundamental role of the Muslim reformers in the revival of Arabic and of a sense of Arab identity is undisputed. Even the rather less consistent record of Islamic reformism in the matter of female emancipation can be accepted. One need only recall the importance of Zitouna graduate Tahir al-Haddad and his *Our Women in the Sharia and in Society*.[20]

Yet all of these ideas—self-reliance, a strong sense of national identity, the drive for a certain concept of "modernization," female emancipation, etc.—are not necessarily deemed by present-day North Africans as being linked in any special way to Islam. Rather, these ideas, admittedly championed by reformist Islam, were always advanced—often more effectively—by other groups as well; and today the fervent believer, the indifferent, and equally the handful of aggressively anti-religious can all join hands in acceptance of such a program. On the basis of today's accepted ideology, Islam—reformist or otherwise—is in a position of appearing, not antithetical, but rather more or less irrelevant. This is hardly a position of strength.

However, there is even more cumulative evidence of Islam's decline as one moves from the realm of ideas and principles to existing institutions.

Consider the changes in education since independence. As has been already noted, in the last decades of French rule the Muslim

---

19. *Sijil mu'tamar jam^ciya al-^culama al-muslimin al-jaza'iriyin* (Constantine, 1935), p. 50. This should be compared with the remarks of the French scholar, William Marçais, who noted in 1937 the striking change among the Algerian natives "who now want to 'do things for themselves'. Even a few years ago one still could observe a sort of total resignation of initiative on the part of our Muslim subjects. They did not dream of acting even for their own affairs. When they wanted to forbid women from visiting the cemeteries they had recourse to the authorities. When wedding expenses seemed too heavy they did not have the courage for self-reform. They asked the French authority to pass a law fixing the limits of wedding expenses and forbidding mutual gifts, the source of impoverishment of families. Today, one sees the birth of a spirit of initiative which is, at the same time, systematically anti-administration." Cf. Henri Pérès, "Le Mouvement Réformiste en Algérie et l'Influence de l'Orient d'après la Presse Arabe d'Algérie," *Entretiens sur l'Evolution des Pays de Civilisation Arabe*, I (Paris, 1957), 57.

20. *Imra'atuna fi al-Shari^ca wa al-mujtama^c* (Tunis, 1930).

reformers were actively engaged in education—the "free school" or "modern Koranic school" system. These schools, based in large measure on private contributions and often (especially in Algeria) hampered by a hostile administration, quite naturally stressed Arabic and Koranic studies. It cannot be argued that they were comparable in standard to the French or Franco-Arab system, or that graduates of this system assumed leading positions in the nationalist movements. Nevertheless, these schools trained a not inconsiderable body of students who otherwise would have been denied any formal education,[21] and at the same time served as a real basis for Muslim reformist political strength.

With independence in each country has come a tendency for unification of the school system modelled on the secular French pattern. In Tunisia this solution was accepted openly as a blessing. Zitouna University has become simply the *faculté* of Islamic and Arabic studies in the University of Tunis and the Zitouna secondary school annexes (which had much greater emphasis on Arabic and Islamic studies as preparatory schools for Zitouna) integrated into the single national school system. Many Zitouna graduates who had been serving as teachers were quietly dropped as substandard.[22]

In Morocco essentially the same position was reached after much soul searching. The dominant impulse in the first two years of independence was for a more traditional education spearheaded by rapid arabization, but in 1958 Moroccan education policy switched to an acceptance of French methods and of French as the language of instruction in some subjects in order to halt declining standards.

In Algeria there was really no feasible alternative to the continuation of a basically French system. The Ministry of Habous (dominated now by officials formerly active in the Algerian Association of Ulama) still has responsibility for some four or five schools which thus remain outside the jurisdiction of the Ministry of Education, but there is no doubt that Algeria, as her neighbors,

---

21. In Tunisia just before Independence there were 35,000 enrolled in the modern Koranic schools or roughly one Tunisian for every four in the governmental Franco-Arab primary school system.

22. An article in *L'Etudiant Tunisien*, No. 3 (1958) claims there were some 800 Zitouna-trained teachers in this category. To appreciate fully the radical nature of this action it is important to realize the crying need for schoolteachers at that time. A few years later the Tunisian government tackled another aspect of the Zitouna "problem" by instituting retraining courses in manual skills for unemployable Zitouna graduates. (Cf. "Jeunesse: De la Grande Mosquée à la Fraiseuse," *Afrique Action*, April 3, 1961.)

is adamantly opposed to the extension of a dual system of education fostering the continuation of a dual culture.[23]

Paradoxically, in independent North Africa the French cultural impact is stronger than ever. This is necessarily somewhat at the expense of Arabic, but even more, of Islamic culture. For the school year 1962-63 there were over 25,000 French teachers in North Africa: 15,200 (60 percent of the entire teaching corps) in Algeria; 8,136 (40 percent of the entire teaching corps) in Morocco; and 2,264 (almost 25 percent of the entire teaching corps) in Tunisia.[24]

This is not to suggest that the modern North African feels threatened in his political independence or his cultural identity by this French effort. On the contrary, he welcomes it and feels it very much part of his own world, but those who speak for the Muslim hierarchy do see this as a real threat to their way of life. A good representative of the Muslim tradition in North Africa at its intellectual best, Shaykh Mohammed al-Fadl Ben Ashur of Tunis wrote in 1955 that the major barrier to the acceptance of French culture at the expense of the Arabo-Islamic culture had been its link with political imperialism. Thus, with the end of imperialism the outside threat to the native culture could become even more formidable.[25]

The official Muslim class has taken similar losses in the field of law. Independent Tunisia and Morocco have both passed legislation unifying the legal system and making certain changes in that last undefiled sanctuary of Muslim jurisprudence—the field of personal status (marriage, divorce, inheritance, etc.). In Morocco these changes have been cautious, accurately reflecting the greater importance which remains with the official Muslim and traditional classes in general. In Tunisia, however, the changes have approached the revolutionary. As a result, both the *Sharia* as an ideal model and the Muslim legal class as the group expected to represent and interpret that ideal have suffered a loss.

This is not to overlook the steady intrusion of Western-inspired codes in North Africa (as in other Muslim countries) since the 19th century nor the concomitant decline of the Muslim judges

---

23. An interesting indication of this sentiment, Mohammed Ibrahim al-Mili, editor of *Al-Chaab* and son of the late Shaikh Mubarak al-Mili, one of the most influential leaders of the Algerian Association of Ulama, speaks with feeling against any role whatsoever for the Ulama of the Ministry of Habous in education.

24. Cited in Charles A. Gallagher, "Co-operation," *American Universities Field Staff Reports*, North African Series, Vol. IX, No. 10, 1963.

25. Ben Ashur, *Al haraka al-adabiya wa al-fikriya fi Tunis* (Cairo, 1956), p. 221.

vis-à-vis their Western-trained colleagues, but previous changes had been justified as subsidiary or at least not in opposition to the principle of *Sharia* jurisprudence as interpreted by previous generations of *ulama*.

However, the Tunisian Personal Status Code adopted on August 13, 1956, made fundamental changes without resorting to legal terminology which could at least save appearances. For example, polygamy was outlawed, a Muslim woman may marry a non-Muslim, and the exclusive power of divorce previously given the man was withdrawn and judgment for divorce became a prerogative of the court. It is interesting to note that the Committee drafting this legislation[26] had generally tended to arrive at these results by use of rather more cautious language, but the Council of Ministers under Bourguiba, who felt the psychological importance of clear language showing the thoroughly revolutionary intention of the legislation, opted for the forthright language used in the final text.[27]

The governmental campaign in support of this legislation also emphasized the inefficiencies and delay in the previous system of *Sharia* courts and thus by implication attacked those members of the *ulama* who served as judges.[28] Bourguiba at his satirical best in the weekly speech of August 3, 1965, recalled how a friend had remarked to him during the "naturalization" crisis of 1932-33[29] that the French did not know how to manage this campaign of attracting Tunisians to demand French citizenship. Obviously, the friend continued, the French had only to set up an office outside of *Sharia* courts and they would obtain citizenship applications from all the exasperated Tunisians who had dealings with those courts.

In this campaign revolving around the new Tunisian personal status code, the issue was directly joined with members of the Tunisian *ulama*, fourteen of whom issued a *fatwa* denouncing the new code. That the government weathered this storm with really very little trouble and that Tunisians today take pride in this "daring" piece of legislation as a symbol of modernity is the best measure of the defeat of the Muslim official class.

26. Ahmad Mistiri, Mahmud Annabi, and Mohammed Ben Salama.
27. Interviews by the author with Mahmud Annabi and Ibrahim Abd al-Baqi in December 1960.
28. In fact, a few days before the new code of personal status was announced, twenty-four judges in personal status courts were dismissed or retired including three from the Tribunal Supérieur du Chara. Cf. *Journal Officiel*, August 3, 1956.
29. Referred to on pp. 104-5.

The first year of independence in Tunisia also saw the abolition of public and private *habous,* which amounted, *inter alia,* to the removal of just one more factor of prestige and potential power for the Muslim official class.

The decline of Islam in the realm of ideas and the radical loss of prestige and power by the Muslim official class in the fields of education and law certainly add up to a fundamentally different picture of Islam in modern North Africa by contrast with the classical concept of Islam as a "total system" in which it was deemed quite unnecessary if not impossible to seek dividing lines where Islam ended and politics, law, the family, business, etc., began.

However, in a modern North Africa, admittedly greatly influenced by many Western norms, perhaps as in the West the Muslim "church" is now separated from state and society. Assuming this to be the case, one might be tempted to extend the analogy and ask whether the Muslim "church" in losing its temporal position might not be in a better position to further its spiritual one.

If such a state of affairs were demonstrated it would certainly tend to discount most of the arguments previously advanced to suggest Muslim decline in North Africa. In this case even the argument that Islamic doctrine is confused—perched precariously between the old medieval synthesis and a reformism which did not prove intellectually satisfying—might assume less important proportions. As a standard text of the sociology of religion observed:

> The essential fallacy, so prevalent today, of confusing the intellectual formulation of religion with its basic nature and function, could be avoided if we recognized the fact that theory is not the most significant or essential part of religion. Worship is, in fact, so integral to religion that it is doubtful if the latter could continue to exist without it.[30]

What then about the vitality of Islam in North Africa today in the restricted sense of worship? Even superficial observance indicates a decline in worship as well. The mosques are poorly attended, public prayer is rarely seen, many educated North Africans admit they have abandoned most of the required ritual of Islam, even the polite formulae with an Islamic context are apparently less in use.

---

30. Joachim Wach, *Sociology of Religion* (Chicago: University of Chicago Press, 1944), p. 26.

THE COUNTERARGUMENT: NOT DECLINING, EVOLVING . . .

Such would seem to be the major points of the argument that Islam is steadily declining as a major factor of importance in North African society. An attempt at rebuttal might well take the following approach.

It is not unimportant to record right off that Islam remains the state religion in all three countries. Nor is this merely the result of inertia. Islam has been affirmed as the state religion in the post-independence constitutions of Tunisia (1959), Morocco (1963), and Algeria (1963). The preamble to the Tunisian Constitution lists as one of the purposes of the state "to adhere to the teachings of Islam." Further, in Tunisia the President of the Republic must be a Muslim.[31] In the Moroccan Constitution the king is given the caliphal title of Commander of the Faithful.

Nor is the existence of Islam as the state religion in any way a matter of controversy, one of several ways to indicate that although religious indifference may well be widespread there is not now and has never been in North Africa anything comparable to European anti-clericalism. Nor is this simply because North Africa has escaped exposure to such ideas. Not a few Frenchmen attached to anti-clerical parties of the left lived in North Africa maintaining more or less intact this aspect of a political program made in France. There is reason to believe that as in metropolitan France anti-clericalism was strong among French schoolteachers living in North Africa. One need only refer to the articles appearing in *Tunis Socialiste* in the 1920's and 1930's to see how some Frenchmen of this persuasion could argue that the Christian church in France and the Muslim "church" in North Africa were both obstacles to progress and human freedom.

Yet although French leftist thinking had a profound influence on the intellectual development of the present ruling elite in North Africa, anti-clericalism fell on barren ground.[32] Anti-clericalism was, in part, unattractive because Islam, like the colon-

---

31. There is no such restriction in the Algerian Constitution which also notes among the fundamental objectives of the state (Art. 10) "the struggle against all discrimination, in particular that based on race or religion."

32. The late Mohammed al-Farid Ghazi in a speech at the Aziza Uthman Woman's Club in Tunis castigated what he considered the baleful influence of Muslim "clerics" in modern Tunisia. He was interrupted by a university-educated young Tunisian woman who retorted sarcastically, "You mean by 'cleric' someone like the Prophet Mohammed?"

ized society itself, was under attack and thus linked with the forces of counterattack which manned the nationalist movements. This is of course true, but it merely pushes the problem back one step further, for it would then remain to determine where the Islamic impulse ended and the nationalist began.[33]

It might also be argued that to compare present-day Islamic reality with the Islamic ideal is rather less meaningful than a comparison with past Islamic reality. It is important, as Tunisia's Dr. Tahir Khemiri has pointed out, not to idealize the past. Answering a questionnaire about the present state of Tunisian culture, Khemiri observed that the previous "culture" had been confined to the low-standard school system epitomized in the *kuttab*, to the stories and tales of the coffeehouses and the superstitions of women in the homes, but today

> We have schools to prepare men and women teachers and hundreds of graduates of European and Eastern universities. We have discovered Al-Jahiz, Abu Hayyan, Al-Ma'arri, and Ibn al-Rumi. The Koran is cited in political speeches as was the case in the time of the orthodox caliphs as well as in articles and newspapers. . . .[34]

This argument, valid to a lesser extent in Algeria and Morocco as well, which recognizes the harsh reality of the previous "age of faith" tends to view with rather more optimism the prospects for Islam in the coming age of mass culture and pluralistic society.

In fact, in the last turbulent decade where the educated class (and thus the participating if not the ruling class) has more than doubled[35] this much can be said of Islam by way of lowest common denominator—Islam is readily accepted by everybody either as a religion or as a necessary element of cultural identity. As the Tunisian Ameur Ghedira affirmed:

> I believe that the irreligious among us who does not believe in God and who does not carry out his religious duties remains nevertheless a Muslim in his culture, his mentality and his responses. Even though he might attack men of religion

---

33. In another sense, Islamic reformism pre-empted the field from any possible "anti-clericalism." The fight became one within the Muslim religious hierarchy, with the reformist *ulama* challenging both the conservative *ulama* and the *marabouts*.

34. *Al-Fikr*, June 1956, p. 63.

35. I.e., as a result of the imposing educational programs in Tunisia and Morocco. In Algeria there was also a manifold increase in the proportion of *participants* in society as a result of the peculiar circumstances of the war.

in a certain question he would invariably defend Islam whenever it is exposed to criticism by a foreigner.[36]

The tendency to "nationalize" Islam can also be seen in the platform of the General Union of Algerian Muslim Students:

> French colonization having as its objective the depersonalization of the Algerian people by oppression and the stifling of its own culture, the General Union of Algerian Muslim Students fixes for itself as essential task the restoration and flourishing of the national culture. *This is why* [the Union] affirms its attachment to Arabo-Islamic culture without which the Algerian intellectual would feel uprooted and cut off from his people.[37]

It would be absurd to argue that such sentiments reflected anything more than the secularized residue of Islam's time-honored emphasis upon the importance of the totality—the *umma* which as *dar al-Islam* presents a solid front to the rest of the world. However, such a residue is important in placing a certain limit on what some would insist is a process of de-Islamization. In another sense this secularized approach to Islam at least maintains the outer shell of Islam and provides a reprieve for more genuinely Islamic forces to come forward and create a new synthesis consistent with their new world.

Do such genuinely Islamic forces exist? Certainly remnants of an older traditionalism are still to be found in Morocco, but that is not really the question being posed. The post-independence insistence in Algeria on a public posture of Muslim conformity extending to such items as denying Algerian Muslims alcoholic beverages in bars may impress the outsider as religiosity instead of religion, but it is strikingly similar to the centuries-old pattern in times of Muslim recrudescence. In the same way one can question the reconsecration of mosques which over a century earlier had been converted into churches during the period of French Algeria. Was it simply the revenge of an outraged society or a religious act?

Perhaps, however, the most impressive sign of a genuine if ill-

---

36. In "Letter from a Friend," *Al-Fikr*, April 1956, p. 6. It should come as no surprise that a disproportionate number of those addressing themselves to these problems should be Tunisians. This is no more than a reflection of the greater advances in Tunisian education and social reforms plus the fact that Tunisia has always tended to be more responsive to outside influences.

37. Cited in André Mandouze (ed.), *La Révolution Algérienne par les Textes* (3rd ed.; Paris: Maspero, 1962), p. 141. Emphasis added.

defined religious sentiment took place in Tunisia—the reaction to President Bourguiba's attempt to circumvent the Ramadan fast.[38] This campaign was inaugurated before Ramadan (February-March), 1960, and met immediately with stubborn resistance. Bourguiba argued that the fight against underdevelopment, so urgent as to make the lassitude and lost time of Ramadan fasting unthinkable, was a modern form of the *jihad* (holy war) and that one engaged in *jihad* is exempted from the Ramadan fast. Compared with venerable precedents of perfectly legal stratagems (*hiyal*) for getting around difficult points of Islamic law, this argument is plausible enough. Significantly, in this campaign to "suspend" the Ramadan fast, Bourguiba did resort to a reasoning that would at least save appearances—something he had refused to do in the Personal Status Code of 1956. Yet the latter was, as has been seen, accepted without too much difficulty while the Ramadan question was resisted and caused great soul searching among both intellectuals and the masses.

In addition, the issue chosen in no way involved Islam as an aspect of Tunisian national identity *vis-à-vis* the outside world. Rather, it seemed yet another example of the option Tunisia usually chooses with enthusiasm, i.e., modernism and the idea of decisions based on rational process as opposed to traditionalism and unquestioned acceptance of custom.

There remains only one satisfactory answer: Tunisians sensed that this move somehow struck at the heart of their religion and refused to accept it. The Ramadan incident seems to indicate a deep-rooted Muslim sentiment which remains in Tunisia and *a fortiori* in the rest of North Africa.[39]

38. The rise of Al-Qiyam (Values) Society in Algeria in early 1964, protesting alleged tendencies in the Algerian government to take a non-Islamic or even anti-Islamic position, might well be another example, but this dispute between the "Muslims" and the "Marxists" is not all that clear, at least to the present writer. It could be little more than the political protests of a group of traditionally trained finding themselves poorly trained and thus bypassed for the important posts in a modern state and society. However, the Tunisian *malaise* over the Ramadan question extended to the modern Westernized élite.

39. The fate of Bourguiba's campaign in later Ramadan fasts only confirms the analysis. In 1961, to the manifest relief of all, Bourguiba soft-pedalled the idea. Then in 1962, the first Ramadan after the Bizerte incident, there was an obvious return to observance of the fast which the government in no way discouraged. In the Ramadan fast of 1964, a *New York Times* (February 9, 1964) dispatch reported that 70 percent of the pupils at the teachers' training college and 60 percent of the university students were keeping the fast. If such a percentage of this group keep the fast, the dispatch concluded, perhaps 90 percent of all Tunisians are fasting.

However, even if one is inclined to go this far in accepting the argument of the rebuttal the most imposing hurdle remains. How can Islam survive as a vital force in North Africa when its official spokesmen (*marabouts, qadis, ulama*) have either disappeared or are in disarray and when the most basic tenets of the religion (especially its institutionalization, that is the day-to-day social role of Islam) are up for reexamination? Even assuming the continued existence of a deep-seated Islamic sentiment in North Africa, who will give it concrete form? Who will speak for Islam?

Some would argue that primitive Islam has no clergy, and thus the decline of an *ulama* class who did not really represent the Islam of the *salaf* hardly poses a problem. There is a certain semantic difficulty here. Suffice it to say that any *institutionalized* religion has its spokesmen, be they called clergy, learned men, saints, or medicine men. This is especially the case of a revealed religion with sacred texts which has spawned a universal culture.

Others adopt quite fascinating syncretic solutions. For example, Farhat Dachraoui, presently a professor at the University of Tunis, argued at the time the Personal Status Code was being considered that *ijma* (consensus) had always constituted the legal Islamic means of finding adequate solutions for new situations, and although "traditionally" *ijma* was the consensus of the body of those learned in the law (*faqihs*) it was always "by definition that of the *umma* in its entirety [here, the Tunisian people]." Thus, "Bourguiba who acts and speaks in the name of the overwhelming majority of the Tunisian people can incontestably claim to speak for the Tunisian *umma*."[40]

Still others point to the crisis in present-day Islam and talk of the need for a new Ghazzali. This has long been the major theme of the many homiletical short articles and radio broadcasts of Tunisia's Mahjoub Ben Milad who also delights in pointing out how Ghazzali, too, had to combat an unimaginative, tradition-bound *ulama* class.[41]

This seems to bring the problem up to the threshold of prediction and "prophecy." At the beginning of this chapter it was noted how at the turn of the century several competent European observers proved completely incapable of seeing that the static,

---

40. *L'Action*, October 15, 1956.
41. Ben Milad, *Tahrik al-Sawakin* (Kitab al-Baath Series) (Tunis, 1956) and *Tahrik al-Sawakin fi shu'un al-Tarbiya* (Tunis, 1950), *passim*. Ben Milad is director of the Ecole Normale d'Instituteurs, of Tunis.

theocentric Islam of their daily research was about to burst asunder. It would be equally foolhardy to suggest today with any great confidence what will happen to Islam in North Africa.

However, some sort of prophecy is customary in studies of this kind. In the secularized use of the word, one role of the prophet can be to suggest at appropriate times that everyone is looking in the wrong direction, operating on false assumptions. Today, most observers foresee an inevitable process of secularization in North Africa. North Africa tends to be measured, analyzed, and classified as one part of the non-Western world or underdeveloped world or *tiers monde* or among the "emerging" nations. It is not fashionable at present to measure, analyze, and classify North Africa within a Muslim context.

This trend may well be based on a false assumption. A new Ghazzali or a new group who will arrive at a reformulation of Islam in North Africa may even now be tackling these problems. One is inclined to go further and suggest that if such a group exists it is not from among the traditionally trained *ulama*.

Individuals meeting this description exist—men who have mastered the thought processes of modern science, who remain Muslims and who have begun to wrestle with the intellectual problems of adjustment. This small group—they are by no means a formal "school"—are in no way related to earlier generations who remained on the level of apologetics.[42] They have a highly developed critical spirit. They eschew the myth of the golden age. They are beyond the fundamentalist fear of how to reconcile this or that new "discovery" with the faith.

An example is Algeria's Malek Bennabi arguing in 1954 that the Muslim had remained devout but his faith had lost efficacy since divorced from the social scene. In a sense, the problem was not as that of "proving" God but of "manifesting" Him.[43]

The new spirit can be seen also in the official Tunisian Ministry of Education pamphlet setting out the secondary school program for those concentrating in Islamic thought:

---

42. Reference is made here to the typology suggested by W. Cantwell Smith, *Islam in Modern History* (New York: Mentor Books, 1959). If Smith had included North Africa in his book, he would have discovered an interesting pattern of apologetics from as early as *L'Esprit Libéral du Coran* (1905), written in French by Tunisia's Abd al-Aziz al-Thaalbi with French-speaking colleagues, through the various Muslim reformist movements in each country and right down to the kind of argument used by the Old Destour newspaper *Al-Istiqlal* in combatting the 1956 Personal Status Code.

43. *Vocation de l'Islam*, p. 49.

> The methods to be relied upon in teaching Islamic thought should be those employed in what is today called the study of religion from the sociology of religion viewpoint. This is the method which attempts to go beyond the investigation of any given mental formation to discover the substantive factors which determined its various viewpoints just as they determined the solutions and the problems arising from that very mental formation in any given age. This method, in short, calls not for simply receiving and believing but for thought, investigation and criticism.[44]

Coming closest to suggesting outright that perhaps a new *ulama* class might emerge from the ranks of the Western trained is Tunisia's Mohammed Taalbi. He is aware of the present bleak picture:

> A medieval restoration is not the desired solution . . . The masses are not perhaps "de-Islamized," but they are certainly not "catechized" either . . . Left to themselves they vaguely sense Islam as a factor of cohesion, a sort of patriotism, of belonging to a common community, history, civilization and destiny . . . [but] such an Islam is at the mercy of every demagogue.[45]

There is, however, modest hope, according to Taalbi. It depends in the final analysis on the maturity of the community.

> Already Muslim scholars trained in the disciplines of European universities, if they have not actually already begun to relieve—as a new Muʻtazila?—the traditional *faqihs,* are nevertheless concerning themselves in greater number with the history of ideas in Muslim civilization and are attempting to define the importance of the spiritual values which have modelled its humanism.[46]

Taalbi, himself, concludes "the perspectives and exact lines of evolution are still indiscernible." Certainly, any conclusion drawn here must be even more modest. However, it can be affirmed that such a small group of thinkers does exist, and when they can pose their problem and that of their society in the following challenging manner, they merit our attention:

44. Translated from the Arabic.
45. "L'Islam et le Monde Moderne," *Confluent,* No. 8 (June-July 1960). Judging from his ideas and his works already published one would be inclined to say that Taalbi, himself, is perhaps one of the best examples of the kind of man he describes.
46. *Ibid.*

A religion lacking restlessness and searching, which is not a quest and a thirst for an ideal, for perfection of the absolute, which is not in a certain measure tragic is not really a religion. Ghazzali was a great Muslim because he had a great anguish.[47]

BY WAY OF POSTSCRIPT

It is useful and appropriate to consider how the experience of Islam in modern North Africa can be compared with that of the Middle East. The following major themes might be suggested as a point of departure:

1. There is first a time lag. Islamic reformism—and for that matter related questions such as female emancipation—tended to reach North Africa a full generation later.

2. Perhaps at least in part for this reason reformism in North Africa was less original in doctrine and had less of an intellectual tradition. In terms of social activity it was, as has been suggested, extremely important, but there was no intellectual equivalent to Shaikh Abduh, Rashid Rida, and the *manar* group.

3. Muslim reformism could blend more easily into the nationalist movements in North Africa since there was nothing quite comparable to the Arab nationalism of the East, of which one important element was the rapprochement of Christian and Muslim Arabs. This necessarily involved a certain transcending of the religious theme in Eastern Arab nationalism.

4. As a corollary of the above point, in North Africa (and especially in Algeria) the colonial experience was both longer and much more intensive. In reaction, the need to embrace Islam as part of the tactic of defense, of establishing one's own cultural identity, during the struggle for independence, was more pressing.

Finally, a word should be said about Libya, which was excluded from this chapter not because the role of Islam in modern Libya has been unimportant (quite the contrary) but rather because the Libyan cases did not fit into the shared experience of the other three countries. Here again, in the field of religion, as in several others, it would appear that the most useful and meaningful comparison would be between Libya and Saudi Arabia (cf. Chapter I, p. 18).

47. *Ibid.*

SELECT BIBLIOGRAPHY ON ISLAM IN MODERN NORTH AFRICA

As the preceding chapter has intimated, Islam is not easily (or properly) separated from the general history of the modern Maghrib. No attempt has been made here to list even a few of the better general works which also devote pages to the role of Islam in modern North Africa. Such a bibliography can be found at the end of the book. However, the reader should remember that some of the most perceptive insights into the present role of Islam in North Africa are often tucked away in a few pages of more general works.

The following bibliography attempts to include (1) the handful of works more specifically devoted to this subject of Islam in modern North Africa plus (2) enough references on rather more specialized subjects (such as changes in Sharia law in North Africa) to be of some help to the reader seeking more detail on these matters.

Abun-Nasr, Jamil, "The Salafiyya Movement in Morocco: The Religious Base of the Moroccan Nationalist Movement," *St. Antony's Papers, No. 16, Middle East Affairs, No. 3,* London: Chatto and Windus, 1963.

Bennabi, Malek. *Vocation de l'Islam.* Paris: Editions du Seuil, 1954.

Berque, A., "Les Capteurs du Divin: Marabouts, Ulemas," *Revue de la Méditerrannée* (May-June 1951).

Bousquet, G. H. *L'Islam Maghrebin: Introduction à l'Etude Générale de l'Islam.* 4th ed. Algiers: La Maison des Livres, 1954.

Brown, Leon Carl, "The Islamic Reformist Movement in North Africa," *Journal of Modern African Studies,* II, No. 1 (March 1964).

Busson de Janssens, Gérard, "L'Indépendance du Culte Musulman en Algérie," *Revue Juridique et Politique de l'Union Française,* V (1951).

Colomer, André, "Le Code du Statut Personnel Tunisien," *Revue Algérien, Tunisien et Marocain de Législation et de Jurisprudence,* No. 73 (July-August 1957).

Confluent (special issue June-July 1964), "Comment les Musulmans du Maghreb Comprennent, Vivent et Pratiquent l'Islam?"

Delisle, René, "Les Origines du F.L.N.," *La Nef,* New Series, Nos. 12-13 (October 1962-January 1963).

Evans-Pritchard, E. *The Sanusi of Cyrenaica.* Oxford: Clarendon Press, 1949.

Gallagher, Charles F., "New Laws for Old: The Moroccan Code of Personal Status," *American Universities Field Staff Report,* North Africa Series, Vol. V, No. 1 (1959).

———, "Ramadan in Tunisia," *American Universities Field Staff Report,* North Africa Series, Vol. VI, No. 1 (1960).

Halstead, John P., "The Changing Character of Moroccan Reformism, 1921-1934," *Journal of African History,* V, No. 3 (1964).

Lapanne-Loinville, J., "Le Code Marocain du Statut Personnel," *La Revue Marocaine du Droit* (1959).

Le Tourneau, Roger, "North Africa: Rigorism and Bewilderment," in *Unity and Variety in Muslim Civilization*, ed. G. von Grunebaum. Chicago: University of Chicago Press, 1955.

Lings, Martin. *A Muslim Saint in the Twentieth Century: Shaikh Ahmad al 'Alawi, His Spiritual Heritage and Legacy*. London: Allen and Unwin, 1961.

Massignon, Louis, "Africa," in *Whither Islam: A Survey of Movements in the Moslem World*, ed. H. A. R. Gibb. London: Gollancz, 1932.

Pérès, Henri, "Le Mouvement Réformiste en Algérie et l'Influence de l'Orient d'après la Presse Arabe d'Algérie," *Entretiens sur l'Evolution des Pays de Civilisation Arabe*, I, Paris, 1957.

Roussier, J., "Le Code Tunisien de Status Personnel," *Revue Juridique et Politique de l'Union Française* (April-June 1957).

———, "L'Application du Chra' au Maghreb en 1959," *Die Welt des Islams*, New Series, VI, Nos. 1-2 (1959).

Valin, Raymond, "Socialisme Musulman en Algérie," *L'Afrique et l'Asie*, No. 66 (1964).

Vidal, F. S., "Religious Brotherhoods in Moroccan Politics," *Middle East Journal* (October 1950).

Ziadeh, Nicola. *Sanusiyah: A Study of a Revivalist Movement in Islam*. Leiden: Brill, 1958.

The question of Islam in modern North Africa fits, of course, into the larger problem of the tensions and problems of adaptation of Islam in the modern world. The two best works dealing with the general problem are:

Gibb, H. A. R. *Modern Trends in Islam*. Chicago: University of Chicago Press, 1947.

Smith, W. Cantwell. *Islam in Modern History*. New York: Mentor Books, 1959.

6

Implications of Rapid Urbanization

Roger Le Tourneau

It is not necessary to insist upon the worldwide feature of urban development. Suffice it to recall that the city of Aix-en-Provence where I live grew from about 30,000 in 1936 to 80,000 in 1964. But the effects of this phenomenon vary considerably from one country to another, according to the individual's capacity for adaptation.

For the so-called industrial nations, where even the country-dwellers participate in the general way of life, the adaptation problems are relatively easy to solve. But when the phenomenon concerns a population rural in its overwhelming majority and living since the remotest times according to archaic standards, adaptation problems become very difficult. The new town-dwellers lack capital and initiative in an environment entirely unknown to them and have everything to learn in their new situation—a new rhythm of life as well as administrative intricacies and the ways of the old-time residents. Such is the case of the North African population.

Before the area was affected by Western influence, migrations from the country to the cities did exist. As early as the 16th century, for example, Algiers was partly peopled by Kabyles and individuals coming from the Saharan region of Biskra. Sometimes, in case of drought or very heavy rain, such migrations would even take on a torrent-like aspect; but as soon as conditions had become normal again the peasants would return to the country because they did not feel at ease in the cities. Starvation would have resulted in voids in the country areas and workmen would be needed. So, the temporary migrants would quickly go back to their village or tribe, happy to resume their ancestral habits.

Besides exceptional circumstances, a regular but very thin stream would bring individuals or even families from the country to the cities: ambition, venturesome genius, unforeseen family circumstances might be the causes of individual migrations. Arriving in small numbers, the newcomers were obliged to adapt themselves to the life of the city which certainly would not change to accommodate them. At first they would live in peripheral, still semi-rural, quarters,[1] sometimes even in straw huts. Such was the case in a quarter of Fez at the beginning of the 20th century. Then, if things went well with them, they would mingle with the urban society, retaining from their origin only a tribal name which showed that in the past—but when?—their ancestors had come from a sometimes remote region: for instance, in Fez, the Filalis, Serghushnis, Fishtalis, Sanhadjis, and many others. These people, however, were too few to affect urban affairs and so, from a general point of view, the question of their adaptation was not of great importance.

All changed when Europeans permanently settled in North Africa and introduced their economy and hygiene. As a matter of fact, in the cities where they established themselves in great numbers, they needed more and more manual labor as their activities developed, and the towns, both traditional and newly founded, became powerful centers of attraction. Moreover, as crude but efficient sanitation spread over the country and resulted in almost complete elimination of starvation and epidemics, the rural population began to grow at an increasing rate, so that manpower which sometimes had been lacking in the past, became superabundant, and there was a rush to urban centers.

It was about 1930 that this evolution became conspicuous, the first inquiries on the *bidonvilles* were published, and people in charge faced the problem of the new city-dwellers. At the outset it was of limited significance, but the phenomenon continued after World War II to increase in magnitude and reached its highest point to date during the Algerian war. Within seven years the population of the city of Algiers and suburbs nearly doubled from less than 500,000 in 1954 to more than 800,000 in 1960. Such an evolution is general in North Africa. The population of Casablanca grew from 350,000 in 1936 to 682,000 in 1952 and 965,000 in 1961; that of Tunis from 300,000 in 1936 to more than 700,000 at present and that of Sidi Bel Abbes from 76,000 in 1954 to more than 100,000 in 1961.

The largest cities are generally also those with the highest rate

---

1. See the novel of François Bonjean, *Les Confidences d'une Fille de la Nuit* (Paris, 1939).

of growth, because their activity is greater and employment is thought of as more abundant than elsewhere, but the increase affects also cities of less importance like, for example, Taza in Morocco or Medjez al Bab in Tunisia. Everywhere in North Africa the general urbanization rate of the Muslim population grows very fast. At present it is near or over 30 percent, while it was under 20 percent twenty years ago.

This rapid and sudden development surprised everybody, the administrators as well as the scholars. It has not yet been studied as a whole and that is understandable, because it has probably not yet reached its acme and is so complex that it requires thorough and careful research for which material is not always easy to find. One may read at present only incomplete studies differing vastly in approach and content.

Many investigators, however, have been attracted by a particularly conspicuous, offensive, and upsetting aspect of the urban phenomenon in North Africa—the *bidonvilles* ("tin-can" cities). From the first inquiries made by R. Baron, R. Huot, and L. Paye in 1936 at Rabat to the recent investigations of the African Center for Applied Human Sciences (CASHA) of Aix-en-Provence, through the monograph of André Adam about Ben Msik *bidonville* in 1948, the writings on those para-urban agglomerations are abundant and of great interest.

However, if the *bidonvilles* present a particularly important problem, one must not forget that urbanization in North Africa presents many other aspects which, although less conspicuous, must not be neglected. Here an attempt will be made at establishing a sort of balance sheet, and in addition to noting results drawn from many good inquiries, a number of questions still without answers will be proposed.

Even before the country poured its overflow population over the towns, the old city-dwellers were transformed in a manner which, though not dramatic nor even conspicuous, did indicate some serious changes.

Very soon after the advent of colonialism, Muslim businessmen and clerks in frequent contact with their Western counterparts came under this influence and began to modify their own way of life. The first things to be modified were clothes and food, which, at length, led to many changes in the old economic equilibrium of the traditional cities. Then Muslims began to use cars and thence to change houses. The old dwelling in the heart of a city with narrow and meandering streets was considered by youth as stifling, access to it in a car was generally impossible, and the arrangement of the rooms did not fit with new ideas on domestic and social life. Consequently some Muslims left the old *medina* and settled in peripheral quarters or in suburbs, as in Tunis and Algiers, even in specifically European areas, renting or buying houses built for Europeans, or even, if they had money enough, building modern houses in accordance with their own ideas. I know this to be the case in Fez. It goes without saying that the new elite of modern-educated people, many of humble origin, like President Bourguiba, went the same way, even more often than the old families.

Consequently, some central sections of the cities were progressively deprived of their habitual residents who were replaced by petty bourgeois and shopkeepers, and even by a poorer class. This is what happened in the southern half of Tunis *medina* and more plainly in the Casablanca *medina* or Algiers Kasbah (traditional section of the city) which became proletarian quarters. The same is now happening in Fez *medina*. Thus the move initiated by an increasing number of the Muslim elite resulted in the real overthrow of century-old social structures and thorough changes in the traditional urban equilibrium.

The evolution of the urban Jewish societies is still more pronounced. Even the most traditional communities, as those of interior Morocco, quickly turned to modernism because, beyond its own attractiveness, it represented to them a means of liberation from the old restraint of the *mellah* or the *hara*.[2] The well-to-do families moved very soon to European settlements, thus freeing their century-old district for Jews who came from other cities or areas, and even for Muslim families, as is the case happening now in the *mellah* of Fez. Thus the ghetto, which for centuries was one of the fundamental features in North African towns, is giving way to mixed districts where Jews live together with Muslims or Europeans, or both. This is certainly the result of a more general evolution, but the fact of urbanization has an important share in it.

Urban increase also carries along changes in the hierarchy of cities. Bône, Casablanca, Bizerte, Rabat are the most striking examples, but there are many others. When Europeans occupied the country, those four small towns drowsed along an unused sea. All of a sudden, the Europeans made great harbors of the first three and a capital of the last. Casablanca has become the largest

---

2. *Mellah* is the Jewish quarter in Morocco; *hara* is the same in Algeria and Tunisia.

city in North Africa, Rabat a town of more than 200,000 inhabitants, Bône and Bizerte the fourth largest cities in Algeria and Tunisia, respectively. On the contrary, some others which were prominent in the past, as Fez, Marrakech, or Tetuan, have lost much—not in number, but in relative importance—a fact which has led their elite to settle elsewhere. This change had already begun before Moroccan independence. Many Fasis (inhabitants of Fez) had already left their native city to go to Casablanca for business purposes, or to Rabat for administrative or political purposes. After independence, there was a real exodus of the Fez bourgeois, which carried along with it a conspicuous proletarianization of this city which was so elegant in the past. It is quite likely that the same thing will happen to Constantine and Tlemcen in independent Algeria.

Up to the present, the most stable social group of the traditional cities has been the petty bourgeoisie—the shopkeepers and artisans, old town-dwellers faithfully devoted to their original habitation—without money enough to try their luck elsewhere, and often lacking also the necessary audacity and taste for risk. They continue to like their city, their surroundings, their houses; they are like a firm point amidst the whirls of urban development. Faithfulness or passivity? That is a question of individuals. But their conservatism will not last long, because their children aspire to modernism and will not hesitate to leave their childhood homes.

One may foresee that within a short time the old *medinas* will disappear more or less completely. That is what is happening at Monastir in Tunisia because President Bourguiba's will is to transform his native city into an entirely modern one. The only monument of the past which will continue to exist, on the seashore, apart from the town and entirely restored, is the ancient *ribat* or fortified monastery which was built in the 9th century in order to guard the Muslim territory against attack from the sea. The old district of Tunis has also been transformed. In Morocco, a plan has long existed and is now taking definite shape to build a new road for automobile traffic above the picturesque and dirty Wadi Fez which separates the old city into two sections, and to open streets for vehicles in the ancient quarters.

The reason is that however picturesque and dear to the heart of old residents, the traditional cities have been built for ways of life quite different from modern conceptions, and can be adapted to our time only at the price of profound dislocation. Some venerated monuments will certainly remain, like the Great Mosque of

Tunis, the Qarawiyin Mosque or Moulay Idris Shrine at Fez. Some beautiful gates will be kept, just as in Paris the St. Denis and St. Martin gates have been preserved; probably also the central market or *suq* of Fez, Tunis, and Marrakech; but private houses will be pulled down or completely made over, streets will be widened. This is an inevitable change, unless the men in charge and the inhabitants decide that some cities must remain as they were centuries ago and become museum-towns. Such an idea is unfamiliar to North African city-dwellers and can be envisaged in any case only for small towns devoid of economic prospects, certainly not for vigorous urban centers like Fez, Marrakech, or Sfax.

Long-range change sets very difficult problems. At first, leaving aside the case of earthquakes as at Orleansville (now Al-Asnam) or Agadir, account must be taken of what exists, that is to say the buildings previous to European settlement which represent an old way of life, some aspects of which still exist; then delapidated European buildings, dating before the general use of cars, as in some districts of Algiers or Tetuan; and, last, the examples of modern European urbanism which flourished often successfully at Rabat, Tripoli, or Tangier, for example. In a city like Casablanca may be seen in a confined area the coexistence of very different, if not opposed urbanistic conceptions—in the center, the districts built up previous to 1912 with zigzag streets rarely wide enough for carriages between low windowless buildings; close to them, the remains of the first European city, with straight but narrow streets fringed with arcades and four- or five-storied houses; at a little distance, villas surrounded with flower gardens; and again close to the old *medina*, skyscrapers of some twenty stories; finally, farther off, *bidonvilles* and sections built up with new low-income housing which look like barracks.

From all this comes an impression of disparity, of attempts in diverse directions and with unequal means. Aesthetics apart, one may ask what sort of lesson independent North Africa will draw from those buildings constructed by and for such different ethnic and social groups.

At length, but only at length, a new North African urbanism will emerge from this sometimes attractive jumble. One may be sure that it will be far from the *medina's* urbanism; but will it not be as far from the endeavors made by town-planners of goodwill, but not a part of the civilization for whose benefit they worked? The new *medina* of Casablanca was praised in its beginning as one of the most successful conceptions of Lyautey's town-planners. Less than fifteen years later, however, it already appeared obsolete and unsatisfactory to some of its inhabitants. Will it not be the same for the present city of Ain Qadus, built in Fez after 1950 for the modern bourgeois car owner?

In brief, the North African town-planners of today—they are still very few—have two kinds of problems to solve. They must find a formula to carry out the desires for modernity of most of the town-dwellers, at the same time being consistent with certain fixed rules of the community in question. Moreover, they must devise solutions that can be readily adapted to new requirements because, as experience proves, these change very fast in North Africa. Today's North African city is the result of traditions that are in transition and of strong but vague aspirations and human pressures which are not easily foreseen. One gets an impression that the stability which it knew for centuries, when the Islamic civilization was immobile, will not be found again for a very long time.

One of the uncertainties in urban life today comes from the unceasing flood of newcomers pouring into the city from rural areas which are no longer able to feed them. For a long time, as a consequence of European settlement, North African cities had received a great many newcomers, but these were Europeans who were usually from urban areas, possessed some capital, and the "know-how" to build houses on credit. Moreover, they were encouraged to settle in North Africa by the colonial power, which placed important material facilities at their disposal. There was congestion at certain periods, but, as a whole, urban growth developed without major difficulties.

The situation was quite different when, after the thirties, crowds of Muslims invaded first the main cities, then the other less important ones. These poor people were attracted less by the brilliance of urban life than by sheer necessity. To them the city was above all a place where nobody died of hunger, whereas in the country, as a result of population growth, they lived in a state of perpetual scarcity, even close to starvation if the crops were bad. Such was of course the case of the poorest areas—in Morocco, the Saharan regions and Tadla; in Algeria, the Saharan border, the high plains and the Kabylia range; in Tunisia, the southern zone, the islands of Djerba and Kerkena, and the central steppe between Kairouan and Gafsa; Djebel Nefusa and Djeffara, in Tripolitania.

The more prosperous agricultural areas contributed very few

migrants to the cities—only some individuals who, for personal reasons decided to settle in town, but were not compelled by necessity. Contrary to a widespread legend, the colonized areas were scarcely affected by urban immigration; for a long time the Moroccan ranges (relatively well watered), the Algerian plains, the Medjerda Valley, and the high plains of western Tunisia sent almost no one to the cities.

It may thus be said that population movements toward the towns were first determined by the enormous need for manpower to create and maintain a European type of settlement, later by the overpopulation of rural areas affected by an almost complete stagnation of agricultural output in many regions.

As a consequence of the unceasing and sometimes torrent-like flood of newcomers, the housing capacity was soon exhausted; afterward—although much later—the possibilities of employment. Those who arrived between the years 1925 and 1930 succeeded in finding room in existing houses and, since offers of employment were abundant, were soon in a position to get decent lodging in new buildings, often erected by the employers themselves. But, since building did not keep pace with the influx from the country, traditional centers were rapidly overcrowded—for example, the old *medina* at Casablanca (studied by Andre Adam)[3] despite the already existing new *medina,* or the extraordinary congestion of Algiers' Kasbah invaded by Kabyles as described by Father Le Tellier. Probably this was the pattern in all the large North African cities around 1930.

But the time came when all the traditional areas were saturated, the smallest room being occupied beyond its normal capacity, every empty space being used for new emergency construction. Then *bidonvilles* began to appear. On vacant land nearly always without streets or drains, newcomers settled with or without the owner's permission, paying a small rent for the ground and erecting strange shelters—tents, wooden huts, shanties made of shells or oil cans put together (thus the word *bidonville*), of cardboard boxes, of tar paper, etc. It was even possible to see a few stone or brick houses in some *bidonvilles:* the houses of "rich" *bidonville* residents.

These settlements reminded Parisians of the ragmen's shanties in the *non aedificandi* area which bordered the ancient fortifica-

---

3. "La Prolétarisation de la Medina de Casablanca," *Bulletin Economique et Social du Maroc* (1950).

tions of Paris. The "tin-can" towns experienced varying fortunes according to the place where they had first been built. Some of them, when space was not restricted, became genuine small towns, however ugly and sordid; such was the Ben Msik *bidonville* at Casablanca, with 40,000 inhabitants in 1948; that of Mahieddine in the center of Algiers with 10,000 in 1956; that of Melassine close to Tunis. Others, on the contrary, could not grow because of lack of space, or were stopped in their development by new urban buildings, or were razed to make room for normal urban districts.

In general the town councils were caught unawares by the suddenness and extent of the phenomenon and could not block it. Some of them preferred to ignore what they could not control and let *bidonvilles* develop without paying attention to them for some time. Others intelligently planned new housing units which, once built, would facilitate the removal of the *bidonvilles;* but usually the newcomers moved into the evacuated lodgings before the town authorities had time to pull them down. Many town councils submitted to this unavoidable development and provided water supply and electricity, accepting the fact, not without reason, that the *bidonvilles* would not disappear for many years. It must be added that, during the Algerian war, the *bidonvilles* in Algeria became an object of concern for political and military, as well as humanitarian, reasons, and a considerable effort was made to equip them and establish decent housing for their inhabitants, but the problem has not yet been solved because of the flood of new immigrants.

A *bidonville* creates an offensive impression. It is ugly. It is miserable. The occupants live packed in it like herrings in a barrel. It evokes the idea of a nasty breeding ground for germs where any epidemic may develop at a terrifying speed. Fire may spread easily because of overcrowding and of the heterogeneous material used in its construction, and as a matter of fact many fires have broken out, destroying lodgings and killing people.

However, a distinction must be made between diverse kinds of *bidonvilles.* Some are badly located, as that of Scala-Nador at Algiers, described by Robert Descloitres.[4] It is wedged in a hole which becomes a slough when it rains, where air does not circulate and heat is severe in summer. But there are others which present a better appearance. I saw some of them on the hills of Algiers

4. R. Descloitres, J-C. Reverdy and C. Descloitres, *L'Algérie des Bidonvilles: Le Tiers-Monde dans la Cité* (Paris: Mouton, 1961), pp. 13-22.

where light and air abundantly circulate and the slope provides drainage. André Adam[5] says the same about Ben Msik and adds, statistics in hand, that sanitary conditions are appreciably better there than in the old *medina* of Casablanca. It can be pointed out here that country people who come to the cities are accustomed in many cases to houses which are not much better than those in the *bidonville*. Poor apology, let it be said, for an intolerable situation. It must be understood that I am not pleading in favor of *bidonvilles*, but one has to admit that, as a temporary solution, it is not inevitably the worst. Overcrowding in Algiers' Kasbah or the old *medina* of Casablanca is less obvious to anyone who only walks through the streets, but it is far worse than the *bidonvilles* for the inhabitants' health.

Chance certainly played a predominant role in the peopling of the *bidonvilles*, but kinship patterns also had a part. In the small *bidonvilles*, ethnic homogeneity is nearly complete: such as that of 20, rue Fransois Gray, in the center of Algiers. In 1961, 250 to 300 people lived there of whom 70 percent were members of the Ulad Sidi Hadjeres tribe (high Algerian plains, west of Shott al Hodna); 20 percent belonged to the Ulad Sidi Brahim tribe, who were from the same neighborhood and of the same parentage; and only 10 percent came from elsewhere. In the largest *bidonvilles*, ethnic divisions were spontaneously constituted, where families coming from the same region, if not from the same tribe, may be found living together.

The first comers were somehow content with such poor housing because they had no basis for comparison. But, according to Reverdy,[6] their children's attitude is quite different. The latter consider themselves as urbanites and think they have a right to live as such, that is to say in true houses. What had for years been bewilderment and submissiveness of countrymen happy to be in a town is now changing into a revolt of people who feel humiliated because of their miserable condition and sense deeply that the situation has been going on much too long.

Unfortunately, even when North African cities enjoyed a perhaps artificial, but real, colonial activity, they were still not able to give employment to everybody, particularly to unskilled

---

5. André Adam, "Le Bidonville de Ben Msik," *Annales de l'Institut d'Etudes Orientales de la Faculté des Lettres d'Alger*, VIII (1948).

6. J-C. Reverdy, *Recherches sur les Attitudes du Sous-Prolétariat Algérien à l'égard de la Société Urbaine* (mimeographed; African Center for Applied Human Sciences [C.A.S.H.A.] Aix-en-Provence, 1963), p. 47.

workers, who on the whole came from rural areas. Even now most of the newcomers must be satisfied with temporary work, which is by no means obtained without difficulty. Reverdy tells the story of an applicant for a longshoreman's job who was obliged to fight other applicants in order to obtain a token-for-hire which had been thrown among them.[7]

However, efforts have been, and are always being, made in behalf of these unfortunates. An enormous number of new houses have been built around the big cities such as Algiers, Casablanca, Tunis, and many others, but after experience they appear inadequate from many points of view.[8] First, however low their rent from a capitalistic viewpoint, they are still too costly for people who are employed only a few hours a week and, even more, not every week. The conclusion is that only privileged people have access to the new houses. Further, the apartments are terribly small (some are not over 20 square meters), giving the housewife, who does not often go out, the impression that she lives in a prison cell, making impossible any gathering of family or friends. Last, they are overcrowded, because in many cases the happy possessor of an apartment takes in with him his old parents or a married brother or sister. Astonishing figures result from this practice— seven sleeping in a space of 29 square meters or nine in less than 40 square meters. The question is whether the remedy is really better than the evil.

As a consequence of independence, many Europeans went back home, leaving many lodgings vacant and nearly whole city districts deserted. This is particularly obvious if we consider the Algerian towns, even Algiers, and the Tunisian and Moroccan cities of minor importance. The first result of this changed condition is that the tenseness which existed previously between European and Muslim communities, at least in time of political uneasiness, has practically disappeared and is almost unimaginable, since everywhere, without any exception, the Europeans are now only a minority and not in a position to oppose the Muslims. Only in Casablanca and Rabat is the European minority still relatively important and could theoretically cause trouble, but solely as a consequence of extraordinary circumstances which cannot be envisaged in the present situation. Let us add that new Europeans

---

7. *Ibid.*, pp. 42-43.
8. J-C. Reverdy, *Habitations Nouvelles et Urbanisation Rapide: Conditions Ecologiques de l'Adaptation au Logement en Algérie* (Aix-en-Provence: C.A.S.H.A., 1963).

have come to Tunisia, Morocco, and even Algeria after independence in relatively important numbers, but to my knowledge no precise study has yet been made on this point. Those newcomers did not know the pre-independence period and therefore, far from making unceasing comparisons with the past, have brought with them a new state of mind.

The human geography of North African towns has been deeply modified: one may still find districts mostly peopled by Europeans, but fewer than in the past; the cities have become, or have returned to the situation of, Muslim cities under a European shell. Contrast with a very recent past is particularly striking in Algiers where a Muslim crowd may now be seen walking in streets where, two or three years ago, Muslims would come only occasionally and where their presence still appears odd, because the shops, cinemas, and houses have all kept their European appearance.

In an enormous number of mansions, the residents, if not the owners, have changed. It would be very interesting from a sociological point of view, to study in detail the changes which have occurred, to examine the circumstances in which the new residents have taken the place of the former ones—whether they simply adopted existing arrangements or made changes; to what social groups they belong; whether they are anxious to maintain the building or only to live in it without caring about tomorrow; by whom they were replaced in their previous housing. A sociological inquiry of this sort should be made over a period of years, because in Algeria at least the situation is so mobile that limited inquiries for a short period could not possibly be of value.

The maintenance of buildings now occupied by Muslims is of great importance. The Europeans, when they left, more or less abandoned a huge capital in real estate, houses newly built in many cases and generally well maintained. If maintenance goes on normally, this capital may last a long while; but will it be so? It may be questioned whether the new occupants will realize the importance of the problem—they may let things slide; one may wonder also whether they can afford proper maintenance, even if they want to provide it. In many cases they may lack capital, skilled labor, and necessary materials. It seems to me that the problem of maintenance of real estate will have to be carefully studied not only by sociologists desirous of making investigations, but also by town councils and even governments.

Some have hoped that such movements within the cities might ease the problem of the *bidonvilles,* since many vacancies occurred here and there more or less rapidly, and in Algeria quite suddenly. It does not seem that this has been the case, although the inquiries about the *bidonvilles* published up to now are all anterior to the Europeans' mass departure. The question is therefore whether, all things considered, vacancies have been only partially filled or, as is probable, the flood of newcomers is more pressing than ever.

As a result of the increase of population, which is not slowing down at all, and the economic stagnation that has followed the end of the colonial régime, it must be envisaged that the situation will continue to deteriorate. At best, deterioration will perhaps be tempered by drastic measures. It is not impossible that the leaders of the now independent countries will be able to establish a program to provide new houses, rented at very low cost, and better fitted to the newcomers' needs.[9] Perhaps also the efforts being made everywhere in North Africa to establish a program of accelerated vocational training will allow a greater number of people to find stable and decently paid jobs, thanks to which they will be in a position to pay more for housing.

But it is obvious that those measures are only poor remedies and cannot eradicate the evil at its very root. Rural development alone will make possible new employment on the spot and the reduction of the exodus toward the cities. On that point, the Tunisian government has launched interesting experiments which to date seem to have produced good results. When peasants earn at home what they need for their daily life, they will not try to leave, at least for a while. As a matter of fact, migration to the cities does not proceed, as in Europe, from a desire for greater welfare and more sophisticated social life, but only from a vital necessity. Therefore, in a better organization of rural economy and a gradual decrease of rural birthrate lie the true remedies for urban overpopulation.

It must be added that North African leaders can only hope to slow down or, at best, to stop immigration toward the cities, for it will be impossible to drive back to the countryside people who have tasted city life, even in *bidonvilles*. In this connection it is advisable to reflect on the following statement, made by a good

9. On that point, indications, unfortunately hazy, may be found in Dr. Benhima's article, "Les Problèmes d'Urbanisation posés par le Développement des Agglomérations," *Bulletin Economique et Social du Maroc, Nos. 94-95* (December 1962), principally pp. 183-188. See also the provisions of the Three Year Plan (1962-1964) in Tunisia, as published by the Secretary of State for Plan and Finances, and a pamphlet published by the same Minister, *Progrès Economique*, No. 3 (April 1963), pp. 9-18.

observer, about the children's villages established in Tunisia for orphans by President Bourguiba: "The experience of Kasserine," he says, "has shown how difficult it was to direct toward agriculture the children of the villages. Most of them have been accustomed since their infancy to an urban environment: they demonstrate in their manner this well-known truth that going back to the countryside is nothing else than a luxury for sophisticated people ... with rare exceptions, due to atavism or childish remembrances, nothing in their imagination or sensibility brings them to agriculture: this job is devoid of prestige and it is extremely difficult to fight against such a prejudice.... At last one must admit that the atmosphere of community life to which they became accustomed in the villages, the improvement, however modest it may be, of their material life, prevent them from taking again the rough and individualistic style of life that prevails in the Tunisian countryside."[10] Mr. Bourguiba's government tried to drive people back from Tunis to central Tunisia but was not successful and was obliged to let many people return to Tunis.

Admittedly, the cities, whether their administration's planners like it or not, will have to assimilate those who have already arrived. They can only at best hope to slow down the pace of new arrivals.

Is it necessary to add that the conditions of life in the *bidonvilles* bring serious psychological and social consequences? As has just been said, overcrowding in the *bidonvilles* becomes more and more unbearable to people who have not known extreme rural poverty, and they unceasingly make comparisons with the opulent districts of the city on the fringe of which they live. The Algerian revolution developed among peasants without land, but it could proceed on its way among city-dwellers without houses. When to the vain all-day-long search for a job are added promiscuity, children's cries, women's quarreling, and the impossibility of relaxation and of a quiet evening among the family, it is easy to understand that a fury of despair is smoldering.

Moreover, even for the privileged, housing is no more the spacious mansion of the past where old parents lived among their married sons. The family is now reduced in general to a couple with young children, due to the necessities of urban housing. Such family dispersion is well known in Western countries and is not considered as catastrophic, but it may be a cause of difficulties for

10. J. G. Magnin, "Les 'Enfants de Bourguiba' grandissent dans leurs Villages," *Institut de Belles Lettres Africaines*, No. 85 (1st quarter, 1959), p. 77.

people who knew another way of life and are accustomed to make decisions with the help of their family. Individual behavior is not easy to learn for people who only knew a collective life.

Here enters, of course, the woman's problem. The well-known writer Frantz Fanon in his book *An V de la Republique Algérienne* applauded the fact that the Algerian war was bringing emancipation to Algerian women. This is true for some of them, but when one sees the streets of Algiers today, it seems much less true. As a matter of fact, Algerian women continue to stay mainly at home, much more, in fact, than their Moroccan or Tunisian sisters. The struggle for independence, in which women largely participated, has had an impact on North African society which will probably bring long-range results, the more so since it was accompanied by the development of education in female circles. But it is only an evolution in its first beginnings. Election days excepted, urban women participate very little in public life and spend most of their time at home; there they perhaps enjoy more responsibility and authority than previously, but that is hardly seen from the outside. The society which may be seen in public is essentially a male society. Development of education at all levels, the part taken by some women—who set an example—in political, administrative, economic, and intellectual life all over North Africa, the enactment in Tunisia, and Morocco to a lesser degree, of a legislation much more favorable to women, all indicate that urban women in the future will be no more what they were previously. But it must be admitted that change will come slowly, because it offends all sorts of venerable traditions deeply rooted in social consciousness in the cities and still more in the country. On that point it must be remembered that more than one-half of the city-dwellers were born and lived for years in villages or tribes. Sex segregation is, and will long remain an essential feature of the urban society in North Africa.

From another point of view, the old collective ties are fading away: the religious brotherhoods have not the same appeal as in the past, the guilds of artisans are practically dead, the ties of solidarity between the inhabitants of a particular district have seriously weakened, because such a solidarity presupposes a relatively stable society where personal ties are strong. As for tribal ties among the newcomers, they remain alive for the first generation but soften soon afterwards in the urban situation.

New relationships are now replacing the previous ones, but they still lack consistency in most cases: on the economic plane there are labor unions and professional associations of every sort; then sportsmen's and sportswomen's associations and youth clubs; but, above all, political parties which gained the support of urban popular masses during the struggle for independence. In Morocco, where a multi-party system is recognized by the Constitution, the political parties maintain great vitality. It is still too early to judge what will be the case in Algeria, although there is provision for a single-party regime in the Constitution. In Tunisia, only the Neo-Destour Party is actually on the scene: it has taken an official and administrative aspect which is certainly much less attractive to the masses than its *élan* when the struggle for independence was developing. In any case, political parties are too young and unstable to form the frame of a well-organized social life. Like other institutions in North Africa they are still too hazy.

We must also pay attention to the economic aspects of urbanization. What remains firmly in the traditional pattern is retail trade. Shops have sometimes been modernized, but the shopkeeper remains so far a man satisfied with a modest turnover who has faithful customers whom he personally knows and who know him. To be sure, some big stores of the *Monoprix* type begin to attract the Muslims but are not yet able to compete seriously with the shopkeepers. This is a fact which deserves careful study; it would be interesting to examine how retail trade is developing (it certainly has new aspects) and why the Muslims prefer small shops in general to anonymous big stores. Such an inquiry should combine data of economics and social psychology.

On the other hand, the artisans seem to be in a very bad situation. Nothing important to my knowledge has been written on them since the book by Lucien Golvin published some years ago.[11] That does not mean that nothing is going on. The creation of basic goods by craftsmen is not conceivable in a modernizing society. The artisan class, long since dead in Algeria, is moribund in Morocco and Tunisia. It can be maintained only if it is occupied in artcrafts subsidized by the government and intended chiefly for tourists or exportation. The prosperity of such people is therefore related in large measure to the efforts to draw tourists to North Africa and to make North African craft work known abroad. The Moroccan and Tunisian governments are making serious attempts in these directions: the Three Year Tunisian

11. Lucien Golvin, *Aspects de l'Artisanat en Afrique du Nord* (Paris: Presses Universitaires de France, 1957).

Plan (1962-1964), for instance, is concerned with this problem, but admits that statistics are often lacking. One may find in the plan provisions for the establishment of cooperative unions for production and commercialization, as well as the allocation of a sum of 3,000,000 dinars for different investments. But the results as regards the artisans are not well known.

Some utilitarian crafts are still practiced. In 1963 I saw in Hergla (Tunisia) people making baskets for oil mills and I suppose that many artisans still succeed in making a living at Fez or Marrakech, but that is only a temporary survival, because mechanization is on the way. One is sure of the fact when he visits the spinning mills and weaving plants of Sousse and Ksar-Hellal in Tunisia. The problem therefore is how the artisans can succeed in getting new jobs. On this subject, a definite investigation should be initiated, which could be useful for men in charge.

Everywhere, modern industries are in existence or are being introduced, and industrial workers are now numerous in all the big cities in North Africa. Thinking of them, the governments in charge tried to maintain the industrial activities created before independence and to create new ones. Although this is related to general economic problems beyond our subject, the point must be stressed because it is pertinent to some previously indicated ideas.

It was said that the new city-dweller encountered considerable difficulties of adaptation, because the town is a complex body where one can easily live only if he knows its whole structure. Among those difficulties is that of learning a new rhythm of work, a regular rhythm which cannot tolerate periods of idleness or inattention, because a machine works well only if it operates according to a fixed routine. The country-dwellers who come to the cities are accustomed to the discontinuity and the changeable rhythm of seasons and weather: they are capable of considerable, but intermittent, effort. Now, without a transition period, they are obliged to yield to the continuous and tyrannical rhythm of the machine, which represents for many of them a true psychosomatic revolution. This must be partly responsible for North Africa's lack of skilled workers. To pass from the habits of farmer (or worse, of a shepherd) to that of a factory worker is difficult. Many take a long time to adjust and others never succeed. Perhaps the situation will improve when the urban population becomes more stable.

Modern industrial workers were led to trade unionism by

European or Europeanized fellow workers, that is to say they were put into a mold they had not shaped and which had not been shaped for them. Later, when the national struggle became acute, exclusively Muslim unions were created, such as the General Union of Tunisian Workers (UGTT), the Moroccan Federation of Labor (UMT), or the General Union of Algerian Workers (UGTA). But, owing to the force of circumstances, those unions first devoted their main efforts to the national struggle, labor interests being more or less set aside. When the struggle for independence ended, the Neo-Destour in Tunisia reduced the unions to the role of satellite-groups which more or less willingly back any action of the party and the government. This did not happen in Morocco. The UMT immediately got rid of the tutelage of the Istiqlal and, after having been closely associated with the National Union of Popular Forces (UNFP) seems now to keep this party at a distance and plainly indicates its intention to remain autonomous.

All this proves that North African trade unionism, which is alive only in the big cities and in some industrial centers, has not yet found its place; it is still too much under the influence of politics and, in two cases out of three, too domesticated to appear as truly representing the interests and aspirations of the workers. Summing up, one can say that in some urban centers trade unionism forms a sort of hidden force which will probably develop with increasing membership but that it has no precise program, no traditions, no doctrinal training, and finally no well-defined identity.

As these statements indicate, North African cities now completely lack stability. To the eye, they first appear as jarring agglomerations (*medina,* European districts of different epochs, new Muslim districts, workers' housing, *bidonvilles*), which were generally built as a result of certain circumstances and more or less fit together. In the field of urbanism, French authorities generally showed themselves conservative, owing to a genuine regard for Muslim civilization, or to timidity, or to a desire for each community to live separately, which avoided a good many difficulties. The national authorities are not concerned with the same problems. On one hand, they are forced by necessity to provide decent housing for people who live in the cities; on the other hand, they want to modernize the urban centers. Urban renewal would also give employment to a substantial labor force. But it cannot be said that a North African urbanism is yet born.

For the time being, North Africans generally use European devices, without perhaps taking sufficiently into account the distinct and special needs of North African society. The only certainty is that the urban centers of any size, but mainly the big cities, will continue to grow for some time to come. In an industrial society it would be easy to deal with such a development, since capital and technical skill would be readily available. But this is not true in North Africa, and we have briefly pointed out how many difficulties and problems have resulted from a development which has been imposed from outside.

If we turn from urbanism to social psychology, we discover that the urbanized human mass has no more found its equilibrium than has the mass of buildings. Individuals of rural but diverse origins have gathered in the towns in great numbers and as a result have not been easily assimilated. In the big cities, at least, they form a sort of alien body which is no longer rural in its occupations and housing, but is not yet urban in its individual and collective reactions or rhythm of life. Accustomed to an unsophisticated way of life that has been shaped by the vagaries of seasons and weather, those people are faced with complex organizations that are almost completely unrelated to the phenomena of nature. Illiterate for the most part, they live in a society where writing is essential, where everyone is expected to know laws and regulations, and where all services must be paid for (and they have no money). The result is great confusion at first, then the integration of some exceptionally gifted individuals, followed by the bitterness of the rest, who know they have a miserable life, do not know how to get out of it, and begin to complain of injustice.

The evolution has been accelerated and exacerbated in recent years by political events: the national struggle and the massive departure of Europeans (as in Algeria) for whom the city lived but who at the same time made it live; by economic events, the increase of rural immigration particularly in Algeria; and by the changes of a society which is dying from some points of view, being born when it is viewed in another light, and ultimately always uneasy because it is in search of an identity, still far out of sight. The situation is still further complicated by the facts of modern mass communication: e.g., enormous gatherings of people for political or sporting events, which keep the masses continually in suspense, thus increasing their excitability.

Finally, all these conditions combine to make North African cities, particularly the larger ones, powder kegs requiring extremely delicate handling. In order to avoid disasters, the officials in charge should have at their disposal precise and up-to-date analyses of current developments; a firm authority so as to avoid or resolve serious crises; and at the same time the poise, judgment, and diplomacy to settle with flexibility everything that can be so settled. Those conditions are not joined together easily, and always lie at the mercy of unforeseeable circumstances. In conclusion, it seems prudent to recognize the fact that urban development in North Africa will not take place without a certain amount of turmoil. North African revolution is on the way, but far from its goal, particularly in the cities, and it seems impossible to foretell how, where, and when it will stop.

URBANIZATION IN NORTH AFRICA

BIBLIOGRAPHY OF THE PRINCIPAL BOOKS AND ARTICLES
Published from 1956 to 1963

Books

Bureau d'Etudes et de Réalisations Urbaines. *L'Urbanisme des Grandes Villes Algériennes et les Equipements Résidentiels*. Paris, 1961.

Délégation Générale du Gouvernment Algérien Résultats Statistiques du Dénombrement de la Population Effectué le 31 Octobre 1954. *Données Statistiques sur les Immeubles et les Logements*. Alger, 1958.

Descloitres, R., J-C. Reverdy and C. Descloitres. *L'Algérie des Bidonvilles: Le Tiers-Monde dans la Cité*. Paris: Mouton, 1961.

Ecole Pratique des Hautes Etudes VIème Section Paris—Les Villes. *Entretiens Interdisciplinaires sur les Sociétés Musulmanes*. Paris, February 18-20, 1958.

Herzog, Monique. *Recherche Bibliographique sur les Causes et les Conséquences de l'Accroissement de la Population Urbaine en Algérie Depuis 1936-1962*. Memoire INTD.

Le Tourneau, Roger. *Les Villes Musulmanes de l'Afrique du Nord*. Alger: La Maison des Livres, 1957.

Marie, M. *L'Urbanisation des Grandes Villes Algériennes*. Cahiers du Centre Scientifique et Technique du Bâtiment, 1962.

Pelletier, Jean. *Alger 1955: Essai d'une Géographie Sociale*. Paris: Les Belles Lettres, 1959.

Reverdy, J-C. *Habitations Nouvelles et Urbanisation Rapide: Conditions Ecologiques de l'Adaptation au Logement en Algérie*. Aix-en-Provence: C.A.S.H.A., 1963.

———. *Recherche sur les Attitudes du Sous-Prolétariat Algérien à l'égard de la Société Urbaine*. Aix-en-Provence: C.A.S.H.A., 1963.

Sebag, Paul. *Un Faubourg de Tunis: Saida Manoubia.* Paris: Presses Universitaires de France, 1960.
_____. *La Hara de Tunis: L'Evolution d'un Ghetto Nord-Africain.* Paris: Presses Universitaires de France, 1959.
_____. *La Grande Mosquée de Kairouan.* Paris: Delpire, 1963.
Secrétariat Social—A la Recherche d'une Communauté. *La Cohabitation en Algérie.* Alger, 1956.

Articles

Anon., "L'Action Entreprise au Maroc pour faire face au Problème des Bidonvilles," *Industries et Travaux d'Outre-Mer,* No. 79 (June 1960), pp. 387-394.
_____, "Algérie. Aménagement du Territoire, Urbanisme Construction," *Urbanisme* (Paris, 1961).
_____, "Les Bidonvilles, Genèse et Résorption. Perspectives de Promotion Humaine. L'Expérience du Clos-Salembier," *Alger-Revue* (Spring 1961), pp. 24-29.
_____, "Comportement des Familles Musulmanes dans les Habitations Nouvelles à l'Oran," *Cahiers du Centre Scientifique et Technique du Bâtiment,* No. 49 (April 1961).
_____, "La Crise de Croissance de l'Agglomération Algéroise," *Alger-Revue* (October 1956), pp. 10-18.
_____, "Etude Sociale du Bidonville de Boubsila dit Berardi à Hussein-Dey," *Nouvelles Réalités Algériennes,* No. 1 (1956), pp. 2-25.
_____, "Familles Nord-Africaines en Bidonvilles," *Cahiers Nord-Africains,* No. 89 (April-May, 1962).
_____, "Loger un Million de Personnes," *Actualités d'Algérie,* No. 11 (February 24, 1962), pp. 11-19.
_____, "Le Problème de l'Habitat et de l'Aménagement des Zones Urbaines en Algérie," *Actualités d'Algérie,* No. 3 (October 16, 1961), pp. 13-20.
_____, "Recensement des Villes de Tunisie," *Encyclopédie Mensuelle d'Outre-Mer,* No. 74 (October 1956).
_____, (L'Urbanisation de l'Algérie), *Actualités d'Algérie* (February 24, 1962).
_____, "Les Villes du Maroc," *De l'Ancien au Moderne Perspectives d'Outre-Mer* (1956).
Aquilina, V., "Les Bidonvilles d'Alger," *Honneur et Patrie* (June-July 1956).
Aujard, R., "Problème du Logement au Maroc," *Bulletin Economique et Social du Maroc,* No. 22 (1959), pp. 320ff.
Barbé, R., "Quelques Données Récentes sur le Logement en Algérie," *Economie et Politique,* No. 69 (1960), pp. 73-79.
Benhima, Dr. "La Cité du Derb Jedid," *Bulletin Economique et Social du Maroc,* No. 22 (1959), pp. 415-435.
_____, Les Problèmes d'Urbanisation posés par le Développement des

Agglomérations," *Bulletin Economique et Social du Maroc,* Nos. 94-95 (December 1962), pp. 163-192.

Berque, Jacques, "Medinas, Villeneuves et Bidonvilles," *Cahiers de Tunisie,* Nos. 21-22 (1st quarter 1958), pp. 5-42.

Brechet, Ch., "Etude sur les Besoins de Logements de la Population Européenne à Casablanca," *Bulletin Economique et Social du Maroc* (June 1956), pp. 771-98.

Coquery, M., "L'Extension Récente des Quartiers Musulmans d'Oran," *Bulletin de l'Association de Géographes Français* (May-June 1962), pp. 169-187.

Descloitres, R. and J-C. Reverdy, "Recherche sur les Attitudes du Sous-Prolétariat Algérien à l'égard de la Société Urbaine," *Civilisations,* Nos. 1-2 (1963).

Descloitres, R. and C. and J-C. Reverdy, "Organisation Urbaine et Structures Sociales en Algérie," *Civilisations,* No. 2 (1962).

Faidutti, A. M., "Les Grandes Lignes du Développement Urbain de Constantine," *Bulletin de l'Association de Géographes Français* (March 1961), pp. 38-51.

Franchi, J., "Urbanisation d'un Bidonville Bordj Moulay Omar (Meknes)," *Bulletin Economique et Social du Maroc,* No. 23 (1960), pp. 255-291.

Inform. Geogr. 20 (5), (November-December 1956), pp. 176-186.

Jovy, René, "L'Urbanisme Algérien," *L'Afrique et l'Asie,* No. 47 (3rd quarter, 1959), pp. 35-47.

Montmarin, A. de, "Les Conceptions Actuelles en Matière d'Habitat Economique au Maroc et leur Application à la Reconstruction du Derb-Jdid à Casablanca," *Annales de l'Institut Technique du Bâtiment* (1960), pp. 611-619.

Nouschi, André, "Croissance des Villes Nord-Africaines (Tunis): Vue par un Sociologue," *Annales,* No. 2 (March-April 1962), pp. 362-367.

Olivier, S. and A., "Alger, Ville Cancer," *Economie et Humanisme* (September-October 1960), pp. 32-47.

Paskoff, R., "Oujda Esquisse de Géographie Urbaine," *Bulletin Economique et Social du Maroc,* No. 21 (73) (July 1957), pp. 71-80.

Planhol, X. de, "La Formation de la Population Musulmane à Blida," *Revue de Géographie de Lyon,* No. 3 (1961), pp. 219-230.

Potier, R., "Alger Ville Pilote," *Encyclopédie Mensuelle d'Outre-Mer* (April 1956), pp. 172-174.

Prenant, A., "Questions de Structure Urbaine dans Trois Faubourgs de Sidi Bel Abbes," *Bulletin de l'Association des Géographes Français* (1956), pp. 62-72.

Ruais, P., "Etudes d'Urbanisme et d'Aménagements Urbains en Algérie," *Etudes et Réalisations* (November-December 1961), pp. 42-51.

Saigot, M., "L'Habitat en Algérie," (Alger, Baconnier, 1960).

Sanson, Henri, "L'Habitat et la Famille en Algérie," *Notes Documentaires du*

Secrétariat Social d'Outre-Mer, No. 29 (October-December 1958), pp. 7-32.
Sebag, Paul, "Le Bidonville de Borgel," Les Cahiers de Tunisie, Nos. 23-24 (2nd quarter 1958), pp. 267-309.
Selosse, J., "Contribution à l'Etude des Attitudes d'une Population Citadine Marocaine Musulmane; Etude des Effets de la Scolarisation et de l'Urbanisation," Psychologie Française, VI, No. 3 (July 1961), pp. 218-230.
―――――, "Perception du Changement Social par une Population Citadine Marocaine," Revue Française de Sociologie (April-June 1963), pp. 144-158.
Suisse, P., "Physionomie du Douar 'Doum'," Bulletin Economique et Social du Maroc, No. 69 (June 1956), pp. 100-122.
Taieb, J., "Une Banlieue de Tunis: l'Ariana," Les Cahiers de Tunisie (4th quarter 1960), pp. 33-76.
Travers, Lucette, "Bône, la Formation de la Ville et les Facteurs de son Evolution," "Annales de Géographie" (November-December 1958), pp. 67, 364, 498-520.

7
Trade Unionism

Eqbal Ahmad

Trade unions in underdeveloped countries are still in their infancy. Some are undergoing the pangs of birth. The growth of the others has been stunted by economic and political circumstances. Only a few show some vitality, and they too are having teething problems. Mr. Bruce Millen in his "profile" of new unions lists amorphousness, fragmentation, lack of structure, financial weakness, outside leadership, opportunism, corruption, and dependence on government among their characteristics.[1] This description is accurate. A catalog of the economic, social, and political problems yield somewhat pessimistic perspectives for trade unionism in an area where the majority are peasants, industry is underdeveloped, unemployment is high and skills are low.

Trade unions in the Maghrib face the same problems as their counterparts in underdeveloped countries and particularly in the Arab world.[2] The growing surplus of the unemployed weakens the unions' bargaining capacity and necessitates their dependence on government for adjudication and arbitration. The majority of workers are unskilled, without power to bargain, and lack the occupational stability necessary for organization. Newness to in-

---

1. Bruce Millen, *The Political Role of Labor in Developing Countries* (Washington D.C.: Brookings Institution, 1963), pp. 17-36.

2. "Indeed, in the sixteen countries under consideration here, trade unions are non-existent in three (Afghanistan, Yemen, and Libya), outlawed or else too small to be more than sporadically active in six (Jordan, Saudi Arabia, Sudan, Iran, Syria, and Pakistan), and sizeable but subservient to government guidance in one (Egypt). In Lebanon they owe their modest strength (about 5,000) to the spirit of traditional guilds and the traditional division of labor among various religious and ethnic groups. In Algeria, Turkey, and Iraq, trade unions are growing in importance, but only in Tunisia and Morocco are they already organizationally and politically strong." Manfred Halpern, *The Politics of Social Change in the Middle East and North Africa* (Princeton: Princeton University Press, 1963), p. 318.

dustrial discipline, persistance of village and communal ties and continued urbanization further militate against commitment to unionism and labor solidarity. Ideological differences and intra-elite conflicts have exposed the unions to interference by parties and politicians. Furthermore, governments and parties in their efforts first to consolidate power, and then to promote industrial growth have tried to ensure political conformity, and to contain the unions' drive toward higher wages and benefits. The context of single party regimes headed by heroic leaders in Tunisia and Algeria has further compounded the risk of total union subservience to the state and the party.

Yet the Maghrib's labor unions are remarkably free from the blemishes of unionism in new nations. The UGTT (*Union Générale Tunisienne du Travail*), the UMT (*Union Marocaine du Travail*) and the UGTA (*Union Générale des Travailleurs Algériens*) are among the few non-Western unions which have succeeded in organizing the majority of employed industrial and urban workers.[3] The UGTT and the UMT are highly professionalized, well structured, centralized, and financially independent organizations led by working class leaders. The UGTA has yet to unify its leadership and launch a well defined program of social action in independent Algeria. Nevertheless, it has successfully restored and expanded its organization after six years of clandestinity during the revolutionary war, and it justifiably boasts of what may well be the best trained core of cadre and leadership in the Middle East and Africa, for a very large proportion of its cadre received their training in the metropolitan CGT (*Confédération Générale du Travail*) and in the countries of Eastern Europe. In the aftermath of independence the UGTA has been facing difficulties but there is little doubt that the Algerian trade unionists have the will and the capacity to surmount them. Indeed, of the four countries in the Maghrib, only in Libya is the workers' organization somewhat typical of non-Western unions. The LGWU (Libyan General Workers' Union) founded in 1952

3. The UGTT, UMT, and the UGTA, respectively, claim memberships of 150,000, 576,000, and 200,000. From spot checks and personal observation it appears that these figures indicate the permanent clientele of the union but actual dues paying membership is considerably less. Total employed persons—wage earners and salaried workers—were estimated at 509,000 in Tunisia (1956), 930,000 in Morocco (1952), and 1,300,000 in Algeria (1954). The figures include workers in the agricultural sector, the majority of whom are not organized as well as the de-unionized services like police, customs, and national guard employees. International Labour Office, *Labour Survey of North Africa* (Geneva, 1960), pp. 151, 153, 154.

has suffered, since 1956, from repression, rival movements, and internal conflicts.[4] The case of the Maghrib's trade unions seems to demonstrate that there is nothing inherent in a situation of underdevelopment to make the emergence of viable trade unionism impossible. It further points out that given a combination of historical and political circumstances effective trade unions may emerge not so much in response to industrialization but as instruments and initiators of modernization.

The Maghrib's labor movements have many similarities among them. They were born in the French colonial setting and were exposed to varying combinations of the same dialectic. All three originated in, and still bear, the influence of the French CGT. All successfully contended against Communist rivals. They played vital roles in the nationalist struggle for independence and are today taking a major part in shaping the political, economic, and social life of these countries. Each of the three has experienced governmental repression no less than governmental benevolence, and has engaged in periods of violence no less than peaceful political participation. Yet the contrasts among them are many. The Tunisian Union, like the Algerian, must operate in a single-party state, the Moroccan in a multi-party system. The UGTT has restored its cohesion after a brief rupture following independence, the UMT split in 1960 and has to contend against a rival union,[5] while the struggle for power within the UGTA does not yet seem to have resolved. The Tunisian organization, its long history, past accomplishments and organizational strength notwithstanding has, willy-nilly, acquiesced to mild taming by the ruling party. The UMT despite the threat of a rival union has displayed exuberant energy and hot temper in opposing the government and rival political groups, and it has forcefully asserted its independence even in its relations with its political ally—the UNFP (*L'Union Nationale des Forces Populaires*). The Algerian movement struck by the revolutionary storm which it helped sustain is now struggling hard to regain its feet.

Leaders of the three movements are committed to the develop-

4. Since the political and economic milieu of Libya has been markedly different from the rest of the Maghrib's, and because the labor movement there is in a very early stage of development it bears little resemblance to its sister organizations. Libya, therefore, does not figure largely in this essay.

5. The UGTM (*Union Générale des Travailleurs Marocains*) was formed in March 1960 at the initiative of Istiqlal leaders—a sequel to the earlier split in the party which was spearheaded by the UMT. This federation claims a membership of 100,000. Informed observers estimate its actual strength at 20,000.

ment of autonomous workers' organization, and seek a constructive role for the unions in the task of economic development. However, the UMT has so far concentrated on political action. The UGTT, while emphasizing social work and workers' cooperatives, accepts sacrifice and hard work and voluntarily renounces strikes in the hope of attaining a viable future through modernization. The UGTA while attempting reorganization and adjustment to independent Algeria waits the consolidation of a regime in whose development programs it can play a significant role. In their differences the labor movements in the three countries reflect their contrasting political milieu.

The fortunes of the Maghrib's labor movement have, to some extent been conditioned by historical circumstances, social conditions, and economic opportunities. But the most important factor in shaping their history, ideology, structure, and leadership has been the nature of their relationship to the political order. The dialectic of colonialism and the dynamics of rapid social change which these countries are undergoing subject their unions —one might say all institutions and individuals—to political, social, and economic pressures. In societies which are undergoing revolutionary transformation all forms of freedom are interrelated, all realms of activity interdependent. It is futile, therefore, to analyze them in terms of political versus economic unionism. It does little good to decry the politicization of unions and see in it the threat of radical or communist infiltration, nor does it help to deny the validity of a union which, due either to weakness or conviction, renounces its right to collective bargaining and wage strikes. And it scarcely helps to contrast the dangers of trade unions consumptionist drive with the need for capital formation, and recommend, as does the eminent Indian socialist Asoka Mehta, non-consumptionist sacrifice prescription which if taken in raw form will reduce the trade unions into ciphers, and freeze the present authoritarian regimes of the third world into despotisms.[6] At best, it seems to me, one might assume the *scope* of trade union activity as including political, social, and economic domains, but view their development in terms of the *intensity* of their concentration on one or the other aspect of activity. The future development of trade unionism would depend not so much on their present activity as it would be governed by their ability to generate and adjust to continuing change in such a way that ultimately

6. Asoka Mehta, "The Mediating Role of Trade Unions in Underdeveloped Countries," *Economic Development and Cultural Change* (October 1957).

they would be clearly differentiable from a political party as well as a philanthropic organization.

Viewed in this way the example of the North African, and particularly the Tunisian, labor movement, yields a model of development which, stated normatively, conforms to three stages in which the labor movements shift the intensity of their activity from the political to general social and economic goals, to increasing emphasis on corporate demands.

In the first stage intense union involvement in politics is inevitable because requisites for economic unionism—a sound industrial base, stable internal or protected external market, and skilled labor force—are lacking. Second, growing unemployment, rural migration, and anomy created by social dislocation lead to generalized grievances and search for political solutions. Third, trade unions in underdeveloped countries have risen not so much in response to industrialization as due to imbalanced modernization whose nature up to now has been primarily political—a fact which led Farhat Hached, the founder of the UGTT to assert, "It is in effect politics which determines conditions of people."[7] Fourth, industrial capitalism insofar as it existed was associated with the colonial setting and therefore elicited a political and nationalist rather than economic response. In this stage the unions resemble political parties in that they are interested mainly in the achievement of political goals and are concerned more with power than welfare. This is especially true during the period of intensified nationalist struggle against colonialism. While opposing an external enemy the union leaders may join conservative or traditionalist political parties but in the absence of attitudinal and ideological congruity this alliance remains a temporary expedient. After independence, the unions might ally with left wing political groups and continue their hyper-political orientation in an effort to displace a traditionalist regime. In either case union leaders may have to justify their continued political concern on ideological grounds and invoke the necessity for political change as a preliminary to social and economic reform. For this reason (and through association with left wing middle-class leaders) the union is likely to sharpen its ideology with increasing emphasis on social and economic questions. Furthermore, since most governing elites

---

7. Farhat Hached, "Le Syndicalisme en Afrique du Nord," *Synthèses* (Brussels), VI (July 1951), pp. 185-190, 186. William H. Lewis, "New Nomadism in North Africa" *Middle East Journal*, II (Summer 1957), 269-281 is an excellent essay on social dislocation and its relationship to trade unions.

have inhibitions against repressing trade unions and because they fear the union's capacity to paralyze urban centers and crucial sectors of the economy, it is often the last organization to face governmental repression. Thus the union carries on the struggle and takes over the apparatus and functions of its clandestine or repressed ally which help it gain legitimacy, organization, ideology, and political skills. If it manages to keep its structure functionally differentiated from the political party, then it is more likely to emerge from the first stage as an important force on the national scene.

The second stage begins after emancipation when the nationalist political elite starts consolidating power and the political party begins to press the trade union into a subordinate place. The labor movement is now faced with the need for adjustment from political to social and economic activity, from revolution to reconstruction. The shift involves continued sacrifices but requires different techniques, tactics, and resources from those needed during the period of political agitation. Yet at this point a trade union can avoid operative commitment to social goals only at the cost of compromising its present or sacrificing its future as a workers' organization. Failure to make this choice may lead a union to sterile political agitation and may ultimately invite repression. The price of the shift is not complete depoliticization. It does, however, represent a definite disentanglement from politics. A trade union may still remain a promotional and political organization in that it might seek broad social and economic goals for an idealized, enlarged working class embracing the majority of population. Yet if its commitment to modernization is genuine it should not exhaust in politics the full range of its activity. It must, then, to retain its identity, legitimacy, and cohesion as a labor organization turn increasingly to the task of providing security, integration, and welfare for the worker. The labor union may perform these functions as a partner of a political party or, in multi-party states, independent of them, but must maintain functional differentiation from the party while stressing its role as an integrative class welfare institution. This is a period of transition which constitutes a necessary bridge between political and corporate unionism. The unions reduce corporate demands and wage strikes to the minimum necessary for maintaining workers' morale and union solidarity while helping labor commitment, increased productivity, and industrial discipline. During this period intermediate levels of activities help a union to maintain its ethos and fulfill its major role as an organization which looks after workers' interest. For example through social work projects, workers' clubs, and vacation colonies it may provide them security of belonging to a group, integrate them to the new way of life and cushion the shock of urbanization; by successfully managing workers' cooperatives it not only reduces their cost of living but inculcates a spirit of self-reliance and cooperation while strengthening union finances and foundations.

A trade union's adjustment to a reconstructive role may be helped or hampered by several factors. First, given the psychology of deprivation from which most elites in underdeveloped countries suffer, its leadership may jockey for positions of power and wealth while the rank and file fall prey to the general apathy that often follows independence. Nevertheless, if the union's ideology has consistently stressed the principle of accountability and if it has gained a measure of institutionalization then the union is likely to avert the danger of degenerating into a springboard for ambitious politicians. Also if the union has developed a core of working-class leaders and cadre they are likely to act as brakes on middle-class (white collar workers) union leaders intent on exploiting the organization for opportunistic reasons. To varying degrees this has been true in Tunisia and Morocco.

Secondly, a trade union with a key role in the nationalist struggle might miscalculate its actual strength and bid for power. The temptation may be considerable. On the eve of independence such a trade union stands out as a more unified, better organized, and effective institution than either the political party or the "resistance."[8] Unlike the party it is a homogeneous organization relatively unhampered by conflicts of right and left, and able, therefore, to project a consistent program of development. Its membership consisting largely of urban workers and state employees is not only easily mobilizable but also holds a strategic control over national life. Having largely escaped repression and clandestinity the union is less exhausted than the party or the resistance, its structure is more intact and its ranks more disciplined. Furthermore, its leaders have had the opportunity to gain national recognition and political skills so that they may be convinced not only of their mission of modernization but also of

---

8. The term excludes an army in exile like Houari Boumedienne's Algerian forces on the Tunisian frontier. A frontier army of this type is perhaps the only group that can more than match the strategic importance of a trade union in the post-independence struggle for power.

the viability of a labor group leading a predominantly peasant nation. The temptation increases when independence is achieved. The cementing factors of common struggle disappear, and the alliance of antagonistic collaborators breaks down. As rival groups scramble for power the party is threatened with disintegration and the country with internecine strife. Thus a trade union with a national mystique and sound organization may either demand too high a price for political support or even try to ride to power over an exhausted nation. The examples of Tunisia and Morocco suggest that a labor movement may be deterred from overplaying its hand by the presence of a heroic leader as the head of the state or party. Also its choice of playing a subordinate political role becomes easier if it can find a popular leader or party with whom it finds an identity of view. Yet the acceptance of a subordinate place and commitment to the constructive task of modernization results from a painful introversion, and deep commitment to trade union ideals. It calls for a functioning union ideology, a leadership and structure capable not only of maintaining but also of reappraising old and adopting new values and attitudes.

Thirdly a union's transition to the second stage may be helped or hindered in accordance with a country's *stage* of modernization.[9] As the representatives of an uprooted and expectant proletariat the trade unions do not accept the status quo and are engaged in an effort to change it radically. Therefore, as the examples of the Old Destour's relations with the first Tunisian labor movement in the 1920's and UMT's relations with the Istiqlal suggest, a conservative or moderate elite which prefers to introduce change without radically altering the traditional economic, religious and status interests view a revolutionary mass movement with distrust. The antagonistic nature of their attitudes and the mutually exclusive content of their ideologies introduce cleavages and not simply differences among them. Since total retirement from politics and concentration on corporate demands is not a realistic alternative in underdeveloped countries and since a trade union cannot successfully transform itself into a labor party in a predominantly agricultural country, it tends, under these circumstances, to ally with an elite having a similar

---

9. Reference is made here to Leon Carl Brown, "Stages in the Process of Change" in Charles A. Micaud, Leon Carl Brown, and Clement Henry Moore, *Tunisia: The Politics of Modernization* (New York: Praeger, 1964), pp. 3-66. Brown traces ideological change in Tunisia in four stages, the last being the displacement of the traditionalist, legalist, and socially conservative Destour by the progressive, socially radical Neo-Destour led by Bourguiba.

view on modernization. Should a conservative or moderate elite come to power, the union is likely to continue its oppositional orientation.[10] Conversely, a union's shift to the second stage is eased if the ruling elite adopts a policy of rapid modernization. In a regime which is keen to ensure the participation of the masses in the task of modernization a trade union is likely, due to the special skills of its leaders and members, to play a significant role in the formulation and execution of progressive policies. It may thus enhance not only its prestige and influence but also its future through industrialization.

The transition to the third stage—to increasing concentration on specifically corporate demands and labor welfare—is perhaps the most delicate task facing the trade union leaders and politicians for it has to be introduced gradually, and much imagination and understanding is needed on both sides. Politicians should understand that the key factor in determining the prospects of a trade union is its ability to cater to the needs and maintain the loyalty of its members. Without working-class support a union would become the bureaucratic arm of the state, or at best a philanthropic organization which lives on, and occasionally distributes, state or party sponsored charity. Politics has prime importance in giving the labor movement the power and purpose which later renders possible effective social and economic action. Deep social concern which may entail acceptance of sacrifice and voluntary surrender of some rights during the developmental stress is a condition for creating the climate in which trade unions can fulfill their classical functions. But the pursuit of corporate interests is an obligation which unions can postpone, and not cancel, only as a temporary concession to common interest and not as a renunciation of inherent rights. No trade union can indefinitely neglect the economic problems of its members without losing working-class support. As the Secretary General of the ICFTU (International

---

10. It should be noted that ideological congruity does not exclude differences of opinion. In some cases excessive consensus and intimacy among the elite may be self-defeating in that it "becomes impossible for any form of conflict to be perceived as other than an expression of aggressive personal hostility." Thus trade unionists in an intimate political community may find it difficult to prevent policy disputes from becoming personal aggression and "adopt as a permanent political posture an attitude of seeking cooperation and unanimity." Moreover, consensus, so crucial to nation-building, may become under the personalized rule of a heroic leader a compelling instrument for ensuring conformity. The Tunisian situation, I suspect, comes perilously close to this pattern. Quotes are from Lucian W. Pye, *Politics, Personality and Nation Building: Burma's Search for Identity* (New Haven: Yale University Press, 1962), pp. 161-162.

Confederation of Free Trade Unions) has put it, "if the trade unions are to accomplish their broader tasks they must command the allegiance of workers and must be able to maintain that allegiance in the first place by effective action to improve the wages and other conditions of the people they represent."[11] Nothing but a common occupation and subjection to specific demands associated with it differentiates a workers' organization from a political party.

One might concede that between the strictly corporate and totally promotional there are intermediate levels of activity which a union may fruitfully pursue. Collective bargaining and wage increases are important but not the only criteria for job satisfaction. Insurance benefits, vacation policy, educational facilities for workers' children, vocational training for the unskilled are others. Workers' participation in hiring and firing policy, in the production councils in industry and union participation in governmental planning also boost labor morale. Also a trade union which can successfully initiate and police the enforcement of social and labor legislation performs genuine union functions in underdeveloped countries. Yet governments and planners realize that labor demands and protests are inevitable reactions to industrialization. As industrialization proceeds pressures on unions increase. A government which is keen to offset violence and promote social harmony should be willing to risk some inflation for the sake of favorable social and political climate. Furthermore, it may be argued that the trade unions' inflationary impact is exaggerated, and that occasional and controlled wage increases may help rather than hinder economic development.[12] A government will benefit from encouraging a union with broad autonomous roots and labor concern. It should ease the task of modernizing a crucial segment of the population for national reconstruction. It also institutionalizes the outer limits of authoritarian rule by assuring continual discussion and bargaining among a significantly large group of socially concerned leaders.[13]

As a conclusion to this general discussion I propose that trade unions which conform most closely to this normative pattern, viz., those which 1) start out as a political and protest movement then

11. Omar Becu quoted in Everett M. Kassalow (ed.), *National Labor Movements in the Post War World* (Evanston, Ill.: Northwestern University Press, 1963), p. 250.
12. See Paul Fisher, "Unions in Less Developed Countries: A Re-appraisal of their Economic Role" in Everett M. Kassalow (ed.), *National Labor Movements*, pp. 102-118.
13. Manfred Halpern, *Politics of Social Change*, p. 339.

2) make the shift to becoming the initiators and supporters of modernization and 3) gradually increase their corporate concern are most likely to contribute to a balanced process of modernization.

A second set of conclusions emerging from this discussion leads us to the hypothesis that the most important conditions for close conformity to the above norm are: 1. A coherent, consistent and functioning trade union ideology. 2. A progressive and radical leadership consisting of working class as well as white collar leaders. 3. Ideological congruity between the trade union and political elite to the extent that there might be differences but not cleavages of opinion on approaches to modernization. 4. Institutionalized structure and mechanism designed to maintain and inculcate trade union values and open enough for reappraisal of old and adoption of new values and attitudes. 5. Commitment of the ideology as well as the elite to the necessity for maintaining and institutionalizing the principle of accountability to the rank and file. 6. A permissive political system.[14]

Of the three labor movements only the Tunisian has made a fairly complete shift to the second stage. The UMT has taken a few steps in that direction, while the outlook of the UGTA is still unclear. By and large the same factors which explain the differences in the degree of modernization in these countries have also contributed to the varying stages and style of trade unionism. Since the UGTT is the oldest, and in our terms, the more advanced union, and because it is still likely to set the pattern for the others, its development is sketched in greater detail while less space is devoted to the UMT and the UGTA.

The history and ideology of the Maghrib's trade unions have been shaped by the interaction of colonialism, socialism, and nationalism. Trade unions rose in the background of colonial expropriation, social dislocation, pauperization, and urbanization unaccompanied by a corresponding rise in industry. The existence of a dual economy and the physical presence of Europeans served further to alienate the masses from the colonial power. The disparities in salary, living standard, and working conditions between the Arab and European settlers were too marked to have escaped envy and resentment. It was only normal that workers should

14. I am indebted to Charles F. Gallagher, Manfred Halpern, and Mohammed Guessous (Center for International Studies, Princeton University) for some of these ideas.

have associated colonialism and capitalism in a single protest. The Maghrib's workers drew their sense of exploitation from their colonial status. Class war took a nationalist content, and given the active influence of French syndicalism, nationalism took on a socialist content.

Political, economic, and social discontent could have led the Maghrib's working classes to fundamentalist religious or paramilitary totalitarian movements, had it not been for the constructive ideological influences to which the North Africans generally, and Tunisians particularly, have been exposed. The ideological influences on the present Tunisian labor movement can be, broadly speaking, traced to two major sources both of a reformist, socialist and humanist nature—French socialism and early Tunisian trade unionism.

The French socialists in Tunisia, an extremely active though small group, provided the major link between Western ideas and the native population. They disseminated and debated their ideas with the Tunisian trade unionists who were at first apprentices in the socialist CGT, then partners, and finally, when Tunisian labor had become avowedly nationalist, its political opponents. The Tunisian laborers' ideological orientation was sharpened by earlier membership in the CGT as well as the necessity for justifying their nationalist commitment.[15]

The initiative in organizing the first trade unions in Tunisia came from socialist leaders like Robert Louzon, Joachim Durel, and Duran-Angliviel. The departmental union of the CGT founded in 1919 consisted mainly of French professional and white collar workers but numerous Tunisians particularly dockers and miners were also members. (One of the earliest demands of the union was "equal pay for equal work," a demand, thanks to the efforts of the socialists, conceded by the government in 1936.) Although a majority of Tunisian workers joined the short lived CGTT (*Confédération Générale des Travailleurs Tunisiens*) founded by M'Hammed Ali in 1924, they returned to the French controlled union after their own had been repressed. Except for another abortive attempt at reviving the CGTT in 1937 under the guidance of Neo-Destour, the Tunisian trade unionists militated in the CGT until 1944 when Farhat Hached, then Assistant Secretary General of the CGT and a trusted associate of Bouzan-

---

15. See Leon Carl Brown, "Stages in the Process of Change," pp. 45-54.

quet, resigned from the union to found the UGTT. Like Hached, practically all the working-class leaders who later played important roles in the UGTT had been active CGT members. During the struggle that ensued between them and the mother organization after the establishment of the UGTT the Tunisian leaders had to demonstrate not only their organizational ability but also to justify themselves in ideological, universal, and moral terms. Replying to the charge of nationalism being antipathetic to international proletarian solidarity, Farhat Hached wrote "In normal times the worker is a natural ally of his proletarian comrades whatever may be their nationality, race or religion. But when two nations are in armed conflict patriotic duty and obligations of citizenship take precedence over syndical obligations, and workers have to fight alongside with industrialists and bankers. Such is the situation now, and it has been created by man." Yet he was quick to concede and warn "However, a trade union may inadvertently slip into the political arena if it becomes symbiotically attached to a political party."[16] CGT charges of negativism and politicization of trade unionism kept the UGTT leaders on the alert even during the feverish days of nationalist struggle when considerations of future were normally forgotten in favor of immediate goals. Stressing the temporary nature of union involvement in agitational politics, Hached reminded the workers of more fundamental union aims: "The working class movement should never become fixed in the negative posture of opposition, and demands for immediate material benefits. The construction of schools, professional training, industrialization and nationalization represent constructive demands and make our workers the veritable artisans of our country. We must attack the roots of our problem."[17] Hached and his companions have had sound trade union schooling. When faced with professionally tough and ideologically alert adversaries they had to meet the challenge creatively. Rarely in new labor movements does the level of debate reach the sophistication and clarity it did in Tunisia and the rest of the Maghrib.

The second ideological influence on the UGTT had indigenous, nationalist roots, and centers around, at first, the legendary figure of M'Hammed Ali. Not much is known about his actual ideas despite Tahir al Haddad's detailed book on the first Tunisian national trade union.[18] The UGTT's present attitudes, however,

16. *Mission,* June 16, 1948.
17. *Ibid.,* May 5, 1948.
18. Tahir al Haddad, *Al Ummal al Tunisiyun Wa Dhuhur al Hakarat al Naqabiyya* (Tunis, 1925).

have been shaped partly by M'Hammed Ali's ideas and schemes, partly by its image of his movement. Some contemporaries accused him of being a fanatic pan-Islamist. Others alleged he was a Communist. An eclectic revolutionary he was probably a bit of both, but above all he was a Tunisian nationalist. A poor peasant's son, he came to Tunis from the South in search of employment, and served in European households. He was exposed to nationalist and pan-Islamist ideas by his association with leaders of the Young Tunisian Movement, and by his participation in the Italo-Turkish War where he is said to have been Enver Pasha's chauffeur. Then in Germany he had mingled with Communist and socialist groups during the heyday of the Weimar Republic. In 1924 he returned to Tunisia with visions of starting workers' cooperatives to help the unemployed and reduce the workers' cost of living, as a necessary complement to a trade-union organization.

In Tunis he associated with modernizing intellectuals like Tahir al Haddad, Tahir Sfar, Arbi Momen, and Othman Kaák. This small elite, which included at least two religious scholars, gave help and legitimacy to the idea of a reformist unionism, and for themselves found a popular forum to express their opinions on social and economic reforms. At the founding of the Society for Tunisian Economic Cooperation in July 1924 Tahir Sfar, then a student in Paris and later one of the founders of the Neo-Destour spoke of economic planning: "We are today swimming in a great sea where ships and vessels are economic plans. Those possessing these plans are able to cross the sea, but those lacking them drown or are tossed by the waves on to the shore."[19] Tahir al Haddad's statement of CGTT goals and purposes are still part of UGTT's attitudes and dreams. Al Haddad accepted much of Marxist ideology but rejected its total application to Tunisia. To him the idea of a class war, though valid, had no meaning in a colony where all classes must cooperate to fight a common enemy. The Tunisian movement is moved more by the idea of reform than revolution. He praised the idea of trade unions starting "workers' consumption, production and agricultural cooperatives, developing productive aptitude of workers, providing education, and banking facilities, and acting as clubs to inculcate the spirit of self-reliance, cooperation and fraternity."[20]

The plan for cooperatives and social work projects as the base

---

19. Quoted in Leon Carl Brown, "Tunisia under the French Protectorate: A History of Ideological Change" (unpublished Ph.D. dissertation, Harvard University, 1962).
20. Tahir al Haddad, *Al Ummal*, pp. 9-10.

for a Tunisian trade-union movement did not materialize. Within half a year of its foundation M'Hammed Ali and other CGTT leaders were exiled, and the nationalist union was dissolved. The movement, however, succeeded in laying the ideological foundations of Tunisian trade unionism. The succeeding generations, particularly that of Hached and his associates improved upon it. Since 1946 each of the nine congresses of the UGTT has devoted a major part of its effort to broad economic and social problems, and one of these—the report of the Sixth Congress (September 1956)—served as a guide to the Tunisian Ten Year Plan. Furthermore, the UGTT's cooperative scheme forms today one of its main strengths, and a major promise. At the time of Tunisia's independence her trade union, more than the Neo-Destour, wielded a coherent, consistent, and functioning ideology. It stressed self-reliance and autonomy of trade unions within the framework of national cooperation. It possessed a reformist outlook which emphasized the educative and integrative functions of a labor organization. And it claimed a program of social and economic development which its leaders were intent on promoting in the national interest.

The labor movement's greater preoccupation with questions of economic development and social change attracted to it the progressive members of the intelligentsia and white collar workers who often disagreed with the moderate position of a broadly based nationalist party on questions of internal reforms. The role of men like Sfar and Haddad has already been noted. When the UGTT was founded it attracted young intellectuals like Mahmoud Messadi (now Minister of Education) and Ahmad Ben Salah (Minister for Planning and Finance) both of whom held posts as Secretaries General of the UGTT. It also attracted young party leaders like Abdullah Farhat (member of the party's political bureau and President of the National Investment Fund) who needed a freer forum to advance their economic and social ideas. These men further enhanced the progressive image of the UGTT by preparing detailed programs of reform and development, by making their special skills available to the party and the government, and by helping the programs of the union to become policies of the state. Since independence, however, many of these men have departed from the union to become high officials in the government.[21] Had it not been for the existence of a devoted and

21. Ahmad Tlili and Habib Achour are the only two leaders of national stature still on the union's executive bureau. There have been drastic changes in the

trained cadre, the union could have been seriously damaged by their loss.

The CGTT experience served also to clarify the conditions and prospects of trade unionism. The movement had its origin in the anti-French feeling of the Tunisian workers who felt that the CGT was not treating them equally. During the docker's strike, which lasted for forty-five days, M'Hammed Ali received support from the Destour which helped the strikers draw national attention and popular acclaim. The unionists won their demands largely because their cause had become a public issue. The experience demonstrated that it was in the framework of popular and party support, based on nationalist appeal, that the workers had best chance of winning their immediate objectives.

Yet the alliance between the Destour nationalists and the labor union collapsed at the first sign of crisis. The elitist Destour leaders could use the trade union as a convenient instrument of political agitation, but they were not ready to face the demands inherent in organizing the masses for political participation—the necessity for changing the traditional forms of economic and social relationships. A basic cleavage existed between the attitudes and aspirations of the two groups. By and large, the Destour elite was concerned with constitutional changes leading to national independence as an end in itself. The trade unionists were interested in fundamental social and economic reforms; and politics for them was only a means to that end. The nationalist movement had so far gained neither the momentum nor the militancy to allow a marriage of necessity, as it did in the case of the Istiqlal and UMT, two incongruent groups. It is understandable that when a socialist coalition in France (Edouard Herriot's) came to power and raised Old Destour hope for constitutional concessions, a militant mass movement appeared to be an unnecessary embarrassment. They felt free, therefore, to abandon the movement and, in an effort to please the socialists, appealed to the Tunisian workers to join the CGT.[22]

UGTT since this chapter was written. The union's relations with the government came to a pass in July 1965 when Achour, his legislative immunity having been withdrawn, was imprisoned and charged with mismanaging union cooperatives. Ahmad Tlili has gone in exile. Early in August Bechir Bellagha, former Governor of Tunis and active in the UGTT during 1945-1956 was elected as the Secretary General of the UGTT. Tlili and Achour were not re-elected to the executive bureau and were expelled from the party political bureau.

22. The communiqué was signed by representatives of the Destour, the Reformist Party, and the Grand Councillors. It spoke of "the disastrous consequences of the

A viable alliance between the labor and nationalist movement, had to await the emergence of a more radical and revolutionary elite. In 1934 when some youthful leaders led by Bourguiba founded the Neo-Destour this condition had been nearly fulfilled. In 1937 the Neo-Destour attempted to revive CGTT and had considerable initial success. But the movement collapsed under colonial repression. Then the war intervened.

The recent history of the Tunisian labor movement began in 1944 when Farhat Hached, a transport worker from Sfax and veteran trade unionist, established an autonomous union in the South. Helped by the Neo-Destour and encouraged even by the protectorate authorities who were keen to diminish the influence of the now Communist-dominated CGT, Hached extended his organization, by the end of 1945, to the entire country while carefully avoiding the charges of politicizing the workers. In January 1946 the UGTT was founded, and its alliance with the Neo-Destour was openly acknowledged. Prominent nationalist leaders took active interest in union affairs. Union leaders were consulted on all major party decisions. As the nationalist struggle intensified the trade union backed the party's agitation with successful general strikes and demonstrations. During the years 1952-1954 when the Neo-Destour faced intermittent repression and clandestinity the UGTT served as cover for nationalist activities. In the absence of exiled or imprisoned Neo-Destour leaders the trade unionists carried on the struggle and helped keep the party structure intact. When armed resistance started in Tunisia, the UGTT used its membership contacts both in the urban and rural areas to organize and keep the terrorist groups under the discipline of the nationalist movement. By its membership in the ICFTU, the UGTT gained an international forum for the Tunisian cause, and with the help of the AFL-CIO and other Western labor movements it helped to internationalize the question of Tunisian independence. With the assassination of Hached in December 1952, the Tunisian nationalist and labor movements acquired their greatest martyr-hero and the symbol of Tunisia's sacrifice for freedom.

A close partnership between the labor union and the party had

---

existence of the CGTT side by side with an international CGT" and added "although we have no direct rights over the workers we decide to use our influence through the press and public addresses to advise the workers to be united within the CGT in order that collaboration may be accomplished in this field also," *Al Nahda*, February 22, 1925.

been established and cemented by common struggle. With the support of the labor union the party had been able to broaden its mass base, withstand repression, and obtain international support. By participating in the struggle for emancipation the labor union had gained legitimacy, acquired valuable skills, and moral claim to a significant role in Tunisia's development. Now a part of the national, rather than class protest, movement its leaders were to belong to the ruling elite dedicated to the task not only of ensuring the workers' welfare but committed also to national reconstruction. Yet this could have led the union, as Hached had warned, to a symbiotic tie with the party. Or it could lead the union leaders to forget the temporary character of their intense political involvement. Aware of this danger Hached and his associates endeavoured to keep the union functionally and organically differentiated from the party. Moreover, they made these distinctions clear to their members and cadre. Speaking to a cadre meeting in 1948, Hached declared: "Trade unionism is a movement against exploitation of workers. It is national, and nothing that concerns the nation is a matter for indifference. . . . But it must seek to remain apolitical and above political competition which divides the working class. . . . In pursuing its goals the trade union must impose its doctrine on and influence the policies of the state which alone has the responsibility for maintaining harmony and equilibrium in the national community. The trade union must have its defendents in national institutions. It should provide the state with technical skills, its will to reconstruct and its ardent faith in the ideal of progress. But it will loose its character, and contradict itself if it consents to share power."[23]

The generation following Hached has not always lived up to this ideal, but events after independence have indicated, on numerous occasions, that these values were successfully inculcated, and large segments of union members still cherish them. In recent years, however, the UGTT's capacity and its leaders' willingness to actively inculcate and appraise union values and attitudes have declined. For example, the union program for cadre formation has been spotty and insufficient to present needs. Its national leaders have been losing touch with the union locals and the rank and file were beginning in 1962-1963 to complain of indolent central direction and too much identification with the party.

23. *Mission,* June 23, 1948.

Ideological commitment to democratic processes, pressures of the cadre, and habits developed through participation in the French CGT have led the UGTT to maintain the principle of accountability in the organization. The union constitution requires election of officials at all levels, and the practice was maintained even during the difficult years following the assassination of Farhat Hached when many unionists were in jail and holding elections was a perilous undertaking. At present elections are held at regular intervals; plurality of candidates is not discouraged and elections are normally contested.

The structural changes introduced in 1958 have greatly centralized and professionalized the organization. Regional unions, which were previously the centers of union activity and political agitation, now have ceded much power and many functions to the ten professional federations, whose offices are located in Tunis.[24] The 132-man National Council which theoretically supervises the organization between the triennial national congresses, and the enlarged administrative commission, which groups general secretaries of the regional unions and federations with the central executive bureau, have met frequently though not as often as the constitution requires. Congresses have been held regularly. The last two congresses (1960, 1963) were occasions of considerable debate over important issues, including union policy vis-à-vis the state and the economic demand of workers. There was much open criticism of the leadership and their conduct of union affairs by delegates of local unions. At the last congress I witnessed a touching demonstration of UGTT's commitment to democratic ideals. It was clear from the start that a strong group within the organization was intent on displacing Ahmad Tlili, a long time trade-union personality and also a prominent member of the party political bureau, from the office of UGTT's Secretary General. Bourguiba's opening speech and later activities of some party members made it apparent that the president and the party had sanctioned his ouster, and there was little doubt left about his departure from the post. Tlili, it seemed, was determined to go down in defeat rather than surrender to pressure for withdrawing from the slate of candidates. The anti-Tlili faction and some party members who were keen to maintain the facade of unanimity and harmony suggested the creation of an office of president

24. Since the union has to adjust to party and government structure the creation of a *comité du coordination* confirmed by the last party congress may again increase the importance of the regional unions.

of the union so Tlili could be honorably accommodated. The proposal raised a furore against "honorary offices" as being inimical to republican and trade-union principles. Put to vote it fetched an overwhelming "non." Tlili having refused to withdraw his candidature, contested the election and lost the secretary generalship. During the intermission before the election Tlili was asked why he was intent on running for the office when his defeat was so imminent. He replied that he wanted to be the first Tunisian to be thrown out of power by democratic means. It is true that he is the first national figure, and the UGTT the first national institution, to have set this precedent in Tunisia.[25]

The above discussion suggests that the UGTT fulfilled, in varying degrees, five of the six conditions (the sixth being a permissive political system) which I have proposed as being important for a union's successful passage through the three stages of development. The UGTT possessed added qualifications, for, by its successful participation in the nationalist struggle it had won a permanent place in Tunisia's history. By carrying on the struggle during the party's clandestinity it had gained not only a national "mystique" but also martyrs and heroes, and a membership which shared the memories and pride of being part of this movement. Its leadership and ideology had won for it the image, at least among the students and urban masses, of an organization equipped to launch a program of modernization. When Tunisia became independent the UGTT appeared to be the only serious contender against a one-party system, and indeed, tried to play this role for a brief period. It was soon forced to make adjustment to a subordinate place in the political system. And the image of the UGTT as an organization parallel with the party disappeared as the latter consolidated its monopoly of power.

Those who regret the decline of the union "mystique" have a nostalgic view of a moment in history. The fact is that the UGTT on the eve of independence enjoyed a glory and appearance of power out of proportion with its actual worth. In 1955 when an exhausted Neo-Destour split between supporters of Bourguiba and Ben Youssef and the infant government was threatened by intransigent terrorist leaders in the countryside, the UGTT looked trim, smart, and poised for action. Its structure, discipline, and cohesion uneroded by clandestinity, its political skills and capacity for maneuver sharpened by experience, and its self-confidence in-

---

25. Tlili was, nevertheless, elected to the 9-man executive committee of the union.

creased by success it looked as if the UGTT could take what it wanted. It was a powerful illusion and even Ahmad Ben Salah, the Secretary General of the union was caught by it. For a brief period the trade unionists considered remaining neutral in the Youssefist crisis so that the warring factions might exhaust each other.[26] The UGTT contemplated assuming power, and decided it should not. Some trade-union leaders were against it in principle and referred to Hached's teaching. Some had militated in the party also and were loyal to Bourguiba. Most felt that there was no reason to suspect Bourguiba's progressive commitments and hence no point in assuming direct control of the government. When the UGTT decided to throw in its lot with Bourguiba its leaders knew they were opting for a subordinate role in a one-party state. They did not know how much and in what ways the union would be subordinated. The question was answered without much delay.

Soon after the Youssefist insurrection was under control, it became clear that Bourguiba and Ben Salah had divergent views on the role of the trade union and on the immediate economic and social solutions for Tunisia. Bourguiba's longtime distrust for division and his penchant for national unity had been reinforced by the struggle against the Youssefists. He was seeking political consolidation and integration within the party of all groups and classes. This called for non-controversial policies. Ben Salah considering UGTT as the "national instrument of social and economic revolution" insisted on a "profound revolution of the economic structure."[27] "We must have full realization of our sovereignty" said Bourguiba. "We must have a socialist plan" announced the secretary general of the union. "Whoever tries to sow distrust and division is acting against the national interest" warned Bourguiba. "Nationalize all national resources" insisted Ben Salah. Such was the dialogue between March and September 1956.[28]

Bourguiba alternated between persuasion and threats—a characteristic of his political style. The UGTT group was allowed to pilot a resolution at the party congress (Sfax) calling for a socialist plan. But when the union staged strikes of farm workers

26. This and the following discussion is based mainly on interviews. I have also drawn on Clement Henry Moore, "Tunisia's Single Party Regime" (unpublished Ph.D. dissertation, Harvard University, 1962), pp. 135-151; 361-376.
27. UGTT, *Economic Report,* Sixth Congress, September 1956, p. 6.
28. See *Le Petit Matin,* April 7, 1956; April 13, 1956; August 18, 1956; *L'Action,* September 3, 1956.

Moroccan Women . . .

. . . voting in a municipal election

. . . posing in a hand-woven Berber blanket

Agriculture

A Berber nomad in the Middle Atlas mountains © Miss M. Bull

Moorish women beating wheat at harvest-time © Miss M. Bull

Weighing the harvest
in an experimental plot

Learning the mechanics
of modern farming

Koutoubia Mosque at Marrakesh

Bourguiba criticized them severely for undermining production. A week after the strike ended, he promised a *statut* for agricultural workers. When Bourguiba offered him the Ministry of Social Affairs, Ben Salah stormed in and out of the Prime Minister's office demanding the portfolio of finance but eventually supplied four UGTT ministers to the new government. The union attended a round table on economic planning with the representatives of the party and other national organizations but rejected its carefully worked out report. Ben Salah blasted the report publicly which infuriated the party leaders who had compromised to accommodate the UGTT demands. In reply, Bourguiba defined his economic policy in a public speech stressing respect for property rights and inviting foreign investments. The UGTT demands had been rejected.[29]

As the Sixth Congress of the union approached (September 1956) the UGTT showed signs of splitting. Habib Achour, a working-class leader and veteran party militant, led the powerful Sfax regional union and was joined by others in protest against politicization of the UGTT. Ahmad Tlili moderated between the contending factions, and in his efforts to save trade union solidarity persuaded Bourguiba to interrupt his vacation in Europe to address the congress. Bourguiba promised satisfaction of two UGTT demands—retirement benefits for mine workers and a statute for state employees—and called for harmonious relations between the government and the union. Ben Salah called Bourguiba "the benevolent father of the nation," and against his opponents defended the UGTT participation in the government and its role in the Constituent Assembly.[30] But the trouble was not over.

The congress called for "organic participation of the UGTT with the action of the Neo-Destour on the basis of a truly democratic social and economic program." Organic participation was defined as "this participation which lays the foundation for a Tunisian labor movement but which nonetheless remains subordinated to the approbations of the party."[31] This alarmed some party leaders who distrusted Ben Salah's ambitions and dreaded the idea of a party-union organic fusion. They encouraged Habib Achour to split. It is clear, however, that the political bureau did not discuss the impending split and Bourguiba gave it his support

29. Speech, August 17, 1956.
30. *Le Petit Matin,* September 21, 1956.
31. *Ibid.,* September 25, 1956.

only by keeping silent. Trade union unity ended when Habib Achour left the UGTT with some 50,000 members and founded a rival union—the UTT (*Union Tunisien du Travail*). Achour demanded removal of Ben Salah and UGTT renunciation of direct participation in politics as the price for unity. Many union leaders felt that continued division of the working class was intolerable, and there was pressure for unity also from the members. Bourguiba, however, wanted Ben Salah out of the union, and in December 1956 the UGTT administrative council met to remove him and to elect Ahmad Tlili as the Secretary General. In April 1957 Achour was coopted to the party political bureau, and in September 1957 a trade-union unity congress met to confirm the change.

The Ben Salah affair defined and limited the role of the trade union. The major issue at stake was the role of politics in trade-union affairs. Ben Salah wanted a continued political role for the UGTT as an instrument of economic and social revolution. Achour insisted on pursuit of trade-union goals, and the unity of the union was achieved by a compromise solution. The UGTT ministers and high officials in the government were no longer considered "members on vacation," and they resigned. The UGTT was defined as an "essentially trade union movement in theory apolitical, . . . working for an increased living standard for the Tunisian proletariat." The 1960 report added that the UGTT still played a political role as in the past because "independence to be effective must be completely and definitely freed of all aftereffects of political and economic servitude and permit the evolution of national institutions toward maximum democracy."[32] This was a justification for the UGTT's participation in the National Front. The substitution of Ben Salah by Tlili, who was already a member of the political bureau and treasurer of the party, and cooption of Achour to the political bureau assured close coordination between the party, the government, and the union. On the whole the relationship has benefited both the party and the union. But there is now a growing need for readjustment, reappraisal, and sympathetic understanding from the party of UGTT's difficulties.

Contrary to many pessimistic forecasts, the UGTT since 1956 has not only maintained its organizational cohesion but has even improved its structure and administration by stressing the prin-

---

32. *UGTT Eighth National Congress, Activities Report* (April 1960), pp. 7-8.

ciple of professional (as against regional) loyalties. By participating in workers-management committees, in the social security program, and in various consultative bodies of the government it has improved its professional competence. It claims a membership of 150,000 of which some 80,000 pay their dues under the check off system. It has been financially not only independent but has even contributed to national and party funds and regularly paid its dues to the ICFTU. It has successfully promoted the movement for workers' cooperatives. In early 1963 the UGTT owned 27 cooperative establishments and employed 3,678 full time workers. In 1964 its long projected People's Bank was serving its expanding cooperatives. The UGTT was also a proud host to some three hundred foreign diplomats and labor delegates who came to attend the inauguration of Tunisia's largest tourist hotel owned by the union.

As an interest group it has campaigned for and obtained advanced social and labor legislation, which include a progressive law for agricultural workers (1957), the introduction of workers-management committees (1959), and a unified social security legislation revised to provide more comprehensive coverage and generalized to the benefit of all workers in the private sector (1960).

As an organization associated with the party and other "interest" groups (UNFT, UNAT, UTIC, UGET) in the National Front, it enjoys a place of importance second to that of the party with which 80 percent of its membership overlaps. Two members of its 9-man executive committee are also members of the party's political bureau. The 21 trade-union deputies in the 90-member National Assembly sit on important legislative committees and are regarded as among the more active, skilled, and even independent deputies. UGTT statute forbids trade-union members from holding executive positions in the government but three of its former executive committee members are ministers, and many high officials in the government are ex-UGTT members. Through them the influence of the UGTT ideas has penetrated the decisions of the state. Through its policy of close cooperation with the Neo-Destour regime, it has promoted not only specific labor legislation but also even more generalized national goals. It justifiably lists as major UGTT "victories" the government's ambitious policy for mass education, the creation of consultative bodies in which the UGTT has an important voice, the government's commitment to the cooperative movement, and an effective public works project which now provides work and subsistence, in American wheat and Tunisian money, to some 250,000 of Tunisia's nearly 400,000 unemployed.

The UGTT today performs, vis-à-vis the workers, some of the party's functions. It articulates and represents the interests of the workers as is evident from its record of achievements. But it also collaborates in the National Front on government and party projects. It represents, as well as subordinates, specific interests to the national interests and thus helps maintain consensus. In the strict sense of the word it is neither an autonomous pressure group devoted solely to wage increases nor a blind instrument of the party. The party profits by respecting a trade union that has broad working-class support. It eases the task of mobilizing an important segment of the population for modernization. It provides the state with the needed skills of trade-union leaders who have often been the initiators and planners of Tunisia's social and economic development. Above all, the union's participation in the party and state councils has helped to blunt the authoritarian edge of a one-party state.

Relations between the party and the union have not been free of tensions, which exist mainly in the regions where the trade union is strong, and in areas of activity in which the union resents having to compete with the party. In Sfax, Gafsa, and Tunis—UGTT strongholds—union officials have clashed with, and complained of, party and government officials hampering their growth by withholding licenses and favouring rival cooperatives which the party is also beginning to organize. Another issue leading to union-party tension has concerned the party professional cells paralleling union locals. These professional cells first emerged during the party's clandestinity to serve as a cover for political activity. Then they were briefly resuscitated during the Ben Salah crisis. Since 1960 the party cells have been revived, some twelve of them in Tunis, six in Sfax, and four in Gafsa. In August 1962, the UGTT administrative council bitterly criticized the professional cells as "creating confusion" and "threatening the concept of a harmonious national front." Then Ahmad Tlili issued a circular asking trade-union militants to take over the professional cells in the forthcoming elections, which they did, and the party temporized and assured the union that the professional cells would not usurp their functions. In April 1963 following Tlili's defeat in the UGTT, a joint communiqué was issued in which the union accepted the existence of the cells and the party promised they would only concentrate on political education. The issue is not yet settled, and at the last party congress (October 1964) trade unionists complained against the cells again without getting any satisfaction.

Similar clashes have occurred in governmental bodies also. These have been less frequent because most issues are settled in the party and national front meetings, and through more informal channels. Occasionally UGTT leaders bring these disputes to the public by debating them in open forums. In the 1962 Congress of Cooperatives, Achour clashed with Mustafa Filali, then director of the government cooperative bank and a former member of the trade union executive bureau. Filali favored centralized credit with governmental supervision and planning, while Achour insisted on diversified credit and competitive cooperatives. Sometimes trade-union deputies are mildly critical of government policies. But normally they tend to promote union interests through their membership in the legislative committees. On very rare occasions have trade-union leaders taken a public stand against party or government decision. In November 1962, Ahmad Tlili publicly criticized the regime for banning the Communist party as an attack on civil liberties and a dangerous precedent at a general meeting of trade-union members.

The UGTT's greatest problem now is that of maintaining the loyalty of its members without being able to satisy their demands. This is an issue which is also the most sensitive in its relations with the party and the government. Its future will probably depend on whether or not the present government will permit the union some indulgence in corporate activities. For eight years it has made invaluable contributions to Tunisian polity and society while holding down wages and endeavouring to step up economic development. Now it is beginning clearly to register losses, and the membership has been complaining over the absence of wage increases. Take-home pay has remained unchanged but the cost of living has substantially increased. The right to strike, considered sacred by Bourguiba in 1956, is nowhere mentioned in the Tunisian legislation, and the union voluntarily refrains from strikes in the "national interest." In the absence of some tangible gains union exhortations to sacrifice and hard work sound hollow, and many delegates to the last congress said so to the national leaders. The number of spontaneous strikes increased in 1962-1963, and in one case the phosphate miners were on strike for three days in defiance of local unions. In a country where discontent is rarely expressed in public and where institutional conformity is a mark of political virtue such deviations may be interpreted as acts of desperation. Discontent among the more educated and political-minded members of the union has taken the form of disaffection which though minor in magnitude is yet indicative of a trend. In March 1962 a group of youthful high-school teachers had discussed the "smothering of trade union liberties with the accord of UGTT leaders who use all means to keep the rank and file members from making their claims heard."[33] Late in 1962 Ahmad Tlili complained that the teachers' union had lost much of its vigor and despite educational expansion had failed to increase its membership.

Ahmad Tlili's displacement as the Secretary General of the UGTT was, at least partly, related to the question of government policies on wages and consumption. Feeling that the government's prescription of continued austerity under the Ten Year Plan was eroding the UGTT membership loyalties, he started advocating some diversification in the plan to include more small-scale industry and some relaxations in favor of basic necessities. By doing this he only increased the irritation of Bourguiba who, since 1958, had been disturbed by his trusted disciple's growing interest in introducing internal opposition within the party. When Ben Salah, the Minister for Planning and Finance complained that Tlili was threatening the execution of the plan the stage was set for his departure. There is no doubt though that there was genuine opposition to Tlili within the union, and he had not endeared himself to his colleagues on the executive bureau. Habib Achour, the new Secretary General is the last of the original leadership still active in the union. Although a veteran party man, loyal to Bourguiba, he is a genuine trade unionist. Following the devaluation of the dinar in 1964 there were strikes in Tunis, and the UGTT administrative council met under Achour and made its protests to the government. At the last party congress (October 1964) Bourguiba publicly chided Achour and other trade-union leaders and warned against narrow class interests jeopardizing national welfare. He did, however, promise some redress.

On the whole, Tunisia's leaders, and particularly Bourguiba, have helped the UGTT to shift its emphasis increasingly from political to social and welfare activities. With the adoption of all its program and with the party now championing socialist ideology

---

33. *Tribune du Progrès* (March-April 1962).

the union needs to evolve new programs and activities to help maintain its functional separateness from the party and government. It has to find ways and means that will make membership in the union satisfying and meaningful. In order to maintain workers' support the UGTT must, from time to time, win material benefits for its members. Without this it will be increasingly difficult for the union to perform the many educational functions which are invaluable for economic development.

MOROCCO

The history of the Moroccan labor movement has been marked by dramatic successes and numerous, though surmountable, setbacks. Its development since independence reflects the complexity, imbalances, and uncertainties of the Moroccan political setting. Its relative newness, as well as its origin, denied the union the time and the opportunity to define and clarify its ideology and program. The exigencies of agitational politics which led to the creation of the UMT, and the conflicting character of political forces in Morocco have cast the labor organization in a revolutionary mold. The UMT has played this role with heroic exuberance, unfailing confidence, and considerable political acumen. Today its opponents as well as its allies consider it the *enfant terrible* of Moroccan politics. The Istiqlal Party, the government, and even its ally, the National Union of Popular Forces (UNFP) have successively experienced its cooperation as well as its opposition. In the political setting of shifting alliances, divisive and alternating palace patronage, and swiftly changing fortunes, the UMT has successfully maintained its position as a powerful and the best organized element in Morocco. Its role in shaping national politics has been significant. It precipitated the split in the Istiqlal, was instrumental in the establishment of the UNFP, and has influenced the government's foreign and domestic policies as an ally no less than as an opponent. It is as much an indication of its importance and strength as its capacity for maneuver that while political parties, and particularly the UNFP, have experienced eclipse and organizational decay, the union has by and large evaded governmental repression as well as institutional decline.

The UMT's achievements in the labor field are no less impressive. Through its participation in labor courts, commissions for professional training, price and wages, social security fund and bureaus of placement, it has advanced the interests of the working class. It has obtained progressive legislation establishing a system of labor courts, basic union rights, the right to organize agricultural workers and cooperatives, regulation of child labor, womens' working rights, minimum wages, and a Superior Council for Collective Conventions. It has bargained for favorable collective agreements with employers and has staged successful strikes at the factory and federation levels. A measure of UMT's success as a labor organization is that although it has a leftist orientation, demands nationalization of key industries, and campaigns against foreign capital, the French industrial employers of Morocco prefer to deal with the UMT rather than the relatively docile and moderate UGTM. They feel that the UMT not only has the support of the majority but its leaders possess the bargaining competence and disciplinary capability needed for stable industrial relations.

The structure of the union, considerably improved since 1958, is an impressive monument of the organizational skills of its leaders. The UMT headquarters in Casablanca has an air of bureaucratic efficiency and modernity rare even in civil secretariats of underdeveloped countries. Its twenty-five professional federations have a total of 136 affiliates. Eight regional unions coordinate the local groups and ensure control and supervision by the 9-man national bureau headed by Secretary General Mahjoub Ben Seddik.[34] Its program of cadre training has been effective. The union's administrative task is considerably facilitated because under government regulation a majority of its full-time workers remain on their employers' payroll. The UMT does not publicize its finances but evidence suggests that it has an annual income of about $400,000 from dues and special collections. It is a measure of the union's self-confidence that it rejects the check-off system as a valid method for dues collection. In view of its financial and administrative resources it is surprising that the UMT has not developed social, educational, and cooperative programs comparable with those of the Tunisian and Algerian trade unions. The explanation for this probably lies in its preoccupation with politics and its opposition role.

Notwithstanding its successes the Moroccan union has paid a price for its political activism. Its leaders, preoccupied with

---

34. The bureau is chosen from the administrative council which is elected by the congress. A national council groups federation and regional secretaries with the administrative council, and meets between congresses.

politics, have tended to neglect the needs and demands of the membership. To evade criticism and to defend themselves from membership pressures they have sometimes disregarded the rules of procedure which govern the organization. Discontent among members led, four years after independence, to two national "centrals" and a few autonomous unions. The UMT has ever since been vulnerable to attacks and splits. There are indications, however, that its leaders have learned from losses and are trying to renew professional contacts with the membership and to disengage the union from political agitation. A more detailed discussion of these developments follows.

The UMT, founded on March 20, 1955, is the first national trade union of Morocco. Employed and skilled Moroccan workers had, however, been CGT members since 1936 when a *dahir* granted trade-union rights to Europeans. The protectorate authorities possessed but did not use the power to prevent Moroccans from forming the union. After the war, the CGT made a concentrated effort to recruit Moroccans. The Istiqlal Party elders at first opposed the move on grounds that membership in a French organization would weaken the nationalist position, that extra legal participation in the union would render the nationalist workers vulnerable to repression, and that it might lead to an association of the nationalist movement with Communism. The party's left wing, however, won a significant victory in 1948 when the Istiqlal reversed its 1946 decision against joining the UGSCM and started large-scale nationalist infiltration into the Moroccan branch of the CGT. At the 1950 Congress of the UGSCM the nationalists outvoted the Communists. By December 1952 when without Communist support, they organized a protest demonstration over the assassination of Ferhat Hached, the break with the CGT was complete and the union became fully controlled by the nationalists. The demonstration, however, was mercilessly suppressed, the union abolished, and its leaders imprisoned.

Released in September 1954, the labor leaders reorganized quickly, contacted the ICFTU, and in March 1955 announced the creation of the UMT. Presented with the *fait accompli,* the French authorities recognized the union in October. Thus while the Istiqlal leaders did not begin reorganization until the king's return, the union expanded rapidly, and within a year was claiming a membership of 650,000. Its success was dramatic, having received impetus from, and being developed in the context of, intense nationalist agitation. The union leaders' achievements were based on successful infiltration and exploitation of the parent organization's rules of procedure. In contrast with Tunisia, Morocco's trade unionists did not have to justify their position in open debates and had few opportunities and little time for ideological clarification. As trade unionists trained in the CGT they are influenced by Marxist ideas, and even today Marxist undertones are strong in their pronouncements because they serve as an excellent tool for social and political criticism. Yet their programs and plans do not relate clearly to the Moroccan context and give evidence neither of the disciplined consistency of the Algerian, nor of the pragmatism of the Tunisian movement.

In independent Morocco the UMT emerged as the second largest group after the Istiqlal. It had some advantages over the latter in the fact that reorganization and centralized control was easier because its members were concentrated in a few urban centers; and by supporting terrorist activities it had reached a better understanding with the Resistance. Through its membership in the Istiqlal political committee it had a direct voice in the party, and ten of its representatives sat in the 76-member Consultative Assembly. Also, union leaders sat on the Superior Council for the Plan. On the council of government it had supporters in Ibrahim and Bouabid. Yet it was uncommitted to governmental decisions and party discipline, and was free to advocate policies without the responsibility to execute them. The UMT was in a position to choose its allies and to cooperate with or oppose the government. During 1956 the union backed the Istiqlal attack on the government with strikes and increasing union demands. After the formation of the predominantly Istiqlal government in October 1956 these objections, and with them the number of strikes declined although the union maintained a posture of independence by mildly criticizing the government's foreign policy and slowness in introducing reforms. In return the union was rewarded with favorable legislation. The honeymoon lasted but briefly.

As the tension between the right and left wing of the Istiqlal boiled over with the formation of the Balafrej government in April-May 1958, the UMT backed the left wing of the party.[35] A rash of strikes led to considerable violence in Rabat and Casablanca because the Istiqlal elders encouraged dissenting workers

---

35. For a detailed discussion of the Istiqlal split and the UMT role in it, see Douglas E. Ashford, *Political Change in Morocco* (Princeton: Princeton University Press, 1961), pp. 93-131, 260-269, 290-301.

to disobey UMT orders. Hopes of reconciliation disappeared when the union responded by stepping up its attack. A full scale assault on Balafrej's government in the UMT journal *Al Tali'a* preceded the resignation of Bouabid and the fall of the government in December. The party split followed. The new government of Abdullah Ibrahim had full UMT support until May 1960 when Mohammed V decided on direct rule with his son as deputy.

The immediate repercussion of the party split was felt within the labor movement. Signs of discontent in the UMT had appeared in 1956 when Jorio, an expelled union leader, formed an autonomous union and threatened the UMT's hold in Rabat until the king intervened in its behalf. Jorio's motivations may have been personal but his appeal lay in his criticism of UMT association with the Istiqlal in an effort to change the government and in his defense of the "sacred principles of syndicalism." When the UMT launched its attack on the Istiqlal, the party elders exploited the existing discontent and trade-union unity crumbled amidst violence and rioting. The dockers of Casablanca were the first to rebel, in September 1958, over their right to choose their local leaders without central interference. After the party split a series of autonomous unions starting with the Rabat section of the Teachers' Federation were announced. These included Rabat's construction workers under Jorio, some factory workers in Casablanca and the miners of Khouribga, Djerada, Bou Arfa, and Kachkate. Morocco's oldest union members were leaving the UMT. The top leadership, too, was divided over the question of the union's role in politics. Before the long-delayed UMT congress was held in April 1959, six members of the executive council had resigned and were later joined by others in forming a revival committee which cooperated with an Istiqlal-sponsored coordination committee to group the dissenters/splinters into a general union. The fact that Assistant Secretary General Taieb Bouazza, a mine worker and CGT official who had disagreed with the UMT handling of dock and mine workers and who had opposed politicization of unions, was forced to resign and sent as Morocco's ambassador to Yugoslavia, did not help the UMT's popularity. In March the UMT's rally on the anniversary of its foundation drew less support than subsequent rallies by its opponent.

Of those who left the UMT, only the Free School teachers were sympathetic to the conservative wing of the Istiqlal for many of them had had traditional education and their schools were founded and financed by the Istiqlal elders. The causes of the dock and mine workers' defection was the UMT's inability to live up to their trade unionist expectations. As workers with some twenty years' of membership in the CGT, they were sensitive to procedures of accountability. They resented the excessive control and manipulation of union locals and the neglect of their specific grievances by the central leadership. They attributed these failings to their leaders' preoccupation with politics. That their protest derived from their disinterest in politics is also indicated by the fact that the majority of the dissenting dock and mine workers did not join the UGTM. Some have remained in autonomous unions; others rejoined the UMT and, today, are a source of worry and irritation to its leaders who are impatient with their assertiveness.

The UMT recovered much of its organizational strength because it had obtained, and during the Ibrahim government continued to make, specific gains for the working class. The government gave its full support to the UMT also by refusing recognition to the splinter movement. The king addressed the UMT rally on May Day and in a reference to dissenting unionists warned against trouble makers. However, on March 20, 1960 the UGTM was founded under Istiqlal sponsorship and promptly complained to the ILO against the government's refusal to give it recognition. The issue was further complicated in May 1960 when the Ibrahim government resigned and the Istiqlal and the *Mouvement Populaire* joined the king's government. In October, a government decree on trade-union rights gave full recognition to the UGTM despite UMT's violent campaign against it.

During the battle against and following the recognition of the rival union the UMT demonstrated a cautious attitude toward openly political strikes. The split and subsequent UGTM attacks had demonstrated the union's vulnerability to charges of politicization and undemocratic handling of union affairs. Moreover, when the government threatened to use force to ensure the right to work, strikes based on generalized demands became all the more risky. Following a clash between the police and strikers in Larache, and the failure of a general strike in the northern zone the UMT tactics changed in favor of piecemeal labor agitation backed by specific labor demands. New directives were also issued to federation and local leaders against discussing political issues in union meetings. This change, however, contributed to increasing tension between the union and the UNFP.

The UMT-UNFP relations have been complicated by personal rivalries among the leaders, UNFP expectation that the union should submit to party directives, and UMT insistence on treating the party as an equal, if not a junior, partner of the union. These differences were accentuated after the new king, Hassan II, refusing to accept UNFP demands for an elected assembly as a condition for participation, formed the government without the UNFP. The party desired a trial of strength along the lines of their 1958 campaign against Balafrej. The union was not willing, but was being pressured to back the campaign with strikes. In June 1961 a civil servants' strike led to suspension of some functionaries. The strike did not have support of the union central and its political character was publicly admitted by Hachemi Bennani who held party office as well as that of union secretary in Rabat. UMT leaders intervened to negotiate a face saving agreement. At the end of 1961 the union gave but lukewarm support to renewed UNFP attacks on the government. These differences came to a climax in December when, encouraged by the UNFP, employees of the foreign office went on strike. The government dismissed sixty of them. The UNFP, through Bennani again, called for a general strike of civil servants which failed. The government dismissed a few more employees and even refused to see a Civil Servants' Federation delegation which was desperately looking for compromise. The UMT rejected the party's importunities for a general sympathy strike, and a few days later Ben Seddik was in direct contact with the palace to secure reinstatement of the dismissed workers. The incident damaged the image of the party as well as the union but the UMT derived satisfaction from the fact that the politicians had learned a lesson against manipulating union members without the central's support.

The incident marked the virtual end of UMT agitation in behalf of its ally, and the beginning of a bitter controversy between the two organizations. The UNFP argued, on the basis of its statutes, that the union was obliged to accept political direction of the party. The UMT asserted its independence as a non-party, non-political organization. At the UNFP congress in May 1962 effort was made to reach a settlement. Ben Barka, the General Secretary of the party, publicly stressed the independence and functional separateness of the union. Four UMT leaders were elected to the nine-man General Secretariat while the union obtained eleven of the twenty-eight seats on the administrative commission. Yet suspicions prevailed and personal jealousies increased when under Ben Barka's capable direction the party's organization began to expand even in industrial centers like Safi and Khouribga. The dispute was renewed when the union refused to support actively the party's decision to boycott the constitutional referendum, and it became public when the two groups used the struggle between the FLN and the UGTA as a cover for debate against each other. At the second UMT congress in January 1963 Ben Seddik bitterly attacked political parties in general, and in the General Report the union was described as being completely independent of all political organizations. The union's Secretary General further confirmed the break by announcing the (unfulfilled) possibility of putting up independent candidates for the elections to the lower house of the parliament.

The UMT today remains a protest movement. It has become cautious about political agitation, and it is now relatively more sensitive to pressures from the rank and file. But it would be incorrect to assume that there has been a fundamental change in the nature of Morocco's labor movement. UMT leaders argue that their intensive, and often negative, involvement in politics results from their not finding national institutions in which they can make their social and economic views explicitly and effectively felt. Their grievances are numerous and these are often generalized to questions of national concern. Yet direct access to power is blocked, and the channels of communication that might relate labor to those in power are either non-existent or ineffective. Furthermore, in Morocco full scale and effective plans for social and economic development have yet to be introduced. In the absence of such plans there is neither the climate nor the means available to the trade union for channeling its energy to the task of national reconstruction.

ALGERIA

Algerian workers participated in the CGT since 1932, and many rose to prominence in the organization in France as well as Algeria. The UGTA, founded in February 1956 as an arm of the FLN, faced repression and violence from the outset. During the first year of its legal existence it had to reconstitute its secretariat seven times because its officials were either arrested or assassinated, or had disappeared. After the merciless suppression of strikes in January-February 1957 and following the battle of Kasbah the union established its external delegation in Tunis and went underground in Algeria. The underground worked with the FLN without having its own structure. The external delegation, through its membership in the ICFTU and status as the representative of Algerian workers, helped win international allies for the revolution. In addition it ran, with outside material and technical help, successful programs of social aid, education, and technical training for displaced Algerian workers and their families. Its cadre training programs in Tunisia and Morocco were effective and the elite of the trainees were sent for advanced work abroad, especially in Eastern European countries. These included trainees in agricultural cooperatives and workers-management in China, Yugoslavia, the Soviet Union, and Czechoslovakia. During the war the UGTA, more than the FLN, was able to devote its energy to the development of skills which it considered necessary for constructing a "socialist" society.

Unlike the Tunisian and Moroccan labor movements the Algerian was not represented in the GPRA and the CNRA, the highest councils of the liberation movement. This indicates its relatively small importance to the FLN. A clandestine trade union was of little help to an organization which had the monopoly of terror and popular support. It also suggests the distrust in which the peasant-oriented revolutionary leaders held an organization of urban workers. This, however, did not deter the UGTA from discussing and advancing plans for the reconstruction of independent Algeria. On the contrary, unhampered by the exigencies of conducting the war and of reconciling diverse interests and opinions in order to maintain a unified front, they were relatively free to advocate revolutionary prescriptions for social and economic development.

Ideologically the trade-union leaders made up the extreme left in Algeria although most are not Communists. This is mainly because the extent of European domination and colonial expropriation not only brutalized their struggle for independence but also sharpened the radical edge of their demands and aspirations. It is due also to the fact that they had militated in the CGT during the period of Communist rather than socialist domination (1944-56). The training of an elite corps in Communist countries further strengthened their radical socialist orientation. The UGTA leaders have been consistent in their concept of a socialist Algeria. In calling for a scheme of workers' management of factories and farms they, more than the Tunisian and Moroccan trade union leaders, have tended to distinguish clearly, if more theoretically, between etatism and socialism. In their distrust of political and administrative dominance by "bureaucrats-turned-bourgeois" they display a closer affinity to the French syndicalist tradition than do their other colleagues in the Maghrib. Also their advocacy of continued political role for the trade union as the avant-garde and guardian of socialism has been more open and direct. Given its vigor and consistency the union point of view progressively gained support among Algerian students and workers. The Tripoli Program incorporated many recommendations made by *L'Ouvrier Algérien,* the UGTA newspaper.

At the time of independence the UGTA enjoyed less prestige than had the Tunisian and Moroccan unions. It had little national mystique and no structure, but did have the potential for becoming a strong organization. It claimed its martyrs and heroes. It had acquired special skills and aptitude for organization. It had built a cadre which any first rate trade union could envy and which though yet small for Algeria's needs, was trained to carry on its social, educational, and cooperative plans. It had the support of foreign trade unions, including the ICFTU and AFL-CIO, which were desirous of helping its efforts at reorganization. It advocated progressive policies in a country where ideologies and classes were not seriously conflicting and where a national consciousness and common outlook had been forged by seven years of common struggle. Yet in the scramble for power that followed independence many gains made during the revolutionary war were wasted and many hopes for new Algeria lost. Today the UGTA, like the rest of Algeria, awaits a vigorous definition of governmental and party policies and controls, and the establishment of a harmonious pattern of authority.

During the struggle for power between the GPRA and the Tlemcen group led by Ben Bella the union leaders at first favored the former because they were suspicious of Ben Bella's "bourgeois" supporters like Ferhat Abbas and Khider, and had greater sympathy with the radical views of Boudiaf. However, as the crisis prolonged, the success of Ben Bella became imminent; and when public disgust took the positive form of masses shouting "enough" to their warring leaders, the union adopted a neutral posture and actively organized demonstrations and deputations to stop the civil war. When the dispute was resolved the union leaders began a campaign for reorganization but had conflicts with the FLN which, in some cases, is alleged to have forcibly installed its own nominees over elected trade union delegates. On November 1,

1962, copies of *L'Ouvrier Algérien* were seized because it charged that the party was willfully destroying the union and compromising its autonomy. In December an agreement with the party promised free union elections, the union's exclusive right of representation in labor affairs, and the party's non-interference in trade union congresses and meetings. The UGTA confirmed the party's supremacy in political matters and its commitment to the Tripoli Program. With this agreement in hand the union called its first congress for January 1963.

The congress was attended by 360 delegates, representing federations and locals from different regions, who were presented with carefully worked out reports on organization, education and orientation. The election of the steering committee indicated that the organizers had the support of the delegates. In his opening speech President Ben Bella promised complete autonomy in the management of union affairs, stressed the need for national unity, asserted the supremacy of the party in defining "political thinking" and warned the trade union against "corporatism" and "ouvrierism" while promising them participation in the self-management of farms and factories. In an obvious reference to its urban character Ben Bella said that the "UGTA would have accomplished its mission and won its place in society only when 80 percent of its delegates will wear turbans."[36] Later, the congress orientation report insisted on the independent character of the union and the revolutionary political and social role of the working class as the guardian of socialism against bourgeois deviation. There were also complaints from some speakers that the party had tried to "fix" the congress delegates. Divergencies between the viewpoints of party and union leaders were clear, and Mohammed Khider, then Secretary General of the party, was known to be hostile to the UGTA. On the second day debates over the orientation report had been heated. When delegates arrived for the third session they were presented with a *fait accompli*. A new group had taken over the direction of the congress with obvious party support. A leadership loyal to the party was then presented for election. Some foreign delegations, including the ICFTU, walked out in protest. The coup d'état was complete. The Algerian example, like the more subtle Tunisian case, demonstrated the vulnerability of a trade union in a one-party state.

36. *Al Chaab,* January 18, 1963.

The UGTA since its last congress has made some progress. It has been supervising the *autogestion* in factories and some farms. In many industries the *autogestion* has successfully functioned. In early 1964 it called on workers in these enterprises to renounce their share of profits and plough it in a special investment fund to reduce unemployment. Some enterprises actually voted to support this position but the government rejected the idea fearing widespread discouragement if it were applied. In the provinces, in major cities, and in key farm areas the local unions are now well organized and active. Central authority and unified direction however are still weak and the persistent, though understandable, restiveness of local and regional unions are not yet counterbalanced by the authority of the national leaders. In a sense Algeria's trade union movement reflects the politics of the country.

* * *

A brief reference to the most recent events in Maghrib trade unionism is in order. A few dramatic turns and sharp political encounters notwithstanding, Moroccan politics retained their familiar character and so did the posture of the UMT. Following serious riots in Casablanca, in which many workers were involved but which the UMT did not actively generate, the king exercised his constitutional power to dissolve the Parliament in June 1965. Then a "rightist" royal government stole "leftist" thunder by nationalizing export trade. At the same time, evidence suggested that the king was placating the left in order to form a government of national union. While rumors of palace-left wing rapprochement were afloat, UNFP's exiled leader Mehdi Ben Barka was apparently kidnapped in Paris, presumably by his conservative opponents who feared an opening to the left. In this background of continuing unstable pluralism the UMT has cautiously but consistently maintained its posture of autonomy from political parties and of opposition to the government.

In Algeria the trends discussed earlier were somewhat confirmed at the second UGTA congress in March 1965. After considerable discussion and an agonizing public re-appraisal of their failures, the participants accomplished three major tasks:

(1) They realistically defined the relationship of the union with the party as an affiliate "national organization representing the workers" devoted to the "achievement of FLN goals as stated in the Charter of Algiers."

(2) A program was outlined which stressed the necessity of

guarding against risks of bureaucratization, sought to promote decentralized communal reforms and self-management in enterprises while discouraging etatism, and called for union participation in the elaboration and execution of programs for economic development.

(3) The congress elected a new and perhaps a more representative Central Secretariat which included several leaders who had been eliminated by the party at the 1963 congress and others who had shown qualities of leadership at the regional and local levels. Despite President Ben Bella's reported advice, no one from the out-going Secretariat was re-elected. After the congress, the new leaders were touring the country recruiting rural and urban workers and reactivating existing locals. Their efforts were reported to be bearing fruit. Its greater representativeness and the fact that it was not backed by Ben Bella's men will, hopefully, help the union's relationship with the ruling Revolutionary Council. UGTA's response to the coup d'état was measured and reserved. It waited more than a week to criticize the cult of personality, and while giving support to the new regime its communique stressed UGTA commitment to the policy of "self-management." Subsequent statements by the new Secretary General, Mouloud Oumeziane, suggest a desire to develop a union capable of carrying on a dialogue with and within the party, and to lend support to a regime in accordance with its ability to carry out the Charter of Algiers.

The UGTT faced what may well be the greatest crisis of its history and one from which neither the trade union nor the political system are likely to recover easily. The trends already noted in this chapter came to a climax in July, 1965 when the government and the party decided that the time had come to reduce the union to an instrument only of policy execution and not of aggregation and representation of even the most pressing interests of its membership. Three major reasons seem to underlie the decision to rid the UGTT of all traces of autonomy. The first is the conviction of President Bourguiba and his immediate associates that they are the repository of Tunisia's national interest and therefore their policies reflecting the interests of the nation need only to be faithfully implemented. Moreover, to admit the existence of class interests appears to deny the force of nationalism and interferes with the "collective conscience" essential for eliciting the sacrifices needed for development.

Second, the UGTT insofar as it provided an actual (as against formal) institutional framework for the expression of dissent, became increasingly galling to the party whose authoritarian tissues have been hardening since the congress of 1958 and which at its last congress (October 1964) was invested with additional autocratic and elitist characteristics. That the UGTT, through the expansion of its cooperatives and social works program was strengthening its autonomous roots made it all the more suspect with the party which was driving toward a total monopoly of power.

Third, to a group of planners and to a President who is wholeheartedly committed to a planned program of rapid economic development, anyone who questions, however mildly, the government's economic policies appears to threaten national goals and therefore deserves punishment. In a sense this attitude is a function also of the cohesion and unity which is so prized for Tunisia by its leaders as well as scholars.

The events leading to the imprisonment of Habib Achour, exile of Ahmad Tlili and the purging of UGTT started in September 1964. The Administrative Council of the union had then demanded wage increases to compensate for the steep rise in cost of living following devaluation of the dinar. At the party congress Bourguiba deplored the "Khobzists" (bread and butter unionists) whose "short sighted view prevents them from rallying to the party . . . . in other words, from joining those who are imbued with the spirit of self-sacrifice." He was critical of union cooperatives—"I tell them that before constructing hotels and housing they should awaken the conscience . . . and prepare them to work for the good of the nation." He reminded the trade unionists who belonged to the party and "particularly those who are in the political bureau" of their "obligations to the party. It signifies belonging . . . . to a movement which is committed to serving the entire nation and not to serving the interests of a class." He deplored the persistence of obsolete trade unionists ideas acquired in the past for "today everything has changed. Nothing remains of the historical conditions which produced and nourished the perspectives, goals and methods of trade unions." Finally he warned that if "persuasion and education failed the state will use means at its disposal" to bring "recalcitrants in line with the policy of planning and investment."[37]

The trade unionists accepted this admonishment quietly and

---

37. Speeches, October 19, 20, 1965.

in public continued to reaffirm their loyalty to Bourguiba, to the party and to the labor union. At the same time, the trade union fought a defensive battle against government and party take over. In December 1964 a new law on cooperatives gave the government additional inspection and regulatory powers. Pressures on UGTT cooperatives increased as the government investigated them for alleged mismanagement and malpractices. However, evidence subsequently released by the government does not confirm earlier charges of bad management and corruption.[38] The party also tried actively to take a controlling interest in the union. When UGTT locals were electing their leaders in April 1965 the party insisted on presiding over the election meetings. In the region of Tunis the then Governor Bechir Bellagha (now the Secretary General of the UGTT) is reported to have presided over most of those meetings.

In his 1965 May Day speech Achour publicly defended UGTT's position on the devaluation question: "For twelve years we have ... exhorted you to work, to produce ... As leaders of the working class it was also our duty to note the effects [of devaluation] on the purchasing power of workers ... to caution the government ... A worker cannot labor on empty stomach; a hungry man cannot be productive. That is why we considered our demand for wage increases as being identical with the demand for increasing production." Later in the month Achour defended the union cooperatives in a speech to the fourth African Congress of the PTT International Confederation: "Their active capital has now increased to nearly two million dinars of which the largest portion goes for wages ... profits support our social works projects."[39] On May Day Achour also announced plans for an extraordinary UGTT congress with the obvious intent of obtaining a note of confidence in union leaders, an affirmation of their representativeness and legitimacy, and thus to make them less vulnerable to governmental repression.

The government needs to act before the congress. But the forthcoming PTT international conference scheduled in Tunis for May 30–June 2 made it an unfavorable time for measures against the UGTT. Bourguiba, therefore, demanded postponement of the congress. On June 21 and 25 the party Presidium

---

38. *L'Action,* July 4, 1965 lists eight UGTT cooperatives which were found guilty of "mismanagement" or "suspected of corruption" or else had been unable to return their loans on time. The UGTT then owned some forty enterprises.
39. *Maghreb,* September–October 1965, p. 19.

and the Central Committee respectively met and decided to take the offensive. Achour, who was then in charge of union cooperatives, was faced with prosecution on charges which he denied and which, he asserted, were only a pretext to curb the union and destroy its cooperatives.[40] On June 28 the National Assembly withdrew Achour's parliamentary immunity while its Vice-President Ahmad Tlili and UGTT Deputy Nouri Boudali protested vigorously. The same day his expulsion from the Political Bureau was announced. On July 2, Achour was arrested. On July 6, the local press announced that two days earlier the UGTT Administrative Council had suspended Achour and nominated Boudali as the provisional Secretary General until the congress, scheduled for July 31, elected a new leadership. No mention was made of the Committee on Discipline or the National Council which, rather than the Administrative Council, had the constitutional powers to take the action against Achour. Complaints were also heard that the decision was made by a minority of the Council membership.[41] Five of the nine members of the Executive Bureau were not present at this meeting. The rules of procedure and the principle of accountability which the UGTT had, by and large, tried so far to respect, appear to have been ignored.

The scene then shifted to Amsterdam. Ahmad Tlili who was also Vice-President of the ICFTU and a possible successor of its present Secretary General Omar Becu, received word from Tunis relieving him as the head of the Tunisian delegation to the 8th World Congress of the International Confederation. He contested the order and the ICFTU confronted two Tunisian delegations. It was an unpleasant choice. Says Professor Windmuller: "Bluntly expressed, the choice consisted of upholding trade union freedom from external controls . . . a cherished ICFTU principle . . . as against the probable disaffiliation of the UGTT. To accredit Tlili would be tantamount to condemnation of the Tunisian government. To recognize the newly designated mandatories could only be interpreted as a retreat from a fundamental principle."[42] The Confederation of Free Trade Unions decided in favor of seating the new delegation. On July 13 Tlili publicly entered into opposition of the government and declared his determination to work for democratization in Tunisia. At the end of July the

40. *Combat,* June 28, 1965.
41. *Le Monde,* July 6, 1965.
42. John Windmuller, "Cohesion and Unity in the ICFTU: The 1965 Amsterdam Congress," Unpublished Draft.

union and the party announced his expulsion from their ranks.

The UGTT special congress met on July 31, and was attended by the Secretary General of ICFTU. Bechir Bellagha, who had resigned his governorship on July 13, was chosen Secretary General by acclamation which indicates that again constitutional procedures were ignored.[43] The Administrative Council and the Executive Bureau were purged. All except one member from the old Bureau were eliminated including the interim Secretary General Nouri Boudali, UGTT's most conciliatory figure, companion of Ferhat Hached and his successor as Secretary General from December 1952–July 1954, a prominent member of the party Central Committee and governor of Cap Bon. With Tlili and Achour out he was the most likely candidate for Secretary General. But Boudali is not only a loyal Destourian. He is also a veteran trade unionist, and after his experience with Tlili and Achour President Bourguiba is perhaps wary of loyal party leaders who also have strong trade union ties. Boudali's vote against the withdrawal of Achour's parliamentary immunity and his cautious defense of a union cooperative scheme and union autonomy during the interim period must also have made him unacceptable to the government.[44] The new Secretary General had been active in the UGTT during the 1945-55 period when the party was often clandestine. Since 1956 he was not known to have taken any interest in the union.

At the opening of the congress President Bourguiba told the delegates that in the battle for development it is "vital for people to accept a discipline as strong as military discipline."[45] He told the new union officials that "The prerogative of speaking on questions of national interest belongs to the party and the party alone." He said "in Tunisia there is no working-class distinct from a non-working class. We are all workers. We must eliminate parasites wherever they appear. Those guilty will be sent to the Camps of El-Haouareb or will be re-educated."[46] These are the hardest words the UGTT had from the President who had always singled it out as a historic and most important national organization.

It is difficult to foretell the future of the UGTT. Since 1956 it has been losing its most experienced and prestigious leadership.

---

43. *La Presse*, August 3, 1965. *Le Monde*, August 3 reported that Bellagha received 191 out of 197 votes which indicates there was some form of voting.
44. See *La Presse*, July 7, 1965.
45. Speech, July 31, 1965.
46. Speech, August 2, 1965 while receiving the new Administrative Council.

This latest crisis has deprived it of its last major leaders. It is now in the hands of second-rate men who have neither the experience, nor the stature to stand up to senior government and party officials unless the latter encourage them to do so. Their present attitudes do not promise such a policy. There is, however, some reason to hope that Bourguiba himself might rescue the UGTT. A flexible and pragmatic politician, he might see the need for permitting a measure of dissent and the usefulness of occasional consumptionist relaxation for economic growth. (In September Ben Salah announced substantial wage increases in the near future). The president has in the past secured the services of those who had differed with him. Most recently Mohammed Masmoudi, expelled from the Political Bureau in 1961, was readmitted and nominated to the Central Committee. It is likely that he would want Tlili and Achour to return to the party and the union. There is yet another possibility which may create an environment free and favorable enough for the UGTT. Some Tunisians, like Tlili, wish to work for the democratization of Tunisia as defined by Bourguiba. If Bourguiba, like Ataturk whom he so admires, sees the need for introducing a loyal and constructive opposition through his faithful yet independent minded colleagues he would probably meet with a greater success than did Ataturk; and this might save Tunisia considerable turmoil in the future.

BIBLIOGRAPHY

Since the publications of Tahar al-Haddad's work in 1925 no book has been published on the Maghrib's trade unions. The best sources of information are the publications and Congress reports of the unions. These include the trade union organs—*Al-Shaab* (Tunis), *L'Avant Garde* (Morocco) and *Al-Ommal* (Algiers). The following is a list of the scant material available in print:

Ashford, Douglas E., "Transitional Politics in Morocco and Tunisia," in *Current Problems in North Africa*, The Princeton University Conference. December, 1959.

Ashford, Douglas E., *Political Change in Morocco*. Princeton, Princeton University Press, 1961. Chapter IX.

Berenguier, H., "Le Syndicalisme Marocain." *L'Afrique et L'Asie* I-trim; 53, 1961, pp. 25-36.

Bourguiba, Habib, "Le Syndicalisme Tunisien de M'Hamed Ali al Ferhat Hached." *Le Temps Moderne*, Vol. 9, no. 96, November 1953.

Denis, A. "Problèmes du Syndicalisme au Maroc." *Cahiers de la République.* Nov.-Dec. 1958, pp. 89-99.

Despax, M., "Observations Sur le Droit du Travail Tunisien depuis L'Independence." *IBLA,* XXIV, 1961, pp. 379-389.

Fischer, George, "Syndicats et Décolonisation." *Presence Africaine,* October 1960-January 1961, pp. 17-60.

al-Haddad, Tahar, *Al-Ummal al-Tunisiyun wa Dhuhur al-Harakat al-Naqabiyya,* Tunis, 1925.

Halpern, Manfred, *Politics of Social Change in the Middle East and North Africa.* Princeton, Princeton University Press, 1963. Chapter 15.

I.L.O., *Labor Survey of North Africa.* Geneva, International Labor Office, 1960.

Lacouture, Jean and Simonne, *Le Maroc A L'Epreuve.* Paris, Editions du Seuil, 1958. Chapter XII.

Lacouture, Jean, "Au Maghreb, Les Organisations Ouvrières Participant à La vie Politique." *Le Monde Diplomatique,* March 12, 1963.

Lambert, Bovy, "Histoire du Mouvement Syndicale nord-ouest Africain." *Africa* (Rome) Vol. XVIII, no. 3. May-June 1963, pp. 123-131.

Lewis, William H., "The New Nomadism in North Africa." *Middle East Journal.* Summer 1957, Vol. II, no. 3. pp. 269-281.

Meynaud, Jean and Anisse Salah Bey, *Le Syndicalisme Africain.* Paris, Edition Payót, 1963.

8
The Rural System of the Maghrib

Jacques Berque

Let us define a rural system as the organization—diversified and subject to evolution—of relations between human groupings and their land. These relations can take many forms and operate at many levels. We shall try, here, to study them from the standpoint of a system of land ownership, which is itself inseparable from the physical setting and methods of land utilization. Since these elements change with the vicissitudes of environment and history, the situation under study will vary both in its individual terms and in their relation to one another. The present period in North Africa exhibits this variation to an acute degree. Observation reveals, among a great tumult of passions and efforts, the application of—or at least a search for—social reforms and economic innovations that will meet the demands of both hunger and justice. Since the violence of such a major change overshadows all previous developments, it may mislead analysis into dissociating contemporary events from their near antecedents and from their fundamental bases. To avoid this error, one must always keep in mind certain constants of the rural Maghrib and the contribution of the legal systems which dominated it in succession. Only under this condition can one identify reality correctly.

ECOLOGICAL CONSTANTS AND PLURALITY OF CIVILIZATIONS

Located in the sub-arid Mediterranean zone, the whole of the Maghrib is subjected to a climate which deprives the major part of its soil of the annual 12 inches of rain necessary for the dry-farming of grains. Two types of land are therefore in a privileged situation: the plains and hills close to the shoreline on the one hand, the irrigated zones on the other.

These are the places where social activity reaches its maximum:

intensive and diversified production, culminating in vine, fruit, and wheat growing; individualized use of energy and active mobilization of agricultural resources. Here, private property can be defined according to one or the other of two types of law—or according to some intermediate formula: 1) the Islamic type (*milk*) whose area of application has progressively shrunk as a result of the extension of its rival; 2) a modern type, born of colonial legislation and based on procedures clearly defining title and boundaries (land registration in Tunisia and Morocco, "*francisation*" in Algeria).

In contrast to these forms of land property, extensive land utilization is the rule in the wide zone subject to irregular or insufficient rains. This calls for a looser appropriation of the land and a preponderance of animal husbandry that becomes increasingly marked as one goes farther south.

This second sector was, in the traditional Maghrib, the center of tribal life; and it is still one of underdevelopment. In the course of the last century, it suffered not only from its own difficulties, but also from a sort of typological "disgrace." Economic dominance, whether it followed the colonist or the *fellah*, was shifting from the steppe, the high plateaus, and the desert to urban activities and coastal farming. This was enough to upset the balance and the process of exchange between coast and hinterland, between agriculture and cattle raising, between individualism and group solidarity, all of which must have characterized the Maghrib before French intervention. In particular, the annual cycle of herd migrations (transhumance), from the Sahara to the coast, or from the mountain to the plain, often contributed a certain rhythm of life and a factor of integration. Since the colonial phase coincided with the propagation of industrial civilization and social dispersion, the disequilibrium which it introduced seems just as irreversible as its technical contributions. The North African states are still too young to have shown thus far a capacity or even a desire to bring a fundamental change into this situation. It is always in the direction of more intensive economic relations that independent countries see progress—it could not be otherwise. But the accent is sometimes put on the necessity of integrating again into the privileged regions the somewhat "forgotten" South.[1] It is true that the regional imbalance worries economists. Yet they do not transpose, in terms of modern techniques and

1. For example, by the *Rapport Economique* of the Sixth Congress of the *Union Générale Tunisienne du Travail* (UGTT), September 1956.

organization, the extensive forms of land use and the examples of group solidarity which, in the past, matched in their own way the physical realities of the country.

To show the permanency of these factors is not to reduce the importance of the geographical, historical, and cultural discontinuities which characterize the Maghrib. The recent or remote past of the region, as well as its present, shows a pattern of successive renewals, of conflicts between norms, of breaks in institutions and behaviors. Early ethnology easily classified these patterns into three groups:

1. A "primitive" one, generally called Berber, viewed as the substratum.

2. Another, Islamic and Oriental, reflecting the intervention of a conquering culture that came along the twin paths of urban civilization and tribal invasion.

3. A modernization of the Western type which can be imputed to the negative or positive effects of French intervention.

Much could be said about this classification, but, to be brief, it evolves from too simple a vision: a stratification buttressed by value judgments, all too firmly tied to the vicissitudes of the power structure. The analysis of Maghrib societies requires, not a distinction between what may be "Berber," "Arab," or "French," but criteria that would trace, with respect to the Maghrib personality, the greater or lesser coherence or dynamism achieved in the integration of heterogeneous characteristics and in the response of a group to its milieu. If this is the correct point of view, we have two possible ways of classifying social facts in North Africa.

First, one would attempt to group the facts in more or less organized sets, according to their degree of relative consistency, whether they have a territorial basis (e.g., the farm community of the Tunisian Sahel) or are tied to an institutional function (e.g., the *fiqh* or "Muslim law"). Second, the facts would be viewed in terms of the several levels at which collective endeavor stands with respect to its material foundations. The distinction would thus be between:

1. An ecological level, to which can be assigned a number of elementary economic behaviors and juridical forms.

2. The level of cultural elaboration which may indeed, in its pure state, reach into Arabo-Berber or French institutions, but which materializes commonly as a complex amalgam, diversely accentuated and qualified according to what is contained in the given situation.

3. A level of legislative action, which evolves in part from the above acquisitions, in part, and mainly, from an attempt, more or less informed, at acting on situations. It is at this third level that governmental action belongs, face to face with the conditioning imposed by the physical and social milieu. It is the level of the citizen, of the plaintiff, and of the judge, and this level is too often the only one reached by observation. But it could in no case be understood without reference to the underlying levels: the level of dialogue between group and country on one hand, and that of conflict or contamination between competing cultures on the other.

SIGNIFICANT FORMS OF LAND TENURE[2]

Where, in the rural Maghrib, the precariousness of climate and other unfavorable factors still uphold the tradition and convenience of extensive farming, certain types of tenure translate this reality into institutions and mores.

Where the group, with its burden of conformism, indifferentiation, and solidarity, outweighs individual initiative, collective tenure outweighs private property. Whether the system is tied to habits of group crop rotation or, more frequently, to the primacy of grazing, or even to job insecurity, communal structures then develop and thrive, in which the true concern of the law is the group itself (*jemaᶜa*). The *blad l'jemaᶜa*, "collective land," thus reappears under a multiplicity of forms over considerable areas—from Agadir to Gabes. In Algeria, it bears the significant name *blad ᶜarch*, "of the tribe," or *sabqa;* and it is under this name that positive law identifies it. This is reminiscent of certain analogous forms in the Near East, where they are called *muchaᶜ*, "collective"—in Syria, for example.[3] There, this concept almost always merges with that of state domanial land, which the term *miri*, "of the prince," conveys. This domanial status, the origin of which is the subject of an age-old controversy in Muslim law, can be considered as the original clay from which, by way of "vivification," *ihya'*, and of state concessions, individual acquisition was born. This evolution is still traceable, and its stages can be dated with precision in the case of Egypt all through the 19th century. Colonial legislation had available some special procedures

---

2. J. Berque, "Droit des Terres et Intégration Sociale au Maghreb," *Cahiers Internationaux de Sociologie* (1958).
3. Where they have been studied particularly by Latron and Weulersse.

(*"enquête partielle"* type in Algeria) to favor, or more exactly to control, this shift from the collective to the individual, but it is so far from being completed that a country like Morocco still has six million hectares in collective land, out of which one-tenth can probably be recorded as wheat land.

Such an indistinct system, favoring the assertion of rival claims, could only generate a development—depending on the vicissitudes of the economy and of the power structure—leading either toward a collective statute, to which immense areas have indeed been subjected, or toward some other statutes under which the occupying collectivity would enjoy no more than a usufruct. In the latter case, evolution has been either toward a true domanial pattern or to a form of *latifundia,* where the former concept merges with that of *iqta͑* or "concession."[4]

In reality, the large manorial holdings, in a form which itself carries special names: *͑azib* (Morocco), *͑azel* (Constantine), *henchir* (Tunisia), balanced the expansion of what was an archaic capitalism, the monopolization of provincial power, and the development of a land use tied to ownership of cattle, rental income, and plowing capacity (*zuja*). A precarious system, based on very loose ties between an absentee landlord and an underemployed worker, constituting only a fragile and scattered form of land utilization—such was the picture at the time the colonist settled. He often proceeded (in Tunisia for instance) to substitute for the previous loose (often absentee) ownership, an implantation that was more productive, but also much more deadly with regard to the former tenants.[5] This was the source of many conflicts.

It also happened at times that the subject around which appropriation crystallized was neither prince nor rich man, but a person drawing his power from religious prestige (*marabout*) or an impersonal religious or ritual symbol: monastery (*zawiya*), or "pious foundation." The latter tenure, called *habous* in the Maghrib (*waqf* in the Near East) has experienced many vicissitudes. In several cases, it has eventually been absorbed by the state domanial system (Algeria, Egypt) or has been turned over to the tenants (Tunisia, 1956). At the beginning of colonization, it assumed considerable importance, to the extent of covering one-third of total landed property in certain countries.

---

4. In Egypt at the time of Mohammed Ali, it was the *iltizam,* or "tax farm on state land." It is in Iraq, due to political circumstances, that this evolution is least advanced.

5. This substitution has been examined, in North Tunisia, by J. Poncet.

Collective, large domain, and "foundation" constituted three forms of land tenure, which were tied to a still extensive agriculture and closely adapted to ecological requirements as well as to the transitory vicissitudes of the milieu. The rural history of the Maghrib has been in large part a back and forth movement between these three forms, and notably between the domanial claims of the state and those of the tribe. What all three forms had in common was the distinction between a dominion right, *raqaba*, devolving to a political or religious master, and a right of usufruct, *tasarruf*, more or less precariously held by the peasant. In the colonial period, these conditions could not fail to appear inappropriate for productive land utilization, a process that requires active use of mortgage credit. As a result, the colonial legislator viewed these ancient tenures as anachronisms. Even more frequently, he liked to think of them simply as a mass of available land resources from which new farm operators (colonists and, to a lesser extent, native members of the new rural bourgeoisie) could draw to increase their holdings. Much loss of indigenous property resulted from this state of affairs.

This was not all. Starting with the colonial conquest, there began to develop a new, rival form of property based on fixed boundaries and intensive labor. It does indeed resemble the manorial domain in its ample dimensions and in the political influence from which it evolves and to which it aspires; but it differs radically in terms of juridical basis and economic significance. The colonial power—and this is shown in detail by the oscillations of Algerian legislation from 1830 on—was always torn between two tendencies: (1) systematic offensive or, on the contrary (2) a relatively sympathetic treatment in regard to indigenous property. The second aspect bore in Algeria an ambiguous but important fruit: the statute which consecrated the property right of the tribes on collective land (Sénatus-consulte of 1863).

The systematic offensive, on the other hand, limited itself to legalizing the eviction of the *fellah*. This process of dispossession was unfortunately carried far beyond the limits of the legal framework. Beyond the areas of official colonization, which had often drawn on former collective land, brokers and speculators brought further havoc, not always justified either by juridical decision or productive utilization. It is to these painful aspects that agrarian reforms in North Africa, either planned for the future or already carried out, are meant to bring riposte and remedy.

The form of rural property that emerged through these vicissitudes, in the hands of the colonist or of his Maghribi emulators, recalled only vaguely the classical model of property law (*milk*) in Islam. Everything conspired to make the new model—theoretically subject to ordinary civil procedure—exceptional. The goodwill of governing bodies, the mood of modern times, all clearly worked in favor of precise boundaries, exact titles, and intensive land utilization. The technical revolution, represented after 1920 by mechanical power and chemical fertilizers, accentuated further the contrast between the two systems. It provoked a real break in the rural continuity of the Maghrib: on the one hand, a property that was registered, defended by law, of European aspect even if it remained in the hands of indigenous members of the bourgeoisie, exploited with the help of advanced techniques, based on large private capital investment or on a "cooperativism" (*mutualisme*) itself monopolized by the dominant class. The *ferme* (so it is called) tends to resolve, and does resolve in many cases, the technical problems of the milieu; but it is hardly "populating." In the whole Maghrib area, it involves only thirty to forty thousand operators and employs too small a number of "permanent" workers, although, it is true, some "seasonal" ones are added periodically.

At the other extreme from this preponderant type, a multitude, clinging to small holdings on difficult terrain, maintained itself not only below the threshold of profitability, but below even that of economic survival. This museum of ancient techniques and archaic ways (as for instance the *khammessat:* sharecropping with the tenant entitled to one-fifth of the net yield) remained vigorous only in certain sectors, protected either by distance or by the roughness of the ground (for instance Kabylia), or yet, in the most favorable case, by a peculiar vitality of the local peasantry (Tunisian Sahel, Doukkala, Moroccan Chaouia). But, its statistical dominance was overwhelming.

This kind of contrast, which was not wholly the effect of colonization, had nevertheless been stretched by the latter, especially in its terminal phase, to an unbearable degree. It must be considered as one of the causes, if not of the independence movement, at least of the broad response it enjoyed among the rural masses, even though the French administration had always given them favorable political treatment because their relative archaism promised to shield them for a long time from the imperative of new ideas.

PROBLEMS OF AGRARIAN REFORMS

Whatever the responsibilities, the situation inherited by independence called for readjustments which, aside from ending the colonial relationship, would restore, or rather initiate, a healthier relationship between the groups and their milieu. This suggests the amplitude of the task, with its problems of 1) national reconstruction, 2) economic innovation, and 3) social reintegration.

The struggle for emancipation made it clear that the Maghribi people were rejecting far more than the simple fact of political dependence, and perhaps most strongly rejected was the situation in the rural districts. The fallen regime bequeathed to the new states a state of affairs for which it must assume responsibility, in the same way it had until then monopolized the principal benefits. There had indeed been some positive as well as negative sides, and any plan of action had to take account of both the one and the other. On the one hand, some obvious flaws would have to be remedied, and, on the other, a valuable technical experience ought to be drawn upon. This balancing of merits and demerits did recede, however, and will recede more and more, in the face of objective observations which may be summarized as follows:

1. The productive utilization of North African resources, until independence geared to exports, especially of wines, citrus fruit, and off-season produce, has accentuated the distortions between north and south, disorganized the balance between agriculture and animal husbandry, and sacrificed the wide areas traditionally devoted to an extensive economy, to the benefit of greater intensiveness in the circumscribed regions.

2. The depletion of Maghrib soils, caused by the excesses of "mining" type farming and by deforestation, creates a menace, the acuteness of which has been demonstrated by the recent floods of the Gharb. However, conservation projects have gone beyond the experimental stage and receive, in the general opinion, the urgent attention which they deserve.

3. Engineers have been able to develop hydraulic techniques adapted to large and small scale projects. From now on, the problems raised with respect to the agrarian reorganization which any irrigation scheme over large areas does entail, are less technical than social: on this precise, but essential point, hardly anything has been done.

4. Specific innovating projects in the areas of wheat, off-season

produce, and citrus fruit have proved their worth, but they ought not to draw the attention of legislators away from undertakings of greater social significance, such as medium-size grain-producing units or basic foodstuff production. In this regard, many economic value judgments still need revision.

5. Agricultural mechanization has won the day, even more through its psychological appeal than because of its material effectiveness, but it poses delicate problems of technical and human adaptation.

Now, all these facts have contributed, in a more or less direct way, to emphasize the inadequacy of a land tenure pattern that had the following characteristics:

1. Below the level of the traditional agricultural unit (area worked by a plowing team = about 10 hectares), Maghrib agriculture is not profitable and its preservation along traditional lines leads only to proletarization and, finally, eviction of the *fellah*. A dangerous alienation of the small peasantry is observable almost everywhere; and everywhere the crowd of landless peasants and partially employed is growing.

2. Accompanying the breaking-up of traditional land tracts, there has been at the other end of the spectrum a concentration of property in large domains. This imbalance was made worse in that an important portion of the better land (2,200,000 hectares in Algeria, 1,000,000 hectares in Morocco, and 850,000 hectares in Tunisia) was held by the colonists.

In Algeria, according to figures quoted by Michel Launay,[6] 69% of European or indigenous farm operators owned between them 15% of the aggregate area, or an average of 3 hectares each; 2.3% owned 40%, or an average of 266 hectares each.

In Morocco at the present time (without reference to the colonial period), the average area of farm properties is 7 hectares; 5 to 10% of the operators own 60% of the land, 50 to 55% hold less than 40%; and 40% own at most a small tract under 0.5 hectares.

In Tunisia, in the Sahel, an olive region untouched by Europeans, 22% of the farmers occupy 66% of the land. In the Cap Bon area, 25% of the owners have 75% of the land at their disposal. These proportions would be, respectively, 6% and 30% for the Kef province, 2% and 40% for that of Souk al Arba, 2.3%

---

6. Michel Launay, *Paysans Algériens: La Terre, la Vigne et les Hommes* (Paris: Editions du Seuil, 1963), pp. 61ff.

and 33% for the region of Tunis, Mateur, Bizerte, and Medjez al Bab.

The necessity for an agrarian reform in the three North African countries arises therefore not from ideological or emotional requirements, which must nevertheless be taken into account, but from a context of which inequality of land distribution constitutes only one aspect, for it encompasses all conditions of social equilibrium and physical survival of the population. What is in question is not just equal distribution or productivity but the very commitment of the Maghrib people to their soil.

Naturally enough, it is as recovery from the foreign colonist, or as appropriation back from feudal owners, that an agrarian reform draws the most support and attracts the most notice in a newly emancipated country. No analysis should overlook such feelings, tied as they are to pressing demands which evoke a broad response the world over. Still, even if the moral, or even ideological, aspects of such measures cannot be dissociated from their global context, it is only by taking this global context into account that one can reach their true meaning and establish criteria to test their validity.

An agrarian reform is, or should be, first of all a procedure for reconciling man to the land around him. The relationship between the group and the land, wherever it has broken down, must be re-established by the reform. Yet, a restoration of the old Maghrib community such as it existed before the colonial regime is clearly out of the question. Industrial civilization, its instruments, its imperatives, and its promises have now penetrated the deeper layers of the bled. All the more urgent, therefore, is the necessity for new group structures in which social solidarities will become readjusted to the physical substratum, to the system of production, and to patterns of behavior. It is only too true that the proportion between human population and available space is worsening in these countries, as elsewhere in the underdeveloped world; true also that, in the territories adapted to productive utilization, there is a widening gap between population and the mass of resources than can be mobilized. Still, this imbalance does not in itself modify the permanent facets of the problem. It is by having eluded, or ignored, these demands, by having withdrawn 5,000,000 hectares of the best land to benefit only a minority, without offering a level of employment, ensuring a supply of basic commodities, or generating a way of life that could, even to a small degree, make up for the damage it had done (by again bringing into harmony the material and the human elements of the Maghrib) that colonization kept extant a vacuum through which the tide of revolution was finally to sweep. It was only bringing to an extreme form, technically more valid but psychologically less acceptable, the scandal of the indigenous *latifundia*. Thus it was normal that the forces of change should associate "colonialism" with "feudalism," (*isti°mar* with *iqta°iya*), and the aspiration toward socialism with the struggle for emancipation. Such is the stage now to be observed in North Africa.

Other arguments, of closer interests to the economist, also militate in favor of modifying the pattern of landownership. The growing mass of landless peasants and the fall of many others below the level of economic viability as individual operators, make it a matter of life or death for new governments to keep pace with demographic growth. However, the cost of the operation cannot be covered out of already insufficient savings without compromising investment. Government leaders entertain the hope that they can escape this vicious circle by compensating the effort at the expense of land reserves still in the hands of the minority. If the operation were to succeed, it would, by a single stroke, rekindle an interest in production among rural masses and would mobilize important resources which are normally tied up in archaic management and subsistence level farming. The group that will bear the cost is not numerous. If it happens, in addition, to be of foreign origin or compromised by being linked with the foreigner, the task is made even easier, or more legitimate. One can even, in the "soft" version of the procedure, nationalize some land against payment in bonds, the latter hopefully to be reinvested in industry: this is for instance what, at an early stage, Egyptian reform had counted on. Between the two extremes of straight eviction and capital transfer, all intermediary procedures are theoretically possible, and all have been or will be, at some time or another, contemplated by these new states.

A third aspect, tied to the first two, fits even more closely the mode of production and the changes which it has undergone under the impact of agricultural machinery. While the traditional community in the Maghrib combines a set of small units, each tied to its instruments of production, i.e., the harnessing unit available for plowing, the new economic unit combines an important mass of mechanical tools with matching amounts of land and capital. Both the area needed to use such equipment profitably and the investment required for its rational utilization, are indeed considerable. The colonist's mechanized farm used to represent by itself, on the average, the potential of a whole community.

PROBES AND REALIZATIONS[7]

The first problem for any socio-economic effort is to choose the sector to which it will direct its efforts. Two theses confront each other in this area, and each arms itself with technical arguments and calls forth the evidence of actual experience.

For a long time, the idea of widespread but slow popularization of techniques dominated in full the approach to indigenous agriculture. Such was the action of the *Sociétés de Prévoyance*[8] or of the *Inspections de l'Agriculture*,[9] the influence of which was supposed to extend over the whole country, with progress more or less sincerely expected in the long run. These policies had no interest in immediate results and even less in economic performance. That would have required a concentration of effort in a circumscribed area, seeking both a psychological shock and the attainment of the "take-off" stage into modern production methods. Although from 1945 on, the Moroccan *Secteurs de Modernisation du Paysanat*[10] broke with the former viewpoints, as had in its own way the *Office des Beni Amir*,[11] the farm policies followed in the last days of the French regime in Tunisia and, more clearly, in Algeria were admittedly a compromise between the two points of view.

The independence regime, interested at the same time in mass action within the rural milieu and in demonstrable results in

7. The facts given here are taken from official documents, but obviously not the commentary or interpretation.

8. *Sociétés Indigènes de Prévoyance*, or SIP. Government agencies for agricultural credit, specializing in medium-term loans to Maghrib farmers. They have functioned in Algeria since the Law of April 14, 1893, and have been extended, approximately on the same pattern, to Tunisia and Morocco.

9. *Inspections de l'Agriculture*. Provincial administrative units specializing in agricultural matters, and notably in the popularization of technology.

10. *Secteurs de Modernisation du Paysanat*. These organizational units, designed to be integrated into the customary collective management of vast agricultural surfaces on the traditional *jemʿa* model, but with the incorporation of mechanization and social action, were innovated in Morocco in 1946, on the initiative of this author and of the agricultural expert, J. Couleau. This innovation met with severe opposition from the forces of colonization, was abandoned in its spirit, and was not revived—in its essentials—until the accession of Morocco to independence.

11. *Office des Beni Amir*. Vast undertaking of the "state farm" type which developed on irrigation land in the Moroccan Tadla, integrating in the process—on a "dirigist" pattern which, at times was restlessly received—the Beni Amir and Beni Mousa tribes that owned the land.

certain sectors, was to orient its efforts toward synthesis—efforts both wider and much more intensive than those pursued in the previous period. Without abandoning the work of education and popularization, to which general and specialized agencies still apply themselves along the same lines as before, it has continued and mostly innovated, in the direction of "shock" results, paradoxically following in this the example of the colonial period. Thus, in Tunisia, the *Office de la Medjerda*[12] brings into play some avant-garde techniques and an interesting notion of redistribution of the surplus income created, for the benefit of the farmers, by the treatment of soils and their irrigation.

This is at any rate the only case until now where, as in Tunisia, a rule limiting the size of appropriated surfaces is in effect. This idea constitutes, as is well known, the basis of the Egyptian agrarian reform, the example of which has a certain impact in the North African states. Morocco is engaged in the same socioeconomic processes, concentrated on an advanced sector in the Gharb plain, i.e., the *polygone betteravier* (area of sugar beet production) of Sidi Slimane. The expansion of dam irrigation will lead to similar developments in the Doukkala, lower Moulouya, and Tadla regions. In all cases, technology recasts in instructive fashion the mode of land utilization, the habitat, and the social behavior of the affected group.

Every aspect of reform is thus linked, in the mind of the leaders, with some economic options, which are in any case under consideration because of obvious necessities. The importance of this preoccupation in fact compensates for that of emotional and ideological themes. Thus it is that Tunisia, for example, has engaged in delicate soil desalting operations, or that Morocco initiated and won, in a remarkably short time, the battle for the mechanization of agriculture. King Mohammed V personally presided over it, in an atmosphere of national unanimity, while tractors trespassed happily over the limits—until then thought of as inviolable—of individual tracts (1956). However, some gloomy spirits objected that the accent thus put on agricultural technique did not allow as much radicalism in the over-all plan. This was the time when the *Centrale d'Equipement du Paysanat*, founded in a more universal framework, was turning into just another machine warehouse. Once more, the "economic" was being

12. *Office de la Medjerda.* Important agency of agricultural modernization which functions on the land of the Medjerda Valley in Tunisia and has undertaken interesting projects of a technical, economic, and social nature.

divorced from the "social." To tell the truth, this divorce appears inevitable as long as knowledge and action, repudiating any dislocation of the whole, do not recognize their profound and reciprocal identity.

Finally, in Algeria, the last country to achieve independence, the problem of what rural areas to modernize was both resolved and posed—for it posed more questions than it resolved—by the existence of *terres vacantes,* which were infinitely more decisive for the social, economic, and political future of the country than the sectors aimed at until now by the *Paysanat*. Obviously, the technological aspect only developed here as a consequence of prior recovery from the owner.

From the soft formula, consisting in a simple repurchase of land from the holder, to the hard formula which evicts him without compensation, the Maghrib has known and will know every experience. Recovery operations, however, have not yet been extended to the large national domains, although this measure has been announced in Algeria where the most audacious experiments are to be observed.

In Morocco, on the contrary, recovery has until now only affected the lands under official colonization. This action, still far from being completed at this writing, has concerned only a few tens of thousands of hectares, taken formerly from the collective property of the tribes and awarded to the colonists under excessively favorable terms. A recent *dahir* (September 26, 1963) announced an extension of the measure, but remained silent on the subject of compensation. At any rate, this last point—in the three North African countries—seems to depend increasingly on obscure negotiations between the former home country and the emancipated nation, rather than on doctrinal concepts. Colonization thus ends up within the perspectives of public international law where it was born. This is no cause for surprise. These perspectives being subject to the vicissitudes of relations between the parties, one cannot be surprised either if, in a country like Tunisia, for instance, where the search for a "happy medium" and for skillful tactics seems to have marked government initiative from the start, the recovery of colonized land—still far from being completed—is carried out one section at a time and in response to urgencies that are sometimes tied to chance events (as one saw after the Sakiet Sidi Youssef and Bizerte incidents). More recently, the Tunisian government has taken a more radical approach in the recovery of colonial land and has shown vigorously, in the

Sahel, its will to modernize arboricultural techniques by cooperative means.

It is in Algeria that this recovery has gone the farthest, even though at the beginning, at least, not proceeding from any plan independent of chance political considerations. From the start of independence, Algeria has been faced with the problem of "vacant" lands, whose owner had left the country under the menace, real or imagined, of violent evictions. Then a few expropriations occurred, affecting notably the large domain of La Trappe, taken as symbolic of colonialism (spring 1963). At last, some internal difficulties in the fall of 1963 led President Ben Bella to nationalize the remaining foreign properties, a fact which confirms, if need be, the intimate tie between such measures and political vicissitudes or movements of opinion.

The proclamation of the principle of *autogestion* (selfmanagement) (decree of March 22, 1963) constituted a resounding innovation, but it was only organizing and legalizing an existing fact. Sometimes spontaneously, sometimes under the initiative of political or union leadership, the taking over of vacant property by groups of workers had begun as early as the fall of 1962. This experiment promptly became one of the features on which the most anger and the most hope were to fasten. The agricultural year just past has neither disarmed the one nor disappointed the other. What was a chaotic situation has been to a large degree kept from disaster by measures in which, in different ways and through various vicissitudes, the spontaneous initiative of the people and the authority of the state have come into association. The personal part taken in these beginnings by the President of the Republic and by Minister Amer Ouzegane emphasized the value which the country attached to the undertaking. The movement was thus proving itself in its progress. While important problems may have been left aside, a radical orientation had been resolved upon, sometimes against the wish of narrow specialists.

While the basic elements of the situation in the other two North African countries do not strike one as very different, the solutions proposed so far differ from the Algerian record by their amplitude, their orientation, and their degree.

Independent Tunisia has turned its attention first to disseminating some *cellules de mise en valeur* (cells of productive utilization) in the countryside, thus giving Tunisian agriculture the benefit of a technology too often reserved until then for European colonization. Then the doctrine evolved further. The Three Year Plan provides for the creation of 200 producing units covering 100,000 hectares: private lands are regrouped around a domanial core, which assumes a pilot role. Still more than a cooperative, what we have is a joint holding company, the shares of which are, in principle, exchangeable. The practice of crop rotation and the technological sharing of means of production do not erase the individualization of land tracts. The administrative leadership seems, for the time being, to give preference to educational objectives over those of an autonomy tending toward spontaneous initiative. These groupings are planned so as to ensure participants an adequate minimum income (250 dinars per family per year); the area per family is estimated at about 15 hectares. This enlargement of what is considered the minimum space requirement is without doubt a "must" from the standpoint of classical agricultural thought and of strict accounting criteria. Must we for all that give up the continued existence of a mass peasantry?

The transfer of a significant number of persons from the primary to the secondary and tertiary sectors, and from the farms to the cities, is not only an objective, but a fact which can be observed in the three countries of North Africa, similar in this to the rest of the world. This "rural exodus" does no more than shift the difficulty, moving the re-employment problem from the farm sector to the "bidonvilles" and "gourbivilles."

Let us note also that the option of Tunisian legislators in favor of private appropriation shows not only in projects affecting new economic units, but also in regard to former collective tenures. The decrees of May 21, 1958, and of May 18, 1957, extend the *milk* regime to the former lands of the pious foundations, *habous*. The law of May 10, 1959, institutes a *certificat possessoire* (ownership certificate) granted by the administrative authority to owners of collective lands: this facilitates mortgage credit, individual farm operation, and finally the private registration of the land.

There is no doubt that personal recovery of the land constitutes, in a rural society long constrained and largely dispossessed, a motivation that needs taking into account. One must revise in this respect the ideal built around what is a seemingly very sketchy collectivism. Yet it would not do for this progress along the path of psychological realism to lead into new processes of landed wealth concentration and to anarchy in production. Can the cooperative bond, the administrative leadership, and the technical solidarities on which the Tunisian experience is founded, eliminate the dangers of land fragmentation and the ever-recurring menace of inequality? Only the future will tell. The appetites of a new rural bourgeoisie, harshly repressed in Algeria, are apparent also in Tunisia, where, in the northern region at least, the lessons contributed by the colonists' techniques had a rather late but effective impact. The repurchase of machinery and, where it was possible, of land, as well as the practice of renting surplus equipment, could be observed from the first years of independence.

These same years saw, in Morocco, the "modernization" of a half million hectares of indigenous land, a phenomenon which undoubtedly reflected the accession of a rural bourgeoisie at a stage of economic expansion. It is not by chance either that one of the first actions taken after independence was to annul the *dahir* of 1946 on the *Secteurs de Modernisation du Paysanat*, thus cutting short the perspectives of collectivist utilization opened by this premature statute.

All these themes are kept alive today by the opposition in the three North African countries. Although this is not the place to insist on controversies that are still raging, the very existence of the debate underlines an apparent readiness to question existing statutes, matching the readiness to question modes of land utilization. The gropings of the legislator where he is not, as in Algeria, swept by the revolutionary tide, the urgency of the situation, the abundance of experimentation, and the controversy over results, all confirm in our view the existence of a searching effort, the very hesitations of which, when arising from a clash with conservative options, denote an open attitude toward the future. This is the case in Morocco where the discovery of the ills of agriculture causes various types of remedial suggestions to be proposed: family farms, production units of a cooperative nature, indirect large-scale operation of individual farms through some public agency, direct state operation, agricultural production cooperatives, state farms, etc. Failures in this area are obviously more numerous than successes, and this is no cause for surprise either.

TOWARD NEW RURAL INTEGRATIONS

In a general way, the problem of which unit, or rather which grouping, to help develop its productivity, faces every government action. It presents itself today under conditions that are strikingly different from those of the previous period. The responsibilities and possibilities open to the administrative apparatus have grown exceedingly since the colonial period, and the basic human background has been quite modified. The attachment to archaic ways of life yields everywhere to the need and attractiveness of more active exchanges. Traditional groupings are almost everywhere discredited, and so deeply affected by dispersion and disuse that they collapse in whole blocks. What will the new morphologies of the country be like? One can say at least that tomorrow's equilibria depend in large part on the measures brought under study today.

However shifting such a context may be, and loaded as it is with both possibilities and risks, it is the context within which actions must be taken. We once more come across the idea from which we started; the necessity for an integration or reintegration of the social group with its material activities and its territorial support. This operation which, at the national scale, is synonymous with independence, has been, we already know, vigorously conceived and pursued by the Maghrib. The same does not hold at the more modest scale of the province, in spite of many plans of regional development, and still less, for the time being, at the scale of the production unit. Besides, another debate occurs at this level: that of the interference more or less fruitful, more or less arbitrary—of the central power in the exercise of spontaneous initiative by the people. As a matter of fact, this problem occurs under a variety of forms, depending on general and local conditions, in the whole Maghrib.

The most advanced experiment, for the time being, seems to be that of the *comités de gestion* (managing boards) in Algeria. The balance sheet of their first year of operations, drawn up in October 1963, seems to bring out, among other things, two points of great theoretical and practical interest. On the one hand, it was noted that the success of the operation was attributable in large part to the structure: the size of the territory covered, its internal coherence, the validity of its economic foundations, etc. On the other hand, it appeared that the cooperation between the *comité de gestion* and the local administrative unit had not yet reached maturity.

We have seen that the problem of appropriating "vacant" property had not been resolved by the decree of March 1963. The problem comes to the fore, indirectly, too, but in explosive fashion, at the time of sharing the profits. The decree had provided for a dual assignment of income: one part going to the collectivity, the other to members of the *comité*. When the time came to apply this provision, two points of view developed, one more aware of psychological expediency and keen on giving the workers a stake in the operation, the other (which was that of the UGTA) anxious to return the surplus to society at large and notably to have it contribute to unemployment compensation. It seems that a middle way was chosen, in which workers enjoy a flat end-of-year bonus, the amount of which varies according to whether the year's operations have shown a profit or a deficit.

Beyond this debate, the problem has to do with the social ownership of this property, its function, perhaps even its definition. Were it only a matter of recovering a colonist's farm, it would be enough, while nationalizing it, to preserve its character of economic cell: wheat factory or wine factory. The less manpower employed, the more profitable the operation would be. Such is often the argument of the technical specialists. But at this moment the sociologist calls to our attention—and the grassroots leader perceives—that this simple transfer would leave intact the menace of a dissociation between the economic role and the "structuring" mission of agriculture. This dissociation, even though less irritating than in the days of the colonist, would nevertheless promise great difficulties for the future.

The audacious experiment of the *comités de gestion* must, I believe, steer away from the cult of the "precedent," and from ideological sketchiness as much as from the technological prejudices inherited from the colonization. It must, in my opinion, attempt to operate:

1. The adjustment of human density on the farm to create the maximum number of jobs, which postulates the progress of a technique of implementation of this new orientation.

2. The formation of new territorial units in which the life of the group, the structure of managerial responsibilities, the economic performance, and the evolving landscape itself would be integrated in the most active manner, achieving by the same stroke a balance between organization and spontaneous initiative.

OF A MAGHRIBIAN UTOPIA

But wouldn't that amount to reconstructing, under conditions of advanced technology and according to a new communal order, this Maghribian bled, in which so many traditional solidarities have foundered on political compromise or residual archaism? A new sort of *jemaᶜa* would then reappear, endowed with political responsibilities and creating, from the basic human clay, a new citizen. Admittedly, this perspective has not to my knowledge yet been formulated. My personal opinion is, nevertheless, that it would be adapted to what we know of reality and to the movements of history. Perhaps this vision shall not be substantiated, and others will take its place. But if I may be permitted some hypotheses, I should like in conclusion to propose a certain image of the future Maghrib.

This Maghrib would rest on three kinds of activities, themselves founded on the geographical structure and on the complementarity of ways of life and cultural vocations. The industrial sector would share with tertiary occupations a growing labor force concentrated in the cities and around well-distributed "complexes." A "wide spaces" economy would transpose the extensive system, notably animal husbandry, along lines adapted to modern productivity, and would in a general way initiate styles suitable to the steppe and to the South. Between the two, grain farming and fruit growing, tied on the one hand to animal husbandry, on the other to processing plants, would join their irreplaceable energies across a multitude of free households.

Such a vision may seem quite fanciful. At the very least, the agrarian reforms which even now are in effect or under consideration in the Maghrib, have enough in them already either to confirm or deny whatever truth it contains.

9

Political Aspects of Rural Development in North Africa

Douglas E. Ashford *

In the midst of the Algerian crisis of the summer of 1962, an official observed that "organization is the absolute weapon."[1] Chaos produces unanimity on the importance of organization, but the most difficult organizational decisions remain to be made when a new nation achieves the minimal stability needed to engage in energetic development programs. The Maghrib is rapidly emerging from the epoch of post-revolutionary disorder, and the pattern for more intensive efforts to organize human resources for development can now be detected. The analysis of how the various political systems of North Africa have responded to the challenge of reconstructing human relationships for intensive economic and social change in rural areas involves some judgments of the political forces unleashed by the revolutions of the past decade.

"Organization" will refer to the formal efforts of government to hasten development and social relationships designed to increase agricultural productivity rapidly. The term is being used to distinguish developmental efforts stemming directly from government action from more diffuse, unstructured changes in the society. Important as exposure to Western techniques and gradual social change through education, etc., may be, it has become increasingly apparent that few African or Asian countries are content to undergo national reconstruction by the slow accumulation of new habits and goals over generations. In the Maghrib, as in most developing countries, the government has actively inter-

---

*The travel and research for this article was made possible by the Joint Committee on the Near East of the SSRC and ACLS, to which the author is grateful. Neither organization shares the responsibility for errors or opinions stated therein.

1. *Jeune Afrique,* July 16-22, 1962.

vened in the development process with formal organizations that will hopefully encourage, cajole, and persuade the citizen to enter rapidly into more productive, specialized roles.

The political system must generate the impulse for change and direct human resources into constructive channels. In the area of political choice optimum alternatives are obscure, the resources of a human being are difficult to measure, and the final decision may be heavily influenced by very reasonable, but totally incalculable concerns. Thus, from the beginning this inquiry assumes that there are no panaceas and that each country must seek its own solution to the imponderables of human reorganization for developmental purposes.

A developing country's ability to gain the confidence of its people and to communicate to them the essentials of the complex tasks to be performed does not rest on its material resources. In monetary terms Libya is by far the most generously endowed country of the Maghrib, but it faces rural problems that are probably unparalleled in scale and complexity in the whole area. Tunisia is certainly the poverty-stricken member of the North African community, but the determination and ingenuity of the Neo-Destour have gone far toward overcoming material handicaps. Morocco has displayed great caution in embarking on experiments in rural reorganization, while Algeria has turned to some extremely radical innovations whose outcome remains in doubt. It would be foolish to predict universal success or failure in any of these cases, but each represents a response based on an essentially incalculable judgment of how human beings can learn and work in a rapidly changing environment.

In analyzing approaches to rural development in the Maghrib, the most important factor is the existing government's orientation to change itself. Lest this become a platitude, it should be added that the general characteristics of complex organizations assisting development can be specified. In addition, their relation to political forces in each country and their implications for the existing regime can often be anticipated with relative ease. The qualities of an intricate organizational structure can be phrased in either psychological or sociological terms. A good deal of speculation about developmental problems has already suggested the major characteristics of such complex organizations.[2] By virtue of

---

2. See Joseph La Palombara (ed.), *Bureaucracy and Political Development* (Princeton: Princeton University Press, 1963) for a survey of progress in different regions of the world. The attitudinal implications have been explored in Lucian

our individual involvement in a modern society we all have a crude knowledge of such problems, though there remains a vast amount of research to relate our common sense to developmental efforts.

The nature of the transformation can perhaps be most easily summarized by noting the extent to which highly intricate relationships become self-regulating in a highly organized society. Quite regardless of the ideological choice to be made, the participants in complex organizations display a remarkable capacity to absorb information, to evaluate its relevance to their tasks, and to adapt their behavior to such innovations as may be indicated by new knowledge.[3] The tendency for social organization to become hierarchically stratified and functionally specific has been noted repeatedly. The defined structural characteristics of modern organizations enable the individual to play specialized roles in a wide variety of activities, to transfer his skills and learning to various endeavors, and to introduce adaptations on the basis of experience.

Each government's orientation to dealing with self-regulating and self-sustaining activity has, of course, been different. How the challenge of dealing with a less calculable society is received is an important indicator of the social and political development to follow. The variations in the government's response can be largely explained by the political style of the regime itself. Indeed, the Maghrib is probably one of the most fertile areas of the world for the comparative study of developmental responses. The North African countries have been endowed with very different political vehicles in order to mobilize a rural population that reflects many

---

W. Pye, *Politics, Personality and Nation Building* (New Haven: Yale University Press, 1962); and also Gabriel A. Almond and Sidney Verba, *The Civic Culture: Political Attitudes and Democracy in Five Nations* (Princeton: Princeton University Press, 1963).

3. For example, see O. J. Harvey, David E. Hunt, and Harold M. Schroder, *Conceptual Systems and Personality Organization* (New York: John Wiley, 1961); and Milton J. Rosenberg, et al., *Attitude Organization and Change: An Analysis of Consistency Among Attitude Components* (New Haven: Yale University Press, 1960). For a theoretical treatment of the social implications of these organizational changes, see S. N. Eisenstadt, "Sociological Aspects of Political Development in Underdeveloped Countries," *Economic Development and Cultural Change*, V (1957), pp. 289-307, and Eisenstadt, "Modernization and Conditions for Sustained Growth," *World Politics*, XVI, No. 4 (1964), 576-594. Essentially, I am suggesting that in order to interrelate political factors with development in manageable form, one might focus initially on how new organizational devices of various governments reflect the needs and interest of the régime itself.

similar cultural and historical conditions. Each of these governments is actively engaged in development and has established a wide variety of organizations to mobilize the energies and talents of the rural sector.[4]

With the foregoing general thoughts in mind the government's approach to rural change and reorganization will be examined. In the first step, the decision to engage in a large scale national reconstruction effort will be reviewed. Secondly, some comments will be made on how the changes emanating from the planning activity have affected the peasants. The aim will be to show how efforts to organize unexploited human resources contrast according to the type of regime. In conclusion, some tentative conclusions will be drawn on future prospects for development based on the approach to rural development manifested in each country.

Despite the almost universal support for more intensive planning activity, nearly every developing country has experienced great difficulty in settling down to an explicit plan that embodies applicable guidelines for national reconstruction. Of all the North African countries, only Tunisia now possesses such a plan, and Tunisian progress has been the product of prolonged political dispute. The Neo-Destour has been ostensibly committed to serious planning since the 1955 Sfax Party Congress, which explicitly charged the political bureau with the "elaboration of a national program of economic expansion and social progress."[5] But Bourguiba was preoccupied in much of 1956 in eliminating Youssefite opposition to the regime, and in reducing the social appeal of Islamic sentiments.[6] In a report that characterized the

---

4. The following analysis will omit general consideration of the background of each of the four North African countries. On Morocco see the author's *Political Change in Morocco* (Princeton: Princeton University Press, 1961); and I. William Zartman, *Morocco: Problems of a New Power* (New York: Atherton Press, 1964). On Tunisia, see Charles Micaud, Leon Carl Brown, and Clement Moore's *Tunisia: The Politics of Modernization* (New York: Praeger, 1963). North Africa has also been covered in three survey volumes: Nevill Barbour (ed.), *A Survey of North West Africa (The Maghrib)* (2nd ed. London: R.I.I.A., 1962); Charles F. Gallagher, *The United States and North Africa* (Cambridge: Harvard University Press, 1963); and I. William Zartman, *Government and Politics in Northern Africa* (New York: Praeger, 1963).

5. Neo-Destour Party, *Les Congrès du Neo-Destour* (Tunis, 1958), p. 79. In the 1964 Bizerte Congress, the party adopted the name, Constitutional Socialist Party.

6. Salah Ben Youssef was Secretary General of the Neo-Destour before Tunisian independence, and came under Nasser's influence during the organization to the North African resistance in the early 50's. As the major spokesman for Arab socialism, he strongly opposed Bourguiba's gradualist policies, and allied himself

government's planning effort as "small and derisory," the UGTT *(Union Générale des Travailleurs Tunisiens)* Congress of late 1956 called for a major governmental reorganization to permit effective, comprehensive planning.[7] The inspiration for the proposal came from Ahmad Ben Salah, who has since quite appropriately become Secretary of State for Planning and Finance. Before assuming the post, however, he was rather forcefully detached from the independent support available to him as Secretary General of the labor unions, and served three years' penance as Secretary of State for Public Health, a job which he dispatched with his customary energy and ingenuity.

Although Bourguiba has been well aware of the economic misery of his country, it was not until 1961 that he committed himself to serious planning and reinstated Ben Salah. Indicative of the dissatisfaction was the report of the 1960 UGTT Congress, which noted that the rudimentary National Planning Council formed in 1958 had never met over the past two years.[8] At this time Bourguiba was still thinking in terms of a virtually unchallenged party leader, and there is little evidence that he had begun to reformulate his views on the reorganization of Tunisian society. It is important to note his political position when the crucial decision was made in 1961. A little over a year before he had emerged victorious and virtually unopposed in national elections. In 1959, the Neo-Destour was reorganized on highly centralized lines according to his wishes.[9] Despite occasional rumblings from the workers, the UGTT was firmly allied with the Neo-Destour.

---

with more conservative Islamic elements who also distrusted France. For a brief account see Charles Debbasch, *La République Tunisienne* (Paris: Librairie Générale de Droit et de Jurisprudence, 1962), pp. 126-136 and pp. 141-151. Also, Charles Micaud, *et al., Tunisia: The Politics of Modernization,* pp. 89-101. The major alternatives for leadership in this period are analyzed in their revolutionary meaning in the author's "Tunisian Leadership and the 'Confiscated Revolution'" *World Politics* (January 1965).

7. "Rapport Economique," *6ème Congrès National de l'UGTT,* September 20-23, 1956, pp. 7-8. This report compares dramatically with the subdued observations of the UGTT when it again came under Neo-Destour auspices. See *Rapport d'Activité: 8ème Congrès National,* April 1-3, 1960, p. 24.

8. Union Générale des Travailleurs Tunisiens, *Sur le Chemin du Développement* (Tunis, n.d. [1960]), p. 31. There were, of course, reservations by middle-class Tunisians at even this preliminary stage. See Union Tunisienne de l'Industrie et du Commerce, *Vème Congrès National: Rapport Economique,* October 28-30, 1960, pp. 10-15.

9. The reorganization of the Neo-Destour in 1959 is discussed in Clement Henry Moore, "The Neo-Destour Party of Tunisia: A Structure for Democracy?" *World Politics,* XIV, No. 3 (April 1962), 461-482. On the recent changes, see "Le Néo-Destour repense ses Structures," *Jeune Afrique,* March 11-17, 1963.

Only then was Ben Salah permitted to form the super-ministry for planning purposes and to fill the job description he had written for himself some five years before.

Perhaps the most fascinating aspect of the Tunisian response has been the mobilization of the single party's forces to provide support. First, all the most influential Neo-Destourians were convened early in 1961 in a seldom-used body, the Economic and Social Council.[10] Additional meetings were held with the party's auxiliary organizations. In the fall of 1961, the party went to the grass roots of the society, and Bourguiba's doctrine of "Neo-Destourian Socialism" emerged. The original version of his new policy is a skillful combination of the political and material rewards to be obtained from planning. The president called for discipline, appealed to individual dignity, and firmly condemned active opposition in the form of hoarding or dishonesty. Lastly, he stoutly defended Ben Salah, still regarded with suspicion by merchants and militant Neo-Destourians. Shortly after Masmoudi's removal, the new minister received the ultimate recognition of being appointed to the party's political bureau.[11]

Both the *Perspectives Décennales* (1962-1971) and the *Plan Triennal* (1962-1964) placed emphasis on the "disinherited regions" of the south, and on measures to improve living conditions in the entire country. The organizational measures to exploit collective tribal lands and state lands, and to provide marketing and credit structures were presented in an integrated fashion.[12] The Tunisian experience is important evidence of how controversial massive attempts to reorganize a society can be in even well-organized, politically-united countries. Very early in

10. Although mentioned in Article 58 of the Tunisian Constitution, the Council was not organized until the country became committed to development activity. See *Journal Officiel de la République Tunisienne*, no. 2, 104e année, "Décret-loi no. 61-4 du 16 janvier 1961 (28 *redjeb* 1380), instituant un Conseil Economique et Social," p. 69, for additional details.

11. Masmoudi represents a school of opinion very like the Western liberal tradition in its emphasis on civil rights and individualism. The conflict with Bourguiba came to a head in the fall of 1962 in a controversy aired in *Action Africaine*, October 7-18, 1961, on the theme of *pouvoir personnel*. Masmoudi was removed for his indiscretion and thinly veiled opposition to Bourguiba's methods. See also *Le Monde*, November 18, 1961.

12. The notion of the "disinherited regions," meaning the semi-arid and arid southern half of Tunisia, appears repeatedly in Tunisian political and social literature. It was a major aspect of the 1956 UGTT proposals, influenced, in part, by the large numbers of miners and port workers in the south. The idea appears again in the *Perspectives Décennales*. Since many of the *fellagha* came from the south and were influenced by Ben Youssef, this concern has political significance. The slow pace of efforts to ameliorate conditions in the south was related to the discontent behind the attempt on Bourguiba's life.

1962 it appeared that many Tunisians had "certain reserves, and some reticence," concerning the plan.[13] Although the president had promised the National Assembly that the plan would not be imposed "by force, propaganda or insult, but by Tunisia's success alone," it was obvious that restrictions on importing, new organizations for marketing dates, olive oil, and other commodities, and plans to reorganize transport would strike heavily at middle-class support for the Neo-Destour.[14] Most important of the repercussions was the realization, partly brought about by the attempt on Bourguiba's life, that the Neo-Destour itself must somehow accommodate the more complex organizational forms concomitant with planning.

Early in 1963 the president announced that the party would revive the provincial councils of the Neo-Destour, which would work in cooperation with the governors. It was admitted that the political commissioners had sometimes clashed with the governors, and handicapped regional development efforts.[15] The new councils for each province were to include officers of Neo-Destour cells, chairmen of the municipal councils,[16] representatives of the auxiliary organizations, as well as government officers. The new organization for participation is an interesting manifestation of the cumulative effects of rapid development and the political repercussions of building a more complex society. It is also an indication of the caution that even a seriously committed government exercises in establishing new organizational links between locally rooted groups and the government.

Tunisian determination to reconstruct the country even at the price of reorganizing the Neo-Destour contrasts sharply with Moroccan experience. Though much more richly endowed than

13. *Jeune Afrique,* March 26-April 2, 1962.
14. The developmental reorganization under Ben Salah also had an impact on the *fellagha,* and contributed to discontent over 1962. As in Morocco, many guerrillas were given lucrative transport licenses. An important aspect of the plan was to consolidate and improve transportation services by bringing small firms under some sort of central supervision. For a frank exposition on the problems of assimilating the resistance movement see Habib Bourguiba, *Analysis of the Plot* (Speech of January 18, 1963), Tunis, Secretary of State for Information, 1963.) See also *Jeune Afrique,* April 1-7, 1963.
15. A comparison of Moroccan and Tunisian early policy toward local councils is the author's "Local Reform and Social Change in Morocco and Tunisia," in *Emerging Africa,* ed. William H. Lewis (Washington: Public Affairs Press, 1963), pp. 113-127.
16. *New York Times,* March 14, 1964. For more details see *Journal Officiel de la République Tunisienne,* No. 60, 107e année, "Loi no. 63-54 du 30 décembre 1963 (14 *chaabane* 1383), relative aux Conseils du Gouvernorat," pp. 1873-1875.

Tunisia, the Moroccan monarchy has probably lost ground over the past two years.[17] To some extent the creation of more intricate organizational ties among the populace represents the classical threat to the monarchical regime, although substantial progress had been made under Mohammed V. Under the urgings of the Istiqlal left wing, now largely absorbed into the UNFP, (*Union Nationale des Forces Populaires*) a super-ministry was set up in late 1956, well before similar action in Tunisia. From 1956 to 1960 under Bouabid, planning was merged with a super-ministry for economic affairs, although it never received the forceful impetus given planning in other North African countries.[18] The attempt to create an integrated planning agency with popular support did not take place until 1957, and the Superior Planning Council held few sessions until 1959. By then, differences between traditional leaders and the progressive wing of the Istiqlal had erupted, in part because the younger leaders wanted to press the King for more substantial delegations of power to engage in developmental activity.[19]

The 1959 meetings were discouraging. Bouabid noted the group's "complete indifference" to problems of financing the interim plan and their failure to utilize programs for grass-roots involvement. One could be more sanguine over the Moroccan approach if any opposition group had been successful in working with the King. However, the same complaints were made by Douiri, the more conservative Istiqlal minister who replaced Bouabid in 1960.[20] After the Istiqlal broke completely with

17. This criticism could be substantiated in several ways, but refers here specifically to the lowered organizational capacity of the Moroccan régime reflected in the fragmentation of the parties, the decline of the labor unions, the failure to build on the rural commune system introduced in 1958, and the dismantling of national planning offices. Since 1962, the king has found it difficult to get support from political leaders, and has relied heavily on Palace functionaries for cabinet posts. The deterioration of the Moroccan situation was first spelled out unmistakably in *La Situation Economique du Maroc en 1960* (Rabat: Ministry of the National Economy and Finance, Division of Economic Coordination and of the Plan, 1961), which made it very clear that little had been done to accomplish the goals of the Moroccan *Plan Quinquennal*, and that poor organization had unleashed many forces detrimental to economic growth. The plan was finally abandoned officially last year, and rural reconstruction efforts doled out in the form to be discussed more below.

18. For a summary of Moroccan planning organization see Albert Waterston, *Planning in Morocco* (Baltimore: Johns Hopkins University Press [for the IBRD.], 1962).

19. *La Vigie Marocaine*, November 23, 1958; and *Le Monde*, November 27, 1958.

20. See *Al Istiqlal*, May 14, 1958; January 16, 1960; and May 12, 1963. The Moroccans knew in 1961 that they would not fulfill the goals of the plan. Not allowing

Hassan II in early 1963, the party came out more strongly against the "simple budgetary measures" that has been substituted for planning. By late 1963 it had become apparent that the country would fall so far short of the goals of the interim plan, combined with serious inflation, that the plan was dropped. In the cabinet appointed in November 1963, the advances made under Bouabid in mobilizing the government were largely undone by dismantling the super-ministry for development purposes. The Moroccan approach indicates the monarchy's apprehension over the encouragement of new organizational ties at lower social levels, which is reflected in other aspects of Moroccan development. Planning became inextricably involved with the creation of new political institutions, as it tends to do in every country making a substantial commitment. Faced with the requirement of delegating power and diffusing avenues for participation, the Moroccan alternative was to withdraw.

Much less is known of attempts in Algeria and Libya. Both are firmly committed to planning, but for very different reasons. In Algeria, the process of involvement was virtually reversed, because the Ben Bella regime was installed well after revolutionary groups had seized large amounts of property and occupied thousands of acres of rich farmland. It is difficult to tell at this time the extent to which Algerian planning may be in fact handicapped by the demands of revolutionary groups, but reports have made clear the hazards of overzealous attempts to create organizational bases for modernization in the absence of appropriate governmental supervision. Ben Bella himself changed from supporting a syndicalist approach to one emphasizing the need for coordination and priorities. The fact that in doing so he assumed the position of his earlier rival, Ben Khedda, is certainly not new in the annals of politics.[21]

---

for demographic pressure, a study done in 1960 concluded that investment was "stagnant" and that no impact had been made in traditional agriculture. See *La Situation Economique du Maroc en 1961, op. cit.*

21. Ben Khedda was President of the Algerian Provisional Government in 1962. See the excellent comparison of the Egyptian and Algerian revolutions by Lacouture, "Pourquoi Ben Bella?," *Le Monde,* July 6, 1962. At the Tripoli meeting the now discredited "centralists" had taken the position that Ben Bella's views led to an "abusive concept of authority, the absence of rigorous criterion and political disorder." *Le Monde,* July 15-16, 1962. It is precisely these problems which Ben Bella attacked after consolidating his position. See the interesting article of *Jeune Afrique,* March 16, 1964, on how the ALN opponents to the "Tlemcen group" were brought back into the régime, including Lt. Allouache, Col. Mohand Ould Al Hadj and Cmdt. Azzedine.

Although the complete story has yet to be unraveled, Algeria moved, during 1963, from a state of affairs approaching Russia's period of "War Communism" to a more conventional form of socialism. Nevertheless, the Ben Bella regime was the most ambitious government in North Africa in terms of a government's proposals to reorganize an entire populace. To a large extent the government was committed to major reforms by the tide of the revolution and the tenuous control of the central government until early 1963. As in the other countries, fundamental decisions about human reorganization also produced bitter controversy within the political bureau, and Khider's disaffection was related in part to differences over party and governmental roles, and also urban and rural priorities. The systematic nationalization of French property began in the spring, the seizure of *La Trappe* being one of the more dramatic moments.[22] Early in April the *Bureau des Biens Vacants* became the *Bureau du Secteur Socialiste*. The reorganization took a firm direction in favor of helping the rural masses, a decision implied in part by Khider's removal.[23] The government's determination to take firm control alienated Abbas and Ait Ahmad. With the arrest of Boudiaf and resignation of Bitat, by the fall the famous *club de neuf* had only one member remaining in a position of power, Ben Bella.[24]

To a large extent, the government was faced with the problem of providing a superstructure for reorganization that had taken place spontaneously with the departure of all but a handful of French farmers, the conversion from military to civilian command

22. *La Trappe* had now gone a full cycle of governmental seizures. It was first taken from the monks by the French government under the Separation Laws early in the century. Ben Bella himself presided over the reorganization ceremony at *La Trappe*, now named *Bouchaout* after a revolutionary hero. *Le Monde*, May 17, 1963.

23. Though yet to be fully documented, the organizational focus for the Algerian internal conflict took place between the army and the party, the FLN. On the eve of independence in 1962, the FLN was poorly organized inside Algeria, and the army, under Col. Boumedienne, was virtually the sole effective national force. Khider hoped to build the party into an effective competitor of the army, and failed. His policy would have relied more heavily on organizing urban elements, while the army favored tactics similar to the Communist Chinese by relying on rural revolutionary feelings. Khider's removal, therefore, indicated new emphasis on rural organization through the army.

24. With the exception of Abbas, who joined the FLN in 1956, all the men mentioned in the last two sentences were among the early militants of the Algerian revolution, and shared Ben Bella's imprisonment from 1956. Most of the political figures went into eclipse in the fall of 1963 with the organization of the second cabinet, when key posts were taken by Ben Bella's confidants. See *Jeune Afrique*, September 23-29, 1963.

in the provinces, and the release of hundreds of thousands of Algerians from detainment camps.[25] The reformulation of the government's policies emerged most clearly with the appointment of a new, primarily Ben Bellist cabinet in the fall of 1963. A superministry, not unlike those in Morocco and Tunisia, was established under Boumaza to control finance, commerce, industry, and planning. The new Ministry of National Economy no doubt worked closely with the Ministry of Agriculture, also under a close friend of Ben Bella, Mahsas, who is credited with saving his colleague's life in the early days of the *Organization Secrète*. Under Mahsas the government sought to impose firmer control over the rural economy and completed the nationalization of the land.[26]

The Libyan case differs greatly from the rest of North Africa, and planning has become a necessity because of an excess of riches rather than the threat of poverty. In terms of the human reorganization confronting the country, Libya is probably facing a more explosive situation than any of the other Maghrib nations. With expected oil revenues in the hundreds of millions for the coming years, there will be difficult problems of preventing the disparity of nomad and urban dweller becoming even greater. As the country gears itself for development, preliminary problems such as the control of the police take on even greater significance and produce the student riots seen in Libya early in 1964.[27] The Muntasser government had a Ministry for Planning and Development under Labidi, but the time gap before ambitious projects to restore desert land can be completed is great. Certainly, we are now witnessing only the prelude to bringing the modern generation and the Bedouin into one society.

The purpose of these comments has been to take the problem of development out of its conventional economic framework and to underscore some of the fundamental political and social problems raised by the massive, rural reorganizations. The Moroccan monarchy has tended to concentrate on industrial projects, not considered here, and has taken an *ad hoc* approach to the funda-

25. The full dimension of these problems has not been clearly established. Up to half a million Algerians had been moved from fighting areas into new villages and detainment camps by the French. The French population in Algeria dropped from over a million to 125,000 in 1962, though there have been reports of some French returning in 1964. For an account of the land nationalization in May 1963, see *Le Monde,* October 4, 1963.

26. *New York Times,* October 2, 1963.

27. Described in *Jeune Afrique,* February 3-9, 1964.

mental issues of rural mobilization. The Tunisians are deeply involved in a detailed planning effort, and the Algerians have already experienced a social upheaval far greater than most planning efforts accomplish in a decade. In Libya, we can detect only the rumblings of basic changes in the regime in the midst of almost bewildering social disparities. The next step is to probe somewhat deeper into the problem of human reorganization on such a vast scale by examining what has been done to provide the rural populace with the organizational infrastructure to generate the social relationships and individual capabilities relevant to a large development effort.

The problems of rural reorganization are particularly indicative of a government's intentions and capabilities because agriculture is too complex and too important an endeavor in a less developed country to modify without consideration and thought. The urban minorities of the North African countries are admittedly of critical and immediate importance both politically and economically, but the urban mass of Casablanca, Algiers, or Tunis has acquired the organizational habits that already make them a responsive and responsible segment of the population. Indeed, one of the hazards of development is that the social gap between this relatively privileged sector and the countryside will be broadened.[28] But development also raises problems of birth control, population migrations, improved public health and education, and modern agricultural practices. The whole complex of modernization activities descends on the *bled,* and a government is ill-advised to take so massive an effort affecting the vast proportion of the people and the foundations of the economy without a clear vision of the goals to be achieved.

Several factors facilitated the Tunisian reorganization of the rural populace, but even with certain advantages the Neo-Destour has not had universal success, nor have the approaches to rural reform been independent of political considerations. For example, the Neo-Destour itself has historic roots in the Sahel, but firm measures to improve cultivation and marketing practices in

---

28. This is perhaps the most serious effect of procrastination, because the highly developed regions have a monopoly of organizational skill and administrative access which enables them to grow without strong government support. Although some economic arguments favor the urban-industrial centers, the potential cost in social dislocation and rural discontent should not be underestimated. For an analysis of the convergence of such dislocations in Morocco, see the author's "National Organizations and Political Development in Morocco," *Il Politico,* XXVIII, No. 2 (1963), 360-374.

olive oil in this region, placed heavy demands on old centers of party strength. Nor was Bourguiba's forthright program to put *habous* and collective tribal land under state supervision without political motive. Because nearly a third of the richest lands was in religious foundations, the government gained considerable leverage over the rural population by acquiring vast holdings, now administered by an *Office des Terres Dominales*.[29] Comparable legislation fixed tribal lands and paved the way for the formation of agricultural cooperatives in the central and southern portions, but was only recently defined in procedures for wide participation.[30]

The government has also had continuing negotiations with the French to recover *colon* lands, having repurchased about a third of the foreign holdings by the end of 1963. By 1964 it became apparent that the voluntary strategy for the formation of cooperative farm units was moving much too slowly to utilize properly the huge quantities of land in state hands. The nationalization of remaining French-owned land in Tunisia created new pressures, and in early 1964 a decree law[31] stated that collective associations that did not succeed in fully exploiting the lands at their disposal could be dissolved by the state. Though the complications of working with the peasants on an equal footing are not fully known, the Neo-Destour was forced to reverse its earlier policy of gradual reorganization.

Considered in its full political complexity, land reform is not immune to international political forces. Bourguiba was prepared to reverse his treatment of the peasant, in part, because the Neo-Destour regime was increasingly criticized for its moderate

---

29. See Habib Bourguiba, *Fixer les hommes sur le terre* (Speech of May 16, 1960), (Tunis: Secretary of State for Information, 1960). Full details on the acquisition and administration of the land are contained in a remarkable handbook prepared by Hervé Sicard. See *Affaires Foncières* (Tunis: Secretary of State for Agriculture, 1960). Though a basic document, the handbook is a good illustration of the fundamental preparations that are often the stumbling blocks for reform efforts.

30. Notice the time span in the following legislation, "Loi no. 57-16 du 28 septembre 1957 (3 *rabia* I 1377), fixant le régime organique des terres collectives," *Journal Officiel de la République Tunisienne* (1957), pp. 250-251. "Loi No. 63-17 du mai 1963 (4 *moharrem* 1383), portant encouragement de l'Etat au développement de l'agriculture," *ibid.* (1963), pp. 745-747.

31. "Décret-loi no. 64-11 du 26 mai 1964 relatif aux associations de développement agricole," *ibid.*, No. 16, March 27, 1964, pp. 380ff. It is interesting to note that Tunisia's strong party organization made this possible with relatively little open opposition, while the much more flamboyant régime of Ben Bella struggled for several years with fiercely independent *comités de gestion*, reflecting peasant parochialism and suspicion of further rural reform.

approach to recovering French-held land, while Algeria moved swiftly to seize French lands in early 1963. In the fall of 1960, Tunisia agreed to pay roughly $2 million to recover about 250,000 acres under French cultivation, and an additional 200,000 acres were included in an agreement in early 1963. In May 1964, the President abruptly announced that the remaining French land, about a million acres, was to be summarily claimed in the coming months.[32] The Tunisians had learned what many other developing countries had discovered. The critical aspect of planning for development is agriculture, and agriculture cannot be reoriented to national requirements in a piecemeal fashion.

These measures provided the Tunisian government with leverage for rural reorganization that has not been developed in Morocco, and that was accomplished in Algeria by the *fait accompli* of the French departure. Until recently, however, the Neo-Destour has been slow to exploit these advances. The government moved swiftly in 1956 and 1957 to undercut the sources of traditional strength in the countryside, and also in the universities and mosques, but tasks of reconstruction moved slowly. The rationalization of scarce technical and financial resources may justify part of the delay, but the Neo-Destour has also been reluctant to establish semi-autonomous centers of development. One of the largest of the Tunisian ventures, the Enfida project, involves a quarter of a million acres, and even larger projects have been begun in semi-arid regions at Souassi and Sidi Bou Zid. The Medjerda Valley scheme to the north of Tunis has also been plagued with problems of getting popular support and other administrative tangles.[33]

Bourguiba himself has confessed that much of the seized land was not being fully exploited,[34] and on some occasions he has made thinly veiled threats that unused land would be taken away from tribesmen. In 1962 the first fifteen farming coopera-

---

32. For the Tunisian position see *Jeune Afrique,* May 18 and May 25, 1964. Their action also received favorable comment in the Algerian weekly, *Révolution Africaine,* May 23, 1964, which had previously chided both Morocco and Tunisia for their cautious approach to land reform. See also, *Le Monde,* May 12, 1964.

33. See M. Callens, "Cinq Années d'Action Administrative dans le Domaine Agricole," *I.B.L.A.,* XXV, No. 98 (1962), 111-134. Also Jacques Chérel, "'De qui s'agit-il?' ou la Mise en Valeur Agricole, Problèmes d'Ensembles Humaines," *Les Cahiers de Tunisie,* VIII, Nos. 29-30 (1960), 17-49.

34. Habib Bourguiba, *Dans Dix Ans, la Tunisie Rénovée* (Speech of March 2, 1959) (Tunis: Secretary of State for Information, 1959). The damage that is thereby done at the local level when the peasants observe that change of ownership has no correlation with living conditions is difficult to calculate, but is very likely great.

tives were begun, and only in 1963 did the government begin to experience the feedback of their program in a congress of cooperative farmers. Without criticizing the Tunisians' careful experimentation in rural reorganization, it appears that the government's first concern has been the consolidation of power in the Neo-Destour. Despite the many historical circumstances justifying this policy, there are certain lessons to be drawn from the reorientation of the political system as the development commitment was made in 1962. The resistance to reform of many of the historically loyal Neo-Destourians suggests: first, that the rationale for mobilizing energies through a single party regime may be over-estimated. Second, the subsequent adjustments in the party organization and in the introduction of regional advisory bodies demonstrates the essential role of intermediary institutions for the expression of differences and communication of operating problems.

The cautiousness of the Tunisian government has been outdone by the apprehensive, and sometimes capricious, approach of the Moroccan government. The relatively rich rural economy of the Gharb, Doukkala, and Meknes plains did not call for immediate action, but the procrastination and confusion that have occurred also involve political considerations. The land reform problem has been frequently discussed since 1956, and Douiri once claimed that over five million acres could be improved under existing conditions.[35] Under the Ibrahim government some effort was made to repurchase small quantities of land from the French, but the project was abandoned because of inadequate organization of skills. It has been revealed that a major land reform proposal was submitted in 1960 when the plan was being studied, and then abandoned.[36] Although Hassan II opened negotiations for repurchase of *colon* lands in 1963, little has been done to relieve chronic underemployment and unemployment in the countryside.

Pessimism in the Moroccan case is produced in part by considering the many organizational advantages the country had at the time of independence. In the more modern rural areas a network of nearly sixty machine stations had grown from the early rural

35. *Al-Istiqlal*, January 19, 1963. See also the analysis of Georges Oved, "Problèmes du Développement Economique au Maroc," *Tiers Monde*, II, No. 7 (1961), 355-398; and also P. Marthelot, "Histoire et Réalité de la Modernisation du Monde Rural au Maroc," *ibid.*, II, No. 6 (1961), 137-168.

36. Mehdi Ben Barka, "Les Conditions d'une Véritable Réforme Agraire au Maroc," in Jean Dresch *et al.*, *Réforme Agraire au Maghreb* (Paris: Maspero, 1962), pp. 119-123.

modernization project of Professor Berque. The use of these stations to make local contact has been minimal, and the massive program of seasonal plowing and harvesting organized by "Operation Plow" did almost as much to antagonize the peasants as to convert them to modern methods.[37] The Moroccan option has generally been to apply effort to the most promising areas first, though action has hardly been more rapid in such cases. Under the French several irrigated areas had been started, the large areas of Beni Mellal being among the most important. Again, poor management and inadequate supervision had created hostility among the peasants.

In 1960 the Moroccan government announced plans to establish an irrigation agency, ONI (*Office National d'Irrigation*), to advance intensive agriculture in several parts of the country. The agency was not in operation until 1962, and the early field projects ended in a controversy in which the first director resigned. The new agency is responsible for nearly three and a half million acres of the country's richest land. Because ONI overlapped with functions of the Ministry of Agriculture and the old machine stations, another organization, ONMR (*Office National de Modernisation Rurale*) was set up in 1962 to use the stations outside ONI's areas for improved agriculture in dry-farming regions. Though it is perhaps too early to pass judgment on these programs, it has been clear that the monarchy has had difficulty in disentangling administrative squabbles in the government itself, and in getting the various field agencies of government to take concerted action.

Many of the obstacles to more effective rural reorganization have been the result of uncontrolled and often unknown intrusion of political considerations in developmental activities. Aside from the major administrative rivalries within the government, there have been careful measures to minimize the number of political figures in some ministries, and since the open break with the Istiqlal those with known party affiliations have been even less welcome.

Perhaps the most disruptive aspect of the Moroccan experience has not been the failure to make a comprehensive attack on rural problems, but the sequence of excessive promises and high hopes followed by poor performance. The Tunisian government, in con-

---

37. See the articles of Oved and Marthelot, *op. cit.;* also F. Clerc, "Rentabilité de l'Opération Labour," *Bulletin Economique et Social du Maroc*, No. 82 (1959), 105-172; and J. Le Coz, "L'Opération Labour au Maroc: Tracteur et Sous-Développement," *Méditerranée*, II, No. 3 (July-September 1961), 3-34.

trast, made careful calculations of fairly limited objectives for rural reconstruction. When the regime unleashed propaganda and took forceful steps as needed, the goals were clearly in mind and both political and social complications were anticipated. The best example of Moroccan uncertainty is the *Promotion Nationale* scheme for public works projects in conjunction with the rural development. In the absence of clearly defined goals such a program has the initial handicap of uncertain purpose, but in the Moroccan case this problem was multiplied by the inability of ministries to coordinate activity locally.

There is no reason why a country should not administer relief to distressed areas, but *Promotion Nationale* was billed as the solution to Morocco's rural problems.[38] In fact, it fell short of its planned employment by nearly two-thirds in 1961 and 1962, and the measure of success that it has had has been largely due to sizable assistance from the royal army rather than from local participants. The report of an interministerial study group noted that each ministry jealously guarded its projects, refused to provide technical support, produced "a multiplicity of definition, passivity, reticence" that were disastrous.[39] The program has been reorganized since 1962, but the possibility of exploiting the opportunity for a major reorientation of the peasantry and involvement at the local level was lost. In this, as in other instances of Moroccan development, the central criticism rests not on what has been accomplished, but on what might have been accomplished given Moroccan resources and organizational advantages.

Neither Algeria nor Libya has had time to become as involved in problems of rural reorganization as Morocco or Tunisia. Libya has made only very preliminary steps by modifying the very awkward and unequal provincial structure of the constitution. When Fikini took office in early 1963, he was given power to set up ten administrative districts with appointed officials, which may serve much more effectively as developmental agencies. The government is now exploring proposals to reclaim desert land for agricultural purposes, but the product of such schemes will not be

---

38. See Guedira's speech in *La Vigie Marocaine*, June 29, 1961. Like ONI, the *Promotion Nationale* had its ordeal concerning its powers of coordination with ministries and local officials, and the first director, an able civil servant, resigned.

39. "Synthèse de l'Examen des Programmes Provinciales de Promotion Nationale," Superior Council for National Promotion, January 5, 1962 (mimeographed). See also the article of A. Tiano, "Une Expérience de Mobilisation du Travail au Maroc," *Cahiers de l'Institut de Science Economique Appliquée*, No. 122 (Series AB), No. 2 (February 1962).

seen for many years. Algeria is also confronted with a problem of redressing the relation of government to rural populace, but in a very different form than Libya. Under the first Minister of Agriculture, Ouzegane, thousands of acres were summarily occupied.[40] While most of North Africa faces problems of insufficient participation, Ben Bella found himself confronted with a rural economy already in the hands of hundreds of *comités de gestion*, each of which spoke in the name of the revolution.

The spontaneous committees that seized vacated land over 1962 are still in the process of being organized, and their reintegration into the Algerian rural economy is certainly one of the most intriguing problems in contemporary North African development. In the most recent legislation on land nationalization late in 1963 it was announced that about four and a half million acres were under self-management committees.[41] As part of the reorganization during 1963, seasonal workers were excluded from the committees. About 100,000 farmers were represented in the congress of self-management (*autogestion*) committees in the fall. This sector of the rural economy, favored by good harvests in the past year, produces over half of Algeria's agricultural exports and over two-thirds of her total agricultural output.

Government supervision has been placed in the ONRA (*Office National de Réforme Agraire*), and recent disclosure reveals the hazards of the rapid conversion. The congress demanded family allowances, paid vacations (including those not given under French ownership), accident insurance, and wage differentials according to skills. The most serious controversies have taken place over the division of farm income. Ben Bella announced in February 1964 that the workers on profitable farms would receive about twice the profit share of the less well managed farms, a policy that has produced some controversy in the Algerian press.[42]

---

40. *New York Times*, November 15, 1962. Though Ouzegane could not prevent the occupation of vacated land, differences developed over how the new committees would relate to government. See the exchange between René Dumont and Ouzegane in *Jeune Afrique*, January 28—February 5, and February 18-24, 1963.

41. *New York Times*, October 2, 1963; and *Le Monde*, October 4, 1963. One can get a rough estimate of how many acres were occupied under the land nationalization laws of March 1963 from an earlier estimate of two and a half million acres in *New York Times*, April 14, 1963. The reorganization and holdings by region are given in *Révolution Africaine*, June 1, 1963.

42. Ben Bella's announcement was the source of some dissatisfaction, which was revealed in the party press. Many of the peasants on less successful farms felt that they had worked as hard as others being paid the full amount. The problem is discussed in *Révolution Africaine*, February 15, and February 29, 1964.

But the fact remains that the new Algerian state has survived a most remarkable agrarian revolution.

The question remains, however, of integrating the fortunate few on the cooperative farms with the untouched problems of rural Algeria. Like the industrial workers managing their own factories, the agrarian committees have indicated that only if exempt from taxes will they be responsible for the masses of rural unemployed. Moreover, with a rural population of some seven million persons, many of them destitute and uprooted, the state will require further sacrifice from the agricultural sector in order to rebuild the countryside. *Le Monde* has already noted that however well the reform responds to revolutionary necessities, it has in fact created two entrenched rural classes, the employed and the unemployed.[43] The potential problem remains of choosing between favoring the organized few or the destitute many.

Though a comparison with Algeria is in some respects unfair, it is apparent that both Morocco and Tunisia have manifested considerable caution in mobilizing rural energies and changing agricultural structures. The most important difference between the latter two is that Bourguiba was eager to take control of the agrarian sector, but slow to provide new institutions and organizations for development. Since 1961 the commitment to planning, however, has brought about important changes, most recently the invigoration of local government and also the party reorganization. Unhappily, it was precisely during this period that the Moroccan regime found it increasingly difficult to reconcile political forces. Throughout 1963, both the Istiqlal and the UNFP were involved in costly legal actions, and effectively barred from participating in local and provincial elections. The monarch has turned to less ambitious rural projects, derived for the most part from vestiges of earlier French programs and directed toward the more productive rural areas, where wealthier Moroccan and French farmers will benefit proportionately or better from improvements.

With no intent to minimize the economic obstacles and social barriers to more vigorous action, it is important to note the full magnitude of the transformation that the North African, and other developing countries, are being asked to make when they seek to mobilize the energies of an isolated, sometimes hostile, countryside. If the country is willing to analyze its own problems, the material problems are not nearly as difficult to anticipate as is that of how the articulate, influential peasant will differ politically

---

43. July 4, 1963.

from the impoverished, disinterested peasant. The countryside cannot be changed without creating more knowledgeable and productive individuals, but there is no way of being certain that the newly created capacities will be directed to the support of the existing regime.

The response to reorganizing the countryside involves delicate and unfamiliar problems for North African leadership. With the possible exception of the FLN, the revolutionary movements have been urban and leadership has been unfamiliar with rural conditions. None of the Maghrib countries has as yet worked out a suitable formula for mobilizing the rural mass, though there are important differences in priority and technique. Despite the advantages of the two monarchies in having a powerful religious appeal, the uncertainty of rural modernization is for them especially great. Morocco learned in the Rif uprisings that religious ties to the monarch were not sufficient to overcome feelings of neglect among tribesmen. King Idris faces an even greater dilemma because the core of his historic support, the Bedouin, are the people most likely to be bypassed by the flood of oil revenues. Islamic appeal does not contribute greatly to the organizational structure by which individuals can express needs, learn new behavior, and communicate with higher levels of authority.[44]

Modernization means, in part, evolving a political system that can respond to human needs that are much more diverse and specialized than those of a village society—indeed, so complex that traditional village organizations may become inadequate.[45] Concomitant with the great diversity of response, the participants tend to express less extreme variations in any single relationship. In reviewing Moroccan developments of the past several years, it appears that the political system has tended to reduce its capacity to coordinate and support a more diverse society. On the level of government itself the Bahnini cabinet represented what has been called the "simple solution."[46] The government has been cautious

44. The problem has been well defined in terms of modernization efforts in Manfred Halpern's *The Politics of Social Change in the Middle East and North Africa* (Princeton: Princeton University Press, 1963).

45. Some of the simplest problems of rural development require more investigation. It is by no means obvious that the village unit, for example, is the ideal unit for development purposes. A good deal can be learned from the efforts of older rural mobilization schemes. See, for example, Henry Maddick, *Democracy, Decentralization and Development* (London: Asia Publishing House, 1963); and Ralph H. Retzlaff, *Village Government in India* (London: Asia Publishing House, 1962).

46. *Jeune Afrique*, November 18-24, 1963. Bahnini was originally Director of Administrative Affairs in the Ministry of the Interior, then Minister of Justice from January to November 1963, when he became president of the Council of

in reaching the rural populace with effective mobilizing activities. The policies of Hassan II have estranged the monarchy from the parties, except the *Mouvement Populaire,* which is poorly organized and has internal divisions. Recent efforts to evaluate Moroccan agriculture suggest that the government looks to the privileged farmers and governmental authority to modernize the countryside.[47]

The one-party regime in Tunisia is very clearly resolved to take the calculated risk that the Neo-Destour can survive a rural mobilization.[48] Despite the hesitance described above, the past several years have seen some remarkable innovations. The first regional development authority was formed in 1963 between Sousse and Kairouan provinces. The relatively ineffective municipal councils have been bolstered, while the *Journal Officiel* shows that numerous loans have been made to local authorities in recent years. Following the coup attempt of December 1962, the cautious policies of the Secretary of State of the Interior were reconsidered and a system of provincial councils has replaced the carefully appointed advisory councils previously selected by the governors. These are certainly not revolutionary concessions, but they stem from the early isolated experiments in development and depart from the pattern of highly centralized organization of the one-party regime.

Both Morocco and Tunisia will be hard pressed, however, to equal the rural mobilization that has already occurred in Algeria. Indeed, Ben Bella himself was hard pressed to accommodate the *fait accompli.* With a peasant population of several million that have been uprooted in the French resettlement scheme, and a rotating group of roughly a half a million Algerian peasants working in France, the Algerian countryside has already felt the shock of modern influences. The rural mobilization has reached a point

---

Ministers. He was reappointed when the cabinet was restaffed in August 1964. A cabinet of technicians, so common among the various military governments of Africa and Asia, is likely to commit the same type of error as the development program aimed at the privileged, urban minority. Accustomed to thinking in calculable, explicit problems, the administrative variety of government may tend to concentrate on the industrial sector. This gives them peculiar advantages in appealing to the working class, apparent in Hassan II's flirtation with the UMT.

47. *Jeune Afrique,* April 6, 1964.

48. *Révolution Africaine,* March 14, 1964. Professor Le Tourneau has pointed out the cumulative nature of the dislocation of countryside and city in a perceptive review of Tunisian affairs, *Le Monde,* July 14-15, 1963. In his words, "disaffection for the régime," may become "more serious as men become more active," in the absence of vigorous efforts to integrate the rural population into modern life.

where Mohammed Harbi, Ben Bella's ex-political advisor, could write that the accomplishments of self-management suggest further radical "transformation of the political and social organization of the State." By intent or default, the Algerians have put the ultimate weapons of development to work, and they may easily set the pace for the entire African continent.

10

Economic Planning in North Africa

A. J. Meyer

Economists contemplating economic development in North Africa invariably end up in wide, mental trapeze swings. The trajectory starts with euphoria over man-land ratios, oil and gas reserves in the Sahara, possibilities for tourism, the magnificent agricultural base created in Algeria and Morocco by the *colons*, and other optimistic elements. It ends in deep depression over economic dualism, political uncertainties of new nationhood, the high costs of international adventuring and military operations, and the other less salubrious aspects of North Africa today. The longer the economist stays at it, the wider becomes the arc of his swings and the higher the peaks and deeper the troughs. No other generalization applies.

Economic planning in North Africa at the moment also lends itself to the generalizations of the broad arc. Plans and the bureaucracies implementing them (or ensuring that they *won't* be implemented) vary widely, from Rabat to Algiers to Tunis, to Tripoli, and on to Benghazi and Beida. The climate in Mr. Ben Salah's *Organisation du Plan* bears little resemblance to that in the Palais du Gouvernement in Algiers. And the gulf between the planning agencies in Rabat and the Ministry of Planning and Development in the Federal Compound (dubbed "the Vatican" by the Libyan Finance Minister of an earlier era) in Tripoli is equally vast. Let us now look at the plans, moving—for no logical reason whatever—from east to west.

LIBYA

The Kingdom of Libya, to put it simply and briefly, did little in the way of economic planning until early 1963. The kingdom, which emerged from long Italian domination, devastation of World War II, and postwar tutelage by the British and the United Nations, had—until very recently—few of the tools associated with planning to aid it. As late as the early 1950's, only a handful (probably no more than a dozen) of Libyans had been to college, a tiny percentage of King Idris' subjects were literate, and Libyans skilled in public administration were in wretchedly short supply. Adding to the nation's woes were depletion of *colon* farms by wartime destruction and emigration of Italians back to Europe, and the political autonomy granted the provinces—Tripolitania, Cyrenaica, and the Fezzan.

To the economic planner, the first thirteen years of Libyan independence emerges as a gestation period in which the main events taking place were political. King Idris was obviously engaged in building his nation in the face of major difficulties—widespread and abject poverty, strong (and often divisive) provincial loyalties, extreme dependence on foreign economic and technical aid, internal problems created by eastern pan-Arabism, to mention a few. To cope, the king remained largely isolated and aloof from his subjects, shuffled ministries frequently, filled the jails on occasion with his subjects whose interests in Baathism seemed overdeveloped, maintained the delicate balance between provinces remarkably well and except for insisting on expensive government establishments in three capitals, did surprisingly well in the face of tremendous odds. Until the spring of 1963, what passed for economic planning in Libya was done for His Majesty almost entirely by foreigners.

There were many of these. Several former officials of the postwar British regime in Cyrenaica occupied crucial administrative posts in the Libyan government throughout the decade of the 1950's. A substantial United Nations Technical Assistance Board mission partially advised, partially itself ran, half a dozen ministries. American academic economists such as Benjamin Higgins visited Libya briefly, wrote papers extolling the evils of economic dualism and returned to their universities with dire predictions about the kingdom's economic future. A large US technical aid mission supplied squads of advisors—an occasional one of whom offered sound advice to a Libyan official capable of putting his ideas to good use. The crowning achievement in this context was the World Bank mission which visited Libya in 1958-59. Its report, typically cautious and conservative in the bank's tradition, recommended the usual improvements in education, highways, agriculture, and public administration.[1] Produced when the oil fields in Cyrenaica were still untested, the bank's study assumed that Libya would remain the economic ward of the United Kingdom, the United States, and the international taxpaper for some time, and suggested that its development aims should be modest.

The nearest thing to planning under local auspices in Libya before 1963 went on in the Bank of Libya. There, several well-educated, energetic governors and an American-educated Director of Research—all Libyans—did a highly competent job of managing the nation's currency and bank reserves and of advising the many prime ministers and the king on monetary policies. In 1963 the Bank of Libya became a full-fledged Central Bank. Over the years it had already developed a very creditable research department, which produced a quarterly bulletin and carried out occasional studies of genuine merit into the economic problems and potentials of the kingdom.

These potentials were, until the late 1950's, uninspiring. In most years during that decade, almost $40 per capita of the estimated average $100 annual income per Libyan came from overseas grants and aid of various kinds—given by the US and the UK for political and military reasons. Output of Libyan agriculture was low, and that of industry almost nonexistent. Exports were limited to hides, olive oil, and esparta grass. Tourism had not yet been thought of seriously. On developing area standards, Libya was an economic backwater.

All this began to change rapidly with the discovery of oil in the Sirte Basin in 1958. The investment of close to $2 billion in petroleum exploration and facilities since then has already uncovered substantial reserves of low cost, high gravity crude oil in several parts of the kingdom; fifty drilling rigs at work during 1964 evidenced their owners' conviction that more oil was to be found; and exports passed the one million barrels per day mark in November of 1964—an output equal to Arabia's of only a few years ago. Libya's earnings from oil exports soared to $180 million during 1964, forecasts for 1965 call for over $300 million, and some experts forecast that the kingdom will reach $500 million yearly within five years. Investment in oil facilities and exploration alone now totals almost $200 million yearly in Libya.

As the dimensions of this bonanza became clearer, the Government of Libya took definitive action in the direction of economic

1. International Bank for Reconstruction and Development, *The Economic Development of Libya* (Baltimore: Johns Hopkins Press, 1960).

planning in 1962. Concomitant to the royal decrees limiting provincial autonomy and creating the "Kingdom of Libya," the petroleum commission (and its earnings) were moved from Benghazi to Tripoli, and a National Planning Council—now a full-fledged ministry—was created. Cursed with staff shortages, the latter spent most of its first year of life seeking advisors, with mediocre success. It also drew up an outline for development. In 1963 an arrangement with the development advisory service of the World Bank afforded skilled advice, and in the autumn of 1963 the Planning Ministry published Libya's first Five Year Plan.[2]

The plan, a forthright document indeed, gets to the heart of the matter quickly in its first sentence:

> The prospects and blessings of economic growth yearned for by the nation to activate and accelerate its progress and to support its independence, which have now become apparent because God has conferred his grace upon the country by revealing its underground wealth, which has been stored for long generations, under the guidance and auspices of our beloved King, Idris the First, may God keep him well, do indeed convey to this nation the happy tidings of a prosperous future and definite progress.

The plan's authors then go on to admit candidly, and in print, that: early oil investments in the kingdom created rapid expansion of imports and service activities but had almost *no* effect on agriculture and industry; Libya suffers from gross shortages of physical *and* developed human resources; its housing boom attests to an economic vigor which is illusory; the price inflation besetting the kingdom is alarming.

The Five Year Plan further outlines a set of general policies for development. It urges that "village inhabitants . . . stay where they are and . . . work in agriculture," while a broad spectrum program of agricultural improvement is set in motion; it proposes massive outlays toward improvement of levels of health and education; it further suggests that the government create a climate favorable to industrial investment—public and private.

The financial magnitudes of the new Libyan Five Year Plan are indeed substantial and testify to the government's commitment to put the major share of forthcoming oil earnings into de-

---

2. Kingdom of Libya, *Five Year Economic and Social Development Plan, 1963-1968* (Tripoli, 1964).

velopment. The plan calls for expenditures of just under £L170 million ($500 million) over the period 1963-68. Beginning with outlays of about $58 million in 1963-64, expenditures are scheduled to move upward sharply—to well over $100 million yearly—as oil earnings grow and Libyan capacities to administer projects improve.

The plan's breakdown of expenditures calls for major outlays in agriculture (£L29 million, just under 20 percent of total outlays), in public works and communications (£L65 million, or almost 40 percent), and health and education (£L35 million, or just over 20 percent of the total). The remaining 20 percent of planned expenditures are scheduled to improve industry, public administration, labor and social affairs and the Planning Ministry itself. The summary in Table I is self-explanatory.

TABLE I*
General Summary
TOTAL ESTIMATES OF THE FIVE YEAR DEVELOPMENT PLAN 1963/1968
(Total Cost: £L. 169,097,000)

Sector	Estimated Cost £L	1963/64	1964/65	Balance to Complete £L
1. Agriculture	29,275,000	2,350,000	4,850,000	22,075,000
2. Industry	6,900,000	545,000	1,245,000	5,110,000
3. National Economy	2,870,000	440,000	680,000	1,750,000
4. Communications	27,460,000	5,067,000	8,678,000	13,715,000
5. Public Works	38,662,000	5,882,000	10,940,000	21,840,000
6. Education	22,365,000	1,975,000	3,895,000	16,495,000
7. Public Health	12,500,000	775,000	2,425,000	9,300,000
8. Labor and Social Affairs	8,690,000	940,000	2,060,000	5,690,000
9. News and Guidance	2,550,000	575,000	655,000	1,320,000
10. Public Administration	6,425,000	2,535,000	1,290,000	2,600,000
11. Planning and Development	11,400,000	650,000	1,600,000	9,150,000
GRAND TOTAL	169,097,000	21,734,000	38,318,000	109,045,000

*Kingdom of Libya, *Five Year Economic and Social Development Plan, 1963-68* (Tripoli, 1963)

The Libyan Plan as outlined above is essentially an eclectic job, resulting from assembly by the revitalized Planning Ministry of the recommendations of the United Nations, the World Bank, and other foreign advisors since 1950, filtered through the appropriate ministries. As yet (spring of 1965) planning in Libya proceeds without elaborate computations and growth models, linear programming, or the other refinements of planning elsewhere. The ministries are occupied for the moment with prosaic—albeit necessary *and* expensive—projects such as sewage plants, highway construction and reconstruction (an enormous task in a nation as large as Libya), and improvements in water supplies, and will probably remain so for at least two years. Meanwhile, the Planning Ministry has begun, with a greatly strengthened staff of younger Libyans and foreign advisors, to focus sophisticated thought and analysis on the plan's sectoral relationships, Libya's need for improvement of health and education levels, and the rest. As these enquiries proceed, the rough outlines and directions and magnitudes of expenditure of the plan will doubtless undergo revision.

TUNISIA

Tunisia presents a different picture. There, independence came later than in Libya—in 1956. Other differences were: Tunisia's French heritage imparted a different character from that left by Italy in Libya; the demographic burden of four million people was far greater than Libya's 1.3 million; the case-hardened economic dualism common to pre-independence Libya (and also to Algeria and Morocco) was not nearly so severe in Tunisia; by early 1965 at least, Tunisia owned only modest proved reserves of oil—and possibly gas; Tunisia faced independence with far better developed human resources than her neighbors—a literacy rate of over 15 percent, more than 1,500 Tunisian graduates of French universities, the beginnings of a middle class of professional men, entrepreneurs, and civil servants, and a hard-to-define sophistication in matters of government and economic life which was uncommon indeed in non-European North Africa; Tunisia also has had the good luck, or whatever, of its uninterrupted political stability—guaranteed by the one-party rule of the essentially able and honest (if not always democratic) Neo-Destour Party and its leader, Habib Bourguiba.

At the outset of independence, from 1956 to 1960, the Tunisian government of Habib Bourguiba concerned itself largely with political consolidation and with eliminating obstacles to long-term economic development. Laws were passed guaranteeing various individual freedoms, abolishing polygamy, eliminating *Sharia* courts, promoting equality of men and women, abolishing *waqf* landholdings and establishing orderly distribution of tribal lands held collectively under French rule. The government also, at first, undertook gradual purchase of the two million acres of Tunisian farmland (out of a total of about ten million acres) owned by

Europeans. In 1960, President Bourguiba even spoke out against the economic retardation of Ramadan.

In other spheres, during the first four years of independence, Tunisia moved in directions which unquestionably reflected the political strength and strong personality of its president. Massive investment went into education, as school enrollments grew from 250,000 in 1956 (about 30 percent of those of eligible age) to almost 600,000 (60 percent of those eligible) in 1963; literacy rates have more than doubled, from about 15 percent at independence to more than 35 percent today; so, too, have numbers of hospital beds, teachers, working women, output of dairy products, canned goods and flour; more startling, and visible throughout Tunisia, has been the massive soil-conservation and tree-planting program —begun immediately after independence and gaining momentum each year since.

Despite their impressiveness, the above efforts were not, in the early years, the result of a coordinated planning effort in Tunisia. They were more the result of President Bourguiba's judgment (shaped by various advisors) about his nation's needs, and what was politically expedient. A political and economic liberal, Bourguiba consistently restrained, and on occasion removed, those colleagues (such as Ahmad Ben Salah of the Tunisian trade union movement) who urged a stronger role for government and more "planification." As in Libya, what passed for planning in the early years in Tunisia was eclectic, and the most important economic advances probably were made in the political and social sphere.

Tunisia did, however, undertake an inventory of its economic potentials after 1956. In the year after independence Professor Ingvar Svennilson became, under United Nations Technical Assistance auspices, advisor to the newly-created *Service du Plan*. He recommended a long-term projection and a short-term plan. To facilitate construction of these, more United Nations experts worked in Tunisia during 1958-59—producing a set of national accounts for 1950-58, input-output tables for 1957, estimates of population, production, consumption, and investment for 1957-71, and a recommended target input-output table for 1971. As this work progressed, the Tunisian government gave permanent status, in 1959, to its *Direction du Plan,* with a ministerial post in the cabinet and a continuing bureaucracy. All this led gradually, during the next two years, to enunciation of what has now become the Tunisian Ten Year Plan.

The Tunisian Plan of 1962-72 is unquestionably the most

sophisticated development outline in North Africa, and probably in the entire Arab East. It contains an impressively contrived set of statistics on every aspect of the development process—Gross National Product and investment projections for the coming decade, consumption estimates, savings forecasts, shortfall calculations, input-output X-rays of the economy as it will look at progressive stages of opulence, and capital coefficients in profusion. Although the plan contains the usual identifiable inconsistencies (and is neither light to read nor to carry) it unquestionably represents an achievement of the economists' art.[3]

More specifically, the Ten Year Plan, and its introductory sub-plan for 1962-64, calls for expansion of Tunisia's national income at about 6 percent yearly, or from about $700 million to just under $1.25 billion by 1972. Investment, the plan hopes, will proceed upward from a beginning minimum of 20 percent of national income. Consumption will be kept in line (by direct controls and inflationary measures) and domestic savings will rise and gradually finance the mainstream of investment—more than half of which is initially scheduled to come from outside sources. Population, meanwhile, will advance, it is assumed, at only about 2 percent yearly—because of retardation resulting from a nationwide birth-control effort being readied during 1964-65. With luck, therefore, the planners hope that the average Tunisian will be at least 40 percent better off in 1972 than he was in 1962—$250 yearly, instead of $150. More important, the nation's economic structure will have changed dramatically, the planners further hope, as will distribution of income and other preludes to a much discussed "take-off" into self-sustaining growth.

The major prelude to the hoped-for "take-off" will, of course, be a large-scale program of investment, public and private. Initially, the investment load (totaling 20 percent of national income) has been borne largely by foreign contributions and loans of various kinds. These outside funds are scheduled to provide about $125 million yearly (out of a total investment of $260 million yearly) in the early years of the plan. After 1965, a dramatic reversal of ratios is contemplated, and by 1972 the plan hopes to see investment going on at well over $250 million yearly, with only $75 million coming from outside. The plan also schedules a gradual shift in the mix, from heavy public investment (in infrastructure projects such as low-cost housing) in the plan's

3. Government of Tunisia, *Tunisian Development 1962-71* (Tunis, 1962).

early phases to greater emphasis on private investment later, as per capita incomes expand.

To raise $125 million yearly abroad is no small feat for a nation of only four million people (and lacking, it might be added, the leverage afforded by a common frontier with the Soviet Union) yet Tunisia apparently did it for a year or two after 1962. United States aid—surplus foods, technical assistance, and economic assistance—for 1962-64 averaged out at nearly $60 million yearly, about $15 per Tunisian. French government aid, including several thousand schoolteachers, was obligated until mid-1964 at about $40 million yearly. To this total of $100 million yearly were added the help of a host of lesser helpers and givers—Sweden, Denmark, Holland, West Germany, Italy, Yugoslavia, the Soviet Union, and various United Nations agencies. Altogether, foreign aid of various kinds came close to the plan's targets for the first two years.

Most unusual among the smaller nations' programs in Tunisia has been that of Sweden.[4] After two unsuccessful foreign aid "adoptions" of underdeveloped nations (Ethiopia and Pakistan), the Swedes undertook to try again with Tunisia under terms of an agreement signed in March 1963. Under a system of loans and untied government aid (which will probably total well under $1 million yearly), Sweden is undertaking sponsorship of the Kelibia project at Cap Bon—a five-part development (financed by a 20-year loan) calling for harbor construction, a school for fishermen, hospitals, and agricultural improvements. In addition, Swedish private firms, operating with their government's approval, and using offices in the Swedish Embassy, have invested (or given suppliers' credits for) more than $20 million in the Sfax superphosphate plant, in the steel mill at Menzel Bourguiba and in the nation-wide telephone grid.

Kuwait is also undertaking to help Tunisia. As of early 1965 the Kuwait Fund for Arab Economic Development had pledged $20 million to assist in strengthening Tunisia's electricity generating capacity and was reportedly considering other commitments. In addition, Kuwait private investors have pledged funds in quasi-public low-cost housing projects and other commercial ventures in Tunisia.

Since mid-1964 all this has been punctuated by an apparent shift by the Tunisian government away from its earlier posture

---

4. Charles F. Gallagher, "A Small Saga," American Universities Field Staff Reports, North Africa Series, IX, No. 12 (New York, 1963).

favoring economic liberalism. Some observers attribute the shift to a growing accommodation between Messrs. Bourguiba and Ben Salah. Others interpret it as an effort by Mr. Bourguiba to counter criticism—from Algeria and several sub-Saharan African nations—that he was soft on "imperialism" and was little more than an African lackey of the West. Other analysts see the growing abandonment of liberalism as resulting from the government's frustration with economic performance in the private sector—where investment had lagged far behind the plan's targets.

Whatever the reasons, Tunisia was moving, by mid-1964, smartly toward a stronger role by government in the nation's economic life. In May of that year, earlier decrees (for gradual turnover, with compensation, of French lands) were rescinded and the remaining *colon* lands were summarily nationalized, and compensation payments were halted. Currency restrictions of all kinds were tightened and then, later in the summer, the Tunisian pound was devalued 25 percent from $2.50 to $1.90. Decrees in support of these measures were myriad and furthered the trend through the autumn of 1964. In a matter of only six months, the liberalism of earlier years was replaced dramatically by belt-tightening austerity.

The effect of the decrees so far has been equally dramatic. France immediately suspended its $40 million aid program and has shown no evidence of reversing her decision. The Europeans in Tunisia grew more restless, and most observers concur that a quiet exodus of French businessmen and professional people gained momentum in the autumn of 1964. New foreign private investment dropped off sharply and was limited in large part to petroleum exploration or to projects already under way—such as the International Harvester assembly plant being built at Menzel Bourguiba. To date (spring 1965) no other government has been inclined to come forward with funds to supplant those withheld by France.

Given the above, one can only emerge with an ambivalent evaluation of Tunisian economic planning to date. On the plus side, figures available indicate that Tunisia's national income advanced at a respectable 4 percent for several years after 1959, and that net per capita improvement was in the vicinity of 1.5 percent yearly up to 1964. Using substantial doses of outside public assistance and much local ingenuity, Tunisia has achieved an impressive record of trees planted, hillsides terraced, *bidonvilles* renovated, new schools and dispensaries built—and staffed remarkably well. The massive unemployment programs, the lack of anything resembling "corruption" in government and the well-timed propaganda effort have undeniably convinced most Tunisians that their government is vigorous and deserving of their support—96 percent voted for the government's candidates in the November 1964 elections.

On the minus side, Tunisia's efforts show equally convincing evidence of difficulties ahead. The Tunisian entrepreneurial class has obviously not been up to investing at anything like the plan's private sector targets. The land nationalization decrees of 1964 added not only a load to the government budget but also eliminated a crucial, and large, source of outside funds—$40 million out of a hoped-for foreign aid transfusion of more than $120 million. Although impossible to isolate, the combination of nationalization and devaluation unquestionably chilled the private investment climate further, and added to the defections of businessmen to Europe. Government enforcement efforts—of currency controls, permits for everything, to mention only two—seem sure to grow and will probably initially create further paralysis.

Given the above, it is difficult indeed to forecast that Tunisia can sustain its modest national income advance of the past five years. To predict that investment levels in excess of 10 percent of national income are possible—given the obstacles listed above—seems foolhardy. The nation could well be in for a line-holding period, with little improvement in net income for several years. Oil discoveries of a substantial nature could change all this, and tourism will undeniably help, but, regardless, it seems doubtful if the planning effort can overcome the many obstacles and generate rapid expansion of national income.

ALGERIA

The Algerian Republic created at Evian began life with the unique distinction of owning, at its birth, one of the world's most ambitious and elaborately contrived development plans.[5] A by-product of the contortions of Franco-Algerian relations of the late 1950's, the Constantine Plan (as enunciated in Algeria by General de Gaulle in the autumn of 1958) was designed to please everybody—proponents of "Algérie Française," advocates of economic development for its own sake, the French critics of economic dualism and Muslim poverty (such as Germaine Tillion) in North

5. "Caisse d'Equipement pour le Développement de l'Algérie," *Plan de Constantine, 1961* (Paris, 1961).

Africa. According to French government publicity brochures, the Constantine Plan departed ". . . from the classic concept of technical assistance by bits and pieces, doled out according to political considerations, and substitutes for it an all-inclusive program balancing the human and material development of Algeria." It was, and remains, a monument to the art of economic planning.

The monument was an ambitious one. Its many volumes are packed with expenditure outlines, calculations of every coefficient known to mathematical man, estimates of future intersectoral relationships (one can estimate, for example, from the charts, the effects on the fishermen in Bône of investments in iron ore facilities near Colomb Bechar) and a lofty set of goals and targets. Briefly, the Constantine Plan called for ten years of forced draft development, divided into two five-year periods. From 1958 to 1963, it was proposed, about $44 billion would be invested—$800 million yearly, or about 40 percent of the estimated Algerian national income of $2 billion! During the five ensuing years, 1963-68, another $7 billion would be ploughed in. The total outlays of $11 billion (half from public sources and the other half from private investors) would lead, French planners hoped, to a doubling of the Algerian per capita income. The resultant $400 per Algerian yearly would, the planners further hoped, permit the revitalized economy itself then to marshall 20 percent of national income for investment—as it soared into "take-off."

It is redundant to note here that there was no "take-off." The French government, for its part, lived up to its plan commitments during 1958-60 inclusive, and more than $1 billion of French public money went to development expenditures. French and Algerian private investors, however—despite the incredibly liberal government guarantees and inducements of all kinds—put up less than $200 million during the same period. So, instead of proceeding at $800 million yearly, total investment under the Constantine Plan went on at less than half that rate. During the same period, moreover, more than $500 million of French private capital flowed northward, back home to the metropole. The net plan in the private sector was modest indeed, and consisted largely of a few new factories, such as Unilever Algerie, and preliminary construction of a steel complex at Bône.[6]

Public investment, on the other hand, yielded impressive and

---

6. Charles F. Gallagher, "The Other Algeria: Notes on a Developing Economy," American Universities Field Staff Reports, North Africa Series, VI, No. 5 (New York, 1960).

visible results during 1958-60. Massive low-cost housing schemes were launched amidst the dreary *bidonvilles* ringing every large Algerian city; school enrollments were almost doubled—from 650,000 to over 1,000,000; the quasi-public petroleum companies made great progress—developing oil installations at Hassi Messaoud and Edjele, and gas fields at Hassi R'Mel and three pipelines linking these to the Mediterranean Sea. The Bou Namoussa Dam and the steel complex at Bône were impressive undertakings indeed.

Although initially impressive, the tempo of public investment dropped sharply with the corrosive violence and political uncertainty which punctuated Algeria during most of 1961 and early 1962. With Evian and the formation of the Algerian Republic came a further massive outflow of funds to the metropole, this time accompanied by Europeans themselves. Most estimates hold that almost 1,000,000 Europeans left by the end of 1962 and that today Europeans total no more than 100,000—mostly newcomers. The resultant combination of shortages of skills and managerial talent, low purchasing power, political uncertainty of every description, other needs of the new Algerian government and pressures by French returnees on their home government led to cessation of the Constantine Plan outlays at the time of independence.

Since independence, the main step by the Algerian government towards orderly planning consisted in the creation (by decrees in August and September 1962) of a *Direction Générale du Plan et des Etudes Economiques,* responsible to the president's office. Further decrees charged the *Direction du Plan* with developing Algeria in keeping with "socialist" principles, such as those enunciated by North African leaders meeting in Tripoli in mid-1962, as well as within the frameworks outlined in the Constantine Plan. Further steps were taken to create multiple arrangements to manage the *biens vacants* lands (farmlands whose owners had abandoned them to return to France), to oversee the national interests in petroleum matters (through the *Organisme Technique de Mise en Valeur des Richesses du Sous-Sol Saharien*) and others.

Little else of moment has been accomplished by the Algerian Republic in the field of planning. Since independence, a stunning set of political, military, and social problems has occupied Mr. Ben Bella and his associates, and there have been neither the funds nor the manpower to keep the Constantine Plan moving.

Massive unemployment (estimated at up to four-fifths of the employable labor force), resettlement of peasants regrouped during the troubles with France, revolts in the Kabyle, a small-scale border war with Morocco, and virtual internal economic paralysis have so far precluded moderate economic measures.

Faced with the above, President Ben Bella resorted to what appear to the outside observer as essentially diversionary moves. Widespread and apparently indiscriminant nationalization of enterprises, Muslim and European owned, proceeded almost daily; so did great public displays accompanying the turnover of *biens vacants* lands to peasant communes; frequent parades of banner-carrying children laboring the theme of "un seul héros, le peuple" marched through the streets of every Algerian city and village; intermittent parades of Soviet, Czech, and Red Chinese visitors offered aid and praise for Algeria's battle against "oppressive capitalism"; the press and radio were full of the government's heroic offers to provide guerrilla fighters for the liberation of Black Africa and to carry the war to Israel, as well as to help the capitalist-oppressed masses in Cuba. Massive doses of dreary and doctrinaire socialist propaganda were ladled out constantly, in every medium.

Bread for the circus onlookers meanwhile has come so far almost entirely from France, the overseas Algerians and the United States. Since Evian, France has provided government aid to Algeria at the rate of about $300 million yearly—most of which has gone to meet the costs of government. The 500,000 Algerians now working in Europe, mostly in France, support an estimated three million citizens at home with remittances; gifts of surplus US food (valued at about $80 million yearly) keep at least another three million Algerians alive. In aggregate, about eight million Algerians are directly dependent upon these outside sources, and the remaining two million exist from earnings of family heads in the more or less "natural" economy.

Given the above, the Algerian government's inability to mount a coordinated planning effort seems understandable. Yet there is some evidence that one is beginning. In March 1964 the Minister of National Economy, Mr. Bachir Boumaza, presented a $440 million development budget to the National Assembly (this was in addition to the ordinary budget of $526 million, passed by the Assembly on December 31, 1963). The proposed budget, presumably following earlier Constantine Plan outlines, calls for one-third of outlays to go to agricultural and rural improvement schemes, and the rest to be divided between industry and infrastructure outlays of various kinds.

Finance for the development budget is scheduled to come largely from outside—just under $200 million from France, another $150 million from other foreign sources (such as the US, UK, Soviet bloc, and Red China), and about $100 million from Algeria itself. Of the latter amount, $50 million is scheduled to come from oil earnings and the other $50 million from earnings of state enterprises and gifts by Algerians to the National Solidarity Fund.

Algeria's planning effort, therefore, remains so far more a hope than a fact. It was launched with accompanying attacks on its major financial supporters—France, for its alleged cupidity in writing off Saharan oil investments at excessively high rates, and the United States for its perfidy in Cuba and for supporting "international Zionism." In view of the utter paralysis besetting private investment in the nation, Algeria's plan aims for most investment to go on under public auspices. Meanwhile, massive unemployment lingers, threats of nationalization continue, and the flood of Muslim Algerians to France, Germany, and Belgium continues at high rates—well over 100,000 yearly by most estimates. Under such circumstances, accurate evaluation of Algeria's planning effort becomes impossible.

MOROCCO

Morocco presents a fourth variation on the theme of economic planning in independent North Africa.[7] There, planning went on from 1949 to 1953 under auspices of the French *Commissariat au Plan*. The "Plan" was little more than a list of infrastructure investment outlines, implemented by a long-term equipment program which managed expenditure of $418 million of public funds, some $100 million yearly, over the five-years. Outlays were heaviest in transport, irrigation, electric power facilities, and education—followed by a list of expenditures of lower priority. Private investment, it is generally concluded (although not affirmed because of lack of statistics), also went on at a high rate and probably equalled public outlays. The high levels were

7. See Albert Waterston, *Planning in Morocco* (Baltimore: Johns Hopkins Press, 1962) and Jane Perry and Andrew Carey, "The Two Developing Worlds of Morocco: A Case Study in Economic Development and Planning," *Middle East Journal*, XVI (Autumn 1962), 457-475.

reached because of a combination of forces—growing French concern over internal Moroccan politics, pressure from US Marshall Plan officials in France, high-priced demand generated by post-World War II shortages for phosphates and output of Morocco's modern sector, a flow of French capital from Indochina (which totaled close to $1 billion according to some experts), and several good crop years.

As elsewhere in French North Africa, what passed for planning was managed entirely by Frenchmen, in Paris and Rabat. So, too, were outlays under the Second Plan for Modernization and Investment. Spanning the four years 1954-57, during which Morocco achieved independence, these totaled about $536 million, or slightly over $125 million yearly. By this time, internal political troubles, collapse of the Korean war boom and one or two bad crop years cut private investments drastically, and most observers view the second plan as having been essentially a public undertaking.

Accomplishments and failures of the first two development programs are readily visible and can be listed quickly. The schemes pushed overall investment up to a respectable 12-15 percent of national income in most years between 1949 and 1957; they made major improvements in Morocco's (already well-developed) system of roads, railways, power generation and transmission, phosphate mining and exporting arrangements, fishing industry, and irrigation facilities for European agriculture; they permitted some impressive rates of crude per capita income advance—3 percent net in many years. In aggregate, the French plans of the 1950's left Morocco with the impressive infrastructure which, as mentioned earlier, induces a first-glance euphoria in development economists.

There were also failures. The French plans did little to train Moroccans, either to make plans or to carry them out, and a mere handful of Moroccans achieved other than menial jobs in the planning organization; the rates of economic advance achieved by the plans fell almost entirely within the modern sector, which contained well under 10 percent of the population, while 90 percent of the populace (all Moroccans) achieved little net improvement in living standard; the plans made no attempt either to recognize publicly, or to launch an attack on the hard shell of economic dualism encasing Morocco.

Morocco's first try at economic planning as an independent kingdom came with the Biennial Investment Plan for 1958-59.

The plan was produced by a newly created *Division de la Coordination Economique et du Plan* (DCEP) staffed almost entirely by Frenchmen and worked as a department within the Ministry of National Economy and Finance. It outlined investments totaling about $213 million for the two plan years, mostly aimed at further infrastructure improvement, but with heavier emphasis (than in earlier French plans) on agriculture, education, and social service.

The Biennial Plan had ambivalent results. Its accomplishments were: it focused on the need to improve traditional agriculture and launched efforts such as "Operation Plow"; it created an industrial development organization, *Bureau d'Etudes et de Participations Industrielles* (BEPI), and arranged several measures to foster industrial investment; it caused, for the first time, a handful of well-informed Moroccans to come to grips with the development process. Its failures were: its investments fell far short of targets in every sector; it dissipated too much of the energies of its staff in elaborate statistical and mathematical model-building exercises (understood by few, implementable by none); and devoted too little staff time and energy to carrying out of schemes; it relied too heavily on Frenchmen, on Algerians, and UNTAB Europeans, and did little to train Moroccans for senior planning posts. Its successes and failures aside, the Biennial Plan afforded, as Albert Waterston has observed, "a much needed interval for the Government to gain more general acceptance for broader planning in both official and private circles as well as for preparing a comprehensive five-year plan."[8]

This came in the shape of the Five Year Plan for 1960-64, the result of three years of work by fifteen commissions (headed by ministers) and dozens of subcommissions and committees. Its formal adoption, in November 1960, served as an anticlimax to a year-long crescendo of confusion over commission reports, political maneuvering and wrangling of all kinds and dismissal by the king of the finance minister (and most of his senior subordinates in the DCEP) responsible for the plan's construction. It called for net public and private investments totaling $250 million yearly ($1.3 billion altogether), aimed to achieve 7 percent yearly expansion of GNP and 4 percent net per capita advance. Its central themes were: to launch an educational and training program; to promote dramatic agricultural reforms; to begin state-involved heavy industries; to "Moroccanize" the kingdom's government; to

---

8. Waterston, *Planning*, p. 21.

promote regional plans and planning organizations, within the plan's overall framework. Fourteen months after the plan's issue (in February 1962) a 10 percent revision of projected outlays and targets was announced.

To judge the Moroccan Five Year Plan's successes and failures at this juncture is quite impossible. Morocco as yet owns no adequate national income accounting arrangements, and the effects of plan outlays to date, in net per capita for GNP terms, is unknown. Morocco's national income is still probably more responsive to weather than to its plan. In view of this, the most that can be tried is a set of random observations, which are outlined in the following paragraphs.

First, the emergence of a carefully conceived plan and its implementation, in Morocco, have been made difficult indeed—some would say impossible—by the combination of a shortage of Moroccans skilled in planning *and* the kingdom's political climate since 1960. There is little evidence that there has been real improvement within the DCEP since that date. A large part of the staff still works in an atmosphere of comfortable irrelevance, toying endlessly with intricate mathematical models and projections. And the constant turnovers of government, musical chairs games with ministers, conflicts between bureaus and departments, and overlapping functions join to keep the planning exercise in a state of virtual paralysis. The result has been essentially to postpone (until very recently) a frontal attack on the agricultural problems, to delay (for several years) any really effective action to convert the former US bases to Moroccan economic use, to avoid confronting the problem of slowing the flood of rural Moroccans to the cities (most of them into *bidonvilles*), and to undertake substantial repair of the earthquake damage to Agadir. Given this situation, the Five Year Plan emerges as a less than significant aspect of Moroccan economic life today.

Next, and more hopeful, there seem to be, at the moment, signs of life in several adjuncts of the planning organization. The chemical complex at Safi appears to be going ahead with much needed foreign private company collaboration; BEPI has achieved considerable vigor under Mohammed Lagzaoui (a former New York supermarket operator) and is now launching a series of new enterprises, among them a super-phosphate complex; the *Centre de Développement Economique et Rural du Rif Oriental* (Centre DERRO) in Fez has produced a massive, three-volume development program for northeastern Morocco; the nation's tourist organizations are exhibiting considerable animation and now are building a network of excellent government hotels, have coaxed European and American investors to undertake others, and have stepped up Morocco's tourist earnings dramatically. These all betray a growing vigor, which may in time reflect backward to the planning organization and Morocco's political structure.

Third, King Hassan, while placating his younger subjects by experimenting with political democracy and moving apparently toward constitutional and representative government, has carefully avoided moves toward planning which might jeopardize his support from France. The land reform program has until recently studiously avoided the *colon* farms (and most observers feel that the decrees will be applied in moderation), pressure against Europeans has been minimal for several years, and a return of Europeans has been under way for some time; encouragement to foreign private investment is an integral part of Moroccan government efforts; the king seemingly pays scant heed to the appeals for harder "planification" from the UNFP opposition, or to the disillusionment of the many leftist French advisors who have left. Meanwhile, foreign experts are welcome in Morocco, and well-staffed missions are now in Morocco from UNTAB, France, USAID, and Yugoslavia, and teams from Kuwait and the World Bank surveyed Morocco in 1964.

SUMMARY AND CONCLUSIONS

The foregoing permits several general conclusions about the state and accomplishments of economic planning as practiced in newly independent North Africa.

First, economic planning in North Africa has so far been almost entirely a national affair, and there is little evidence of concrete cooperation or even of any great knowledge within the four nations about one another's problems or plans. Where such knowledge does exist, it so far has led to heightened competition—as evidenced by Tunisia's forced draft superphosphate undertaking, felt by many to aim at getting markets ahead of Morocco's Safi complex. One exception to this rule has been the marketing arrangement for esparta grass, which has worked surprisingly well. Another has been the talks between Tunisia and Algeria on marketing. Meanwhile North African citizens, and the world at large, are treated to a deluge of pious statements—such as those by Messrs. Bourguiba and Ben Bella about joint use of Saharan oil and gas, the conclusions inevitably reached by North African Arab student conferences, and the news releases after the March 1964 visit of the Libyan Planning Minister to Tunisia.

Next, the most tangible evidence of area-wide economic cooperation in North Africa probably rests in the UN Economic Commission for Africa's suboffice in Tangier. Established in 1963, the ECA branch produced (in February 1964) a report on "Industrialization and Economic Development of the Maghrib." It has outlined needs for further studies, has offered its facilities to North African governments to prosecute these, and is currently working to convene meetings of North African leaders to discuss economic collaboration in the Maghrib. It has also made sensible suggestions about linkage between the Algerian and Moroccan electricity grids.

Third, the national planning exercises give little evidence of any area-wide doctrinal slant or commitment to philosophies such as the Arab socialism of Egypt. King Hassan, as mentioned earlier, has so far shown little taste for the stringent "planification" urged upon him by the UNFP (and his leftwing French advisors) and may well go down in history, as Ernest Gellner has written (*New Society*, May 16, 1963), as the last French pro-consul in North Africa. Tunisia's plan and its application can still be described as moderate. King Idris gives no evidence whatever of founding a socialist state in Libya. And Algeria, while avowedly "socialist," is impossible to categorize in coherent terms.

Next, the planning exercises so far have focused attention on North Africa's extreme dependence on the outer world—for public and private investment funds, technical assistance, schoolteachers, markets for oil, phosphates, fruit and wine, tourist earnings, and the rest. Morocco, Tunisia, and Libya have grasped this fact. Ironically, Algeria—the most dependent of all—has yet to recognize it. Properly controlled and nurtured, this dependence can provide enormous motive force for economic expansion. Capital transfers from oil and other exports and economic aid could total close to $1 billion yearly for the four countries within only a few years. Without this foreign linkage, North Africa would face enormous obstacles to sustained growth.

Fifth, North Africa's plans so far make glaringly evident the basic administrative incompetence which curses many new nations. Without fixing blame, it is enough to say that planning in North Africa has focused attention on the gulf between a nation's capacity to field a plan of marvelous mathematical consistency (invariably a delight to savants at the Sorbonne) and that same nation's utter inability to marshall the men to make it work. Tunisia alone is moving hard to fill the gulf.

Next, economic planning in North Africa will provide an informative (and one hopes not too expensive) training program for several nations in the facts of life concerning oil and gas. As exports of Libyan and Algerian hydrocarbons grow, governments of these nations face a pressing need to shape policies in their long-run interest, and not to commit acts of self-mutilation. In the incredibly complicated energy world today—with its swings from shortage to glut, new (and competitive with North Africa) discoveries of oil and gas (in the North Sea, for example), Soviet oil, subsidized prices, vicious price competition, rapidly changing technology, to mention a few variables—sophisticated policies by producing governments are imperative. Most observers concur that Libya so far has been not only lucky but very astute in this respect, and the soaring output is the result. Few would reach the same conclusion about Algeria. There, the problems over oil were admittedly much more complicated. But, for whatever reason, the Algerian government has, since independence, effectively stopped the search for new oil fields, slowed construction of the "third" oil pipeline (from Hassi Messaoud to Arzew), and encouraged, by its actions, a rush to build gas facilities which will ultimately compete sharply in markets now held (or sought) by Algerian gas.

Further, an important by-product of economic planning in North Africa may well be its effect in shaping the changing character of "cooperation" in France. As Charles Gallagher has pointed out recently,[9] "cooperation" is a very important part of France today and is accepted, not only by intellectuals and economic development theorists, but by lawmakers and "Mr. Durand in the street" as well. This general acceptance, which contrasts with the recoil from foreign aid now under way in the United States, has pushed French economic and technical assistance up to the world's highest levels—in per capita terms and as a percentage of national income. Algeria, Tunisia, and Morocco alone now get close to $400 million yearly from the French taxpayer, including almost 25,000 teachers. These North African ventures, which dwarf US aid efforts in per capita terms, will unquestionably—as they succeed or fail—influence the French aid effort greatly. And

---

9. Charles F. Gallagher, "Co-operation," American Universities Field Staff Reports, North Africa Series, IX, No. 10 (New York, 1963).

they well might become prototypes for enhanced efforts elsewhere by Western nations—or the opposite.

Next, North Africa offers still another arena where the Soviets, Red Chinese, and Yugoslavs can joust with Western nations with economic aid and technical assistance. So far, as shown earlier, France and the United States have served both as whipping boy and provider of aid to Algeria, and as provider of aid to Tunisia, Morocco, and Libya. Soviet bloc efforts so far have been limited to providing aircraft (for Ben Bella and for the Algerian and Moroccan air forces), trading agreements (covering a list of commodities which neither side seems able to deliver, except for Moroccan cobalt to Red China) and to discussions between Red China and Algeria over collaboration in oil matters. One indication of the importance of the latter was that during the same week in March 1964 that the latter discussions (which were on the theme of purchases of Algerian oil by Red China) went on, Red China announced that a new oil field in Manchuria would soon free the nation from dependence on Soviet oil and make it into a net exporter! As in Egypt, India, and elsewhere, it seems a good bet that the Soviets and Red Chinese will meet, in North Africa, the same expensive frustrations which beset Western nations in the region, and will find subversion a hard task indeed.

Next, the planning exercises in North Africa offer an example in the "developing" world where the corrosive competition between arms outlays and those for economic development has not yet begun. Across the board, the four North African nations still (spring of 1965) devote less than 5 percent of national incomes to "defense" expenditures, have avoided the Middle Eastern arms race amazingly well (where outlays on arms average nearer to 10 percent of national income) and have so far failed to saddle themselves with expenditures directly competitive with those for development. To the development economist, the situation is not only surprising, but refreshing.[10]

Finally, the development plans now mounting in North Africa offer still another fascinating new laboratory for those same specialists in economic development. For example, the region's problems of land tenure and ownership (as typified by the *biens vacants* programs in Algeria) are prodigious, and other Arab East

---

10. During the late spring and summer of 1965 there were occasional newspaper reports of arms shipments to Algeria and Morocco. If true, these could well forecast a resumption of tensions between these two nations, and ultimately, increases in arms outlays.

land reform programs offer no sensible guidance; the almost certain onslaught from tourism, now gaining momentum, offers observers the chance to relate North Africa's response to that of Italy, Greece, and Spain; efforts to undo economic dualism will occupy many economists for a long time; Libya will provide a fascinating example of soaring investments, with "before and after" (like Charles Atlas exercises) measurements possible along the way. Attracted by all these, plus the pleasant North African climate, the development experts are sure to come. That they will add another ring to the Maghrib's circuses is certain. Hopefully, they will add also to its bread.

BIBLIOGRAPHY

Bourdieu, Pierre, et al. *Travail et Travailleurs en Algérie.* The Hague: Mouton, 1963.
Byé, Maurice (ed.). *Le Développement Agricole en Algérie.* Paris: Tiers-Monde, 1962.
"Caisse d'Equipement pour le Développement de l'Algérie," *Plan de Constantine, 1961.* Paris, 1961.
Carey, Jane, Perry and Andrew, "The Two Developing Worlds of Morocco: A Case Study in Economic Development and Planning," *Middle East Journal,* XVI (Autumn 1962), 456-475.
Food and Agricultural Organization of the United Nations. *Mediterranean Development Project.* Rome, 1959.
―――――. *Projet FAO de Développement Méditerranéen: Tunisie.* Rome, 1959.
―――――. *Projet RAO de Développement Méditerranéen: Tunisie.* Rome, 1959.
Gendarme, René. *L'Economie de l'Algérie: Sous-Développement Politique de Croissance.* Paris: Colin, 1959.
Government of Tunisia. *Tunisian Development 1962-71.* Tunis, 1962.
Guen, Moncef. *La Tunisie Independante face à son Economie.* Paris: Presses Universitaires de France, 1961.
International Bank for Reconstruction and Development. *The Economic Development of Libya.* Baltimore: Johns Hopkins Press, 1960.
International Labour Office. *Labour Survey of North Africa.* Geneva, 1960.
Kingdom of Libya. *Five Year Economic and Social Development Plan, 1963-1968.* Tripoli, 1964.
Ministère d'Etat chargé de la Réforme Administrative. *La Politique de Coopération avec les Pays en Voie de Développement* (The Jeanneney Report). Paris, 1963.

Nuttonson, M.Y. *The Physical Environment and Agriculture of Libya and Egypt.* Washington, D.C.: The American Institute of Crop Ecology, 1961.

―――――. *The Physical Environment and Agriculture of Morocco, Algeria, and Tunisia.* Washington, D.C.: The American Institute of Crop Ecology, 1961.

Perroux, François (ed.). *L'Algérie de Demain.* Paris: Presses Universitaires de France, 1962.

Rapport sur la Zone d'Attaque Sahéla-SRA. Fez: Centre DERRO, 1962.

Revue d'Information de l'Organisme Saharien (bi-monthly), Algiers.

Stewart, Charles F. *The Economy of Morocco: 1912-1962.* Cambridge, Mass.: Center for Middle Eastern Studies, 1964.

Tillion, Germaine. *Algeria, The Realities.* New York: Knopf, 1958.

United Nations. *Structure and Growth of Selected African Economies.* New York, 1958.

Waterston, Albert. *Planning in Morocco.* Baltimore: Johns Hopkins Press, 1962.

11

Planning: Why, How and What Results?

Charles Issawi

Why are all the North Africans moving towards some kind of a planned economy? What methods of economic planning are they using? What are the likely results?

I believe one can answer the first question by saying that some form of planning becomes inevitable when the government handles a significant proportion of the Gross National Product and a large share of the country's investable funds. This may come about because the government receives substantial non-tax revenues. Thus, in North Africa, as in the Middle East, an important factor has been the combined effects of large oil revenues and foreign aid. This leads to a paradoxical result: the oil companies and the United States, French, and other governments, all of whom are staunch upholders of free enterprise, are promoting planning and socialism. But then, history does have a wry sense of humor and Hegel did make some cryptic remarks on "the cunning of Reason" which uses men's passions and desires to bring about its own ends.

But to return to the main point. Where government non-tax revenues are large their expenditure must be planned, the alternative being to fritter them away haphazardly.[1] (That is why the giving of so much United States and other aid, as well as the granting of loans by the IBRD, is being made conditional on the presentation of some kind of plan.) Yet, where no such outside funds are available, there are four major reasons why planning is even more urgent.

1. Chapter I of the Libyan Plan strikes the right notes: "... The selection, supported by justifications, of the *most suitable projects* which have the *most effective means* for the progress and prosperity of the country. Such projects should be *co-ordinated* so as to give a clear picture of the welfare of the people. This gives rise to the necessity of giving preference to the development schemes in the order of their real *priority*. . . ." (Italics added.) Kingdom of Libya, *Five Year Development Plan, 1963-1968* (mimeographed), p. 2.

First, everywhere today a large, and expanding, sector of the economy is being run directly by the government, for reasons which have often been described.[2] Second, in many countries, including the North African ones, the industrial, commercial, and financial sectors were controlled almost exclusively by foreigners, whose departure—or expulsion—*en masse* has left these countries denuded of entrepreneurship; however, the extent of deprivation varies, Tunisia and Morocco having started their careers as independent states with much larger and more developed native bourgeoisies than Algeria or Libya. Third, planning is the prevailing ideology. The alternative to planning by the government is planning by the heads of the large enterprises that dominate the various sectors of the economy—of course within the limits set by the forces of the market. Now in most underdeveloped countries it is felt today, rightly or wrongly, that *this* business is too important to be left to businessmen. This brings us to the fourth and last, but not least important, factor: fashion. Planning is the *dernier cri,* as was, say, constitutional government in the 19th and early 20th centuries. In most underdeveloped countries today there is a touching belief that socialist planning is the gimmick that will infallibly, painlessly, and simultaneously bring about national power, rapid economic development, and social welfare.[3] In the particular case under consideration, the North Africans—wrongly—identify capitalism with European colonialism, which they believe—rightly—failed to develop their countries in the proper direction or to a sufficient degree. They identify planning

---

2. In the first place, most of these countries have to build up a costly infrastructure—roads, irrigation works, ports, electric stations, etc.—which either constitute an obvious field for government activity or which national private enterprise is unable to undertake while foreign capital is reluctant to do so, or will take up only on terms unacceptable to governments that have just obtained their independence. Secondly, almost all these governments are trying to accelerate development by providing certain forms of credit which the private banking sector was failing to meet, notably long- and medium-term agricultural and industrial loans, through institutions wholly or largely owned by the government. Thirdly, new government-owned industries have been set up where it was judged, rightly or wrongly, that private enterprise would not show enough interest. Lastly, the desire to accelerate development by sharply increasing investment has led many governments to nationalize large chunks of the private sector, in the hope (which may or may not materialize) of using its profits to finance investment.

3. An English economist who was basically favorable to planning stated that he had "a suspicion that planning appealed to many as having the properties of a magic charm which would enable us, not to solve, but to shirk our problems." H. D. Henderson, "The Price System," *Economic Journal* (London, December 1948). If this was true of Britain, how much more applicable is it to the emerging nations?

and socialism with the Soviet world, which is surrounded by an aura of glory, undimmed by close acquaintance.

So much for the Why. As to the How, a survey of the various systems of planning in use today shows that they fall into three broad groups: command, target-project, and indicative planning.

Command planning is exemplified by the Soviet Union. In principle, state ownership of the means of production makes it possible to determine output, prices, employment, and so forth, for each producing unit. Consistency is sought by the method of "material balances" and "labor balances," which seek to equate needs and availabilities.[4] In practice, such balances have been established only for a selected number of leading branches, leaving the rest of the economy to fend for itself as best it can within the broad limits set by "synthetic balances" aiming at equilibrating income, expenditure, investment, consumption, exports, and imports. Such a system results in rapid development of a few sectors accompanied by shortages, queues, black markets, and, occasionally, famine in the other sectors.

Target-project planning is practiced in many underdeveloped countries. On the macro-economic plane, projections and targets are laid down for such variables as income and investment by making heroic assumptions regarding propensities to save and import, incremental capital-output ratios, reinvestment rates, and so on. The flesh on this skeleton is supplied by various specific projects—irrigation dams, factories, roads—more or less adequately studied. Strictly speaking, these plans are more like long-term capital budgets, allocating government investment over the specified number of years. Naturally, the ramifications of any given project and its impact on the rest of the economy are seldom investigated, except in a most sketchy manner. The result is that although quite a few projects are actually implemented, numerous imbalances are created leading to shortages, wastes, under-utilization, inflation, and balance of payments difficulties.

Indicative planning has been carried out most successfully in France. Here, the public sector is very important and has numerous levers of control, but it is not predominant. The objective is to coordinate the public and private sectors, and the various branches of each of the two, so as to achieve the desired rate and balance of growth. This is done essentially by getting together

---

4. See Sh. Ia-Turetskii, *Planirovanie i problemy balansa narodnogo khozyaistva* (Moscow, 1961) and Abram Bergson, *The Economics of Soviet Planning* (New Haven: Yale University Press, 1964).

representatives of various industries and sectors and inducing them to modify their plans so that they become mutually consistent and selfsupporting. The state plays its part by financial policies, generous fiscal and credit incentives, and the coordination of its own investment with that of the private sector.[5]

Given the background of Algeria, Morocco, and Tunisia, and the part played by Frenchmen in the formulation of both their early postwar and their current planning, one would expect their plans to fall into the third category. However, the great paucity of their data and the lack of trained personnel have in fact made their plans much more like those of other underdeveloped countries, i.e., what I have called target-project plans. They therefore show the same weaknesses and are subject to the same objections.

One could, if one wished, make more detailed criticisms of these plans. First, they frequently lack internal consistency, in such matters as: capital-output ratios; availabilities of resources and the demands made upon them; forecasts of foreign exchange disbursements and receipts; availability of trained manpower, and so on. Secondly, the anticipated relationships between the various sectors —e.g., agriculture, industry, mining, and so on—are based on the most conjectural data, and practice is likely to diverge greatly from the lines laid down in the plans. Thirdly, one can predict a good deal of misallocation of resources, due to the fact that the market economy, with its disciplines, is being increasingly replaced by a control economy. Moreover, the investment criteria chosen often leave much to be desired. Still more important are the difficulties encountered in the pricing of the goods and factors of production in the rapidly expanding public sector. Lastly, there is the question of the bureaucracy which is supposed to execute all these plans. Surveying in the mind's eye the host of government officials, one cannot but recall the remark made by the Duke of Wellington as he reviewed his ragged troops before one of the major battles in Spain: "I don't know what effect they will make on the enemy, but by God they scare me!"[6]

---

5. See François Perroux, *Le IVe Plan Français: 1962-1965* (Paris: Presses Universitaires de France, 1962); John and Anne-Marie Hackett, *Economic Planning in France* (Cambridge, Mass.: Harvard University Press, 1963); and Jacques H. Drèze, "Some Post-War Contributions of French Economists," *American Economic Review*, Part 2 (Supplement, June 1964).

6. In practically all underdeveloped countries the civil service is, not surprisingly, cumbrous, lacking in technical skills, and more or less corrupt. But the North African countries suffer from an additional handicap, attributable to the rapid replacement of French (or in Libya, Italian or British) officials by nationals. "In Morocco, for example, in 1955, a year before independence, 33,000 out of 51,000

But rather than continue on this plane of generalities, let us consider one specific case, that of agriculture in Tunisia. Professor Meyer describes the Tunisian plan as "unquestionably the most sophisticated development outline in North Africa, and probably in the entire Arab East."[7] Now it may seem unfair to pick on agriculture, since it is the sector that does least well under planning. The reasons for this are obvious when the planning of agriculture is compared with that of other sectors. Thus, in transport and communications it is relatively easy to plan—indeed it is largely a matter of good engineering which can be hired abroad. And once the road is built or the radio station is in operation, it is very difficult to judge whether or not the project is economic, i.e., whether or not it absorbed resources which could have been used to greater advantage elsewhere. For the benefits are largely social, i.e., not measurable by the yardstick of prices, and cost-benefit ratios are very difficult to establish. The same is true of many other forms of infrastructure and still more of social overheads such as education and health services. Factories, for instance, are relatively easy to build, and even to operate, and the question of their efficiency can be left to be determined later—much later. After all, one can always invoke the infant industry argument to explain losses, and these infants do take an unconscionably long time to grow.

But agriculture is a different matter. Here planning consists in persuading millions of stubborn, cunning, suspicious peasants—who have never experienced any good, and have generally suffered much evil, from the cities—to change the way of life they have been pursuing for thousands of years. As recent Russian and Chinese history shows, force does not seem to succeed where persuasion has failed. To all of which must be added that in agriculture Nature is a major cooperant factor, and that Nature pays

---

civil servants in the central administration were Frenchmen, who had almost exclusive control of the higher positions. An additional 10,000 Frenchmen held posts in public corporations and utilities. Nationalist leaders themselves acknowledged that there were probably no more than 2,500-3,000 experienced Moroccans to take over the French-held posts. Yet by the end of 1958, 21,000 French civil servants had left the administration and 7,500 Frenchmen the public corporations and utilities. . . . Similarly, in Tunisia, Frenchmen occupied 13,500 out of 18,400 civil service positions in 1955, the year before independence. By 1959 there were only 1,800 Frenchmen left, including 1,200 French school teachers, in a bureaucracy that had grown to 23,000." Manfred Halpern, *The Politics of Social Change in the Middle East and North Africa* (Princeton: Princeton University Press, 1963), pp. 343-344. In Algeria the shift has been even greater.

7. See Chapter XII, pp. 240-1.

©Miss M. Bull

The market-place in Tangier

TRANSPORTATION AND INDUSTRY
Hassi Messaoud and the Port of Casablanca

Algiers firemen destroying the bidonville in the old section of Mahieddine. (Government of Algeria)

little heed to the instructions laid down by government planners in the capital city.

The Tunisian Ten Year Plan provides for an annual growth rate in agricultural output of 5.5 percent per annum. One has only to compare this figure with the 2.2 percent rate achieved in Tunisia during the last few years, or with the 2–2.5 percent characteristic of most underdeveloped countries, to begin having serious doubts. Closer inspection merely reinforces these doubts. The area planted to citrus is to increase from 6,500 hectares to 9,200 by 1971, which seems reasonable; but output is to rise from 65,000 tons to 180,000, which is not, seeing that it implies a doubling of yields. Similarly, date yields are to increase more than fourfold and wheat yields are to double, all of which seems highly optimistic. And when one learns that much of this increase is to be achieved by setting up producers' cooperatives—one of the most difficult and delicate forms of social organization—and notices that the plan provides for the reduction of the work force in agriculture from 70 percent of the total to about 33 percent, one's doubts become greater and greater.

As regards Morocco, I cannot do better than echo the following criticisms, made in an address by the Crown Prince to the Superior Planning Council of August 1, 1960: "Morocco lacks significant statistical data, without which there can be no real planning.... [Consequently] ... the conclusions [of the commissions and the DCEP *(Division de la Coordination Economique et du Plan)*] reflect uncertainties and divergences that are often important."[8] To which may be added the following remarks by a well-qualified observer, Albert Waterston: "There was a noteworthy lack of well prepared projects ready for execution.... The Plan did not cover several important economic fields, including credit, money and banking policy, wages and salaries, price policy, marketing problems, international trade and land reform.... There is a dearth of technicians in the DCEP qualified to interpret and apply such econometric formulations."[9] Waterston concludes: "No one doubts, however, that the Plan is lagging seriously."[10]

A few remarks may be made regarding planning in Algeria. The Constantine Plan could not be implemented because of the war, which lasted long enough to tear to pieces Algeria's social

---

8. Quoted in Albert Waterston, *Planning in Morocco* (Baltimore: Johns Hopkins Press, 1962), p. 31.
9. *Ibid.*, pp. 32-33.
10. *Ibid.*, p. 45.

fabric and to make impossible the continued presence of the French, who had run the bulk of economic activity. Since independence, the government has been frantically struggling with the elemental forces released by the war, and trying to divert them into less dangerous channels. Thus the nationalization laws of March 1963 merely confirmed the seizure by the workers and peasants of factories and lands abandoned by Frenchmen in 1962.[11] As in other countries at a similar stage of revolution, Algeria is trying out Workers' Management (*autogestion*). One quotation will suffice to bring out the leading idea behind this system: "The self-management of an enterprise—be it industrial, agricultural, handicraft, commercial, financial or mining—is based on the principle that those who work have the right to make use of it [*en tirer parti*] themselves, *without masters or imposed head*. It is management by the workers themselves."[12]

As for the results anticipated: "The verdict of a year of experience has shown that workers are fit to manage enterprises. . . . Self-management guarantees that each workman will have a stronger and more durable interest, which will arouse him to create new resources and to husband them better, to raise his productivity and increase output."[13] One hates to sound skeptical, but it seems safe to predict that in the not too distant future workers' management will be replaced by the strictest director's control, with all the range of sanctions used in socialist countries.

Libya's plan consists mainly of a string of investment projects, more or less carefully studied and loosely coordinated. Finance presents no problem and technical aid is freely available from abroad, but the rigidity and fragility of the social structure and the weakness of the bureaucracy will not doubt retard implementation.

Returning to more general considerations, I should also like to develop a little further a point raised by Professor Meyer in Chapter X: the lack of any coordination between the various national plans. In the United Nations document, "Report of the ECA Industrial Coordination Mission to Algeria, Libya, Morocco and Tunisia,"[14] the authors start with the implicit assumption that the four countries form a natural economic unit and with the

11. République Algérienne Démocratique et Populaire, *L'Autogestion en Algérie* (Alger, March 1964), p. 3.
12. *Idem*, Ministère de l'Orientation Nationale, *Documents sur l'Autogestion* (Alger, August 1963), p. 3.
13. *Idem, Le Secteur Socialiste Industriel* (n.d.), p. 6.
14. E/CN, 14/248, 5 February 1964.

explicit one that they could greatly profit by coordinating their plans, concentrating certain branches of activity in a given country and others in the other countries, and exchanging products. In this way wasteful duplication can be avoided, division of labor may be carried out further, and plants may be built of a size which would ensure economies of scale. At present, on the contrary, each country is busily setting up small plants, based largely on imported raw materials and producing at such a high cost that they are kept going only by heavy protection or government subsidies. "Examples are the sugar refinery in Tunisia, safety match manufacture in Libya and several North African assembly plants" (p. 19).

Among the authors' suggestions is the supplying of electricity by Algeria to both Tunisia and Morocco. By connecting its grid with that of Algeria, Tunisia could obtain "electric power at 7-8 mills per unit or two-thirds of the present production costs, and avoid the multimillion dollar investment for additional generating capacity" (p. 27). Similarly, Morocco could obtain its power needs at 6-7 mills per kilowatt-hour, compared with an estimated cost of 9-10 for local production; this would reduce its "annual power bill by 900,000 dollars" (p. 30).

Another good suggestion would avoid duplication in the smelting of ores. Tunisian zinc ores could be sent to Algeria for smelting, instead of to a small and inefficient local plant, and the returning ships could carry Algerian lead concentrates for smelting in Tunisia (p. 32).

The same applies to the very promising petro-chemical industry. "The Maghrib's immediate demands could be met most economically from a single ammonia plant, with an output of not less than 150,000 t. per year and working with low cost natural gas. The investment cost would be 25-30 million dollars, compared with about 40 million dollars required for the three smaller plants with a similar total output. Production costs would be reduced by 5-10 dollars per ton of ammonia which represents a combined total annual saving of about one million dollars" (p. 41).

In iron and steel the need for concentration is even more urgent. "Without an agreement in North Africa for a coordinated program of iron and steel production, much of what has already been committed may well prove to have been wasted; the remainder of the investment required is unlikely to be forthcoming" (p. 48). And, to show the magnitude of the sums at stake, present plans call for an investment of some $235 million in iron and steel in Algeria, Morocco, and Tunisia—a substantial sum considering that their combined Gross National Products amount to well under $5,000 million.

Specialization by country is also essential in the assembly industries since it is "the only avenue leading to large scale production. . . . A large number of assembly industries present great possibilities for sub-contracting" (p. 51). At present all three countries have small and inefficient assembly plants and Libya may soon follow suit, as oil brings further affluence and raises the demand for motor cars. Similarly, small and inefficient glass industries exist in all three countries but it is only at an all-Maghribi level "that a flat glass factory would be economic" (p. 63); the example of the Damascus glass factory, which has excellent equipment and is very efficiently managed, shows how steeply unit costs rise when the small size of the market makes it necessary to produce below capacity.

One last point—coordination is at least as urgent in other fields as in industry. Thus the report very sensibly points out the advantages of pooling the miniscule merchant fleets, integrating the airlines, and jointly planning the road systems of the North African countries. To which one could add agricultural marketing and exports.

Of course, such projects come up against a very serious obstacle: the incompatible ideologies of the four countries, their very different social and political structures, and their conflicting ambitions, which have led to more than one armed clash or other incident. Still, while an economist has no right to tell others what ideology to adopt or what political system to follow, and while he must patiently, if reluctantly, submit to inconvenient political realities—while he must accept the "primacy of politics"—he is in duty bound to point out the economic costs of the politicians' vagaries. And not only, I may add, in North Africa or, indeed, in the underdeveloped countries.[15]

From all of this, you may have guessed the answer to the third question: What Results? Of course, in most accepted senses of the word "fail," the plans will fail. One need not go as far as a distinguished friend of mine, the late Nikolai Koestner, who once said that a plan that succeeds 101 percent is one that has failed; strictly speaking he was right, since such a plan could have

---

15. As this chapter was being revised for publication, the North African governments announced the setting up of a body to coordinate their economic policies—surely a step in the right direction. See *New York Times,* November 29, 1964.

achieved its goal with a smaller expenditure of resources—though most of us would gladly settle for this kind of failure. But what of a plan that fulfills 90 percent of its aims, or 80 or even 50 percent?[16] If, as seems highly probable, the vast projected investment does give these countries a big forward push in the economic and social fields, is it terribly important that they did not achieve a better allocation and use of their resources? Is it fair to expect such a high degree of foresight and efficiency from states that emerged only yesterday, some of them after shattering convulsions that almost demolished the very fabric of their society? After all, think of what it is they are trying to do—to refashion their society and economy, hurriedly replacing structures that are thousands of years old by new ones modeled on foreign patterns, *without* undergoing the upheaval or paying the price in blood and suffering exacted from Russia, eastern Europe, or China. As Mehdi Ben Barka put it so well: "The agrarian revolution required two centuries in Western Europe; it cost eight million deaths in the Soviet Union. We do not want to wait so long, nor act so brutally."[17] Granted that they are making many mistakes, because of inexperience, suspicion, rigidity, and over-extension—often induced by political and social forces outside the control of the government—is not all this to be expected?

As was pointed out by a judicious observer: "Indeed, it is arguable that no 'deliberate' industrialization program—such as that being attempted today in India—can obey the traditional laws of economic rationality. The authors of such programs generally

16. Available data indicate a very low rate of growth in the last two or three years, except in Libya where oil has fueled the economy. See Bank of Libya, *Monthly Economic Bulletins* (1962-65); Banque du Maroc, *Etudes et Statistiques, passim;* and République Tunisienne, Secrétariat d'Etat au Plan et aux Finances, *Rapport sur la Première Année d'Exécution du Plan* (1962).

17. Quoted in I. William Zartman, *Morocco: Problems of New Power* (New York: Atherton Press, 1964), p. 118. Of course it may well be that these countries are attempting the impossible and that they will have either to slow down their revolution drastically or, what is more likely, adopt totalitarianism. And, needless to add, totalitarianism by itself does not ensure success.

It also goes without saying that these countries have other objectives, besides reform and economic growth. Perhaps the one to which they attach most importance is the building up of their armed forces and other sources of power to the point where they will be able to deliver a hard blow to the advanced countries whose aid they are at present soliciting but accepting with such bad grace. Pending that day, they are making full use of that convenient weapon of the weak against the strong: the adoption of a high moral tone accompanied by constant pinpricks and a steady barrage of attacks from all the state-controlled mass media. But while this should be clearly recognized by the advanced countries, it should not change their basic attitude of sympathy nor fundamentally affect their policy.

base their thinking on some kind of long-term calculation, and indeed may be right to do so, but their essential decisions are political, or based on a political interpretation of long-term economic desiderata."[18]

Lastly, is there any way of learning other than by doing? If I may conclude with a trite French proverb: *"C'est en forgeant qu'on devient forgeron."* And if, in the course of learning their trade as smiths, these countries waste a lot of good metal, supplied by the more advanced and wealthy countries—Western and Soviet —that just happens to be part of the price which the advanced and wealthy countries will pay for the promotion of the economic development of the world.

18. Alec Nove, *Economic Rationality and Soviet Politics: Or was Stalin Really Necessary?* (New York: Praeger, 1964), p. 54.

12

Oil in the North African Economy

John H. Lichtblau

SIZE AND IMPACT OF NORTH AFRICA'S OIL INDUSTRY

The emergence of North Africa as one of the world's major oil supply centers is the most important economic event to have occurred in that part of the globe in modern times. The impact has been all the more profound because of the suddenness of the development.

Ten years ago all of North Africa contained only a few tiny oil fields supplying a fraction of local demand and no one knew for sure that much more oil would ever be found. In 1965, the region's oil exports will equal those of Iran, one of the giants among oil exporting countries, and total oil income from royalties, taxes, wages, and other local expenditures are likely to equal about $20 for each of the Maghrib's thirty million inhabitants, compared to annual per capita income of about $150 from all other sources. Unfortunately, as we shall see, the newly found wealth is very unequally distributed within the region so that only a minority will benefit from it.

The size of the discoveries and their relative proximity to the world's principal markets has suddenly focused the attention of oil producing and consuming countries everywhere on North Africa. In fact, it has been feared in some quarters, and hoped in others, that as a result of the new discoveries, the center of gravity of international oil operations would soon shift from the Persian Gulf to the Sahara Desert. As of now, such predictions would seem to ignore the realities of the existing situation, namely, that while the two areas will increasingly compete with each other, North Africa is not another Middle East and is not likely to become one in the foreseeable future. The following statistics will bear this out.

Currently, North African oil production is about 1.7 million barrels daily, or just one-fifth of the production in the Middle East. If all scheduled pipelines in North Africa should be completed by late 1966, production will then amount to about 2.1 million barrels daily, while Middle East output will exceed 9 million barrels daily. The total proved reserves on which current production is based amount to 18-20 billion barrels in North Africa and to over 200 billion barrels in the Middle East.[1] Productivity per well is approximately 1,450 barrels daily in Libya and less in Algeria, compared to the Middle East's average of 4,300 barrels daily.

The External Impact of North African Oil

How important is North African oil to the rest of the world? Strictly from the point of view of volume—not very. There was certainly no oil shortage in 1960 when North African exports began to move to markets in appreciable quantities. The Middle East, with a small assist from Indonesia and Venezuela, supplied all the oil needs of the Eastern hemisphere with capacity to spare and at prices well below the postwar high or even the temporary high of the Suez crisis. Given the Middle East reserves, it could have gone on meeting all requirements for the next quarter of a century at least. Why, then, was North African oil developed? There are two main reasons—competition and diversification. Competition is the force which compels oil companies—particularly the large ones—to search for new oil deposits wherever it is geologically indicated, just to maintain their position in the industry. For if company A does not develop a new deposit, company B will, in which case company A's supply position, relative to B, would decline. Thus, new oil supplies may be developed without regard to the developing company's—and hence, the industry's—existing supply-demand relation.

More important in the development of North African oil resources was the quest for diversification of supply sources. Both producing companies and importing countries share this desire not to rely too heavily on any one supply source or area, for financial, political, and strategic reasons. If an illustration of the danger of "too many eggs in one basket" was needed, the Suez

1. However, ultimate reserves, i.e., total reserves in place, may be only four times as big in the Middle East as in North Africa (including Egypt), as was pointed out by Mr. John Ricca in a discussion at the 18th Annual Conference of the Middle East Institute.

crisis supplied it with enough drama to make everyone see the point. There is no doubt that without Suez the development of North Africa's oil resources, particularly those in the Sahara, would have proceeded slower. Whether the shift to North Africa has resulted in a true diversification of Europe's oil supply sources will be discussed later. But the existence of a shift from the Middle East to North Africa cannot be denied.

In Germany for instance, North African crudes supplied about 28 percent total requirements in 1964, compared to 3 percent in 1961 while the Middle East share dropped to 44 percent from 64 percent in 1961. For Europe's six Common Market countries, total North African imports accounted for 23 percent of total oil imports in 1964, compared to 1 percent in 1959, while the share of Middle East imports fell by almost exactly that many percentage points—from 77 to 57 percent.[2] An additional incentive for developing North African oil supplies—foreign exchange savings—applies primarily to France and is discussed in the section on Algeria.

Redistribution of Producing Countries' Oil Revenues

If North Africa's principal impact on the world oil industry has been, and will continue to be, to reduce the importance of the Middle East as a primary supply area, then the gain of the new area is really the loss of the older. From the point of view of economic development this may be considered a desirable change, for it spreads the benefits of oil production over a large number of approximately equally needy recipients. Oil revenues lend themselves better to this reallocation than the earnings from almost any other primary commodity. The oil producing countries are the only raw material exporters among the underdeveloped nations whose incomes have risen steadily and significantly throughout the entire postwar period. The *Economist* recently referred to the oil exporting nations as the "rich poor," in contrast to the "poor poor" nations whose livelihood depends on the exportation of agriculture and mining commodities most of which have declined in volume as well as in value. By a quirk of nature much of the world's oil reserves are located in sparsely populated countries. The extreme case is, of course, Kuwait with a population of 250,-

2. These declines reflect percentages only. In actual volume, Middle East oil exports to all western European countries, except France, have grown substantially since 1959.

000 and an annual oil income of $550 million in 1963, equal to $2,200 per capita. A partial redistribution of such income to other nations in need of development income cannot help but improve the utility of this income.

OIL IN ALGERIA

So far we have discussed North African oil production as a whole. However, this is really an oversimplification, for Libya and Algeria, the Maghrib's two oil producing countries[3] are quite different in character as well as in resources; and this is of course reflected in their oil policies. Let us look first at Algeria since it preceded Libya as a commercial oil producer by about three years.

Oil and the Franco-Algerian War

Efforts to find oil in Algeria were begun in the early 1950's under the active sponsorship of the French government which was concerned over the dollar drain (over $300 million per year) caused by oil imports. Consequently, it wanted to develop a source of franc-zone oil. By 1956, when the search had shown the first positive results, private companies became interested in joining the government companies. Soon afterwards, the Suez crisis added another strong incentive for finding domestic oil. When the first evidence became available that the Algerian Sahara contained major oil deposits, the news had an impact on France far beyond the confines of the oil industry.

One French premier of the time, Pierre Mendès-France, called the discovery of oil in the Sahara the most important event of his tenure, while his successor, Guy Mollet, said "Saharan oil . . . forms one of the foundations of our independence." Stock issues for new Saharan oil ventures were oversubscribed by the French public within hours after they had been put on the market and the whole thorny problem of whether to continue the war against the Algerian rebels took on a different slant. For now, an economic justification could be added to France's emotional motivation for keeping the tricolor waving over Algeria.

The Algerian rebels, on their part, hoped to speed up France's defeat by denying her access to the new oil supplies. The rebels

---

3. A major oil find in Tunisia has recently been announced by the oil company ENI. But it will take some time before the find's true significance can be evaluated.

also warned all non-French companies to keep away from Algeria until independence had been achieved.[4]

As it turned out, France won the battle of petroleum—the rebels did not seriously succeed in interrupting the growing flow of Saharan oil or in stopping the influx of foreign companies—but lost Algeria. The cease-fire agreement of Evian of March 1962, in which France recognized Algeria's independence, contained a special protocol on Saharan oil. This protocol which has formed the basis for all oil operations since independence, was a masterpiece of restraint and reasonableness, especially in view of the bitterness of the French-Algerian war. In essence it provides for the Algerian government to step into the shoes of the French government as far as Saharan oil, gas, and pipelines are concerned. All acquired rights were to be respected by Algeria and the companies were to remain subject to the provisions of the existing Saharan Oil Code, including the 50-50 profit sharing arrangements based on actual (not posted) prices. The grant of new concessions was to be subject to Algerian legislation, but for the next six years, French-controlled companies were to enjoy first choice on all new concessions. A joint Franco-Algerian Commission was to be established to advise the Algerian government on oil legislation and to exercise general supervision over the oil companies. Finally, Algeria was to receive the former Algerian provincial government's 40.5 percent share in the French *Société Nationale de Recherche et d'Exploitation du Pétrole en Algérie* (SN REPAL), which has a half interest in both Hassi Messaoud, the country's largest oil field, and Hassi R'Mel, the largest gas field and a one-third interest in *Union Générale du Pétrole* (UGP), a government-sponsored refining and marketing company in metropolitan France.

The Pipeline Dispute

It is now three years since the Evian Accords and while their basic provisions are still in force, it is clear that the Algerian government is profoundly dissatisfied. At the same time, the French government as well as the foreign oil companies disagree with some of the Algerian government's interpretations of the Evian Accords. A major bone of contention has been private versus state ownership and control of the country's urgently needed

---

4. John H. Lichtblau, "France Finds Treasure", *The Reporter*, December 27, 1957.

crude oil pipeline. Since the two existing pipelines are already operating at capacity, at least 175,000 barrels daily of new Algerian production—equal to over 35 percent of total existing output—are currently shut in for lack of transportation, at considerable loss in revenue to both the Algerian government and the seventeen operating oil companies.

The oil companies have taken the position that under the Evian Accords an exploitation permit carries with it the right to transport any oil or gas produced. The government denies that this right is implied and has insisted on making the line a state enterprise. The companies' opposition to a government pipeline is based on their fear that control over the line's tariff rates would enable the government to exact more revenue from the companies than is provided for under the 50-50 agreement. In all other major oil producing countries, pipelines are owned and operated by the oil companies themselves.

Since the French government agrees with the interpretation of the oil companies, the issue has gone to international arbitration, as provided in the Evian Accords. However, the Algerian government is not awaiting the outcome of the arbitration but began actual construction in September 1964, expecting that the dispute will be settled before the line is completed, as part of the basic revision of the Evian oil agreement currently under negotiation.

The government's project will cost about $60 million, most of which is to be borrowed at five to six percent annual interest, including $28 million from Kuwait and the rest largely from Britain, since a British construction firm is carrying out the project. The principal plus the interest payment plus the loss in revenue, due to the fact that the company-proposed project would have been ready at least a year earlier than the government project, will amount to over $100 million.

The question of financing a project of this magnitude points up the general problem of how resources should be allocated in a developing country with low capital formation and large foreign assistance needs (France's contribution to Algeria for 1964, amounted to $194 million). Should the government undertake major projects in competition with available private foreign capital or would optimum resource allocation not require that the government's capital expenditures be concentrated on improving the country's infrastructure for which private foreign capital is rarely available?

Changing the Evian Accords

Algeria never considered the oil provisions of the Evian Accords as a permanent settlement of her oil affairs. Almost since the beginning of independence, President Ben Bella insisted that his country must have greater control over its principal natural resource and export commodity than is provided for in the Evian Accords. As time went on, his insistence became ever more outspoken and vociferous, reflecting the country's growing national self-assertion and socialist orientation. The relatively low level of oil revenues contributed further to demands for a revision of the Evian Accords.

The French government, after insisting for a time on the inviolability of the Accords, finally recognized the politically explosive potential of the Algerian complaints and initiated renegotiations. As of this writing there is still no agreement, although the two parties are reported to be fairly close to achieving one. It may be taken for granted that the role of the Algerian government in the country's oil affairs will greatly expand under the new agreement. This will apply particularly to new oil reserves in which the Algerian government is supposed to receive a direct stake through a new French-Algerian "Cooperative Association," to be formed for the purpose of finding and developing new fields. Algeria is expected to guarantee the continued operations of the existing foreign companies. However, these companies will certainly have to pay considerably higher revenues to the government than they do now. Revenue rates will probably be raised more for production from new fields than from existing ones.

Algeria's dissatisfaction with the existing revenue provision, which provides that royalty and income tax payments are to equal 50 percent of the companies' net earnings, stems largely from the fact that the revenue provision in the Evian Accords was adopted unchanged from the Saharan Oil Code drawn in 1958 when Algeria was still part of France. Under this code, oil companies are entitled to a temporary depletion allowance, i.e., they may defer from their taxable earnings an amount equal to 27.5 percent of their gross revenue (up to 50 percent of their net earnings) for a period of five years. The code also permits rather liberal amortization of investments. These tax incentives reflect the former colonial power's primary interest in maximizing crude oil production rather than revenue collection. However, the Algerian government, like most oil exporting nations, is more interested in the latter than the former. Neither of these two tax deductions exist in the Middle East, in Venezuela, or in the revised Libyan Oil Code.

It cannot be denied that Algeria's oil revenue per barrel would be higher if these tax provisions did not exist. Since 1960, total government petroleum earnings and total crude oil production have been as follows:

	OIL & GAS REVENUE (in millions $)	CRUDE OIL PRODUCTION (in 1000 b/d)
1960	20.0	180
1961	26.5	330
1962	40.8	430
1963	45.0	502
1964	65.0	557
1965 (estimated)	70.0	580

Thus, in 1964, the government revenue per barrel of oil was only 32 cents, compared to about 75 cents in the Middle East, over 90 cents in Venezuela, and an estimated 50-60 cents in Libya. However, this comparison needs to be qualified. Most oil companies in the Sahara have so far only paid the required royalties (12.5 percent of the sales value of the oil) but no income taxes, because no taxable income was earned after amortization of investment and the deduction of the deferred depletion allowance. However, much of the companies' original investment will have been written off in another two years and the deduction for the depletion allowance will also begin to be returned to taxable income by then. The government's revenue per barrel of crude oil can therefore be expected to rise appreciably from that time on. Furthermore, the Algerian government requires all oil companies to spend 50 percent of their gross export proceeds inside Algeria. While this provision—unusual for the international oil industry—is not particularly costly to the companies at present, since they are all in the exploring and developing phase which requires considerable local expenditures, it could prove restrictive when that phase is completed and the foreign companies wish to reap the fruits of their investments by maximizing the repatriation of their earnings.

Still, even when all these qualifications are taken into account, the fact remains that the tax provisions of the Algerian Oil Code are less favorable for the government than the tax provisions of most other oil exporting countries. The same applies to royalties which are based on the field price of the oil in Algeria; but in the Middle East and in Libya they are tied to the export price which is usually higher.

France's Position

However, these facts are largely offset by certain special benefits which France has conferred on Algerian oil. We have already mentioned one such benefit—free aquisition by the Algerian government of a 40.5 percent share in the large French petroleum enterprise SN REPAL. Of still more importance is the market protection which France has extended to Algerian oil. By compelling refiners in France to take a certain share of their oil need from Algeria a large assured market for this oil has been created at prices considerably above those prevailing in the world market. Since the production cost of Algerian oil is higher than that of either Middle East or Libyan oil and since the quality of Algerian oil is less well suited to the requirements of the European market than Middle East oil, this exclusive market protection is of considerable economic value to Algeria. In 1964 nearly 70 percent of Algeria's total oil exports found their way into this protected market at prices which are currently more than one third higher than Algerian oil could command in the open market.

France has also proposed an energy policy for the European Common Market which would give preferential treatment to crude oil imports from overseas countries and territories associated with the Common Market. Algeria would be the principal beneficiary of such a policy.

Despite the prospects for a new oil agreement during 1965, there is continued uneasiness in oil industry and government circles about the long-term future of Algeria's oil policy. This is seen in the declining values of Saharan oil shares at the Paris Bourse, as well as in the recent entry of France's government-controlled *Régie Autonome des Pétroles* into exploration activities in the Persian Gulf offshore area and elsewhere which reflects official French policy to seek further diversification of the country's oil supply source in order to limit dependence on Algeria. There is no doubt that this decision was influenced by the growth in Algeria's nationalism and anti-Westernism.

Algeria's desire to replace the existing oil policy, which had its origin in the colonial period, with one that bears the country's own stamp is understood and appreciated. The uneasiness is over the Algerian government's ultimate aim.

True, neither Ben Bella nor Houari Boumedienne has ever requested outright nationalization of the Algerian oil industry. But Ben Bella and other top political figures have suggested that in the socialist economy of the future, the role of the foreign oil companies might be relegated to that of sub-contractors producing oil exclusively for an Algerian government company. The cadre for such a company would come from the new Petroleum Training Institute established by the Soviet Union in Algeria. Whether the foreign oil companies could or would accept such a role depends of course on the conditions offered and on the companies' confidence in the government.

If the French and other foreign oil companies in Algeria should ever be forced, by harassment or decree, to curtail their operations, they would not be the only losers. As pointed out earlier, there is no urgent need for Algerian oil anywhere in the world and good prospecting opportunities may be found elsewhere. And if France were ever to withdraw her special protection of Algerian oil and treat it as any other imported commodity, the volume and value of Algerian oil shipments would become greatly depressed. Since oil production and refining is now Algeria's largest single industry and oil exports, at the current annual rate of over $400 million, account for more than half of Algeria's total exports, the country's entire economy would feel the consequences of such a deterioration in French-Algerian relations.

Algeria's Natural Gas Industry

While this chapter is concerned primarily with the problems of oil, a brief comment on Algeria's natural gas may be in order, since oil and gas are, after all, geologically, chemically, and commercially related.

Algeria's proven natural gas supplies of at least 60 trillion cubic feet (nearly 60 percent of which are located in the huge Hassi R'Mel field) are about equal to her crude oil reserves in terms of energy content (British thermal units). Until recently only an insignificant fraction of this supply was produced—all of it for the country's home market, principally the cities of Oran and Algiers. However, a new gas liquefaction plant has raised the output to 70 billion cubic feet. The liquefied gas is being exported by tanker to Britain and France. But given her reserves, Algeria could export fifteen to twenty times that much gas. Whether she ever will, depends principally on the trans-Mediterranean pipeline project which has been under discussion and study for several years now. The project would cost about $600 million and would have an initial capacity to supply Western Europe with 250 to 350 billion cubic feet of Saharan gas per year. Europe certainly needs natural gas in large volume, but, partly because Algeria's growing anti-Western nationalism and talk about socialism has scared European investors and partly because of the giant gas finds in Holland in late 1963, the country may have missed her chance of becoming the continent's principal natural gas supplier. At the time of writing, the pipeline project is not under active consideration. Instead, France is expected to confine herself to the much more modest project of building another gas liquefaction plant for export purposes, as a joint French-Algerian venture.

OIL IN LIBYA

If Algeria is the problem child of North African oil, Libya is the model of good country-company relations. In part this is of course due to the fact that while in Algeria the oil industry was developed by the former colonial power and thus became an intricate part of the whole web of colonial and post-colonial relations, the search for Libyan oil did not even start until about three years after Libya had achieved her independence.

Libya's oil reserves are currently estimated at eight to nine billion barrels, just slightly lower than Algeria's ten to eleven billion barrels. However, at the present early state of exploration these figures mean little, except that much more oil is likely to be found.

Libya's first petroleum law was passed in 1955, the first well was drilled in 1956, the first major discovery (*Esso's* Zelten field) was made in 1959, commercial production and exports started in the summer of 1961 at the rate of 23,000 barrels daily and are currently in excess of one million barrels daily. No country has ever run through the whole gamut of oil development—from preliminary exploration to major exporter—in that short a period.

A total of twenty oil companies are active in Libya. Thirteen of these are US companies, the others are British, Dutch, French, German, Italian. This granting of concessions to a number of different and competing companies is in sharp contrast to the practice in the Middle East where concessions are usually held by one company in each country. The impact of oil on the economy has been much stronger in the case of Libya than Algeria, simply because Libya is much smaller and has a much less developed economy than Algeria. What oil has meant to Libya can be seen by the fact that oil exports last year accounted for 98 percent of total exports. This year the share will be still higher. As a result Libya's balance of trade has turned from a $128 million deficit in 1961 to a large and growing surplus since 1963. Another pertinent statistical comparison is between the $250 million oil company expenditures in 1963 and the approximately $35 million in value added by all Libyan industrial activities in 1958.[5]

What these figures show is that in Libya, much as in Saudi Arabia or Kuwait, the discovery of oil imposed a gigantic export industry on a small subsistence economy with consequent profound changes in the country's basic politico-economic structure. Thus, though the oil industry employs only 10,000 Libyan employees, this has increased total industrial employment in the country by 40 percent.

Not all the changes have been for the better. Agricultural output, for instance, has stagnated or declined for the last six years, as farmers have poured into the cities to participate in the oil boom. As a result, the country's food import costs have risen sharply while the abandoned farms are being destroyed by water and wind erosion.

Government Oil Revenues

Total government revenues from oil are as follows:

	GOVERNMENT OIL REVENUES (in millions of dollars)	CRUDE OIL PRODUCTION (in 000 barrels daily)
1962	36.0[6]	184
1963	76.0	462
1964	158.0 (est'd)[7]	862
1965 (estimated)	252.0[7]	1150

The unit revenues in the above table vary from year to year. In 1962 they averaged only 53.6 cents per barrel, owing to the fact that of the two producing companies in that year only one showed

---

5. United Nations, *The Growth of World Industry* (1938-1961).
6. Abdul Amir Q. Kubbah, *Libya, Its Oil Industry and Economic System* (Baghdad, 1963).
7. Actual cash receipts may be somewhat smaller for 1964 and some larger for 1965, since the timing of the company payments is such that the revenues for a calender year do not fully correspond to the exports of that year.

a profit and hence, paid taxes, the other paid royalties only. In 1963 unit revenues seem to have declined as more companies began production without showing an immediate profit. In 1964, unit revenues improved and in October of that year Mr. Mohammed Geroushi, Libya's representative to the Organization of Petroleum Exporting Countries (OPEC), declared in an interview with the *Middle East Economic Survey* that the "actual figure currently averages around 55¢ to 60¢ per barrel."[8] For 1965, an average revenue of 60 cents per barrel appears reasonable on the basis of Mr. Geroushi's disclosure that *Esso*, which will account for about half of total exports this year, pays about 65 cents revenue per barrel and the other major producers somewhat less. We may assume that by 1966 Libya's average unit revenue will exceed 65 cents. If and when Libya revises its petroleum law to reflect the recent agreement between the member countries of OPEC and the major oil companies operating in the Middle East, unit revenue should rise even higher. The agreement provides that in the future the companies will pay royalties in *addition* to a 50 percent tax on net income; heretofore, royalties and taxes *together* were limited to 50 percent tax on net income. Libya actively participated in the negotiations leading to the agreement.

After 1967, Libya can also expect revenues from the exportation of natural gas. *Esso* has recently proposed the expenditure of $140 million to construct a gas liquefaction plant at Marsa Brega capable of processing 110 billion cubic feet of natural gas per year. The bulk of the exports is to go to Italy.

The reason why Libya's oil revenue per barrel is so much higher than Algeria's lies to some extent in production cost differentials but mostly in Libya's more favorable oil code. Before 1961 the two codes were not too different, since both contained provisions for rapid amortization and percentage depletion deductions. However, in 1961, just about the time commercial oil production began, Libya issued a revised oil code which redefined and increased the companies' taxable income base by permitting fewer deductions. Under the 50-50 principle, which applies also in Libya, the redefinition resulted in higher payments to the government. Abdul Amir Kubbah says in his book on the Libyan oil industry that government revenues under the 1961 code were 37 percent higher in 1962 than they would have been under the 1955 code.[9]

Issuance of the new oil code did not mean that the government

---

8. Quoted in *Platt's Oilgram*, October 15, 1964, p. 3.
9. Abdul Amir Q. Kubbah, *Libya*, p. 79.

abrogated the existing one on whose basis the oil companies had decided to go into Libya. Instead, the government made an effort to persuade the companies to switch voluntarily to the revised oil code. The persuasion was backed by the government's refusal to issue new concessions or permit rearrangements of existing concessions, such as assignments to other companies, unless the applicant accepted the terms of the revised oil code. By now all producing companies and most of the exploring companies have accepted the revised code, so that Libya's oil revenues are computed entirely on the new basis.

Under Libyan law 70 percent of all oil revenues must be allocated to the country's development. A development plan provides for expenditures of nearly $475 million over a five-year period. There is no doubt that oil revenue will contribute its allocated share, and much more, towards achieving the plan's goals, for the future of Libyan oil exports looks very good indeed, as is shown below.

Competition with Middle East Oil

Production costs for Libyan oil are somewhat higher than for Middle East oil. But Libya's more favorable geographic location, relative to the European markets, more than offsets this cost differential. Thus, the basic tanker rate to Lavera near Marseilles, the intake port for the big South European pipeline, is $1.93 per ton of crude from the Libyan port of Brega, compared to $5.32 from the Saudi Arabian terminal of Ras Tanura. For oil shipments to Hamburg the basic rate is $3.62 per ton from Brega against $6.96 from Ras Tanura. Libyan oil is therefore fully competitive with Middle East oil anywhere west of Suez, although its quality, like that of Algerian oil, is less well suited for the European oil products demand pattern than Middle East oil. On the other hand, Libyan crude oil fits very well into the US oil import pattern.

Libyan Oil Revenues and the Maghrib

If oil developments continue as expected, Libya will soon be the Kuwait of North Africa. For Libya herself this would be a very fortunate position. But for North Africa as a whole it would not. For it would mean that the bulk of the region's revenues from natural resources would be concentrated on just four percent of the Maghrib's thirty million people. Such a lopsided distribution of regional wealth is no more beneficial to development in North Africa than in the Middle East. Kuwait has recently begun to share her riches with other Arab countries (although, so far, only on a very modest scale). Libya may eventually have to do the same. In fact, as North Africa's richest and smallest country, she may soon be expected to contribute significantly to the various regional development schemes.

Furthermore, because of her oil earnings, Libya is likely to find herself under increasing pressure from her Arab neighbors to effect the liquidation of the local military bases of the United States and the United Kingdom before the expiration of the base agreements in 1972. Until 1963 the $40 million in aid given annually by the US and the UK, largely in consideration of the rights for the military bases, plus the income from the local expenditures of the base personnel represented Libya's largest single source of income. But by now the contribution from this source seems small, compared to the country's income from oil, so that Libya can no longer justify the existence of the foreign bases on economic grounds.

THE SECURITY OF NORTH AFRICAN OIL SUPPLIES

We said at the beginning of this chapter that one of the principal reasons for the rapid development of North Africa's oil resources was Europe's quest for diversification of oil supply sources. As we have seen, volumetrically, this goal has been largely achieved, with a significant share of Europe's oil supplies having now been shifted from the Middle East to North Africa. But does this shift also represent a strategic diversification of supply sources? This can only be answered in terms of ethnic, economic, and political power blocs and interest communities, and their likely solidarity under stress. In other words, if supplies from the Middle East became again unavailable for political or strategic reasons could Europe count on a continuous receipt of supplies from North Africa?[10] No clear-cut answer to this question is possible. But some of the considerations to be taken into account in weighing the problem are briefly listed below.

Both the Middle East and North Africa form part of the vast bloc of less developed, anti-colonial commodity-exporting nations.

---

10. For an analysis of this problem which arrives at a somewhat similar conclusion, see Harold Lubell, *Middle East Oil Crises and Western Europe's Energy Supplies*, (Baltimore; Johns Hopkins Press, 1963).

All oil producers in both regions (with the exception of Iran) form part of the Arab world and belong to the Arab League. All but one of the producers in both regions belong to OPEC. Algeria has not joined because OPEC's principal function is to engage in collective bargaining with the private international oil companies, whereas Algeria negotiates only with the French government. However, the North African republic is sympathetic to OPEC's aims of obtaining higher revenue and export prices and supports the organization's striving for solidarity among the world's oil producing nations.

Thus, the two regions have sufficient common interests and contacts, economically and emotionally, at least to raise the possibility that a request of support from the oil producers in one region would be heeded by the producers in the other. We all know that during the Anglo-Iranian oil conflict such solidarity was not forthcoming. It may not again in a similar situation. But history does not repeat itself. And the political consciousness of the countries in question has grown considerably in the years since Mossadegh.

None of this is meant to imply the existence of a world-wide monolithic bloc of oil producing countries. There is no such bloc and the fact that North African oil has greatly de-emphasized the importance of the Suez Canal as Europe's principal oil artery is politically, strategically, and logistically quite significant for Europe. But Egypt is Libya's big and very influential neighbor. Hence, Libya's cooperation may possibly be obtained if access to the Canal were again to become a political factor. And Algeria, which was French territory when oil production started, belongs now to the leftist-neutralist bloc of nations and could under certain circumstances be inclined to put emotional over economic considerations regarding oil exports, particularly in the short run.

All of this is of course very much in the area of speculation, since none of the situations hypothecated above are visible on the political horizon of today. But it is speculation within the realm of the possible and thus points up the fact that a gap may well exist between the geographic and the political diversification of Europe's oil supplies, as far as the shift from the Middle East to North Africa is concerned. The importance of this gap depends on the oil industry's never-ending search for new petroleum supplies which, just now, is being rewarded in places as far apart as the Netherlands and Nigeria.

BIBLIOGRAPHICAL NOTE

Most of the factual information in this paper is based on articles and news items which have appeared in the following trade publications which report regularly on international oil affairs:

Petroleum Press Service (monthly), London
Petroleum Intelligence Weekly, New York
Oil and Gas Journal (weekly), Tulsa, Oklahoma
Oil and Gas International (monthly), London
Petroleum Times (biweekly), London
Platt's Oilgram Newsservice (daily), New York
Pétrole Informations (bi-weekly), Paris
World Petroleum (monthly), New York
PIB Newsletter (monthly), published by Petroleum Information Bureau, London
Activité de l'Industrie Pétrolière (annually), published by the Comité Professionel du Pétrole, Paris

13

Problems and Prospects for North African Unity

*Benjamin Rivlin**

If any additional evidence is needed to demonstrate the pervasiveness of the process of change engulfing the states of North Africa since independence, it can be found in the attention being paid to the question of Maghrib unity, even while each state still faces the challenge of setting its own house in order. In fact, Maghrib unity is viewed, by most of those calling for it, as "the solution" to many of the most difficult problems that beset the North African states individually, particularly that of economic development.

Just what is meant by Maghrib unity? What is the status of this unity today? In what directions can closer union within the Maghrib develop? What are the prospects for such development? These are the questions with which this chapter is concerned.

THE VISION AND THE COMMITMENT

Long before independence, the vision of North African unity captivated the imagination of nationalist leaders. Based on the shared cultural values of their Arabo-Berber-Islamic heritage as well as on the region's identity as a distinct geographic entity, *al-jazirat al-maghrib* (the Island of the West), the idea has been a recurrent, although by no means the dominant, theme in nation-

---

* The author acknowledges his gratitude to the Joint Committee on the Near and Middle East of the Social Science Research Council and the American Council of Learned Societies for the grant that facilitated his research in North Africa on the subject of this paper, and to the Research Center for Comparative Politics and Administration of Brooklyn College for aid in its preparation.

alist propaganda since the early formative days of the North African nationalist movements in the 1920's and 1930's. As nationalism developed in North Africa, it was not a preeminent *Maghrib nationalism* but rather individually distinct Moroccan, Tunisian, Algerian, and Libyan movements. The pan-Maghrib dream, often intertwined with pan-Arabism whose apostle Shakib Arslan so greatly influenced the first generation of North African nationalists, formed a part of their respective ideologies from the very outset. Professor Julien points out that the ideal of Maghrib unity, drawing inspiration from the 12th century Almohadins, who united North Africa under one dynasty, spurred Maghrib nationalists to draw together.[1] Moreover, because most of the region was ruled by the same European power—France—Moroccans, Algerians, and Tunisians were inevitably pushed into close contact with each other as students in Paris (e.g., Association of Muslim Students of North Africa, organized in 1927), or as exiles, agitating for North African freedom (e.g., The Arab Maghrib Office, established in Cairo in 1947). While each nationalist movement was fighting essentially for the independence of its particular country, independence for the Maghrib as a whole was always evoked, as evidenced in Mehdi Ben Barka's pronouncement that "... the community of thought, of goals, and of destinies is such among the three peoples of North Africa and their liberation movements, that when one speaks of one part one is necessarily speaking of all and vice versa."[2] But the North African nationalist profession of faith did not stop with assertions of reciprocity and interrelatedness, for it proclaimed that a united Arab Maghrib was a basic aspiration of the peoples of North Africa. Reflecting this faith widely shared by most nationalists in the Maghrib, Allal al Fassi wrote in 1948, "The reality is, that the [nationalist] movements in North Africa, although under different names and labels, are but one movement seeking liberty, *unity*, and rejuvenation."[3]

After independence, this profession of faith was reiterated time and time again in each of the Maghrib countries. Typical of these reaffirmations are Mohammed V's declaration that "... the unity of North Africa is one of our most cherished hopes"[4] and Bourguiba's

1. Charles-André Julien, *L'Afrique du Nord en Marche* (Paris: Julliard, 1952), pp. 22-23.
2. *Premier Colloque Méditerranéen de Florence*, October 3-6, 1958, pp. 59-60.
3. 'Alal al-Fasi, *The Independence Movements in Arab North Africa* (Washington, D.C.: American Council of Learned Societies, 1954), p. ix. Italics added.
4. Embassy of Morocco, Washington, D.C. *Statements and Documents*, "The Tangier Conference," Vol. I, No. 3, May 15, 1958, p. 1.

vision of a "United Maghrib from Sollum to the Atlantic."[5] Eventually, the Maghrib idea found expression in the constitutions that were adopted in North Africa. Most explicit is the Tunisian Constitution (July 1959) which, in its preamble, avows the Tunisian people's determination "of remaining true . . . to the ideal of a Union of the Great Maghrib," and in Article 2 declares that "the Tunisian republic is a part of the Great Maghrib and is working for its unity, within the framework of common interests." Both the Moroccan and Algerian constitutions, while more restrained on this matter, are nonetheless obeisant to the Maghrib idea. Article 2 of Algeria's Constitution (September 1963) affirms that Algeria "is an integral part of the Arab Maghrib," while Morocco's Constitution (December 1962) merely declares in its preamble that "The Kingdom of Morocco, a sovereign state whose language is Arabic, constitutes a part of the Great Maghrib." The Libyan Constitution, drafted under the aegis of the United Nations in 1950-51, when France's hegemony over the other states of the Maghrib appeared impregnable, understandably makes no mention of closer union with these states. However, Libyan leaders have since affirmed Libya's Maghrib identity on several occasions, although Libya's commitment to pan-Maghribism is by no means as pronounced as that of the other three states. For a while Libyan policy envisioned the country as a buffer between the Arab states of the Maghrib and the Mashriq. But in recent years Libya has increasingly become involved in Maghrib affairs and its leaders have publicly reaffirmed their faith in Maghrib unity.

Most affirmations of faith in pan-Maghribism have been in the nature of statements giving unqualified allegiance to the concept of Maghrib unity whose meaning is left vague and whose structure is undefined. A notable exception to this is Algeria's commitment to Maghrib unity. In an address on April 5, 1963 as reported in *Le Monde*, Premier Ben Bella declared:

> We are not for a Maghrib which will be an altered copy of the Fertile Crescent, in the hands of imperialism and opposed to Arab Unity. Geographic considerations are secondary; there are above all choices in domestic and foreign policy to consider. We would align ourselves with Lapland as well as with the Maghrib, if these countries would side with us in

5. From a speech delivered on January 3, 1957, and reprinted in a collection of President Bourguiba's speeches on Africa under the title, *The Advancement of Africa* (Tunis: n.d.), p. 31.

face of the great roar of protest that will be raised when we put our great socialist designs into operation.[6]

In this speech, Ben Bella, in referring to the Arab world, said "I hope that the Arab world will rid itself of the Imam Badrs, the Ibn Sauds and of all the Emirs who hinder it."[7] It is hard not to conclude that Ben Bella had his Maghrib neighbor King Hassan of Morocco specifically in mind when he made these statements. Clearly, Ben Bella was establishing an ideological prerequisite to Maghrib unity. During the Algerian-Moroccan frontier war some six months later, the attack on Hassan as an enemy of socialism, was made very explicit.[8] However, it is most interesting to note that the Algerian leadership had second thoughts about this line because in official versions of this speech, the text has been edited and altered to modify this position considerably. In the revised version, Ben Bella's statement reads as follows:

> As for ourselves, we are ready to cooperate in the creation of this Maghrib. Some of our brothers have expressed this basic desire. The dialogue has begun. We wish to continue it and to make it so that this profound aspiration of our masses becomes a reality. We are for the Maghrib, but certainly not for a Maghrib that will be an altered copy of the Fertile Crescent, in the hands of imperialism and opposed to Arab unity.[9]

The revised version does not implicate King Hassan even by indirection.[10] The intention in these revisions clearly was to tone down the attack on a fellow Maghrib chief of state and at the same time to modify the ideological connotation of Maghrib unity, thus not foreclosing the debate on this issue.

---

6. *Le Monde,* April 5, 1963.
7. *Ibid.*
8. See République Algérienne Démocratique et Populaire, Ministère de l'Orientation, *Actualité et Documents,* No. 22, October 1-15, 1963, and No. 23, October 16, 1963.
9. République Algérienne Démocratique et Populaire, Ministère de l'Information, Direction de la Documentation et des Publications, *Discours du Président Ben Bella* (El-Riath), April 4, 1963, p. 16.
10. Actually two revised versions of this speech have appeared; the one cited in the previous note and one included in a collection of Ben Bella's speeches, République Algérienne Démocratique et Populaire, Ministère de l'Orientation Nationale, Direction de la Documentation et des Publications, *Les Discours du Président Ben Bella,* Année 1963 et 1er Trimestre 1964. The latter version completely eliminates the references to the Arab monarchies, while the former only refers to the Amir Badr and to Ibn Saud without mentioning any "other emirs."

THE MEANING AND PURPOSE OF MAGHRIB UNITY

Up to this point, reference has been made to "Maghrib unity" and "pan-Maghribism" without clearly defining the concept or indicating its purpose. The strong ideological commitment to Maghrib unity by all North African leaders is unmistakably clear; but far from clear is exactly what is meant by such unity and what specifically it is intended to achieve. Most North Africans, when using the term rarely stop to define it, leaving its meaning vague and unstructured. This may be done deliberately by sophisticated leaders who realize the difficulty in trying to give precise meaning to such an idealistic symbol; or, it may be done cynically by demagogues whose major concern is in getting as much political mileage as possible out of the idea. Since most politicians in North Africa, as elsewhere, combine the qualities of the sophisticate and the demagogue, the absence of a clear-cut statement as to the meaning and purpose of Maghrib unity is understandable. But also present is a view of pristine simplicity that finds it unnecessary to define Maghrib unity since its meaning (at least to those who hold this view) is obvious. This concept is epitomized in the statement: "The North Africans constitute a single people and the frontiers that divide them are artificial obstacles."[11] The logical conclusion one is led to by this statement is that the goal of Maghrib unity is the creation of a single polity in North Africa. Official utterances, however, are by no means as definite. The references to Maghrib unity in the constitutions of the North African states, previously cited, aptly illustrate this point. Algeria, Morocco, and Tunisia solemnly affirm in their respective constitutions that they are part of the Grand Maghrib, but that is about all. The various constitutional commitments to the idea of unity do not preclude the ultimate creation of a single state in North Africa, but then again they do not clearly point in this direction. As a matter of fact each constitution stresses the sovereign independence of its country and people, but at the same time each implies a "manifest destiny" process that eventually will unite the peoples of the Maghrib.

The exact form Maghrib unity is to take remains to be established. The alternatives range from the establishment of a single North African polity as the optimum, to the institutionalization of consultations among the four Maghrib states, as the minimum. At the "Conference for the Unification of the Arab Maghrib" held in Tangier in April 1958, "the federal form" was advanced as

---

11. See Julien, *L'Afrique du Nord*, p. 24.

"most responsive to the realities of the participating countries."[12] Taken together with the other Tangier decisions, it is quite clear that the idea of a federated Maghrib was viewed as a long range goal rather than as an immediate objective. In fact, since 1958 the idea of a Maghrib federation has been played down considerably, even by those who had previously strongly advocated it. Instead, the emphasis has been upon more limited objectives labeled "joint action," "cooperation," or "solidarity." These have ranged from King Hassan's suggestion (not taken up) that each head of a Maghrib state speak for all other Maghrib states when visiting foreign countries,[13] to functional economic agreements reached in 1964, under the guiding aegis of the United Nations Economic Commission for Africa.[14] From the viewpoint of actual progress towards unity in the Maghrib, the latter agreements take on great significance since it is generally assumed that they will lead to similar agreements in other functional areas such as education, air transportation, etc., and that the cumulative effect of this process will be the building of a "unified Maghrib."

Implicit in the immediately foregoing discussion of the meaning and form of Maghrib unity is that the purpose of this unity is the enhancement of the Maghrib and its people. It is to be noted in the oft repeated dictum of North African nationalism, that freedom in the Maghrib will not be achieved until every part of the region is independent. This was the real purport of the 1958 Tangier conference, to demonstrate the solidarity of the already free North African states with the Algerian people, embroiled in a bitter struggle for independence. Moreover, the motto *E Pluribus Unum*, is in theory no less appealing to the North Africans than it was 175 years ago to the American colonists. Facing common problems of economic underdevelopment, social stagnation, and political weakness, it is quite natural for North Africans to feel that through unity they will achieve the strength to enable them to solve the problems with which they cannot cope individually.

But the purpose of Maghrib unity is not viewed exclusively within the context of North Africa; it is also postulated as a precursor both to Arab unity and to African unity. Without hesitation, North African leaders stress Maghrib unity as reinforcing both Arab unity and African unity at the same time. Exactly how Maghrib unity would be related to either or both of these broader

12. Embassy of Morocco, *Statements*, p. 11.
13. *The Economist*, February 23, 1963, p. 689.
14. See p. 00.

unity movements is not spelled out. Lacking such definition, Maghrib leaders seem to have no difficulty in proclaiming their loyalty to the three unities simultaneously, pushing aside any incompatibility that may be inherent in such a triple allegiance. Basically, a degree of incompatibility does exist and within the Organization of African Unity the question of "continentalism versus regionalism" has emerged as a contentious issue. With progress painstakingly slow, towards Arab unity, towards African unity, and for that matter, Maghrib unity, the problems stemming from incompatibility are a long way off. For the moment, the issue is largely hypothetical and because it is so, it affords North African political leaders the opportunity to bask in the glory of each unity. At this point in their history, they find it highly convenient to have three such lofty themes to play in their efforts to attune their peoples to the demands of independence and modernization.

That the concept of Maghrib unity does not as yet have a precise meaning or agreed upon purpose hardly poses a problem for those who either advocate it or use it for ends in North Africa, but it does create just such a problem for those attempting to study and evaluate the issue. Without a clear understanding of what is serving as a base, it is impossible to analyze in any meaningful way progress to date and prospects for the future involving this vision and commitment to Maghrib unity. Thus, for the purposes of analysis in this chapter Maghrib unity can be taken to mean any kind of cooperative venture undertaken by two or more of the four Maghrib states through institutions and staff specially created on a permanent basis to work towards a common end. While this definition seems to be pointing away from the creation of a single polity in North Africa, this goal is not ruled out theoretically, even if practically it appears unlikely to take place. However, because of its remoteness it would be most unfair to judge the process of regional integration in the Maghrib in terms of achieving this ultimate of ends. At the same time, this definition rules out any random meetings of two or more states as well as multilateral treaty arrangements that are not institutionalized, i.e., that do not have distinct organs to fulfill the function of the treaty.

THE STATUS OF MAGHRIB UNITY SINCE INDEPENDENCE

Even before independence was achieved by all the Maghribi states, a "Conference for the Unification of the Arab Maghrib" took place. Convened in Tangier in April 1958, this conference was technically unofficial, being a meeting of representatives of the dominant political parties of the Maghrib—Istiqlal (Morocco), Neo-Destour (Tunisia), and FLN (Algeria). Actually, those attending included very high officials such as Ahmad Balafrej of Morocco and Bahi Ladgham of Tunisia, as well as Ferhat Abbas who was soon to become the first president of the Provisional Government of the Algerian Republic. Libya, the fourth Maghrib country, was represented by an observer but did not participate actively. The conference resolved that it was "the unanimous will of the peoples of the Arab Maghrib to unite their destiny in the tight solidarity of their interests," and that the time had come to "cement their desires for union within the framework of common institutions."[15] It also proposed the establishment of a permanent secretariat and an Arab Maghrib Consultative Assembly, and for periodic meetings of the leaders of Algeria, Tunisia, and Morocco to further the development of Maghrib unity. Little was accomplished in the next eight years to implement the conference's resolve and proposals. The permanent secretariat met three times during the first six months after the conference, the Arab Maghrib Consultative Assembly was never organized nor were periodic meetings of the leaders held.

With the attainment of independence by Algeria in 1962, many assumed that the time was ripe to carry out the ideal of unity. The stumbling block of French colonialism had been removed from the scene. Now, all four Maghrib countries were independent states, and they had it within their sovereign power to construct a community in North Africa to their own liking. Actually, the issue of North African unity moved only very slowly onto the political arena of the Maghrib. In 1962, Morocco and Algeria agreed to the creation of an inter-ministerial council for a united Arab Maghrib, but this body never met. Similarly, there was no follow-up to the meeting of Moroccan, Algerian, and Tunisian foreign ministers in Rabat in 1963 which had issued a call for coordination of the three countries' foreign, cultural, judicial, and economic policies. In anticipation of this conference, the *Economist* commented "One foreign ministers' conference cannot make a political summer. It could disperse some clouds."[16] But no positive results, even so miniscule, were evident. In fact, viewing inter-Maghrib relations between independence and 1964

15. Embassy of Morocco, *Statements*.
16. *The Economist*, February 9, 1963, p. 490.

which witnessed a frontier war between Morocco and Algeria, a break in diplomatic relations between Morocco and Tunisia, acrimonious charges by Tunisia of Algerian interference in its internal affairs, plus a host of less serious irritations—one wonders whatever happened to the ideal of Maghrib unity. A deep-freeze descended upon inter-Maghrib relations. The Maghrib states were hardly talking to each other, acting more like bitter enemies than like brothers who were supposed to be "cementing the desires for union" by creating "common institutions."

It was not until May 1963 that the first thaw in inter-Maghrib relations came at the African Unity Conference of the African heads of state at Addis Ababa. A meeting there between Ben Bella and Bourguiba set the stage for a reconciliation which led to a series of agreements establishing the principle of regular consultation on foreign political matters, providing for mutual assistance in legislative matters, and instituting a system to expedite the movement of persons and goods across the Algeria-Tunisia frontier. The rapprochement culminated on November 28, 1963, with the signing of a far-reaching Tunisian-Algerian economic agreement, concerning the use and distribution of energy, establishing a joint commission in the field of electrical energy, and confirming the desirability of harmonizing policy with regard to large economic blocs. According to Bourguiba these agreements dissipated the misunderstandings that had existed between Algeria and Tunisia.[17]

Although the new agreement was hailed both in Algiers and in Tunisia as a step in the direction of Maghrib unity, it was some time yet before the thaw extended to Morocco. King Hassan II had stayed away from the Addis Ababa conference because of the Mauritanian issue, and from the December 1963 meeting of all North African Arab heads of state at Bizerte because he did not wish to come face to face with Nasser. However, within a month of the Bizerte meeting, Hassan found it convenient to attend the Arab summit meeting at Cairo, called to formulate a plan of action in response to Israel's plans to divert water from the Jordan. At Cairo, it is reported that "inter-Maghribian disputes were somewhat dissipated by conversation and breakfast shared by Ben Bella, Hassan II and Bourguiba, along with Nasser."[18]

The fact that the Maghrib leaders were talking to each other,

17. *The Maghreb Digest*, II, No. 1 (January 1964), 31-32; II, No. 2 (February 1964), 8-9.
18. *Ibid.*, II, No. 3 (March 1964), 25-26.

hardly constituted real progress towards regional unity. Given the context of inter-Maghrib relations in the months and years immediately preceding the Cairo Conference, it represented a step, albeit a tiny one, clearing some of the ground standing in the path of unity.

At about the same time, the necessity of more coordinated action by the Maghrib states in the economic sphere was becoming evident. The benefits of a concerted Maghrib approach to economic problems constituted an underlying rationale of all thinking about North African unity practically from the moment the idea was first broached. In the years immediately following World War II, French economic planners argued that under the exigencies of modern economic life, calling for industrialization and economic development, it was necessary to foster regional integration in North Africa, and from their point of view naturally in close association with France.[19] Maghrib economic integration was also espoused by North African nationalists, some of whom were even prepared to accord a special position to France *vis-à-vis* the Maghrib, but only on condition that Morocco, Algeria, and Tunisia first attain complete political independence.[20] Once independence was achieved, little attention was paid to coordinated economic action or planning. Each country proceeded unilaterally, making its own plans, entering into its own economic and financial agreements with France and other foreign powers. The chilled atmosphere of inter-Maghrib relations impeded any efforts at regional economic coordination. At best, there were a series of bilateral agreements—between Morocco and Algeria, Morocco and Tunisia, Tunisia and Algeria—all of which were individually hailed as furthering Maghrib unity but most of which were stillborn.

Of prime economic concern to the states of the Maghrib, was their relationship to the European Common Market. Although Morocco, Algeria, and Tunisia faced very similar problems in this regard and quite logically came up with more or less identical views as to how these problems should be resolved, they did not coordinate their positions and tactics in advance, but rather negotiated individually with the EEC. Only when negotiations

---

19. See for example René de Lacharrière, "Problèmes d'Organisation Politique et Administrative et Projets de Développement Industriel en Afrique du Nord," Chapter IX in *Industrialisation de l'Afrique du Nord* (Paris: Colin, 1952).

20. See for example Bourguiba's statement quoted in Roger Le Tourneau, *Evolution Politique de l'Afrique du Nord Musulmane, 1920-1961* (Paris: Colin, 1962), p. 468.

between Israel and the EEC were in their final stages, did the three Maghrib states undertake joint action in protesting the citrus provisions of this proposed agreement.[21] On this matter, it should be noted, that these states were not alone since other citrus-producing countries of the Mediterranean, such as Italy and Spain, similarly objected to the impending Israeli-EEC agreement.

The experience with regard to the European Common Market clearly underscored what had previously been acknowledged in theory, i.e., the need for closer economic coordination. But the point was strengthened in February 1964 when the Economic Commission for Africa published the report of its Industrial Coordination Mission to Algeria, Libya, Morocco, and Tunisia.[22] The Mission noted the wastefulness in duplication of industrial investment and in the lack of coordinated action in the ten sectors of large scale industry under examination. It urged quick action to stem the disintegration which was setting in because consultations in the preparation of development plans were lacking.[23] The economic ministers of the Maghrib states were supposed to meet on April 6, 1964, to plan action implementing this report; but this meeting was postponed at the last minute. It seems apparent that the countries were in no position to begin serious discussions on specific aspects of Maghrib unity, which holding this meeting implied. However, the meeting was not put off indefinitely for it took place some six months later in November 1964. In a real sense, the Economic Commission for Africa's report served as a prodding instrument. Its mere existence had the effect of forcing the North African countries to think concretely about Maghrib coordination. Thus, from the standpoint of pan-Maghribism, the ECA helped push the issue of Maghrib unity into the center of the political arena in 1964.

Further thawing of inter-Maghrib relations took place at the African summit conference called by the Organization of African Unity in Cairo in mid-July 1964 when personal contacts among Ben Bella, Bourguiba, and Hassan were resumed. Out of these meetings emerged reports of an imminent Maghrib summit conference to deal with problems of North African unity.[24] By the end of the year, this conference had not been held but the summit

21. *The Maghreb Digest*, II, No. 5 (May 1964), 42.
22. U.N. Document, E/CN.14/248, 5 February 1964, *Report of the ECA Industrial Co-Ordination Mission to Algeria, Libya, Morocco and Tunisia.*
23. *Ibid.*
24. *Maghreb* (Paris), No. 5 (Sept.-Oct. 1964), p. 8

idea was not dead. At the conclusion of King Hassan's official visit to Tunis in December, a joint communiqué asserted that agreements reached between Maghrib states serve to clear the way for a four-power Maghrib meeting at the summit, indicating clearly that a summit was in the offing. Why the delay?

Having participated in the Arab and African summit conference at which momentous issues of African and Arab unity were dealt with, the call for a Maghrib summit meeting seemed to emerge quite logically. With the eyes of all the people of North Africa focused on the summit conference, the cause of pan-Maghribism could be greatly advanced through the stirring pageantry and noble words of rededication to the gospel of unity and solidarity. Despite such advantage, if this is all that takes place and no tangible results emerge from the conference, it runs the risk of retarding rather than advancing the cause of Maghrib unity. On the other hand, if tangible agreements are reached, there is risk of another kind—to the individual participants whose political position back home may be compromised by these agreements. For example, Algeria's *Révolution Africaine* editorially supported the idea of a Maghrib summit as it emerged from the Hassan-Bourguiba meetings, stressing that "We [the states of the Maghrib] have no chance of success if we are not united." But it went on to say that "to take into consideration immediate interests" in the summit conference "is a trap" for "it would guarantee the interests of small social groups at the expense of the overall interests of the people of the Maghrib."[25] Inherent in this notion is danger for any leader who would be required to sacrifice the interests of one or another group upon whose support he relies back home. It is quite evident that a summit conference, whose ground is not carefully laid out, can prove risky for the overall idea of Maghrib unity and for the individual participants as well. It is therefore not surprising that the North African heads of state have not rushed into such a conference but have rather moved cautiously. Thus, when the first concrete steps towards Maghrib unity were taken in the fall of 1964, they were taken not at a summit nor a foreign ministers level but on a technical ministerial level. Ministers of economy and agriculture from all four states met in Tunis from September 29 to October 1, 1964, and agreed to create a permanent Advisory Committee to study means of economic coordination in the Maghrib and to formulate a single policy

---

25. *Révolution Africaine*, No. 99, December 19, 1964, p. 8.

vis-a-vis the European Common Market. Two months later, the ministers participated in a two-day conference in Tangier held under the auspices of the Economic Commission for Africa, agreeing to establish the following permanent institutions:[26]

    1. An Industrial Studies Center in Tripoli, Libya, to study industrial projects of common interest.

    2. A nine-man Standing Consultative Committee, composed of high officials, with headquarters in Tangier, Morocco. Required to meet once every three months and charged with the responsibility of promoting the coordination of economic development planning and of studying methods of financing economic development, this committee is regarded as the key institution in the newly emerging pattern of regional economic integration.

    3. A Council of Ministers, with the same chairman as the Standing Consultative Committee, established to act on the recommendations of this committee.

With the establishment of these bodies, the first tangible region-wide integrative machinery came into being. From the viewpoint of regional integration, this initial step is of considerable significance for its represents the first concrete expression of the long-held dream of Maghrib unity. Moreover, it represents an important breakthrough, because while taking the first step towards regional integration in any setting is difficult enough, it was even harder in the dissentious Maghrib atmosphere. However, this is only the beginning. To stop at this point will hardly constitute a fulfillment of the commitment to build a united Maghrib. It remains to be seen whether this first step is a precursor of additional moves in the direction of North African integration.

While actual progress towards unity on a governmental level has been extremely slow, each visit by a head of state, minister, or official delegation from one Maghrib state to another automatically touches off a spate of headlines and newspaper comment heralding the inevitable construction of a unified Maghrib. In addition, the press and semi-official bodies use every other possible occasion to promote the idea of Maghrib unity. A few examples will suffice to illustrate this steady flow of propaganda. At the end of March 1964, a regional Boy Scout seminar in Algiers attended by scout leaders from Morocco, Algeria, and Tunisia was

---

26. For full text of the agreements see *Maghreb* (Paris), No. 7 (Jan.-Feb. 1965), pp. 3-10.

hailed with the banner headline "First Steps Towards the Unity of the Maghrib" and in the story, the scouts are described as "the avant-garde of everything that is about to be done to bring about the construction of the grand Maghrib."[27] Ironically, this news story appeared in the press just as it was also reporting delays in the exchange of prisoners of war between Morocco and Algeria. A second example is to be found in the two-page spread in *Révolution Africaine* in honor of Algeria's noted painter Mohammed Racim. Featured is a picture of the artist working on a large symbolic painting captioned "The Dawn of the Grand Maghrib."[28] Similarly the meetings of Maghrib youth organizations are also used to focus attention on the dream of unity. At their first meeting in Tunis in February 1964 and again at their meeting a year later in Algiers, the representatives of youth groups from Morocco, Algeria, and Tunisia asserted that their coming together constituted "an important contribution towards the supreme objective of unity of the Maghrib peoples."[29] Clearly, the drums of unity are beating in the Maghrib. What are its prospects?

A LOOK AHEAD

Before regional integration can take place, not only in the Maghrib but in any region in the world, it is recognized by all students of the subject that certain "background" or "essential" conditions have to be present in order to generate the quest for unity.[30] The foregoing discussion has amply demonstrated that a quest for unity based on shared cultural values of religion, language, and history and a favorable ecological setting exists in the Maghrib. It has also shown that sound economic reasons exist for regional integration. Together these constitute a significant set of factors, whose existence establishes a propensity for some form of regional integration.

The existence of these regional propensity indicators does not, however, automatically trigger the integration process. Regional integration does not come about because a set of conditions exists. It comes about when the existence of these conditions is taken advantage of by deliberate action and decisions. This calls for active political bargaining among the parties concerned, and,

27. *Le Petit Marocain* (Casablanca), April 1, 1964.
28. *Révolution Africaine*, No. 106, February 6, 1965.
29. *Avant-Garde* (Casablanca), February 20, 1965.
30. On the subject of regional integration, see listings in bibliography at the close of this chapter.

since regional integration involves states, the question of sovereignty and independence quickly comes into consideration.[31] What is involved here are not empty legalistic concepts but matters of national pride, differences in orientation and outlook, and rapidly crystallizing vested interests in titles, positions, and power.

Any step in the direction of regional unity, if it is to be meaningful, must be within the context of the definition of the concept previously established in this chapter, i.e., any cooperative venture undertaken by two or more states through institutions and staff specially created on a permanent basis to work towards a common end. Any such step implies a modification of sovereignty in that it places limitations upon future freedom of action of those entering into the regional relationship. For example, in the case of the Maghrib, a straightforward application of the Tangier economic agreements and their normal evolution, involving coordinated planning for economic development, would affect the economies of the several countries so basically that before very long the separate ministries of national economy would themselves be severely circumscribed. As a matter of fact, this is the very goal of regional integration—*the establishment of regional instruments for the realization of common aims by limiting the freedom of action of the member states.*

Herein lies the crux of the problem of the prospects for Maghrib unity. It can be stated axiomatically, as a rule of inter-state relations, that only under the most unusual circumstances and only after very lengthy consideration and negotiation are sovereign states likely to enter into an amalgamative relationship with a neighbor or neighboring states. Regional integration is, therefore, difficult to achieve even under optimum conditions. Despite the existence of background conditions favorable to unity, there also exist certain background conditions, clearly evident in the foregoing review of unity efforts in the Maghrib to date, that weaken rather than strengthen the region's propensity for unity. Specifically, the prevailing political atmosphere in the Maghrib, marked by conflicting ideologies, personal rivalries, and clashing political styles, is hardly conducive to regional integration. Under these circumstances the achievement of Maghrib unity calls for the highest qualities of statesmanship, the most unselfish of spirits, and a willingness to compromise.

31. On the question of bargaining to achieve regional amalgamation, see William H. Riker, *Federalism: Origin, Operation, Significance* (Boston: Little, Brown, 1964).

Do these exist in the Maghrib? No one can answer this question with any semblance of certainty. Neither can one provide easy predictions as to the prospects for Maghrib unity. What can be said is this: With the creation of the Standing Consultative Committee and the other agreements for economic regional coordination, the process of bargaining entailed in the establishment of any form of regional unity has begun. If the states of the Maghrib permit these new regional instrumentalities to evolve by individually practicing self-restraint, it will be patently evident that they are serious about achieving unity. But if they do not, it will be equally clear that they are unwilling to make the necessary sacrifices and Maghrib unity will remain a vision, constantly evoked by self-seeking demagogues and politicians, rather than a reality, working for the progress of the entire Maghrib and its people.

BIBLIOGRAPHY

On Maghrib Unity

Ben Barka, Mehdi. *Problèmes d'Edification du Maroc et du Maghreb*. Paris: Plon, 1959.
Bouabid, Abderrahim, "Pour faire l'Unité du Maghreb il faut construire de Solides Base Economiques," *Le Monde Diplomatique* (July 1961).
Bouabid, Aberrahim, "Prospects for a United Maghreb" in William Lewis (ed), *New Forces in Africa*, Washington, D. C.: Public Affairs Press, 1962.
Chaker, Abdelmajid, "La Formation du Grand Maghreb est désormais une Nécessité Inéluctable," *Le Monde Diplomatique* (April 1961).
De Lacharrière, René, "Problèmes d'Organisation Politique et Administrative et Projets de Développement Industriel en Afrique du Nord." Chapter IX in *Industrialisation de l'Afrique du Nord*. Paris: Colin, 1952.
Al-Fasi, 'Alal. *The Independence Movements in Arab North Africa*. Washington, D. C.: American Council of Learned Societies, 1954.
Gallagher, Charles F. *The United States and North Africa*. Cambridge, Mass.: Harvard University Press, 1963.
Julien, Charles-André. *L'Afrique du Nord en Marche*. Paris: Julliard, 1952.
"La Conférence Ministérielle Maghrebine," *Maghreb* (Paris), No. 7 (Jan.-Feb. 1965).
"Les Tentatives de Conférences Maghrebines 'Au Sommet'," *Maghreb* (Paris), No. 6 (Nov.-Dec. 1964), pp. 7-11.
Le Tourneau, Roger. *Evolution Politique de l'Afrique du Nord Musulmane, 1920-1961*. Paris: Colin, 1962.
Liska, George. *The Greater Maghreb: From Independence to Unity?* Washington, D.C. Washington Center for Foreign Policy Research, 1963.

Marchat, Henri, "Le Conflit Frontalier Algéro-Marocain," *Revue Juridique et Politique d'Outre-Mer*, XVIII, No. 1 (Jan.-March 1964), 65-82.

Report of the ECA Industrial Co-Ordination Mission to Algeria, Libya, Morocco and Tunisia (Ewing Mission), UN Document E/CN.14/248, 5 February 1964.

Sands, William, "Prospects for a United Maghrib" in *The Arab Middle East and Muslim Africa*, ed. Tibor Kerekes. New York: Praeger, 1961.

Slim, Mongi, "Le Grand Maghreb: Réalité et Perspectives," *Le Monde Diplomatique* (July 1964).

Zartman, I. William. *The Sahara—Bridge or Barrier?* New York: Carnegie Endowment for International Peace, 1963.

On Regional Integration (General)

Deutsch, Karl W., "Toward an Inventory of Basic Trends and Patterns in Comparative and International Politics," *American Political Science Review*, LIV, No. 1 (March 1960), 34-57.

Deutsch, Karl W., and Jacob, Philip E., et al. *The Integration of Political Communities*, Philadelphia, Pa.: J. B. Lippincott and Company, 1964.

_____, et al. *Political Community and the North Atlantic Area: International Organization in the Light of Historical Experience.* Princeton: Princeton University Press, 1957.

Etzioni, Amitai, "A Paradigm for the Study of Political Unification," *World Politics*, XV, No. 1 (October 1962), 44-75.

_____, "The Dialectics of Supranational Unification," *American Political Science Review*, LVI, No. 4 (December 1962), 927-935.

Haas, Ernst B., "The Challenge of Regionalism," *International Organization*, XII, No. 4 (Autumn 1958), 440-458.

_____and Philippe C. Schmitter, "Economics and Differential Patterns of Political Integration: Projections about Unity in Latin America," *International Organization*, XVIII, No. 4 (Autumn 1964).

Nye, Joseph S., Jr., "Unification in Africa: Six Traps in Search of a Scholar," in *Public Policy*, eds. John D. Montgomery and Arthur Smithies. Cambridge, Mass.: Harvard University Press, 1964.

Riker, William H. *Federalism: Origin, Operation, Significance.* Boston: Little, Brown, 1964.

14

The Colonial Imprint

Elizabeth Monroe

During the long period of Algerian resistance to France that followed the French invasion, a leading shaykh remarked to General Bugeaud that "even if, like the Turks, you are here for three hundred years, you will go in the end." He spoke in 1841. Now that his prophecy has come true, it is worth asking how deep and permanent is the mark that colonial experience at European hands is leaving upon North Africa.

When considering the former French territories, and Algeria in particular, there are no criteria on which to found a judgment. No other territory has shared all Algeria's experiences—the advantages of European example, on a major scale and reinforced by proximity to Europe, offset by the chagrin and envy that are generated at sight of strangers making gainful use of domains that native hands had let run to waste. With Libya, by contrast, it is possible to make valid comparisons. There, the Italian colonial experiment was so brief, so late in date, and so unpopular with many of the implanted Italians, that it can be likened to British and French experience in some of the ex-Ottoman mandates. There (except in Lebanon, with its peculiar and ancient Christian affinities with Europe, and in Palestine, which Jewish immigration turned into a special case) the imprint left is much slighter than either mandatory expected; in Syria and Iraq, the standards of justice and political liberty that prevail within a generation of the mandatory's departure show no sign of the influence that France and Britain each worked so hard to instill. Italy's Libyan experiment is likely to show as little trace.

Prophets who turn to the ex-French dependencies cannot be so confident. About Tunisia and Morocco, most of their guesses tally, but they differ about Algeria. There are both social and historical reasons why Tunisia and Morocco are bound to bear less marks of French influence than will Algeria. Their experience of protection was shorter; the proportion of French settlers to indigenous inhabitants was lower,[1] and those who came remained Frenchmen who intended to end their days in France; the Algerian *colon,* by contrast, found it natural to live and die in Africa. Further, Tunisia and Morocco retained, in the bey and the sultan respectively, a living symbol of a national pedigree. Above all, each preserved its Islamic culture and character owing to the influence and renown of a great Islamic university—the Zitouna in Tunis, the Qarawiyin in Fez. The French, who respected local dignity and learning, made no sustained attempt to assimilate the protected peoples, and when they metamorphosed the empire into the *Union Française* in 1946, they gave both protectorates the right to join it on an exalted level as "associated states," related to France by virtue not of colonization but of international treaties. Both waived the supposed privilege.

Algeria possessed no such individuality, identifying marks, or academic poles of counter-attraction. It was, therefore, as its modern scholars ruefully admit, infinitely colonizable. Accordingly, the bulk of this essay deals with the French imprint that is likely to be left upon Algeria—the most unusual and in the long run probably the most influential of the three territories.

Frenchmen are sure that they have left a permanent mark upon Algeria because there, as nowhere else in Africa, their policy of assimilation created a widespread local desire to behave and think like Frenchmen. By their standards, this desire ought to have been increased, and not impaired, by their policy of the 1950's, which was simultaneously to assimilate the Algerians and to grant them a measure of autonomy. Even though the contradiction implicit in these two notions led to the Algerian war and to Algerian independence, they believe that assimilation made such inroads as to produce permanent traits.

Probably the prime factor in favor of this belief is Algeria's physical proximity to France. Algiers is only 400 miles from Marseilles—as far as from New York to Washington and back and, nowadays, a commuter's run. Cross-fertilization of ideas and standards has long taken place in both directions, carried northwards by intellectuals and students bound for the Sorbonne and, on a lower intellectual level, by workers bound for jobs in French mines and factories. Between 1914 and 1954 two million Algerians served in France either as soldiers or as workers, and, even

[1]. Percentage of Europeans in 1946-47: 12.3 percent in Algeria; 7.4 percent in Tunisia; 3.4 percent in Morocco.

now the Marseilles station platform, on the departure of the cheap *train-omnibus* for Paris, shows at a glance that the procession continues. Southbound, the carrier of the past has been the *colon* and official, from prefect to schoolteacher; since the mass exodus of 1962 these have been in part replaced by technicians. There were at the beginning of 1964 still 18,296 Frenchmen serving in Algeria, of whom 12,000 were teachers. But their replacement by Algerians is only a matter of time, and the cultural carrier of the future is the European tourist fleeing the overcrowded beaches of France, Spain, and Italy. The invisible export of sunshine and antiquities is already a substantial item in Tunisia's and Morocco's balance of international payments, and Algeria's need of foreign exchange is bound to cause it likewise to develop a hotel and tourist industry.

Perhaps next in importance as an agency of French influence is the conservatism of trading habits. Algeria, which was in the heyday of the *colons* high on the list of France's overseas trading partners, today vies with Italy for fourth and fifth place. Provided that some differences of opinion about what Ben Bella called "legitimate rights" to Saharan oil and "equitable remuneration for existing investment" can be smoothed over, and provided that Algerian oil continues to enjoy preferential treatment in France, this channel of interdependence is unlikely to grow less. Algeria, out of inclination to demonstrate the break with the *ancien régime*, has sought other suppliers, and bought arms from Egypt or factory equipment from the Soviet Union; but France remains its largest supplier, and if Paris' mood of political magnanimity survives, is likely to continue to do so.

There are always chances, of course, of some unpredictable political rupture, such as that which occurred with Tunisia in 1964, when General de Gaulle brusquely brought an advantageous commercial convention to an end in retaliation for Tunisian nationalization of lands still in foreign hands. As a result, Franco-Tunisian trade fell off, but not disastrously, for French technical assistance was barely curtailed, suggesting that the trade promoted by aid is not subject to political vicissitudes. It is even less likely to be so in Algeria, because, as one French minister remarked during a debate on overseas aid in July 1964: "A break with Algeria would upset the whole of Africa and would jeopardize France's standing in the 'Third World'."[2]

It is nowadays fashionable to question the value of technical

---

2. "Une rupture avec l'Algérie ébranlerait tout le continent africain et remettrait en question la position de la France dans le tiers monde" (M. de Broglie).

and financial aid as a way of making one's mark on a foreign nation. Nevertheless, there is bound to be some result for the effort Frenchmen are making to preserve in the realm of economics some of the 'interdependence" that they tried and failed to set up in politics. French reliance on a *mission civilisatrice* has long been proverbial, and on financial and technical aid as a means of maintaining touch with Africa is fast becoming so. In proportion to home resources, France has spent more in this way than any other nation—in peak years 12 percent of its national budget and nearly 2 percent of its gross national product, as compared with under 1 percent in the United States. In 1962, French Africa and the franc zone got 95 percent of this bilateral public aid. In 1964 (the last full year of the economic clauses of the Evian Accords) 40 percent of total overseas aid went to Algeria; in that year, Algeria, Tunisia, and Morocco between them received as much as the rest of Africa put together. At the peak, Algeria received outright budgetary subsidies, as well as loans and sums earmarked for purchases in France. At one time, public opinion polls were said to show that three-quarters of all Frenchmen were in favor of this massive effort, but, as in the United States, its priority in the scale of national expenditure is beginning to be questioned. In a famous article in *Paris Match* in April 1964, a journalist named Cartier asked when charity was going to begin at home, and since then "Cartiérisme" has become a word that needs no explaining, and has found some influential supporters. From 1965, which is the year in which the Evian Accords end, untied aid is to be drastically cut, and, though tied aid will continue, the proportion of it devoted to the ex-French empire will dwindle and that granted to foreign friends will rise. The givers have calculated that tied aid best serves to maintain their imprint on Africa.

The influences that militate against a permanent French imprint are nevertheless formidable. Judging by experience all over the underdeveloped world, the strongest is the Afro-Asian desire for national identity and dignity, and the consequent wish to expunge traces of the *ancien régime* even at the price of material loss. This powerful emotion stimulates—at minimum—a wish to preserve the lifeline of Islam, to use a national language, and to diversify dependence by getting aid and funds from as wide a range of sources as possible.

Establishment of identity as a Muslim by faith and civilization is a desire shared by all the Arab world, even by nationalists who never observe religious practices. The Islamic nature of the state is written into constitution after constitution, from Pakistan westward, for reasons that are only partly religious; these include a determination to display that Islam denotes a way of life that is different from that of others, that links believers to a great and significant past, and that sets them inside a preserve into which infidels cannot go. In the days when the *ulama* dominated an Algerian political party (which they ran from Constantine, at the end of Algeria nearest to Tunis, Cairo, and Mecca) adherence to Islam signified reaction, and it was arguable that rebellious modernists might hanker after French standards. But two developments have changed their outlook. The first is Algeria's independence and nationhood. Today, many Algerians who had become assimilated to an extent that caused them to live in France (either because they liked it, or because they collaborated during the Algerian war and left in order to avoid reprisals) are ready to admit the pull of the homeland. *"Je suis à cheval,"* they say, *"entre deux civilisations,"* and, pressed to the limit by a crisis, such as a war, most younger men say that their first loyalty would be to Algeria. They are helped in this direction because proofs are multiplying that it is possible to be modern as well as a true Muslim; when President Bourguiba contrived in the early post-independence years to bring certain Islamic laws and customs into line with modern practice (which he did at a pace and with an aplomb that no protecting power could have contemplated), his biggest contribution to North African individualism was the proof he afforded that it is possible to live within the letter of Islamic law in a modern way.

Language, and the survival of the French language as a vehicle of instruction, is a debatable point that is discussed in detail elsewhere in this book. Clearly French will survive as the second language of the educated class, but will it be simply a foreign language or one that Algerians use of choice in the home, much as some educated Lebanese families—Muslim as well as Christian—reserve their Arabic for jokes and talking to peasants and servants.

In Morocco in particular, French is bound to disappear as a language of daily use; already in 1964, the Moroccan government had ceased to replace the surviving 11,000 French teachers with Frenchmen as contracts came to an end; it is even conceivable, since Morocco is situated on the Atlantic, that English could at some distant date replace French as the second language in school curricula. In Tunisia, such a choice is inconceivable. Even under the stress of the de Gaulle-Bourguiba quarrels over Bizerte in 1961 or over nationalization of land in 1964, only a token batch of French teachers was called home; in 1965, over 2,000 remain, and bilingualism, illustrated by Bourguiba's impeccable French together with his racy orator's Arabic, is likely to remain the sign of a first-class education. In Algeria, the survival of French for official use is a more open question. For at least two decades the country will be run by men who had schooling only in French, and to whom the use of Arabic in the presence of critical foreign Arabs causes anxiety. French was the language of the literature of the Algerian resistance and at the time of writing, only two out of eleven Algerian daily or weekly newspapers are in Arabic.[3] For some time to come, even the Algerian who knows good Arabic may speak French at home, as do some Lebanese. But the Arab peasant speaks Arabic; Ben Bella was of peasant birth and determined that the dichotomy between country and town be eradicated. In the opinion of more than one contributor to this book, Arabic will prevail in the end, and French be, as it is in Lebanon, the mark of a good education. But one reservation must be made to this dictum—the existence and toughness of the Algerian Berbers.

In India, where an awkward multitude of languages is spoken, the displacement of English by Hindi after a fifteen-year period as the language of all India communication and the official language was prescribed in the constitution. But when the relevant date came—1965—linguistic separatism had developed to an extent that caused the Tamil speakers of the south to insist that the change must wait. Unless Arab-Berber harmony were unexpectedly good, the Berbers (whose language was for all practical purposes never a written one and who therefore excel at French) might say the same. Yet bilingualism of the kind that prevails in Switzerland or Canada is impossible, not only because French is no one's mother tongue, but because French and Arabic represent two such different ways of life. A period of bilingualism of choice, on the Lebanese model, or of necessity, on the Indian one, is likely for a time, but radio and the television are potent factors for change, and all Algerians are likely to know Arabic before the turn of the century.

Another influence that is tending to erase the French hallmark

---

3. Daily, *Al-Chaab;* weekly, *El-Moudjahid.*

is Algeria's search for a national ideology. This is, as is Egypt's, labeled socialism, but it takes the same vague form as Nasser's doctrine if only because (in the economic straits that have followed independence and the French exodus) the pattern of socialist planning is repeatedly warped by the need to take *ad hoc* decisions in order to keep alive. The economic differential that separates Algeria from France is driving the two countries in different directions more thoroughly than French aid is bringing them together. For, as in any country as dependent on foreign aid as is Algeria, all major funds for investment are dispersed through the agency of the government. Further, if, as in Algeria and Egypt, that government has failed to win the confidence of private investors, the government is forced still further in the direction of state management; willy-nilly, it must adopt patterns that are much closer to the Soviet than to the French model.

At the time of writing, this development is less marked in Morocco or Tunisia than in Algeria because in both the former there is less doubt than in the latter about where the seat of power really lies. The men in control in both Tunisia and Morocco have had long experience of power, and of forging it out of powerlessness in the years of the two protectorates. In both countries, therefore, men of the age-group of Bourguiba and Balafrej are familiar with the problems of power thanks to a continuity of experience that the young Algerian war leaders do not yet possess. What is more, these Algerians are cumbered with economic and financial problems far graver than those which beset their neighbors, and are still further handicapped by the after effects of their struggle not only against France but against dissenters among their own people; these last range from the old-fashioned and the overcautious to Muslims who collaborated with the French authorities and rivals who dispute their tenure of power. Thus the tendency of Algeria to move towards a totalitarian economic and social pattern, and *ipso facto* away from a French one, seems strong. It is reinforced by Algeria's intention to practice neutralism and non-alignment in foreign affairs, and so to obtain part of the help that Algeria needs from Communist countries.

One outcome of the economic differential between Algeria and France could therefore be the growth of a political differential. Under pressure of economic stress a country such as Syria, although at one time bent on the exercise of power by popular consent, is finding itself constrained to adopt a policy of power by repression, to hang citizens for their political beliefs and condemn business men to death for "shaking public confidence." Even in Egypt, where, thanks to the homogeneity of the nation, such ferocity is difficult to imagine, economic stress has forced totalitarianism upon a dictator who set out with quite other intentions.

A lesser, but significant, move to erase the French hallmark is the North African determination to establish a pedigree. For this, Tunisia and Morocco do not have to look far; both possess known Muslim ancestry, a native architecture of distinction, an element of continuity supplied for centuries by a ruling house and—in Tunisia's case—the distinction of having made important contributions to the 19th-century literature of Islamic modernism and Arab nationalism. Each of the two nations is comfortably weighted with a form of ballast that Algerians do not possess. Soon, heroes of the Algerian resistance dating back to Abd al-Kader and perhaps to Numidian battlers with the Romans will take the place of Gaulish chieftains such as Vercingetorix. But a lack of ancestry prior to 1830 is a drawback that irks some Algerian nationalists.

Given modern systems of communication, total independence has ceased to be possible. What are Algeria's alternatives to maintaining some degree of interdependence with France? "Algeria is an integral part of the Arab Maghrib, the Arab world and Africa," says its constitution, showing which way its inclinations lie. Here is a statement of fact in terms of geography and of Islam, and—in spite of much initial wrangling (and, between Morocco and Algeria, a little shooting) it seems that a harmonious Maghrib, or at any rate a harmonious Algeria and Tunisia, might materialize faster than a harmonious Arab League has done. If this were to be so, one reason for the harmony might be a common legacy of French education and a resultant capacity for compromise. Total fusion, on the other hand, is improbable if only because the economies of the three countries compete with rather than complement one another.

Membership of some great and effective pan-African brotherhood is an unlikely development. Continental unity has never yet materialized in the Old World, and experience of the breakdown of Asian nationalism under stress of inter-Asian quarrels suggests that continents unite only on negative issues, such as anti-imperialism. A country at Algeria's or Tunisia's relatively advanced stage of development is gratified at the prospect of special relations with fellow-Africans to whom its nationals can be teachers instead of playing pupil to Europe, but first encounters with Negro Africa have not all been smooth. For instance, the Tunisian contingent that served with the UN force in the Congo discovered that the Congolese rated its members as white, and so alien. It is possible, however, that West Africa (and in particular Senegal where two hundred years of colonization at French hands has produced a high degree of assimilation) may provide a bridge of a kind that cannot yet be foreseen.

All told, France, despite her blemishes in North African eyes, offers advantages that few other countries possess. Communist affiliations make a good counterweight to French primacy, but few North Africans want totally to substitute Russian or Chinese friendships for French ones. Were France to display nostalgia for her former dominance, Algeria's distaste for the French veneer that it now possesses might quicken. But France has shown no such inclination. Apart from pockets of diehards who mourn the good old days of *Algerie Française* (much as their counterparts in Britain mourn the "loss" of India), Frenchmen accept the inevitable about Algerian independence. The French referendum of April 1962 on the issue was overwhelming; over 90 percent of those voting and over 65 percent of the electorate voted *"oui."*

To enquire why they did so would be to open the whole interesting question of why Europe's zest for empire declined in the course of the 20th century. As regards Algeria, the incentive could have been war-weariness, or disgust with the final excesses of the OAS, or confidence in General de Gaulle's slow, skillful moves towards riddance of an incubus that was sapping France's position in Europe; with some, it may have been the knowledge that nuclear weapons had altered the whole criteria and incidence of military planning and expenditure. Whatever the combination of motives, the bulk of the French nation quit Algeria without lingering looks behind, and so increased France's chances of making her mark there a lasting one.

BIBLIOGRAPHY

Ageron, Ch-R. *Histoire de l'Algérie Contemporaine*. Paris: Presses Universitaires de France, 1964.
Berque, Jacques. *Dépossession du Monde*. Paris: Editions du Seuil, 1964.
Brunschwig, Henry. *Mythes et Réalités de l'Impérialisme Colonial Français*. Paris: Colin, 1960.
Cartier, R., "L'Accusé du XXe Siècle: l'Homme Blanc," *Paris Match* (April 1964).

Chevallier, Jacques. *Nous, Algériens*. Paris: Calmann-Lévy, 1958.
Cheverny, Julien. *Eloge du Colonialisme: Essai sur les Révolutions d'Asie*. Paris: Julliard, 1961.
Deschamps, Hubert J. *La Fin des Empires Coloniaux*. Paris: Presses Universitaires de France, 1963.
Gordon, David C. *North Africa's French Legacy: 1954-1962*. Cambridge, Mass.: Center for Middle Eastern Studies, 1962.
Memmi, Albert. *Portrait du Colonisé, précédé du Portrait du Colonisateur*. Paris: Buchet Chastel, 1957.
Mitterand, F. *Aux Frontières de l'Union Française*. Paris: Editions du Seuil.
Mus, Paul. *Le Destin de l'Union Française de l'Indochine à l'Afrique*. Paris: Editions du Seuil, 1954.
Nora, Pierre. *Les Français d'Algérie*. Paris: Julliard, 1961.
Perroux, François. *Problèmes de l'Algérie Indépendante*. Paris: Presses Universitaires de France, 1963.
Pickles, Dorothy. *Algeria and France: From Colonialism to Cooperation*. London: Methuen, 1963.
Savary, Alain. *Nationalisme Algérien et Grandeur Française*. Paris: Plon, 1960.

15

Modernization of the Maghrib

Jacques Berque

The North African nations have attained independence, faithful to their appointment with poverty, injustice, and absurdity: poverty because of a rapidly increasing demography, injustice as a result of inequalities—most strikingly those arising out of appropriation of the best land by foreigners—and finally absurdity—absurdity rooted in the former regime, as well as in some conditions characteristic of our times and which the Arab peoples have in no way been spared. The latter are able to express them through a whole series of synonyms, the most common of which carries the meaning of anguish: *qalaq*. The situation which these countries faced at the time of independence was indeed filled with anguish and agonizing.

I have attempted in Chapter VIII to analyze the main characteristics of that situation with respect to the rural system, to which a majority of the North Africans still belong. Here, I propose to offer a few remarks more in the nature of a synthesis.

The colonial regime meant a growing disparity between the developed part of the world and the underdeveloped—that is, exploited—part. Indeed this dissymmetry can be observed within North Africa itself, with an opposition, already apparent during the colonial period and continuing since independence, between two sectors (as the economists would say): a so-called "modern" sector and a so-called "traditional" one. Unfortunately, rural North African life still fits for the most part into the traditional sector. It can thus be said that the task of independence is to remedy this dissymmetry, or, in other words, to restore the balance between what, in an economy, a society, a mentality, a language, springs from modern civilization (which, whether one likes it or not, means industrial civilization)—and the rest. For the rest contains vital forces which should never have been neglected and which have proven, notably in the independence struggle, their enormous potentialities. This aspect has been underscored recently by various exegeses of the Algerian revolution. They show —to the surprise of some—what share of the emancipation process was assumed by those peasants of the *djebels,* by people who had been labeled—and are still called out of habit—underdeveloped, or at the very least archaic. The task which independence must face is to reintegrate the people by restoring on sounder bases the relationship between what obeys the general laws of world development and what is rooted in the depths and the very foundations of the North African identity, and was too often until now tainted with inherited, but mostly acquired, traits of "underdevelopment."

The job is thus to reintegrate the culture of these people to its natural basis. This calls for strenuous efforts at finding an adjustment between learned and inherited languages, or between traditional attitudes and those which are critical and innovating. The so-called developed and underdeveloped parts will also have to be reintegrated, it being understood that we are talking about geographic and economic zones as well as social and mental ones.

What are the lines along which one can expect a solution or an approach to the problem thus posed? Although the three North African personalities are sharply defined, the substratum on which they rest and the set of problems they share are in my view largely homogeneous over the whole Maghrib. I am one of those who believe in the future unity of the Greater Maghrib and in its desirability. I thus have a certain right, buttressed by a few arguments, to propose unified processes as well.

The first, and the one that first comes to mind, is the technological process. Colonization had imposed itself in the world as the result of a technological lag between already industrialized and not yet industrialized countries. Independence means that dependent peoples have taken this technology in hand. A thousand difficulties spring up at this point. Where the technology was formerly submitted to, it must now be mastered. It is still largely learned from the outside, and thus applied to the country's realities on the strength of theoretical premises. There is no mystery in saying that many excellent theories and excellent techniques have failed in these countries, or indeed in the world, because they did not emanate from the intimate reality of the society. This is not a secret among economists. There is already a whole literature (a literature which has not yet completed its course) to show that, in the end, economic theories must be both worldwide in their inspirations and specific in their applications —and when I say "their applications," I mean this in the most basic sense.

What is true of technology is true as well of social analysis, which at any rate should go hand in hand with technological modernization in such a process. We too often observe that the distinction between traditional and modern sectors dominates all surveys by experts and a good portion of government actions. If one assumes this dualism at the start, the problem is insoluble. North Africa, like many other countries reaching independence, encounters a number of false dilemmas. Every time a choice is proposed to such people in the form: "either ... or ..." the problem thus posed is insoluble. Arabization or occidentalization? An insoluble problem! What the Maghrib wants is arabization through occidentalization, or occidentalization through arabization. Modern sector or traditional sector? This really amounts to accepting the old division of the country between colonized and so-called indigenous sectors. As long as such a division exists, de-colonization has not been accomplished in that country.

As long as, on one hand, a few million hectares of the best land continue to be utilized under methods that imply, for example, mechanized farming, the others being relegated to extensive agriculture, or at the most, to more or less benevolent acts of popularization, the solution has not been found. For the majority of Maghribian *fellahs* still find themselves in the extensive sector, that is, geographically, below the 12-inch rain limit. One hears and reads that indigenous agriculture is not profitable under a unit size of ten hectares; but if this were true, it would mean that there is no place left for a peasantry! The perspectives thus open would be absurd.

It seems to me that, in the face of such dilemmas, the government concerned must turn to its scholars—scholars in technology and scholars in the social sciences—asking them to propose technical means of aligning one sector with another and of modernizing farm life in North Africa, starting at the bottom and not just creating a small privileged area as colonization had done. For a colonization, be it national, is still a colonization. I have spoken of technology and social analysis. I was forgetting a third sector. It is the one that fills the front of the stage: call it passion. It is the affective element, or at least what appears as such to us and to those concerned, but where the sociologist quickly identifies a great release of values, which constitutes the realities of de-colonization. It is in the release of values drawn from itself that independence has a chance of reappropriating to the national personality the methods already utilized by the industrial world, so as to achieve a re-creation of itself that is worthy of its hopes. Thus, the three paths I see for such a progress are scientific analysis, technological progress, and the creation of symbols and values. President Ben Bella once said in one of his speeches: "What is the revolution? The revolution is a dream. Had we not dreamed, we would never have been revolutionaries." What he meant by that is not that positive processes must be dropped in favor of dreams, but, on the contrary, that the facts must be viewed in all their ramifications, or, in other words, with all attendant symbols and values.

Now, the path followed by these countries with quasi-unanimity, and in accord with other countries in the world which share the same circumstances, is the path of planning, which at first sight appears to be that of the most rigorous rationality.

Earlier in this book, we have been presented with a serious examination of planning, and at times even the very legitimacy of planning has been brought into question. I think that planning in these countries must not be considered from the angle of economics. The planning of the Maghrib and of former colonial countries is not an economic tool. It is a way of achieving reintegration. It is a way, for people who have been subjected to historical disintegration and to irrationality, of recovering, by reference to some hypotheses which they themselves formulate, a collective being which they can rebuild to their measure and in accordance with their ends. In truth, we are all—ex-colonials and ex-colonizers—interested in this rationality. For if our present world stands a chance, it is precisely within such perspectives of a reintegration of Man.

Select Bibliography on Modern North Africa

(Attention is again called to the more specialized bibliographies appearing at the end of most chapters in this book.)

A comprehensive bibliographical article is that of Roger Le Tourneau, M. Flory, and J. P. Trystram, "L'Afrique du Nord: Etat des Travaux," *Revue Française de Science Politique,* IX, No. 2 (June 1959), pp. 410-453. Still very useful is the earlier study by Benjamin Rivlin, "A Selective Survey of the Literature in the Social Sciences and Related Fields on Modern North Africa," *American Political Science Review* (September 1954), pp. 826-848. The article by Paul E. A. Romeril, "Tunisian Nationalism: A Bibliographical Outline," *Middle East Journal* (Spring 1960), pp. 206-215, is especially helpful for modern Tunisia but gives some good indications for the neighboring countries as well. A good bibliographical study of Libya is R. W. Hill, *A Bibliography of Libya,* Department of Geography Research Papers Series No. 1 (University of Durham, Eng., 1959). Worthy of note also is the U. S. Library of Congress publication compiled by Helen F. Conover, *North and Northeast Africa: A Selected, Annotated List of Writings, 1951-1957* (Washington, D. C., 1957). Many of the general works on modern North Africa include good bibliographies. Especially useful are those found in books of Barbour, Gallagher, and Le Tourneau (see below).

A number of general studies on modern North Africa are available. A welcome addition to the American Foreign Policy Library series is Charles F. Gallagher's, *The United States and North Africa* (Cambridge: Harvard University Press, 1963), an excellent survey of Algeria, Tunisia, and Morocco with emphasis on the contemporary scene. There is now a second edition of the *Survey of North West Africa (The Maghrib)* edited by Nevill Barbour (Oxford University Press, 1962). Similar in format to the earlier *The Middle East: A Political and Economic Survey* (Oxford University Press) now in its third edition (1961), the *Survey of North West Africa* is successful in what is an almost impossible task—the creation of a reliable one-volume reference handbook. A sure account of the political developments and the nationalist struggle in modern times can be found in Roger Le Tourneau, *Evolution Politique de l'Afrique du Nord Musulmane 1920-1961* (Paris: Colin, 1962). Jacques Berque's *Le Maghreb entre Deux Guerres* (Paris: Editions du Seuil, 1962) should also be mentioned. An excellent exposition of the many-faceted encounter between colonizer and colonized in former French North Africa, it does, however, often presuppose a detailed knowledge of the subject on the part of the reader. There are also the books by Lorna Hahn, *North Africa: Nationalism to Nationhood* (Washington, D. C.: Public Affairs Press, 1960) and the good, compact survey by I. William Zartman, *Government and Politics in Northern Africa* (New York:

Praeger, 1963), available in paperback. Another recent paperbook is Richard M. Brace, *Morocco, Algeria, Tunisia,* in The Modern Nations in Historical Perspective series (Englewood Cliffs: Prentice-Hall, 1964).

The process of decolonization in North Africa—and especially the tragic and brutal Algerian war—occasioned many books which were either avowedly polemical or designed to present a timely report on the then current crisis. As is usually the case most of these works can be considered as superseded by more dispassionate studies now being written with less sense of urgency. There are, however, a handful of books written during the heat of battle which should not be forgotten. Several, indeed, played a role in shaping the events themselves. Foremost in this select category is the pioneer study by Charles-André Julien, *L'Afrique du Nord en Marche* (Paris: Julliard, 1952). The profound insights of Robert Montagne (even though proved wrong in his short-term predictions) in his *Révolution au Maroc* (Paris: Editions France-Empire, 1953) will also stand the test of time. The several works of Germaine Tillion written during the Algerian war contain information of more than passing validity, two of which are available in English: *Algeria: The Realities* and *France and Algeria: Complementary Enemies,* published by Knopf, New York, in 1958 and 1961, respectively. *La Révolution Algérienne* (Paris: Plon, 1959) by Swiss journalist Charles-Henri Favrod should be noted. The second edition was published by Plon in 1962 under the title *Le F.L.N. et l'Algérie.*

Crises and great issues serve to stimulate a scholarly interest which can often maintain itself after the public has moved on to other concerns. If problems of decolonization no longer interest the French man in the street, the overall question of modern imperialism in North Africa still occupies the attention of a small group of French scholars. Something of what might be called a revisionist school can be discerned in the works of several French Marxists such as André Nouschi, *La Naissance du Nationalisme Algérien* (Paris: Editions de Minuit [1962]; Albert Ayache, *Le Maroc: Bilan d'une Colonisation* (Paris: Editions Sociales, 1956) ; and Paul Sebag, *La Tunisie: Essai de Monographie* (Paris: Editions Sociales, 1951). See also Yves Lacoste, André Nouschi, and André Prenant, *L'Algérie Passé et Présent* (Paris: Editions Sociales, 1960). These "revisionists" are not immune from the charge of substituting a new distortion in the place of the previous distortions linked with the heyday of an "Afrique du Nord Française" (No less a person than Charles-André Julien, himself an old militant in the French Socialist Party has so argued.) However, the debate itself and especially the carefully documented dossier of social and economic data being compiled by revisionists should prove a healthy influence in advancing our understanding of modern North Africa.

A basic study on geography and ethnography of North Africa is that of Jean Despois, *L'Afrique du Nord* (3rd ed.; Paris: Presses Universitaires de France, 1964) which contains an exhaustive bibliography. In English, the competent geographical textbook on Africa by William A. Hance, *The Geography of Modern Africa* (New York: Columbia University Press, 1964) is to be recommended. A good collection of maps is found in the *Oxford Regional Economic Atlas: The Middle East and North Africa* (London: Oxford University Press, 1960).

In studying these newly independent states of North Africa at the national level there is always a danger of exaggerating the change and overlooking the continuities. No better antidote to this problem can be found than the works of a good anthropologist. In this connection it is worth recalling that the eminently readable and sound general survey by Carleton Coon, *Caravan: The Story of the Middle East* (rev. ed.; New York: Henry Holt, 1958) draws very heavily on the author's firsthand knowledge of North Africa. No attempt can be made in this general bibliography to list the many anthropological monographs on North Africa, but that of Marvin W. Mikesell, *Northern Morocco: A Cultural Geography* (Berkeley: University of California Press, 1961) deserves mention as a model of clear well-informed exposition which also uses charts and visual aids to excellent advantage. An excellent guide to the growing body of works by sociologists and anthropologists on urban problems in North Africa is given in the bibliography compiled by Roger Le Tourneau at the end of Chapter VI in this study. If one were to choose a single work on this vast subject he might well select Robert Montagne (ed.), *Naissance du Prolétariat Marocain* (Paris: Peyronnet, 1952).

Among the books devoted particularly to economic matters in North Africa the following might be mentioned: René Gallissot, *L'Economie de l'Afrique du Nord* (Paris: Presses Universitaires de France [Que Sais-je? No. 965], 1961); Charles F. Stewart, *The Economy of Morocco: 1912-1962* (Cambridge, Mass.: Center for Middle Eastern Studies, 1964); René Gendarme, *L'Economie de l'Algérie* (Paris: Colin, 1959); Moncef Guen, *La Tunisie Indépendante face à son Economie* (Paris: Presses Universitaires de France, 1961); and Benjamin Higgins, *The Economic and Social Development of Libya* (New York: United Nations, 1953).

Another major source—especially important for understanding the mentality of the ruling elites—are the novels and literary works of a flourishing school of modern North Africans, writing in French. Several have been translated into English as well, e.g., Mouloud Mammeri, *The Sleep of the Just* (London: Cresset Press, 1956) and Albert Memmi, *The Pillar of Salt* (New York: Criterion Books, 1955). The excellent monograph by David Gordon, *North Africa's French Legacy: 1954-1962* (Cambridge, Mass.: Center for Middle Eastern Studies, 1962) discusses, among other things, this body of writers and provides bibliographical details.

Those desiring to keep up-to-date on developments in North Africa and to know of new books and articles on this subject can rely (in English) on the Chronology, Book Reviews, and Bibliography of Periodical Literature sections of the quarterly *Middle East Journal*. In French there is (since 1964) the excellent *Maghreb: Documents Algérie Maroc Tunisie* appearing six times a year edited by La Fondation Nationale des Sciences Politiques and published by *La Documentation Française* (16, Rue Lord-Byron, Paris VIII). Even more comprehensive is the *Annuaire de l'Afrique du Nord*, published by the Centre d'Etudes Nord-Africaines, Aix-en Provence. Volumes I and II (1962-63) have already appeared. The *Annuaire* includes detailed chronologies, book reviews and long articles on selected subjects.

In conclusion, a few books dealing with individual countries of modern North Africa should be mentioned.

MOROCCO

Ashford, Douglas E. *Political Change in Morocco*. Princeton: Princeton University Press, 1961.

Barbour, Nevill. *Morroco*. London: Thames and Hudson, 1965.

Lacouture, Jean and Simonne. *Le Maroc à l'Epreuve*. Paris: Editions du Seuil, 1958.

Landau, Rom. *Morocco Independent*. London: Allen and Unwin, 1961.

Monteil, Vincent. *Maroc*. Paris: Editions du Seuil, 1962.

Rézette, Robert. *Les Partis Politiques Marocains*. Paris: Colin, 1955.

Zartman, I. William. *Destiny of a Dynasty: The Search for Institutions in Morocco's Developing Society.* Columbia: University of South Carolina Press, 1964.

———. *Morocco: Problems of New Power.* New York: Atherton Press, 1964.

ALGERIA

Ageron, Ch-R. *Histoire de l'Algérie Contemporaine.* Paris: Presses Universitaires de France, 1964.
Aron, Robert (ed.). *Les Origines de la Guerre d'Algérie.* Paris: Fayard, 1962.
Behr, Edward. *The Algerian Problem.* New York: W. W. Norton, 1961.
Bourdieu, Pierre. *The Algerians.* Boston: Beacon Press, 1962.
Kraft, Joseph. *The Struggle for Algeria.* Garden City: Doubleday, 1961.
Perroux, François (ed.). *L'Algérie de Demain.* Paris: Presses Universitaires de France, 1962.

TUNISIA

Ardant, Gabriel. *La Tunisie d'Aujourd'hui et de Demain.* Paris: Calmann-Levy, 1961.
Debbasch, Charles. *La République Tunisienne.* Paris: Librairie Générale de Droit et de Jurisprudence, 1962.
Laitman, Leon. *Tunisia Today: Crisis in North Africa.* New York: Citadel Press, 1954.
Micaud, Charles A., Leon Carl Brown, and Clement H. Moore. *Tunisia: The Politics of Modernization.* New York: Praeger, 1964.
Moore, Clement H. *The Dynamics of One-Party Government: Tunisia since Independence.* Berkeley: University of California Press, 1965.
Raymond, Andrè. *La Tunisie.* Paris: Presses Universitaires de France (Que Sais-Je? No. 318), 1961.

LIBYA

Evans-Pritchard, E. E. *The Sanusi of Cyrenaica.* Oxford: Clarendon Press, 1949.
International Bank of Reconstruction and Development. *The Economic Development of Libya.* Baltimore: Johns Hopkins Press, 1960.
Khadduri, Majid. *Modern Libya: A Study in Political Development.* Baltimore: Johns Hopkins Press, 1963.
Owen, Roger. *Libya: A Brief Political and Economic Survey.* London: Oxford University Press, 1961.
Villard, H. S. *Libya, The New Arab Kingdom of North Africa.* Ithaca: Cornell University Press, 1961.

The Contributors

EQBAL AHMAD, Assistant Professor in the School of Labor and Industrial Relations at Cornell University was born in India in 1931 and is now a citizen of Pakistan. He received his B.A. and M.A. from the Punjab University in Lahore and is now completing his thesis for a joint Ph.D. in Politics and Near Eastern Studies from Princeton University. Mr. Ahmad lived in North Africa during the years 1961-1963 first as a Rockefeller Fellow doing research on his doctoral dissertation and later as Associate Director of the International Cultural Center in Tunisia. During 1964-1965 he taught in the Department of Political Science at the University of Illinois, Urbana.

DOUGLAS E. ASHFORD, Associate Professor of Public and International Affairs, Graduate School of Business and Public Administration of Cornell University, was born in Lockport, New York, in 1928. He received his Ph.D. in politics from Princeton University in 1960. He has taught at Princeton (1959) and the University of Indiana (1959-1961), and has lectured at the Foreign Service Institute and the Peace Corps. In 1962-1963, Mr. Ashford was Visiting Professor of Middle East Studies at the School of Advanced International Studies of the Johns Hopkins University. He has done extensive field research in North Africa, most recently in 1961-1962 under a grant from the Social Science Research Council and the American Council of Learned Societies. He is the author of *Political Change in Morocco* (1961), *Perspectives of a Moroccan Nationalist* (1964), and of numerous periodical articles, including "Elections in Morocco: Progress or Confusion?" and "Politics and Violence in Morocco," both of which appeared in the *Middle East Journal*.

JACQUES BERQUE holds the Chair of Social History of Contemporary Islam at the *Collège de France*. Born in Algeria in 1910, he is *Docteur-ès-Lettres*. After many years devoted to government administration and social science research in North Africa, and also service as an international expert in the Middle East, he was named as Professor at the *Ecole pratique des Hautes Etudes* in 1955, and then as Professor at the *Collège de France* in 1956. In addition to his teaching assignments, he has also been consulted by several universities in the Arab World on the organization of their social science departments. He is the author of *Structures sociales du Haut Atlas* (1955); *Histoire sociale d'un village égyptien* (1957); *Les Arabes d'hier à demain* (1960) which has been translated into several languages; *Le Maghreb entre deux guerres* (1962); and of *Dépossession du monde* (1964).

LEON CARL BROWN was born in Mayfield, Kentucky, in 1928. He was educated at Vanderbilt University, receiving his A.B. degree in 1950. He did graduate work at the University of Virginia, the London School of Economics, and Harvard University, where he received his Ph.D. degree in history and Middle Eastern studies.

He spent several years in the Middle East with the Foreign Service in Khartoum and Beirut, followed by independent research in North Africa under the Ford Foundation and the Institute of Current World Affairs. He is co-author, with Clement Moore and Charles A. Micaud, of *Tunisia: The Politics of Modernization* (1964). He is now Assistant Professor of Middle Eastern Studies at Harvard University.

CHARLES F. GALLAGHER was born in San Francisco in 1923. He has the unusual background of having specialized in two different non-Western cultures. During the Second World War he was trained in Japanese, saw service as an officer in the U. S. Navy and afterward served as Cultural Property Adviser to the Supreme Commander for the Allied Powers in Japan. Returning to academic life he was graduated *summa cum laude* from Harvard University in 1951. He then devoted two years in Paris and three in North Africa to a program of study and research on the Arabic and Islamic world. Since 1956 he has been associated with American Universities Field Staff, reporting on North Africa and the eastern Arab world. A member of the Council on Foreign Relations, he has contributed articles to *Foreign Affairs, Virginia Quarterly Review, Middle East Forum, Oriental Art* and other journals. He is the author of *The United States and North Africa* (American Foreign Policy Library) (1963) and the chapter on Tunisia in Gwendolen Carter (ed.) *African One-Party States* (1962). He is now preparing with E. S. Munger a *Political Geography of Africa*.

CHARLES ISSAWI, Professor of Near and Middle East Economics at Columbia University, was born in Cairo in 1916. After completing his studies at Oxford University, Mr. Issawi returned to Egypt and served in the Ministry of Finance and the National Bank in Cairo from 1937 to 1943. He taught at the American University of Beirut for four years, and then, in 1947, came to the United Nations where he served in the Middle East unit of the Secretariat. He has been at Columbia since 1951. Mr. Issawi's most recent works include *Egypt in Revolution* (1963); and (with M. Yeganeh) *Economics of Middle East Oil* (1962).

ROGER LE TOURNEAU, holder of the chair of Islamic civilization at the University of Aix-en-Provence and Visiting Professor at Princeton University, was born in Paris in 1907. After completing his studies at the Ecole Normale Supérieure, he was sent to Fez, Morocco, in 1930 as a professor, and later became director of the Franco-Muslim secondary school. He was appointed Director of Education in Tunisia in 1941 and was arrested by the Germans and sent to France. After the war he was Deputy Director of the Centre des Hautes Etudes d'Administration Musulmane in Paris, and in 1947 was appointed as professor of history and civilization of the Muslim west in the University of Algiers. In 1957 he was offered the chair of Islamic civilization at Aix-en-Provence, and in 1959 was appointed visiting professor at Princeton. His books include *Fès avant le Protectorat* (1949); *Damas de 1075 à 1154* (1952); *L'Islam contemporain* (1952); *Les débuts de la dynastie Sa'dienne* (1954); *Les villes musulmanes de l'Afrique du Nord* (1957); *Fez in the Age of the Marinides* (1961); and *Evolution Politique de l'Afrique du Nord Musulmane* (1962). He revised the second volume of Charles-André Julien's *Histoire de l'Afrique du Nord* (2nd ed., 1952) and contributed to the first *Annuaire de l'Afrique du Nord* (1962), published by the Center for North African Studies at Aix-en-Provence, which he helped to establish. He occasionally contributes to *Le Monde* and to various periodicals.

JOHN H. LICHTBLAU, Research Director of Petroleum Industry Research Foundation, Inc., was born in 1921. He received his M.A. in economics from New York University. He served as an economic analyst with the US Department of Labor, the National Industrial Conference Board, and Walter J. Levy, international oil economist, prior to assuming his present position in 1956. In addition to his regular research work, Mr. Lichtblau has taught at the New School for Social Research in New York, and lectured on oil economics at the American University's Energy Institute, Northwestern University's Transportation Center and the London School of Economics. He is co-author of a report, *The U. S. and Its Foreign Trade Position* (National Industrial Conference Board), and of *U. S. Oil Imports—A Case Study in International Trade; The Oil Depletion Issue;* and *Energy Policy and Competition* (all published by the Petroleum Industry Research Foundation). In addition, he is the author of numerous articles on oil and related subjects in such publications as *The Reporter, The New York Times, The Financial Times* (London) and the *Journal of Petroleum Technology*.

A. J. MEYER, Professor of Middle East Studies and Lecturer in Economics at Harvard University, is Associate Director of the Center for Middle Eastern Studies at Harvard. He was born in Hawarden, Iowa, in 1919 and received his A.B. and M.A. from the University of California at Los Angeles, and his Ph.D. from the Johns Hopkins University. From 1947 to 1955, Professor Meyer was a member of the faculty of the American University of Beirut, and in recent years he has lived and travelled extensively in North Africa. He is the author of *Middle Eastern Capitalism: Nine Essays* (1959), and of *The Economy of Cyprus* (1952).

ELIZABETH MONROE, is a Fellow of St. Antony's College, Oxford. She was born in Great Malvern, England, in 1905, and is an M.A. of Oxford University. She held a Rockefeller Traveling Fellowship in North Africa and the Middle East in 1937-1938. She was Director of the Middle East Division, British Ministry of Information, during World War II, and is a former Middle East correspondent for *The Economist*. She is the author of *The Mediterranean in Politics* (1938), and *Britain's Moment in the Middle East* (1963), and co-author of *A History of Ethiopia* (1955).

CLEMENT H. MOORE, Assistant Professor of Political Science at the University of California at Berkeley, received his Ph.D. from Harvard University in 1963. His *Tunisia Since Independence* (1965) was the result of twenty months (1960-62) research in Tunisia under a Ford Foundation research grant. He is also one of the authors of *Tunisia: The Politics of Modernization* (1964). Under a one-year grant from the Rockefeller Foundation, he is presently lecturing at the universities of Algiers and Rabat while preparing a comparative study of the three North African political systems.

BENJAMIN RIVLIN, Professor of Political Science at Brooklyn College of the City University of New York, received his B.A. from Brooklyn College in 1942 and his Ph.D. from Harvard University in 1949. His long-standing interest in North African Affairs dates back to 1943 when he studied Moroccan Arabic and North African Area Studies at the University of Pennsylvania under the Army Specialized Training Program and was subsequently assigned to the African section of the Research and Analysis Branch of the Office of Strategic Services, serving in Washington and in North Africa. After World War II, he served in the research sections of the Department of State and of the Trusteeship Department of the

United Nations. In connection with his research interest in North Africa, he has made frequent trips to the area since 1951 on grants from the Social Science Research Council and the American Council of Learned Societies. In 1956-57, he was a Fulbright Research Scholar in France, working on North African affairs. Since 1963, he has been Visiting Professor of Public Law and Government at Columbia University, teaching a course on political evolution in North Africa in its African and Middle East institutes. He is the author of numerous articles on North African affairs appearing in *The Annals, The Middle East Journal, The American Political Science Review,* etc., of *The United Nations and the Italian Colonies* (1950, Carnegie Endowment for International Peace), and co-editor of the recent volume *The Contemporary Middle East: Tradition and Innovation* (N.Y., Random House, 1965).

I. WILLIAM ZARTMAN, Associate Professor and Director of Graduate Studies in the Department of International Studies at the University of South Carolina, was born in Allentown, Pennsylvania, in 1932, received his Master's degree from the Johns Hopkins University in 1952 and his doctorate from Yale in 1956. He served as a Naval Intelligence Officer for two years in Morocco and remained in that country to conduct research under a Social Science Research Council grant. His books include *Morocco: Problems of New Power* (1964); *Government and Politics in Northern Africa* (1963); and *Destiny of a Dynasty: The Search for Institutions in Morocco's Developing Society* (1964). Mr. Zartman did research in North and West Africa in 1962-1963 under a Rockefeller Foundation grant for a book on the development of foreign relations among the states of North and West Africa, *Developing International Relations* (1965). Mr. Zartman is currently Visiting Associate Professor at New York University, where he is working on a project covering relations between Africa and the Common Market. He is also co-author of four other volumes, and author of a number of articles on Africa and international relations in French and American journals.

Glossary

Terms

BLAD: The countryside or hinterland.
BLAD AL-SIBA: The territory beyond the authority of the central government, as opposed to the *blad al Makhzan* q.v.
COLON: A European engaged in agriculture in North Africa—often used to refer to all European "settlers."
EVIAN ACCORDS: The agreements signed in March 1962 by France and the Algerian provisional government providing for Algerian independence and regulating the relations between France and the new state.
FELLAGHA: A Tunisian "partisan," or underground fighter against the French.
FELLAH: A landholding peasant, or agricultural worker, Arab.
FIQH: Islamic jurisprudence.
FRANCISATION: The "Frenchification," in culture, of North Africans, particularly in language.
HABOUS: Land or property held in religious trust; called in the Eastern Arab world "*waqf.*"
HARA: Quarter of a city; in Tunisia the Jewish Quarter.
KABYLIA: The mountainous area lying roughly between Algiers and Bougie inhabited by Berber speakers.
MAKHZAN: Treasury; by extension, the government, in Morocco; the opposite of *siba*, q.v.
MEDINA: Literally "city," by usage the older, pre-modern sectors of cities in North Africa.
MELLAH: The Jewish quarter of a city in Morocco.
MILK: "Ownership"; roughly the equivalent in Anglo Saxon law of "freehold."
SAHEL: The "plain," a central region of Tunisia.
SANUSI: Religious brotherhood founded in 1837 by Muhammed b. Ali al-Sanusi. Its principal strength is in Libya, especially Cyrenaica.
SIBA: See *blad al-siba*.
UNION FRANÇAISE: The complex structure of relations between France and her overseas possessions provided for by the constitution of 1946.
ZAWIYA: Meeting-place for Islamic religious brotherhood. Loosely comparable to convent or monastery.

Abbreviations

FLN, Front de Libération Nationale (Algerian National Liberation Front)
OAS, Organisation Armée Secrète (French Secret Army)
OPEC, Organization of Petroleum Exporting Countries
SN REPAL, Société Nationale de Recherche et d'Exploitation des Pétroles en Algérie (Algerian government oil company)
UGTA, Union Générale des Travailleurs Algériens (General Federation of Algerian Workers)
UGTT, Union Générale des Travailleurs Tunisiens (General Federation of Tunisian Workers)
UMT, Union Marocaine du Travail (Moroccan Labor Federation)
UNFP, Union Nationale des Forces Populaires (Moroccan National Union of Popular Forces)

Index

Abbas, Ferhat, 16, 105, 182, 221, 293
Abduh, Mohammed, 101, 102, 120
Accra, 65, 67
Achour, Habib, 167, 168, 171, 172, 186, 187, 188, 189, 190
Adam, André, 125, 130, 132
Addis Ababa, 64, 65, 66, 294
al-Afghani, Jamal al-Din, 101
Aflaq, Michel, 64
AFL-CIO, 162, 182
African Unity Conference, 294
Agadir, 128, 195, 251
Aghlabids, 7
Ain Qadus, 129
Ait Ahmad, Hocine, 23, 221
Aix-en-Provence, 123, 125
al-Alawi, Moulay al-Arabi, 13, 102
Alexandria, 87
Algerian Association of Ulama, 7, 102, 105, 106, 107, 109
Algiers, 5, 7, 12, 64, 68, 123, 124, 126, 128, 130, 131, 132, 133, 134, 137, 184, 223, 234, 278, 304
Almohade, 6, 287
Almoravides, 5, 6
amir al mu'minin, 13
Amman, 64
Amsterdam, 188
Andalusian Moriscos, 76
Angola, 67
ANP (People's National Army), 23, 30
Arab League, 1, 62, 63, 64, 67, 284, 310
Arab Maghrib Consultative Assembly, 293
Arab Maghrib Office, 287
Arslan, Shakib, 287
Arzew, 254
Association of Muslim Students of North Africa, 287
Ataturk, 190
Atlas Mountains, 4
autogestion, 184, 206, 229, 264
Baath Party, 64, 65, 235
Baghdad, 63, 65
Bahnini, Ahmad, 231
Balafrej, Ahmad, 176, 177, 179, 293, 309
Bandung, 68
Bank of Libya, 236
Baron, R., 125

Becu, Omar, 188
Bedouin, 5, 6, 77, 222, 231
Beida, 234
Beirut, 64
Belgium, 8, 248
Belgrade, 68
Bellagha, Bechir, 187, 189
Ben Ashur, Shaykh Mohammed al-Fadl, 110
Ben Badis, Abd al-Hamid, 102, 103, 104, 105
Ben Barka, Mehdi, 179, 180, 184, 267, 287
Ben Bella, Ahmad, 3, 22, 23, 30, 31, 32, 33, 45, 48, 50, 53, 55, 62, 64, 68, 70, 71, 75, 88, 95, 98, 182, 183, 185, 206, 220, 221, 222, 229, 232, 246, 247, 252, 255, 275, 278, 288, 289, 294, 296, 305, 308, 316
Benghazi, 12, 234, 237
Beni Hillal, 5
Beni Mellal, 227
Beni Sulaym, 5
Ben Khedda, Youssef, 220
Ben Milad, Mahjoub, 117
Ben Msik, 125, 131, 132
Bennabi, Malek, 118
Bennani, Hachemi, 179
Ben Salah, Ahmad, 12, 26, 29, 160, 166, 167, 168, 170, 172, 190, 216, 217, 234, 240, 243
Ben Seddik, Mahjoub, 174, 179, 180
Ben Youssef, Mohammed, 104
Ben Youssef, Salah, 23, 63, 165, 166, 215
BEPI (*Bureau d'Etudes et de Participations Industrielles*), 250, 251
Berber, 1, 2, 5, 6, 7, 11, 25, 35, 76, 77, 80, 81, 104, 194, 308
Bernard, Augustin, 16
Berque, Jacques, 227
Bevin-Sforza plan, 19
bidonvilles, 124, 125, 128, 130, 131, 132, 134, 135, 136, 140, 207, 243, 246, 251
Biennial Investment Plan 1958-1959 (Morocco), 249, 250
Biskra, 123
Bitat, Rabah, 221
Bizerte, 28, 49, 50, 56, 57, 63, 65, 68, 69, 85, 105, 126, 127, 201, 205, 294, 308
blad al makhzan, 5

327

blad al siba, 5
blad carch, 195
blad l'jemaca, 195
Bône, 126, 127, 245, 246
Bouabid, Abdul Rahman, 176, 219, 220
Bou Arfa, 177
Bouazza, Taieb, 177
Boudali, Nouri, 188, 189
Boudiaf, Mohammed, 182, 221
Bougie, 5
Boumaza, Bachir, 222, 247
Boumedienne, Houari, 3, 22, 30, 278
Bou Namoussa Dam, 246
Bourguiba, Habib, 3, 12, 22, 23, 24, 25, 26, 27, 28, 29, 30, 33, 34, 38, 45, 49, 52, 54, 55, 62, 63, 64, 65, 70, 75, 98, 105, 111, 116, 117, 126, 127, 136, 162, 164, 165, 166, 167, 168, 171, 172, 185, 186, 187, 189, 190, 215, 216, 217, 218, 224, 225, 230, 239, 240, 243, 252, 287, 294, 296, 297, 307, 308, 309
Bourguiba, Habib, Jr., 50, 57
Bouzanquet, 157, 158
Brega, 282
Britain, 10, 56, 58, 68, 69, 236, 248, 274, 278, 283, 303
Bugeaud, General, 303

Cairo, 7, 63, 64, 65, 67, 68, 75, 86, 287, 294, 295, 296, 307
Camps of El-Haouareb, 189
Canada, 308
Cap Bon, 200, 242
Carthage, 4, 6
Cartier, R., 306
Casablanca, 12, 14, 62, 66, 68, 70, 75, 124, 126, 127, 128, 130, 131, 132, 133, 174, 176, 177, 184, 223
cellules de mise en valeur, 206
Centre DERRO *(Centre de Développement Economique et Rural du Rif Oriental),* 251
CGT *(Confédération Générale du Travail),* 147, 148, 157, 158, 161, 162, 164, 175, 176, 177, 178, 180, 181
CGTT *(Confédération Générale des Travailleurs Tunisiens),* 157, 159, 160, 161, 162
Chaouia, Morocco, 198
China, 17, 56, 58, 69, 70, 181, 248, 255, 267
Chou En-Lai, 70
CNRA, 181
Colomb Bechar, 245
colon, 10, 16, 52, 56, 78, 224, 226, 234, 235, 243, 252, 304, 305

comités de gestion, 209, 210, 229
Conference for the Unification of the Arab Maghrib (1958), 290, 292
Congo, 66, 67, 68, 311
Constantine, 12, 127, 196, 306
Constantine Plan, 244, 245, 246, 247, 263
Coppolani, Xavier, 97
"Council of Sunni Ulama," 103
Cuba, 17, 58, 69, 247, 248
Cyprus, 51
Cyrenaica, 4, 6, 18, 19, 52, 235
Czechoslovakia, 181

Dachraoui, Farhat, 117
Damascus, 86
DCEP *(Division de la Coordination Economique et du Plan),* 250, 251, 263
Denmark, 242
Descloitres, Robert, 131
Direction Générale du Plan et des Etudes Economiques, 246
Djebel Nefusa, 129
Djeffara, 129
Djerada, 177
Djerba, 129
Douiri, Mohammed, 219, 226
Doukkala, 198, 204, 226
Doutté, Edmond, 97, 100
Dozy, Reinhardt Pieter Anne, 6
Druzes, 8
al-Dukkali, Abu Shuaib, 7, 102
Duran-Angliviel, 157
Durel, Joachim, 157

Edjele, 246
Egypt, 1, 7, 18, 58, 62, 63, 64, 65, 66, 87, 195, 196, 253, 255, 284, 305, 309, 310
Eisenhower, Dwight D., 49
Enfida, 225
Enver Pasha, 159
Esso, 281
etatism, 182, 185
Ethiopia, 242
European Economic Community, 96, 271, 277, 295, 296, 298
Evian Accords, 45, 46, 50, 53, 55, 56, 60, 75, 244, 246, 247, 273, 274, 275, 306

Fanon, Frantz, 17, 25, 137
Farhat, Abdullah, 160
al-Fassi, Allal, 25, 35, 38, 62, 102, 287
Fatimids, 6, 7
FDIC (Democratic Front for Constitutional Institutions), 35
Feisal II, 62
Fertile Crescent, 18

Fez, 12, 77, 102, 124, 126, 127, 128, 129, 139, 251, 304
Fezzan, 48, 235
al-Fikini, Muhieddin, 47, 228
Filali, Mustafa, 124, 171
fiqh, 194
Fishtalis, 124
Five Year Plan (Libya, 1963-1968), 237, 238
Five Year Plan (Morocco 1960-1964), 250, 251
FLN (National Liberation Front), 16, 22, 25, 26, 30, 31, 32, 33, 38, 46, 53, 58, 62, 63, 65, 69, 86, 180, 181, 182, 184, 231, 293
de Foucauld, Charles, 100
France, 6, 10, 46, 47, 50, 51, 52, 54, 55, 56, 57, 58, 59, 60, 61, 64, 68, 69, 85, 87, 91, 105, 106, 180, 243, 247, 248, 249, 252, 254, 255, 258, 260, 271, 272, 274, 275, 277, 278, 279, 287, 288, 295, 303, 304, 305, 306, 307, 309, 311
Franco-Algerian War, 272, 273

Gabes, 195
Gafsa, 129, 170
Gallagher, Charles, 33, 254
de Gaulle, Charles, 36, 49, 50, 56, 64, 244, 305, 308, 311
Gaullist, 49
Gellner, Ernest, 253
Germany, 8, 58, 64, 242, 248, 271
Geroushi, Mohammed, 281
Ghana, 66
Gharb, 199, 204, 226
Ghazzali, 117, 118
Ghedira, Ameur, 114
Golvin, Lucien, 138
GPRA, 65, 66, 68, 181, 182
"Greater Maghrib," 1, 20, 74, 314
Guedira, Ahmad Reda, 35, 36
Guinea, 66, 67

Hached, Farhat, 150, 157, 158, 160, 162, 163, 164, 166, 175, 189
al-Haddad, Tahir, 108, 158, 159, 160
Hamburg, 282
Hanbali school, 103
Harbi, Mohammed, 31, 233
Hassan II, 13, 22, 34, 35, 36, 47, 56, 64, 88, 98, 179, 220, 226, 232, 252, 253, 289, 291, 294, 296, 297 (and below)
Hassan, Crown Prince Moulay, 58, 263
Hassi Messaoud, 246, 254, 273
Hassi R'Mel, 246, 273, 278
Hayyan, Abu, 114

Hergla (Tunisia), 139
Herriot, Edouard, 161
Higgins, Benjamin, 235
Hilalian invasions, 76
Hungary, 69
Huot, R., 125

Ibn Khaldun, 5
Ibrahim, Abdullah, 63, 176, 177, 178, 226
al-Ibrahimi, Shaikh Bashir, 102, 107
IBRD, 235, 237, 239, 252, 258
ICFTU (International Confederation of Free Trade Unions), 154, 162, 169, 175, 181, 182, 183, 188, 189
Idris I, 47, 62, 231, 235, 237, 253
Ifriqiya, 7
ILO, 178
India, 255, 267, 308
Indochina, 249
Indonesia, 70, 270
Industrial Studies Center (Tripoli), 298
Inspections de l'Agriculture, 203
Iran, 269, 284
Iraq, 303
Israel, 9, 64, 65, 247, 294, 296
Istiqlal, 22, 24, 25, 34, 35, 38, 52, 67, 89, 140, 153, 161, 173, 175, 176, 177, 178, 219, 227, 230, 293
Italo-Turkish War, 159
Italy, 8, 18, 47, 58, 239, 242, 281, 296, 303, 305

jadid, 73
al-Jahiz, 114
al-jazirat al-maghrib, 4, 286
Jbala, 77
jihad, 116
Jordan River, 294
Jorio, 177
Julien, Charles-André, 287

Kaák, Othman, 159
Kabyles, 123, 130, 198
Kabylia region, 5, 11, 17, 53, 81, 129, 247
Kachkate, 177
al-Kader, Abd, Amir, 310
Kairouan, 129, 232
Kasavubu, President, 68, 69
Kasserine, 136
Kef, 200
Kelibia, 242
Kenya, 9
Kerkena, 129
Kettani, Abd al-Hay, 104
Kettaniya brotherhoods, 104

khammesat, 198
Kharijism, 6
Khemiri, Tahir, 114
Khemisti, Mohammed, 75, 93
Khider, Mohammed, 182, 183, 221
Khouribga, 177, 180
Koestner, Nicolai, 266
Korean War, 249
Krim, Abd al-, 5, 63
Ksar-Hellal, 139
Kubbah, Abdul Amir Q., 281
Kuwait, 242, 271, 280
Kuwait Fund for Arab Economic Development, 242, 252, 274, 282, 283

Labidi, 222
Ladgham, Bahi, 293
Lagos, 66
Lagzaoui, Mohammed, 251
Larache, 178
La Trappe, 206, 221
Launay, Michel, 200
Lavera, 282
Lebanon, 12, 62, 303
Le Tellier, Father, 130
LGWU (Libyan General Workers Union), 147
Liberia, 65
Libyan Oil Code, 276
Louzon, Robert, 157
Lumumba, Patrice, 65
Lyautey, Marshall, 129

al-Ma'arri, 114
Mahieddine, 131
Mahsas, Ali, 222
Mali, 66, 67
Malta, 51
manar group, 101, 120
maquis, 1
marabouts, 97, 100, 108, 117, 196
Marrakech, 12, 127, 128, 139
Marsa Brega, 281
Marseilles, 282, 304, 305
Masmoudi, Mohammed, 190, 217
Mateur, 201
Mauritania, 65, 66, 67, 69, 294
Mecca, 307
Medjerda Valley, 130, 225
Medjez al-Bab, 125, 201
Mehta, Asoka, 149
Meknes plain, 226
Melassine, 131
Mendes-France, Pierre, 272
Menzel Bourguiba, 242, 243
Mers al-Kebir, 49, 50

Messadi, Mahmoud, 160
Meyer, A. J., 262, 264
M'Hammed Ali, 157, 158, 159, 160, 161
milk, 193, 198, 207
Millen, Bruce, 146
Mobutu, General, 68
Mohammad, (the Prophet), 6
Mohammed V, 13, 24, 34, 35, 46, 49, 54, 62, 63, 68, 177, 204, 219, 287
Mollet, Guy, 272
Momen, Arbi, 159
Monastir, 127
Moncef Bey, 25
Monrovia, 65, 66
Monteil, Vincent, 86
Moriscos, (see Andalusian)
Mossadegh, Mohammed, 284
moudjahid al akbar, 28
Moulouya, 204
Mouvement Populaire (Morocco), 178, 232
Moscow, 68
Muntasser, Mahmud, 222

Nasser, Gamal Abdul, 51, 63, 64, 65, 75 294, 309
National Front (Tunisia), 168, 169, 170
National Planning Council (Libya), 237, 238, 239
National Promotion (Morocco), 36, 37, 228
NATO, 69
naturalisés, 105
Neo-Destour Party, 12, 22, 24, 26, 28, 31, 32, 33, 34, 36, 37, 38, 39, 103, 105, 138, 140, 157, 159, 160, 162, 165, 167, 169, 189, 213, 215, 216, 217, 218, 223, 224, 225, 226, 232, 239, 293
Netherlands, 242, 279, 284
Niger, 67
Nigeria, 284

OAS, 16, 311
OAU (Organization for African Unity), 64, 66, 67, 292, 296
Office de la Medjerda, 205
Office des Beni Amir, 203
ONI *(Office National d'Irrigation)*, 227
ONMR *(Office National de Modernisation Rurale)*, 227
ONRA *(Office National de Réforme Agraire)*, 229
Office des Terres Dominales, 224
Old Destour, 102, 103, 105, 153, 161
OPEC (Organization of Petroleum Exporting Countries), 281, 284

INDEPENDENT NORTH AFRICA 331

Oran, 12, 49, 278
Orleansville (Al-Asnam), 128
Ottomans, 7
Oumeziane, Mouloud, 185
L'Ouvrier Algérien, 182, 183
Ouzegane, Amer, 206, 229

Pakistan, 242, 307
Palestine, 64, 303
Paris, 9, 64, 128, 131, 249, 287
Paye, L., 125
Pellat, Charles, 86
Persian Gulf, 269, 277
Perspectives Decennales (Tunisia, 1962-1971), 217, 240, 241, 263
Petroleum Training Institute (Algeria), 278
Plan Triennal (Tunisia, 1962-1964), 217
Portuguese Guinea, 67
PSD (Democratic Socialist Party), 35, 36
PTT International Confederation, 187

qadim, 73, 117
qalaq, 313
Qarawiyin, 304

Rabat, 12, 64, 86, 88, 89, 91, 93, 102, 125, 126, 127, 128, 133, 176, 177, 179, 234, 249, 293
Racim, Mohammed, 299
Ramadan, 28, 116, 240
raqaba, 197
Rashid Rida, Shaykh, 120
Ras Tanura, 282
Régie Autonome des Pétroles, 277
Report of the ECA Industrial Coordination Mission to Algeria, Libya, Morocco and Tunisia, 264, 296
Reverdy, J.-C., 132, 133
Rif, 5, 11, 231
Riffians, 81
Romans, 5
Rome, 6
al-Rumi, Ibn, 114

sabqa, 195
Safi, 180, 251, 252
Sahara, 4, 11, 15, 50, 67, 70, 129, 234, 269, 271, 272, 273, 276
Saharan Oil Code (Algeria), 273, 275, 276
Sahel, 24, 25, 27, 194, 198, 200, 206
Saint Augustine, 4
Sakiet Sidi Youssef, 48, 51, 205
salafiya movement, 101, 102
Sanusi, 6, 7, 18, 19

Saudi Arabia, 18, 75, 120, 280
Sayah, Mohammed, 29
Scala-Nador, 131
Second Plan for Modernization and Investment (Morocco 1954-57), 249
Secteurs de Modernisation du Paysanat, 203, 205, 208
Sénatus-consulte of 1863, 197
Senegal, 67, 311
Serghushnis, 124
Sfar, Tahir, 159, 160
Sfax, 128, 162, 166, 167, 170, 215, 242
shi'ites, 8
shirk, 103
Shott al-Hodna, 132
Sidi Bel Abbes, 124
Sidi Ben Daoud, 100
Sidi Bou Zid, 225
Sidi Slimane, 204
Sirte Basin, 236
Slim, Mongi, 69
Sociétés des Prévoyance, 203
Society for Tunisian Economic Cooperation, 159
Sollum, 288
Sorbonne, 304
Souassi, 225
Souk al-Arba, 200
Sousse, 139, 232
South Africa, 9
Southern Rhodesia, 9
SN REPAL *(Société Nationale de Recherche et d'Exploitation du Pétrole en Algerie)*, 273, 277
Spain, 5, 6, 7, 17, 68, 99, 296, 305
Spanish Morocco, 8, 9
Suez, 51, 62, 282
Suez Canal, 284
Suez crisis, 270, 271, 272
Sufi, 6, 98, 99, 100, 102
Sunnism, 8
Svennilson, Ingvar, 240
Sweden, 58, 242
Switzerland, 12, 308
Syria, 87, 303, 309

Taalbi, Mohammed, 119
Tadla region, 100, 129, 204
Taimiya, Ibn, 103
Tangier, 12, 128, 253, 290, 291, 293, 298, 300
Tarfaya, 8
tariqa, 108
tasarruf, 197
Taza, 125
Tetuan, 127, 128

al-Thaalbi, Abd al-Aziz, 102
Tibet, 69
Tillon, Germaine, 244
Tlemcen, 127, 182
Tlili, Ahmad, 164, 165, 167, 168, 170, 172, 186, 188, 189, 190
Tripoli, 7, 12, 18, 128, 234, 246, 298
Tripoli Program, 45, 53, 182, 183, 237
Tripolitania, 4, 6, 18, 19, 80, 129, 235
Tshombe, Moise, 67
Tunis, 7, 11, 63, 64, 65, 66, 77, 91, 102, 103, 111, 124, 126, 127, 128, 131, 133, 136, 159, 170, 172, 180, 187, 201, 223, 234, 297, 304, 307
Tunis, University of, 109, 117
Turkey, 58

UGET, 169
UGP *(Union Générale du Pétrole)*, 273
UGSCM, 175
UGTA (General Union of Algerian Workers), 32, 33, 140, 147, 148, 149, 156, 180, 181, 182, 183, 184, 185, 210
UGTM, 174, 178
UGTT (General Union of Tunisian Workers), 26, 29, 32, 34, 140, 147, 148, 149, 150, 156, 158, 159, 160, 162, 163, 164, 165, 166, 167, 168, 169, 170, 171, 172, 173, 185, 186, 187, 188, 189, 190, 216
Ulad Sidi Brahim, 132
Ulad Sidi Hadjeres, 132
ulama, 79, 97, 98, 99, 100, 102, 103, 105, 111, 117, 118, 307
Umayyads, 7
UMT (Moroccan Federation of Labor), 35, 140, 147, 148, 149, 153, 156, 161, 173, 174, 175, 176, 177, 178, 179, 180, 184

UNAT, 169
United Arab Republic, 19, 62, 85
United Nations, 1, 48, 68, 69, 71, 235, 238, 240, 242, 250, 288, 311
UN Economic Commission for Africa, 253, 264, 291, 296, 298
UNTAB, 250, 252
UNFP (National Union of Popular Forces), 25, 34, 35, 140, 148, 173, 178, 179, 184, 219, 230, 252, 253
UNFT, 169
United States, 48, 51, 55, 56, 58, 62, 68, 69, 75, 235, 236, 242, 247, 248, 249, 251, 254, 255, 258, 279, 283, 306
United States Agency for International Development, 252
Union Française, 304
al-Uqbi, Tayyib, 102
USSR, 19, 56, 58, 68, 69, 181, 221, 242, 248, 255, 260, 267, 278, 305, 309
UTIC, 169
UTT *(Union Tunisien du Travail)*, 168

Venezuela, 270, 276

Wadi Fez, 127
Wahhabi, 18
Waterston, Albert, 250, 263
Weimar Republic, 159
Westermarck, Edvard A., 97
Windmuller, John, 188
World War II, 18, 24, 124, 235, 249, 295

Young Tunisian Movement, 159
Yugoslavia, 69, 177, 181, 242, 252, 255

Zeltan oil field, 279
Zitouna, 102, 108, 109, 304